JOINING SOCIETY
Social Interaction and Learning in Adolescence and Youth

Joining Society addresses a timely and crucial topic, the socialization of today's youth, asking precise questions: To what are the young socialized? Which skills, modes of thinking, or forms of action are required from them, and what developmental value do they hold? All too often, socialization tends to be viewed within the confines of a particular geographical or cultural situation. The multinational list of contributors brings an international perspective to the problems of socialization to work and to adult life while at the same time emphasizing the common issues that face youth around the world.

Some of the topics addressed are the rules and roles involved in socialization, attaining personal agency through collective activity, the use of new technologies, and the role of intergenerational relationships.

Over the past few decades, social scientists have begun to appreciate fully the importance of social interactions in the development of thinking and the acquisition of the necessary social and cultural skills for active and responsible involvement in society. This book sheds new light on the processes through which this is accomplished and through which society may hope to intervene in positive ways with today's youth.

Anne-Nelly Perret-Clermont is Professor of Psychology and Director of the Institute of Psychology at the University of Neuchâtel. She is editor of *Social Interaction and Cognitive Development in Children* and coeditor of *Jean Piaget and Neuchâtel* (with J. M. Barrelet).

Clotilde Pontecorvo is Professor of Educational Psychology at the University of Rome "La Sapienza." She is author of *Writing Development: An Interdisciplinary View* and coeditor of *Orality versus Literacy: Concepts, Methods, and Data* (with C. Blanche-Benveniste).

Lauren B. Resnick is Director of the Learning Research and Development Center at the University of Pittsburgh. She is the author of *Education and Learning to Think* and editor of *Knowing, Learning, and Instruction.* She has coedited several books, including *Linking School and Work: Roles for Standards and Assessment* (with J. Wirt).

Tania Zittoun is a Research Fellow at Corpus Christi College, Cambridge, where she studies cultural resources in young adult transition periods.

Since 1987, Barbara Burge has been the Senior Assistant to Lauren B. Resnick, Director of the Learning Research and Development Center at the University of Pittsburgh. During 10 of those years she was also the Editorial Associate for *Cognition and Instruction.*

THE JACOBS FOUNDATION SERIES ON ADOLESCENCE

Series Editor: Professor Sir Michael Rutter
Institute of Psychiatry, London

The Jacobs Foundation Series on Adolescence addresses the question of what can be done to promote healthy development around the world. It views this important question from different disciplines in the social sciences. Economists and sociologists may consider how we can promote human capital over time, specifically an individual's ability to become educated and to develop earning power; demographers and sociologists may analyze development patterns over generations; psychiatrists and psychologists may tackle the problem of how much change is possible in psychological health during the life course and over generations.

Drawing from these different domains of inquiry into human development, the Jacobs Foundation Series on Adolescence examines the potential for change across generations and during the life course in three areas: (1) human capital, (2) partnership behavior, and (3) psychological health and the rearing of children. The purpose of the series is to further the goals of the Jacobs Foundation – to contribute to the welfare and social productivity of the current and future generations of young people.

Other Books in the Series

Youth in Cities: A Cross-National Perspective, edited by Marta Tienda and William Julius Wilson

The following titles were published in collaboration with the Jacobs Foundation, before the series was established:

Youth Unemployment and Society, edited by Anne Petersen and Jeylan Mortimer (1994)
Self-Efficacy in Changing Societies, edited by Al Bandura (1995)
Psychosocial Disturbances in Young People, edited by Michael Rutter (1995)
Preparing Adolescents for the Twenty-First Century, edited by Ruby Takanishi and David Hamburg (1997)
Understanding and Preventing Teacher Burnout, edited by Roland Vandenberghe and Michael Huberman (1999)

JOINING SOCIETY

Social Interaction and Learning in Adolescence and Youth

Edited by

Anne-Nelly Perret-Clermont
University of Neuchâtel

Clotilde Pontecorvo
University of Rome
"La Sapienza"

Lauren B. Resnick
University of Pittsburgh

Tania Zittoun
University of Cambridge

Barbara Burge
University of Pittsburgh

 **CAMBRIDGE**
UNIVERSITY PRESS

PUBLISHED BY THE PRESS SYNDICATE OF THE UNIVERSITY OF CAMBRIDGE
The Pitt Building, Trumpington Street, Cambridge, United Kingdom

CAMBRIDGE UNIVERSITY PRESS
The Edinburgh Building, Cambridge CB2 2RU, UK
40 West 20th Street, New York, NY 10011-4211, USA
477 Williamstown Road, Port Melbourne, VIC 3207, Australia
Ruiz de Alarcón 13, 28014 Madrid, Spain
Dock House, The Waterfront, Cape Town 8001, South Africa

http://www.cambridgc.org

First published 2004

Printed in the United States of America

Typeface Minion 10.5/13 pt.   *System* LATEX 2$_\varepsilon$ [TB]

A catalog record for this book is available from the British Library.

Library of Congress Cataloging in Publication Data
Joining society : social interaction and learning in adolescence and youth / edited by
Anne-Nelly Perret-Clermont ... [et al.].
   p.   cm. – (The Jacobs Foundation series on adolescence)
"The 'Joining Society: Social Interaction and Learning in Adolescence and Youth' conference,
held at Marbach Castle, Germany, in 1997 provides the basis for this volume"–P.
Includes bibliographical references and index.
ISBN 0-521-81719-6 – ISBN 0-521-52042-8 (pb.)
1. Youth – Social conditions – 21st century – Congresses.   2. Social interaction in
adolescence – Congresses.   3. Social learning – Congresses.   4. Socialization –
Congresses.   5. Maturation (Psychology) – Congresses.   6. Adolescent psychology –
Congresses.   I. Perret-Clermont, Anne-Nelly.   II. Series.
HQ796J574   2003
305.235 – dc21   2003046179

ISBN 0 521 81719 6 hardback
ISBN 0 521 52042 8 paperback

Contents

Contents

Contributors

Barbara Burge, Learning Research and Development Center, University of Pittsburgh, Pittsburgh, Pennsylvania, United States

Felice Carugati, Department of Education, University of Bologna, Bologna, Italy

Alain Coulon, Department of Education, Université Paris 8 at Saint-Denis, Saint-Denis Cedex 02, France

Annie Fouquet, Direction de l'Animation, de la Recherche, des Études et des Statistiques (DARES), Paris, France

Shirley Brice Heath, Department of English, Stanford University, Stanford, California, United States

Manfred Hofer, Department of Psychology, University of Mannheim, Mannheim, Germany

Karsten Hundeide, Psykologisk Institutt, Universitetet I Oslo, Oslo, Norway

Klaus J. Jacobs, Chairman of the Board, Johann Jacobs Foundation, Zurich, Switzerland

Claude Albert Kaiser, Service de la Recherche en Éducation (SRED), Geneva, Switzerland

Saul Meghnagi, Director, Istituto Superiore per la Formazione, Rome, Italy

David Middleton, Department of Human Sciences, Loughborough University, Leicestershire, United Kingdom

Anne-Nelly Perret-Clermont, Institute de Psychologie, Faculté des Lettres et Sciences Humaines, Université de Neuchâtel, Neuchâtel, Switzerland

Jacques Perriault, Section de Recherche sur les Industries Electroniques du Savoir (SERIES), Université Paris X-Nanterre, Nanterre Cedex, France

Clotilde Pontecorvo, Università degli studi di Roma "La Sapienza," Dipartimento di Psicologia dei Processi di Sviluppo e Socializzazione, Rome, Italy

Dragan Popadić, Department of Psychology, University of Belgrade, Beograd, Yugoslavia

Lauren B. Resnick, Learning Research and Development Center, University of Pittsburgh, Pittsburgh, Pennsylvania, United States

John B. Rijsman, Department of Psychology, Tilburg University, Tilburg, the Netherlands

Laurence Roulleau-Berger, Chargée de Recherche CNRS, Groupe de Recherche sur la Socialisation, Université Lumière Lyon 2-bât K, Bron/Cedex, France

Paul Ryan, Faculty of Economics and Politics, King's College, Cambridge, United Kingdom

Roger Säljö, Department of Education, Göteborg University, Göteborg, Sweden

Ursula M. Staudinger, Psychology Department, Dresden University, Dresden, Germany

Stuart Tannock, Social and Cultural Studies, University of California–Berkeley, Berkeley, California, United States

Jonathan Tudge, Department of Human Development and Family Studies, University of North Carolina at Greensboro, Greensboro, North Carolina, United States

Tania Zittoun, Institute de Psychologie, Faculté des Lettres et Sciences Humaines, Université de Neuchâtel, Neuchâtel, Switzerland

Foreword

The mission of the Johann Jacobs Foundation is international. Currently, its grant-making policy operates through communication networks to influence decision makers and educators, to facilitate interdisciplinary research, and to promote research for incentive and mutual aid.

Each year the foundation sponsors a major conference related to one of these priorities as defined by the board. The "Joining Society: Social Interaction and Learning in Adolescence and Youth" conference, held at Marbach Castle, Germany, in 1997, provides the basis for this volume. That topic is directly connected with the Johann Jacobs Foundation's growing interest in the adolescent phase of human development in the social context of a rapidly changing world. The Foundation promotes research in this area and contributes to the development of action programs with a three-pronged goal: to improve opportunities for adolescents, to promote the development of respect for the environment, and to identify future widespread problems that may result from the unreasonable exploitation of environmental resources. This effort also involves correcting or preventing the marginalization of youth, particularly in inner cities, and proposing ways in which disadvantaged teens can become competitive users of new information technologies.

For the organization of this conference, the Johann Jacobs Foundation invited Anne-Nelly Perret-Clermont, a psychology professor at the University of Neuchâtel, to set up a small international team. She was chosen because of her special interests in the social psychology of education and her extensive research on the importance of horizontal (peer) interactions in cognitive development. Professor Perret-Clermont's group included Clotilde Pontecorvo, a professor at the University of Rome "La Sapienza"; Lauren B. Resnick, a professor at the University of Pittsburgh; and Tania Zittoun, a doctoral student at the University of Neuchâtel. The conference provided a highly productive "thinking space," with participants from 15 countries representing a careful mix of disciplines, theoretical perspectives, and research traditions. This volume builds on and extends the main presentations and debates of this conference.

Our societies are facing formidable new problems; fortunately, new knowledge, resources, and approaches with which to solve them are also increasing. Although this book focuses on serious concerns about the well-being and prospects of contemporary youth, it also reports illuminating research findings and offers promising ideas and strategies for addressing these concerns. Today, postindustrial countries find themselves struggling with a common set of problems, the solutions to which may vary from society to society. Strategies that work in one place may not succeed in another where the culture, politics, and economy differ. Yet decision makers and practitioners can profit enormously from examining relevant research and the successes and problems experienced by others.

We hope that researchers will feel encouraged to pursue their important scientific work in this area.

Klaus J. Jacobs, Chairman
Jacobs Foundation

Preface

Anne-Nelly Perret-Clermont

The story of this volume unfolds like a fairy tale. Once upon a time, a fairy sent a letter to a professor at one of Europe's smallest universities. The recipient was a Swiss social psychologist who was preparing to celebrate the centenary of a compatriot, Jean Piaget, a major developmental psychologist. His prominence was fading in his own country both because of an increasing emphasis on technological and economic problems and because of a diminished concern for the education of youth. This was occurring despite the overwhelming presence of inquisitive young people in the social science departments, who sought help in making meaning of their seemingly ever-changing world; in reflecting on intergenerational relationships, social bonds, and individual autonomy; in trying to understand their cultural diversity and historical heritage; and in worrying about the future.

Upon opening the letter, the professor thought she was dreaming. It was an invitation to "secure the help of two or three colleagues in convening at Marbach Castle a group of 40 scientists of your choice, young promising researchers and confirmed senior scientists from all over the world, to work on an issue that is of primary importance for young people's future." I was the professor, the "fairy" was Klaus J. Jacobs, and the magic wand was the Johann Jacobs Foundation, well known for supporting important innovative projects and encouraging worldwide communication among scientists. A series of annual conferences on youth, sponsored previously by the Johann Jacobs Foundation, had resulted in important publications (e.g., Bandura, 1995; Petersen & Mortimer, 1994; Rutter, 1995).

I turned to Clotilde Pontecorvo, an Italian specialist on the role of talk and conversation in the growth of thinking in the home and in schools, with extensive experience among teachers, educators, and politicians; to

Lauren Resnick, an American cognitive psychologist who, after having studied socially shared cognition and the school-to-work transition, has become deeply involved in the educational assessment of young people; and to Tania Zittoun, a Swiss graduate student whose recent personal experience of youth and professional training in social psychology and the psychology of emotions have made her a keen observer of her contemporaries' creative involvement in music, art, and other forms of social life. She provided a constant reminder of both the importance of transgenerational transmissions and the autonomous role of the young in making sense of contradictions in the "established worlds" into which young people are supposed to integrate.

Thus, on November 6–8, 1997, researchers representing diverse disciplinary perspectives from many European countries, including Russia and Yugoslavia, as well as from North America, South Africa, and the Middle and Far East, convened at the Johann Jacobs Foundation's Communication Center at Marbach Castle in Germany. The success of the conference prompted us to prepare a book dealing with the most important issues. Because our authors represent a range of theoretical perspectives expressed in nine different native languages, it became necessary to add Barbara Burge, an expert in international editing, to our team of editors.

This volume builds on the work and discussions of that conference. The initial question presented to conference participants was: How do social interactions provide opportunities for young people to learn life skills? It aimed at identifying the resources available to youth for fruitful peer interactions and other forms of interactive learning. Our scrutiny of the various facets of this issue led us to restate the question in a broader perspective: In this current period of profound societal transformations, under which conditions and with what kind of vertical or horizontal support do young people develop skills and acquire knowledge? When (and why) are these meaningful to them? The conference debates enlarged the understanding of learning by placing this basic activity at the intersection of expert transmission, self-crafted competence, and social participative activity. It raised new issues, called for theoretical reframings, and established the basis for the genuine multidisciplinary perspective presented in our volume.

We are indebted to the Johann Jacobs Foundation and its board for their exceptionally helpful support and an exceedingly gracious environment for our work. Their open invitation and exhilarating discussions in the early planning stages of the conference foreshadowed their constructive collegiality throughout. I also want to acknowledge the invaluable support of Pierre Ducrey, archaeologist and former Vice Chancellor of the University of Lausanne, for his helpful advice, encouragement, and thought-provoking questions and the decisive impulse provided by Laszlo Nagy, former President of the Johann Jacobs Foundation, who drew on his substantial personal experience and on the Foundation's long history of involvement in projects with youth, notably the Boy Scout and Girl Scout federations. With the diligent help of Judith Kressig, Theo Brenner, the current President of the Foundation, has been a valuable partner in setting the effort in motion and shepherding it, step by step, to publication.

We thank all those conference participants who did not contribute chapters to this book for their stimulating contributions to the debates. In writing their chapters, the authors included herein have drawn extensively upon this collective venture.

Very special thanks are due to the members of the board of the Johann Jacobs Foundation. We greatly appreciate that most of them actively participated in the initial planning meeting and were a vital part of the entire conference. We sincerely thank them for their genuine interest and cogent comments: Paul B. Baltes, Pierre B. Ducrey, David A. Hamburg, Christian Jacobs, Heinrich Ursprung, and especially the Chairman, Klaus J. Jacobs, whose personal commitment to a profound and empirically based reflection on these important matters is an important testimony. From the first draft of the conference design to the very last moments of the 3 days of work in Marbach, Klaus J. Jacobs honored us with his presence and enriched our discussions by sharing his worldwide experiences and in-depth reflections.

REFERENCES

Bandura, A. (Ed.). (1995). *Self-efficacy in changing society.* Cambridge: Cambridge University Press.

Petersen, A. C., & Mortimer, J. T. (Ed.). (1994). *Youth unemployment and society.* Cambridge: Cambridge University Press.

Rutter, M. (Ed.). (1995). *Psychosocial disturbances in young people: Challenges for prevention.* Cambridge: Cambridge University Press.

I

INTRODUCTION

1 Thinking Spaces of the Young

Anne-Nelly Perret-Clermont

When and how can appropriate *thinking spaces* offer young people the resources to face life's challenges? Thinking is considered here in the large sense of a dynamic mental activity, both cognitive and symbolic, an alternative to acting out or to reacting. Under certain conditions that permit it, the individual develops in what may be viewed as the continuation of Winnicott's (1971) *transitional space* or what we designate as *thinking spaces*, which pertain to both the self and the nonself and allow us to elaborate both fantasy and images of reality. The thinking space is the frontier of freedom in the psychic activity in which the individual elaborates the perceived reality in order to represent or symbolize it and to become able to reflect on it.

Expanding still more on Winnicott's model, we also consider the thinking space in its social dimension. Thinking has its roots in collective activities that permit or even provoke it. The child and the young enter communities of practice that make more or less explicit (first during feeding and nurturing time; then, around play and daily routines; later, in more formal teaching, cultural socialization, leisure, professional training, and work activities) their thinking and the discursive fruits of it. In dialogues, the child and later the adolescent are called upon as cothinkers or challenged with issues on which they have to take a stance. This constant confrontation with joint activities, with words and other symbolic mediations, with role-taking, but also with socially built situations, with set problems and their accepted solutions, with memories and expressed feelings, contributes to equipping the individual with the means to think, which he or she in turn learns to use by reinvesting them in new contexts and also in facing new technologies (Perriault, this volume). This merging in socially shared thinking can be vastly different for young people, depending on their circumstances. Young

3

people do not always find spaces that allow for a personal, meaningful involvement and for social relationships that provide resources for thinking, acting, and reflecting on the experience. Thinking spaces are both inner zones of personal psychic activity and social opportunities to carry on this activity in sufficiently secure settings where the child or/and adolescent can risk confronting others with differing points of view and discovering new elements of reality.

The grandfathers of modern psychology (e.g., Baldwin, Vygotsky, Piaget, Mead, and others) were extremely conscious of the importance of social life in the development of higher psychological functions. Each in his or her own way has made efforts to account for the interdependence among such psychological endeavors as integrating perception, cognition, and emotion; being social; asserting an identity; constructing a time perspective; and taking role perspectives and responsibilities. Adolescence has then been described as a period in which social moratoriums (Erikson, 1950) can offer most valuable opportunities to learn life skills and ground self-identity. In the past few decades, systematic empirical investigations have brought further evidence of the importance of expert–novice interactions (teaching, training, and cultural socialization) for one entering the conceptual world offered by a cultural milieu and its practical and symbolic tools (Resnick, Levine, & Teasley, 1991; Pontecorvo, Säljö, Tudge, this volume). Research has also shown the crucial role of more horizontal peer interactions in the development of competencies by the genuinely creative dynamics of a thinking mind constructing its own understandings via personal experience and confrontation with the "otherness" of his or her fellows and partners (Carugati, Staundinger, this volume). The mind and the culture, the personal biography, and the social inheritance of knowledge and of collective emotional experience have all been shown to be closely interdigitated in the daily experiences of young people who strive to survive and discover themselves as agents in ever larger networks of action, discourse, and legitimization.

What is known about the role of various social contexts in fostering or impeding this psychological growth in adolescence? Is it a matter of the growth (or learning) of individual competencies and skills, or is such a metaphor misleading (Kaiser, this volume) because it does not point adequately to the interpersonal processes that people experience when shaping their personalities and crafting their skills (Rijsman, this volume)? Social life can encourage thinking, but it can also resemble an obstacle course that offers neither time nor partners to help young people become conscious of and reflect on their lives. We need to understand better what sustains the development of such basic life skills as the ability to express emotions and revisit experience, to give it meaning, to make choices, to construct time perspectives, and to develop an active sense of coresponsibility toward the future.

Interrelated Levels of Analysis

In trying to examine the thinking spaces of the young, it can be useful to distinguish (Doise, 1982) between different but interrelated levels of analysis: those that pertain to individuals and those that reflect the collective character of thinking as inserted in joint activity and broader social life.

Seen from an individual level, thinking is related to other elements of the psychological growth of the person (e.g., maturation, emotions, language acquisition) and develops within a history of experiencing personal relationships with significant others, via trial and error in devising means (e.g., tools, know-how, strategies, discourse, concepts) via networks in which the person discovers the different roles that can be played. The individual discovers that the course of personal action can be stopped and reflected upon (e.g., imagined, replicated, predicted, modified, compared, criticized, built into an alternative, narrated).

This thinking activity is usually not done in isolation, however. On an interpersonal level, daily confrontation with the thinking of other partners is a powerful incentive that involves facing the *otherness* of his and/or her fellows' perceptions, feelings, wordings, or scopes. Incentives may come from a partner who joins in the activity, reflection, or conversation, reaches into the zone of proximal development (I prefer the term *zone of proximal thinking*), and pulls on the ongoing psychological activity, notably by contributing to its verbalization but also by just creating a differentiation of actions and thoughts. Thinking can also be fostered by formal teaching situations or from reading, the media, or other cultural activities (Zittoun, 2001). But usually these are mediated by someone who has introduced the young person to the school, the book, the play, or another cultural event or joint activity and who is also likely to discuss it with him or her later.

Even if some identification with the partner occurs, sustaining the mutuality, the interaction most often leads one to discover that, whatever the resemblance, the other is never oneself, and that one's own point of view amounts to only one among a number of others and is seldom the whole truth. Confrontation with alternative points of view might be resented as conflictual: a conflict between two modes of responses that, here and now, appear incompatible. But are conflicts always conflicts in the sense of incompatible issues? Answering this question requires examining the problem from different points of view. That is, gaining a deeper understanding of the situation or reformatting the problem may make it possible to account for both positions and even to conceive of other positions. Otherness per se is not adversity; being different brings about dialectical dynamics; conflicts need not be intellectual or emotional fights and certainly not physical fights. The difference of points of view creates opportunities. Sociocognitive conflicts challenge the person to depart from a restricted perception of what is at stake and to decenter and gain an understanding that includes the position of the peer (Perret-Clermont, Grossen, Nicolet, & Schubauer-Leoni, 1996; Carugati, this volume). Whether it is correct or incorrect does not matter at this point. This decentering allows a young person to become capable of accounting for different partners' points of view. It occurs most easily in relational spaces that have sufficient emotional security for the matter to be a cognition under consideration and not the relationship itself (Grossen & Perret-Clermont, 1992; Monteil, 1989; Perret-Clermont, 2000).

Young people need to experience such secure relationships. They might find them in families (Hofer, Youniss, & Noack, 1998; Hofer, Pontecorvo, this volume), schools, churches, or youth movements (Heath, this volume); or in sports, music, or theater groups (Roulleau-Berger, this volume); or in their more informal peer groups (Amerio, Boggi Cavallo, Palmonari, & Pombeni, 1990; Heath, Hundeide, this volume). And what about their experience in apprenticeships, student jobs, formal employment, trade unions (Tannock, this volume), and political parties? These crucial life settings deserve more attention from research in order for us to gain an awareness of when and how such activities can offer youth the necessary framing needed to exercise, through trial and error but still in security, new skills, other perspectives, and new ways of doing and taking the initiative. And yet this will not be sufficient (Perret & Perret-Clermont, 2001). Young people also need to be explicitly encouraged to *reflect upon* such learning opportunities, a necessary step for experience to become learning: that is, not only to venture into them, more or less by chance, but also to express the experience, consider it, remember it, learn from it, and plan new trials.

This leads to another level of analysis: the functioning of social institutions and intergroup relations. Families and school systems (Fouquet, this volume), professional training and division of labor (Ryan, Meghnagi, this volume), and even the boundaries of ethnic and religious groups are undergoing important changes. These changes affect both the conditions in which young people live and their access to the experience of former generations, as well as their understanding of its relevance for the present. The historical and cultural circumstances invalidate certain social modes of functioning, foster new ones, and modify the general scenery in which young people discover themselves sources of agency. What skills do they develop to cope with the apparent diminishing of traditional references? How do drastic events such as war (Popadić, this volume), regained peace, the move toward democratic management of society (or the reverse), and rapid economic changes (e.g., growth or recession) affect their life perspectives (Bandura, 1995; Newman, 1993; Petersen & Mortimer, 1994; Wilson, 1996; Fouquet, this volume) and present attitudes toward self-agency, identity, and social relationships?

The Social, Cultural, and Historical Embeddedness of the Development of Young People's Life Skills

Learning is not just the incidental gathering of information (on the Internet or elsewhere). It is also not only the steady conformation to formal school requirements. Long-term relationships and, hence, sustained interest seem necessary to acquire complex skills (Hinde, Perret-Clermont, & Stevenson-Hinde, 1985). Efforts are more likely to be fruitful when they respond to vital needs in a scenario of plausible success. As Hundeide (2001) states:

We therefore need a broader view of human development and mediation, where the emphasis is not on the development of skills, tools, operations or even cognitive structure as such, but on the mediation of our shared cultural and moral conceptions of the world, of life, of values of persons, identities and human relationships within which cognitive skills and individual coping strategies become meaningful and worthwhile. (p. 6)

The personal appropriation of preexisting knowledge and the development of competence occur if they get crafted within activities that make sense for a personal narrative. Hundeide continues, "Human beings need a conceptual framework of meaning into which they can project their life so that it makes sense. These life-theories or narratives are crucial for psychological adaptation and survival under difficult life conditions" (p. 1). To reflect on one's own practice is also in itself a source of change, but it requires discursive resources. Adolescents will develop skills in those activities that deal with issues that are relevant for them on the personal level (e.g., survival, recognition, reproduction, identity, violence), but these skills will be life skills only if they are also meaningful at the collective level and not just fruits of despair. To be true skills (and not mere reactions), they have to be recognized as such, reflected upon, and adapted to new situations. And this can occur only if adequate frames offer the discursive means, the interlocutors, and the rules of the game that guarantee the security necessary to read past experience in a critically constructive way.

Obviously the thinking spaces of the young will differ according to their social and cultural situations. In the ensuing chapters of this volume, the reader will discover how certain social settings (e.g., families, schools, peer groups, or workplaces) are likely to function at times as very valuable resources, in other circumstances as constraints, or in extreme situations as destroyers of the identity and thinking capacities of the person. It will become apparent how much the wider historical and cultural circumstances affect the possibility of intergenerational or cross-age transmissions. Under pressures such as affective losses, school failure (Zittoun, this volume), unemployment, war, and cultural disruptions, young people might undergo more or less severe emotional anesthesia. Where and with whom can they regain their human identity necessary to make a narrative and revisit their experience? When meaning-making systems have been removed, how can the young return to "normal"?

In some circumstances, adults no longer believe in their capacity to educate or teach. Some educational institutions do not adapt easily to societal change. For instance, in the professional training area, even the dual system does not always manage to keep up with changes in the market. And in places where society requires entrepreneurship and high-risk attitudes, schools might still tend to teach obedience and conformity rather than opening spaces for creativity, initiative, and responsibility. In other circumstances, however, the nonadaptive nature of certain institutions can make them a refuge in a disrupted environment. When adults and young people compete for scarce resources, the criteria for adulthood may become desynchronized. When society is disrupted, the young do not feel welcome to join society, but instead may be inclined to change it or to try to escape from it, as some young Yugoslavians did in the 1990s (Popadić, this volume).

Learning, Meaning Making, and Generativity

Many of the findings reported in the following chapters point to the importance of discourse not only in conveying experience but also in meaning making and learning (Middleton, Pontecorvo, Säljö, Tudge, this volume). Perhaps experience cannot be conveyed, but the meaning of it can be transmitted and permitted to point to goals and relationships that are worth investing in, inviting young people to project themselves into time perspectives, building bridges among the present, the past, and the future. Narratives permit the reconstruction of identity throughout changes from infancy to adulthood and also throughout changes in the environment and in ideological modes.

Discourse as a collective activity creates the tools for transmitting cognitive and symbolic memory, confronting reality and fantasy, and opening the way for distantiated looks at emotions and events. Spaces with adequate frames (i.e., security, rules of the game, mediation tools, know-how) must offer the possibility of putting experience into words and reflecting on it. Frames are required to stop the concatenation of ongoing activities and to invite the actors to face their limits, revisit their experience, acknowledge the new skills learned as well as the difficulties that have been overcome and those that remain, and redefine themselves as conscious agents with goals within their settings. The invitation to the noble task of thinking has to be extended to the young. Frames need guardians whose task is not to possess knowledge as a private property or to repress creativity or critical reflection, but to maintain the rules of the social contracts that permit dialogue and joint creative thinking. Who will take responsibility for this guardianship of thinking spaces that are secure enough for the anxiety-raising activity of revisiting experience? This guardianship is not custody. It is a caring, social awareness, a generativity: the *engendrement* of the meaning of the lives of future generations, the crafting of futures (Resnick and Perret-Clermont, this volume).

REFERENCES

Amerio, P., Boggi Cavallo, P., Palmonari, A., & Pombeni, M. L. (1990). *Gruppi di adolescenti e processi di socializzazione* [Groups of adolescents and socialization processes]. Bologna: Il Mulino.

Bandura, A. (Ed.). (1995). *Self-efficacy in changing society.* Cambridge: Cambridge University Press.

Doise, W. (1982). *L'explication en psychologie sociale.* [Explanation in social psychology]. Paris: Presses Universitaires de France.

Erikson, E. H. (1950). *Childhood and society.* New York: Norton.

Grossen, M., & Perret-Clermont, A.-N. (Eds.). (1992). *L'espace thérapeutique. Cadres et contextes* [The therapeutical space: Frames and contexts]. Paris and Neuchâtel: Delachaux et Niestlé.

Hinde, R. A., Perret-Clermont, A.-N., & Stevenson-Hinde, J. (Eds.). (1985). *Social relationships and cognitive development.* Oxford: Oxford University Press.

Hofer, M., Youniss, J., & Noack, P. (Eds.). (1998). *Advances in applied developmental psychology:* Vol. 15. *Verbal interaction and development in families with adolescents.* Stamford, CT/London: Ablex.

Hundeide, K. (2001). Reactivation of cultural mediational practices. *Psychology and Developing Societies, 13*(1), 1–24.

Monteil, J.-M. (1989). *Eduquer et former* [Educate and train]. Grenoble, France: Presses Universitaires de Grenoble.

Newman, K. S. (1993). *Declining fortunes: The withering of the American dream.* New York: Basic Books.

Perret, J.-F., & Perret-Clermont, A.-N. (2001). *Apprendre un métier technique* [Learning a trade in a context of technological change]. Fribourg, Switzerland: Presses Universitaires de Fribourg.

Perret-Clermont, A.-N. (2000). Apprendre et enseigner avec efficience à l'école. Approches psychosociales des possibilités et des limites de l'apprentissage en situation scolaire classique [Learning and teaching efficiently in school: Psychosocial approaches of the possibilities and limits of learning in a classical school situation]. In U. P. Trier (Ed.), *Efficacité de la formation entre recherche et politique* [Efficiency of training between research and politics] (pp. 111–134). Chur and Zurich: Verlag Rüegger.

Perret-Clermont, A.-N., with the collaboration of Grossen, M., Nicolet, M., & Schubauer-Leoni, M. L. (1996). *La construction de l'intelligence dans l'interaction sociale* [The construction of intelligence in social interaction]. Berne, Switzerland: Peter Lang (revised and augmented from the original version: *Social interaction and cognitive development* [1980]. London and New York: Academic Press).

Petersen, A. C., & Mortimer, J. T. (Eds.). (1994). *Youth unemployment and society.* Cambridge: Cambridge University Press.

Resnick, L. B., Levine, J. M., & Teasley, S. D. (Eds.). (1991). *Socially shared cognition.* Washington, DC: American Psychological Association.

Wilson, W. J. (1996). *When work disappears: The world of the new urban poor.* New York: Alfred A. Knopf.

Winnicott, D. W. (1971). *Playing and reality.* New York: Basic Books.

Zittoun, T. (2001). *Engendrements symboliques. Devenir parent: le choix du prénom* [Symbolic births. Becoming parents: Choosing a child's first name]. Unpublished doctoral dissertation. University of Neuchâtel, Switzerland.

2 Prospects for Youth in Postindustrial Societies

Lauren B. Resnick and Anne-Nelly Perret-Clermont

The industrialized countries of Europe, North America, and Asia are now well into a period of economic transformation that appears to be as profound in its social effects as the Industrial Revolution itself. As strategies of production and distribution change dramatically, and as the movement of people and goods across national borders accelerates, the conditions in which adults live and children are raised are shifting. No groups in society are more profoundly affected by these changes than are adolescents and young adults, who are themselves in a period of personal transition from childhood to adulthood, from appropriate dependence on others to responsibility for the welfare of others, from preparation for future economic and civic participation to actual participation.

It is unclear to young people – and, when they are candid with the young, to their parents, mentors, and advisors – just how they should prepare. Those in positions of political and economic power and influence agree that a more highly educated workforce will be required in the future, a workforce able to participate in defining and evaluating their own work, rather than just following orders, and able to learn new skills several times during their working lives. It is assumed, therefore, that young people should spend substantial portions of their adolescence and young adulthood in some form of education and training. But no one knows exactly how this education ought to proceed. Narrow preparation for a specific trade or professional career is not likely to produce the skills and habits that will enable productive adaptation over a lifetime of work. Yet broader philosophical or "liberal" education seems too isolated from the demands of real-world participation.

Although young people are spending more time in education and training institutions, these may not be the only, perhaps not even the most important, agencies of passage from childhood to adulthood. Traditionally, the workplace has been a locale in which young people were socialized into the roles and responsibilities of adulthood and where they learned many of the skills they would need as workers. As recently as a generation ago, the majority of young people in most countries left secondary school to join the workforce directly, either as fully participating wage earners – usually in unskilled blue-collar occupations – or in some form of structured apprenticeship. On the job, young people learned not only the particular skills needed to do the work but also the *discipline* of work, from punctuality, to following the rules and rhythms of the workplace, to the social forms that governed interaction in and around the workplace. Being a worker or apprentice also gave the young person access to the adult social life of the community. No longer a child, he (and sometimes she) could then join in the informal gatherings of adults, including the after-work drink, church and political meetings, and sports and communal excursions.

Religious (and quasi-religious) and labor movements supplemented the informal socialization opportunities with organized youth programs. These youth programs often provided young people who were no longer in school and whose work required more discipline than thought with *thinking spaces*, as Perret-Clermont has called them (see Chapter 1, this volume): places in which they could learn about ideas and events beyond those of their immediate job and community; reflect on social and personal possibilities; and cultivate personal interests in the arts, politics, religion, science, and technology. Such programs functioned against a backdrop of expectations and socialization provided by the work experience. If factory or other unskilled work was repetitive and not likely to foster human and spiritual development, youth agencies could provide the "antidote." Meanwhile, the experience of regular, respected work provided young people with a structured, adult role in society. They could – often with the support of youth groups – envisage a future that included them as productive members of society.

Today that nexus for socialization of young people has broken down. Traditional entry jobs are disappearing, and high rates of youth unemployment have been the norm in most industrial countries for some years. In other countries, there are plenty of jobs, at least for mainstream youth, but these are often part-time and short-term, so young people *churn* from job to job (Zemsky, 1997). They earn enough to satisfy some immediate consumer desires but not enough to take on family responsibilities. Above all, they do not experience the social induction into adulthood that used to accompany early work participation.

In countries with strong welfare systems, the economic impact of youth unemployment or underemployment is substantially mitigated. Income alone cannot provide the socialization into responsibility that becoming a member of the adult workforce used to provide, however. Official youth groups and training institutions are not adequately filling the *socialization gap*, and to many adults, youth appear to be increasingly alienated from mainstream, productive society. This alienation, sometimes accompanied by increased youth crime, is exacerbated by the presence of mixed ethnic populations with differing social, cultural, economic, and (sometimes) citizenship statuses. At the very least, large segments of the youth population seem to be adrift, deprived of a sense of the future and unsure that they can find a welcoming place in the adult life of their countries.

The problem of alienation and drift is highest for youth from marginal populations: for example, the children of immigrants and members of certain ethnic minorities. But the social dislocation created by changing economic conditions is no longer a problem of just the underclass. Alternative *youth cultures* attract the children of even the most privileged. The reason for this must lie in something more than the appeal of the media that promote these alternatives. Young people clearly want something that the formal institutions of which they are a part cannot, or at least do not, provide. What is that something? Could mainstream institutions do a better job of providing it? Perhaps they could, but only if those in charge are able and willing to examine the alternatives closely and to consider the possibilities of new forms of organization that are better suited to an era in which ideas and information flow without apparent control and in which the boundaries between youth and adulthood are far less clear than formerly.

This massive *de*structuring provided the backdrop against which the conference that forms the foundation for this volume was convened. We were aiming to use recent research on learning, socialization, and identity formation to suggest approaches to *re*structuring that would respect current political and economic realities. We began with an apparently simple question: What would it take to help young people join society?

It quickly became clear that our formulation was filled with contradiction and irony. For what could *joining society* mean? Except in rare pathological instances, children enter the world as social beings, members of a functioning microsociety of family closely connected to others. As several of our authors show in convincing detail (e.g., Pontecorvo, Hofer, Tudge), children and adolescents function as part of intergenerational and multi-institutional groups, and their cognitive competencies, social identities, and preferences are shaped by interactions in these primary social groupings. From the moment of birth, children are joined to the several microsocieties in which they participate. The simple underlying message of these often complex analyses is that, with rare exceptions, people of all ages are socially joined in whatever they are doing.

In everyday language, the term *joining society* sometimes means becoming an adult, that is, behaving and being treated as an adult rather than a child or youth. But what is the definition of *adult*? Adulthood sometimes means being a parent, but what about very young parents, teenage mothers for example? Have they joined adult society? And have others who choose to delay or even to forgo parenthood given up on adulthood as well? It seems clear that a strict definition of adulthood as taking on the position and responsibility of leading a family is not applicable today.

Joining society as an adult is sometimes defined in terms of working: being economically productive rather than economically dependent. Yet this definition provides no more clarity than family status does. Our judgments of what it means to be productive and adultlike, even in economic terms, are very contextualized and nuanced. Depending on his country and subculture, a 30-year-old man still living with his parents but holding down a steady job may be considered dependent, whereas a 30-year-old mother who chooses to stay at home to care for her child is likely considered independent. Joining society means having a career, an adult social identity related to one's economic or work function. But what can this notion of career mean when today's life trajectories are broken or unpredictable or when we are told that many people will have two, three, or even four different careers in the course of their lives, and when technological changes, in particular in the field of information and communication technologies (ICT), modify the times and the places for work and training and induce the creation of new trades (Schürch, 2002)?

Least clear of all is the notion that one joins society by becoming part of the social mainstream. This may mean joining a mainstream religion as opposed to a cult. It may mean voting or otherwise participating in official political or civic life. Or it may just mean being a law-abiding citizen, playing by the rules, avoiding criminal or marginal activities. But what about those for whom there is – or is perceived to be – no place within the mainstream? If society appears to be prohibiting your joining, how can you join? Do you face a life of alienation or opposition? Or might you *create* alternative societies, subcultures that are more receptive, comfortable, and even economically fulfilling?

Such youth-constructed societies in fact exist – *gray zone* organizations that, for the most part, do not have much in the way of official sponsorship and may evoke fear and concern among mainstream citizens. Perhaps a closer examination of these subsocieties can help point the way to more "official" solutions.

What Do Youth Want? Lessons from Youth-Led Organizations

To imagine new forms of social organization that might work for today's youth, we need to begin by asking what the young themselves seem to want and what seems to attract them. What evokes their loyalty and willingness to expend effort? The chapters by Heath, Roulleau-Berger, Hundeide, and Coulon (all in Part II of this volume) describing gray zone youth organizations begin to provide an answer. Each of these chapters describes a microsociety, mostly created and managed by young people themselves, that provides for its members a well-structured environment in which to engage in work they view as productive and within which a range of social and economic needs can be met. The organizations described in these chapters range from those that mainstream society can embrace with little reservation (e.g., the performance and sports groups described by Heath) to the most frightening of neo-Nazi youth groups (Hundeide). Some, such as the gray market cooperatives described by Roulleau-Berger, occupy a more disputed territory. Despite the different political and economic niches that these organizations fill, however, they are stunningly similar in terms of providing basic social functions for their young participants. The following are some core features shared by otherwise very different organizations operating in different countries and in very different political and social conditions:

> *Earned entry.* Individuals become members of youth-constructed organizations by proving themselves, not by right of birth or assignment by an official organization. Some have initiation rites. All have rather elaborate rule structures. Failure to live by the rules leads to expulsion. Membership is thus never permanent but is continuously earned.
>
> *Ritual, belonging, and identity.* Membership is symbolically affirmed by participation in rituals that mark one as an insider. These can be religious and peaceful in nature or may involve ritual violence of various kinds. Participation in such rituals establishes and affirms one's identity as a member – both to oneself and to one's fellow members.
>
> *Group support for individual needs.* Each of the organizations studied has certain communal commitments to its members. Contributions to economic and family needs, including the care of dependent siblings,

is part of what all of the youth-based organizations offer. Backing up the individual in controversies (such as gang confrontations) also provides some sense of stability and protection for young people who may be living in threatening conditions. For youth on the margins, this economic and protective function plays a central role, making it possible to live more comfortably in the larger official society, even if not able to join it fully.

Short-term, visible payoffs. For young people drawn to the kinds of youth-based organizations reported here, the future is uncertain and unreliable. The organizations that attract them are focused on success that is visible in a relatively short time span. In the eyes of the youth who are involved, one attraction of the organizations is that they are focused on action in the here and now rather than on preparation for uncertain opportunities later.

Will to productivity. Youth-based organizations reveal a hunger among young people for productive engagement in society. They want to do something that they view as worthwhile. They want to be recognized for real achievements. They do not want handouts or praise that they do not trust as authentic. They want to earn their way, albeit sometimes in ways that mainstream society finds questionable or disturbing.

Productivity and Work as Elements of Youth Socialization

These features of youth-run organizations point to some features that might become elements of redesigned official programs for youth development. Consider first the central role of work itself – the will to produce in the here and now. Young people may be creating a new version of the *work ethic* described almost a century ago by Weber (2001). Like 19th-century Protestants, participants in today's youth-led organizations seem to value productive work not just as a means to an economic end but also as a mark of identity, a kind of social validation of their importance and membership in a valued group.

These young people may be trying to recapture an important piece of what official society has denied them. William Julius Wilson (1996) brought to our attention the devastating intergenerational effect of the disappearance of work within an entire community. Growing up in a world in which their parents and other older relatives are not living within the discipline – and rewards – of regular jobs, young people lack an image of the possibilities of work and often turn to other ways of getting along or, sometimes, prospering. Catherine Newman, whose earlier work had documented the devastating effects of permanent job loss on the families of managerial and technical professionals (Newman, 1999a), has also shown that, for marginal youth, even low-paid, routine jobs can serve as important routes to social participation. In other work (Newman, 1999b), she demonstrates how young people in the most marginal communities of the United States use low-paid, dull fast-food or similar jobs to earn money (perhaps for tuition in training courses) as well as to define themselves as productive members of the broader society. So work appears to play a key role in youth development, not only for young people in the gray zone organizations described in this volume but also for young people climbing a more establishment-honored ladder of training and preparation.

Here, then, is a most unlikely socialization vehicle for a joinable society. It is work itself – dull, uninteresting, underpaid, but productive work – that can, under certain circumstances, provide a way into the society at large. Young people would certainly prefer that what they do not be dull and underpaid. But they do want to work. It appears that welfare and other social payment schemes, although they may be part of a full youth development policy, do not meet young people's need to feel productive and responsible. Without turning it into simple exploitation, how might we harness this will to effort and responsibility? Some years ago, Steve and Agnes Hamilton (in press) described to American audiences the socializing functions that the German youth apprenticeship system fulfilled alongside its education and training functions. At a time when established youth apprenticeship systems in Europe are challenged by new tastes for higher education, along with shifts in the economy, it will be important to maintain productive work opportunities for youth as an important element in revised programs. Countries such as the United States, whose education systems generally treat youth labor as an annoying fact of life rather than a potential resource for socializing young people, will need to reconsider some very deep assumptions that providing maximum learning opportunities for young people calls for keeping them mainly in some form of schooling well beyond what young people themselves might prefer.

Communities of Practice and the Dilemma of Training

Besides the will to produce, something else can be learned from examining the alternative gray zone organizations that young people inhabit so much more enthusiastically than they do many of the organizations created for their benefit by the establishment. This is the importance of *communities of practice*, a term originally used by ethnographers to describe the unofficial social groupings that mediate between the official rules and defined roles of formal organizations and what it actually takes to get the work of those organizations done (Brown & Duguid, 2000; Lave & Wenger, 1991; Suchman, 1995; Wenger, 1998).

A community of practice is a group of people who engage in coordinated action aimed at a shared goal. There is often substantial learning involved for individual members of the group and for the group as a whole, but the focus of effort is on completing current work. There is also much social interaction, in forms often different from those of formal meetings, official training sessions, or other management events. By observing a community of practice, one sees not just socializing, not just learning, but also productive doing. The task that is worked on has economic or social value; it is not designed as a learning exercise but rather as an effort to provide a product or service valued by someone external to the group: the audience that will attend a theater production, the customers in a street market, or political leaders. This external validation appears to be essential to the proper functioning and the appeal of youth-led organizations as well.

Productive doing through social and cognitive coordination is characteristic of all the many studies that now exist of effective communities of practice in the workplace. In one of the earliest such studies, Julian Orr (1990) described the practices of Xerox copy machine repairmen who, in their down time between repair calls, traded stories about difficult repair cases and worked out possible solutions for challenging new cases. Other examples of such studies have documented how ship navigation (Hutchins, 1993) and airline cockpit crews coordinate their thinking and action (Hutchins & Palen, 1997); how ground control crews in an airport act together to bring a plane into a gate safely and on time; and how a news staff monitors information coming in over a wire service and informally distributes topics to appropriate individuals. In each of these studies, there is a striking contrast between what groups of workers actually do and what the company manual specifies as standard operating procedure. Supervisors of these productive work groups often do not know about the unofficial practices of their workers. And the workers themselves often hold the knowledge tacitly. Knowledge is embodied in workers' everyday actions, and participants often cannot easily articulate their knowledge to others (hence the need for ethnographic research to document and describe the existence and functioning of communities of practice).

Although focused on production, communities of practice can also provide substantial learning opportunities for individual members. For example, Goodwin (1995) showed how novices in a chemical production plant are able to produce pure products and learn new skills at the same time. From a very different theoretical perspective (more concerned with finding ways to include unskilled and undereducated workers in manufacturing that was becoming increasingly demanding technically), Bertrand Schwarz (1994) showed how line workers in an automobile factory could learn technical skills through analysis of their own work processes. Attending specifically to the learning aspects of communities of practice, some scholars have explored how the community-of-practice concept might translate into changed practices of schooling and training.

These community-of-practice approaches to learning contrast sharply with the dominant official approaches to preparing youth for economic participation. Most countries' training programs are organized around credentialing systems in which students climb a *ladder of skills*. Skills are often taught in a decontextualized manner, separate from whatever on-the-job practice may also be offered. In northern Europe's dual systems of youth apprenticeship, for example, the school rather than the workplace has most of the responsibility for teaching specific skills. Furthermore, the focus of most training systems is primarily on preparation for the future. As a result, the here-and-now productivity that characterizes youth-led organizations and other communities of practice is sacrificed. Worse yet, the skills learned in the school or training center are often mismatched to the labor market. Consequently, young people participate in training programs – whether under official school or other sponsorship (arrangements differ by country) – and then often find that there are no jobs for them. The de facto message to marginal young people may be that society does not really intend for them to join. In some other cases, youth understand that they are likely to get jobs if they earn their diplomas, but they do not believe their training is really relevant for those jobs. This can have two consequences: boredom and lack of commitment during their training years, and then lack of cognitive reflective resources during their later professional practice (Perret & Perret-Clermont, 2001).

Communities of Practice for Youth and Adults

A focus on youth alone will give us only a very partial view of what kinds of practices and policies might smooth the path to productive adulthood for young people. Fragmented social conditions indeed create new conditions for the young. But it is worth noting that the new conditions in which adults are living may be part of the reason that so many youth are having such a difficult time joining society. Fragmented conditions for adults incur secondary consequences for youth development: Social roles, identity figures, significant others, and social feedback networks are changing, some-times vanishing. This means that gray zones exist not only in the economic and social spaces that youth inhabit but also in the symbolic space that they occupy. In some cases, these gray zones are vacuums where the young subsist in a cultural no-man's land, with no significant interlocutors; no meaningful frames of reference for values, norms, and ideals; no collective practices or stimulating discourses, exchanges, and thinking. Under these conditions, the *symbolic resources* (Zittoun, 2001) of the young are likely to be scarce, their affiliation moves anchored only in short-term relation-ships, and their opportunities to link past and present experiences poor and unarticulated.

The gray zones discussed throughout this volume can be viewed as the laboratory of the future, allowing the crafting of new interpersonal rela-tionships, the definition of new roles and intergenerational relations, the development of new practices for daily life as well as for cultural, learning, or work activities, for the emotional repair or destruction of disturbed self-assertive and socialization processes. They are in themselves forces of neither good nor evil, but rather *open spaces* either for creativity or for brainwashing experiences (Roulleau-Berger, Hundeide, this volume). The *desinstitution-alization of life paths* (Meghnagi, this volume) can open opportunities to those for whom traditional norms and institutions inhibit creative adapta-tion. At the same time, unstructured gray zones can augment the risks for the most fragile persons and statuses.

Under which conditions can social and symbolic gray zones be places for constructive creativity both for individuals and for communities? And when are they destructive of personal and collective agency? In their illustrations of the interdependency between cognitive and identity processes, between meaning making and self-esteem, both Carugati and Rijsman (this volume) make clear the important role of relational and social frames. The young develop their minds and their understanding of themselves and of wisdom (Staudinger, this volume) throughout their personal history of encounters with others in learning activities. Perriault (this volume) describes the in-terdependency of these life experiences in the case of the learning to use ICT tools. For these learning moments to be fruitful, they have to take place in contexts that are sufficiently sheltered to offer security. Trial and error, a crucial mode of learning, can be carried out only if the risks of vital physical or symbolic damages (e.g., for health, face saving, identity, affiliation, school success) are contained.

It is interesting to note that, in the examples reported by Heath from youth-based organizations, the successes seem to have relied in part on the notable commitments of older peers to protect younger members from social acts that would damage their social survival. These individuals create in-group discipline and present it as training to become a responsible person: that is, someone capable of successfully confronting the need to coordinate personal goals with the outside norms of real life. These older peers become authority figures. They gain their power in the in-group by their capacity to meet the needs of their young partners and to offer them identification figures and affiliation paths, as well as their capacity to receive outside recognition for their successful ventures.

The outside plays a crucial role in youth-based organizations, providing them with recognition via mediating adults who maintain a frame of security for the organization itself in its relationships with the wider society (e.g., housing of the activities, presenting a public image via the media, maintaining relations with the police and other formal or political institutions). The power relationships, and the negotiation processes between these mediating adults and the young organizers, are very subtle and crucial processes (Palmonari, 1987) that deserve more attention, both for their role in the successes and failures of youth-based organizations and for the light they might shed on other institutions that seem presently to be losing contact with the younger generations: trade unions (Tannock, this volume), political parties, mainstream religious congregations, and even some parts of the dual vocational training systems of Germany, Switzerland, and other northern European countries.

The creative gray zone offered by youth-based organizations goes beyond peer relationships and the mixture of security and feedback from "outside" reality that they provide. These organizations also privilege certain forms of discourse as an activity of reflection on individual and collective practice. Youth-based organizations are not alone in providing such opportunities, and much depends on the match between young people's experiences at home or in other informal settings and what they encounter in the outside world. Kaiser's examples (this volume) are cases of discrepancies between the youngsters' discourses and the learning/teaching practices in which they are immersed in school, with consequent inhibition of their feelings of self-esteem and personal agency. Säljö and Tudge (this volume) also treat the school as a potentially nurturing space for reflective discourse but suggest that reflection can be more or less consonant with real-life experience. The (relatively) sheltered opportunities offered by school for some trial and error and reflection exercises can support acquisition of semiotic tools and competencies, but these may not transfer easily to daily or professional life contexts.

Each move from formal to other settings seems to require new meaning-making processes because the move from one context to another changes significant references. For Middleton (this volume), different settings imply different cultures of discourse to which the incomer has to be socialized. In other words, as Carugati states in his chapter, the move is not only (or perhaps not even primarily) a change from a lower stage of understanding to a higher one, but also a lateral move from one cultural setting proper to a given community of practice to another cultural setting pertaining to another collective practice. In an open and complex (and ever-changing) society, the young must be socialized into several communities of practice at the same time, not withstanding the possible contradictions between the ways of doing and the ethos of these various communities (Cesari Lusso, 2001). Only the development of reflective skills over these conflicting demands can foster adaptation capacities, both at the practical and symbolic levels, and permit creative adjustment to these sometimes divergent communities of practice.

These reflective skills seem to be born in interactive processes (Perret-Clermont & Nicolet, 2001; Resnick, Levine, & Teasley, 1991; Carugati and Heath, this volume). They do not develop accidentally, however, but must be deliberately cultivated in planned *thinking spaces* (Perret-Clermont, 2000) under the coaching of peers or adults who assume specific roles in framing the discussion, giving the floor, involving peripheral participants, protecting the dignity of participants, and keeping the discussion on point. This last function calls for a deep understanding of the issues under discussion as well as well as of the symbolic tools specific to different domains of discourse. As Säljö makes clear, this development of discourse tools and processes has been the traditional role of schools. Even in the dual systems of vocational training that give major weight to work involvement and hands-on learning, a very important role is granted to the professional schools. Yet these schools are not always well adapted to their intended role in developing reflective discourse among youth, which leaves a large void in the overall experiences of young people. Experience in helping the young in their transition from school to work helps to reveal the dimensions that present formal education seems to leave unmet (Zittoun, this book).

Families are yet another setting in which young people may learn the discourse skills that will help them shift to adult roles. In family discussions, children and youth often practice the speech behaviors and types of discourse that characterize asymmetrical relationships. Pontecorvo (this volume) shows how this can work around the family dinner table, while Hofer (this volume) describes mother–daughter interactions. In both cases, the discursive activity of the young entails not only cognitive and linguistic learning, as well as emotional and cultural socialization, but also a dynamic process of negotiation and renegotiation of the nature of the relationship, the adolescent's role, and mutual expectancies. In youth-based organizations, at work, in schools, or in the family, the young will learn to take responsibilities in an autonomous, skillful, and socialized way only if given flexible and safe opportunities to negotiate step by step, and with the necessary support, their advancement in participation, reflection, and accountability. This implies, in all these places, a space for discourse, debate, decision making, and feedback from outer reality.

What is meant here by "feedback from outer reality"? As noted earlier, the young seem to seek full social status and a sense of personal agency via the desire to be productive. Having an impact on the outside world, seeing the fruit of one's labors and not just receiving the traditional social gratifications given to children (e.g., praise from parents, marks given by teachers, diplomas conferred by schools), are experiences longed for by adolescents. Yet our capitalist societies allocate to youth mostly a place as consumers. In order to occupy this position, some young people invest their energy in earning money as early as possible, entering the labor (sometimes gray) market at almost any cost (e.g., dull work, low pay, terrible schedules, no on-site training). Being productive comes to mean nothing more than earning money when, as we have seen, there are much broader, socially generous meanings of productivity that can attract the energy and loyalty of young people.

Fouquet's, Ryan's, and Popadić's contributions to this volume make it clear that the transition pathways followed by the young are not only the result of education and self-expectancies but also are framed largely by institutional structures that differ substantially from one country to the next in the status they grant to the young, in the age of involvement in various activities, and in the kind of support they offer. Given this variety of situations internationally, the conditions exist for a set of *natural experiments* investigating how transitions to productive adulthood can best be managed. What are the opportunities for discourse and reflection that transform these transitions into learning opportunities (Perret-Clermont & Zittoun, 2002)? How do individuals and institutions adapt to the structural changes occurring around them? Above all, what happens in the gray zones in which society at large, and the young themselves, develop and test possible futures? If research of these kinds occurs over the next few years, we will be able to have a much more optimistic discussion of joining society the next time scholars are convened to address this crucial set of issues.

REFERENCES

Brown, J. S., & Duguid, P. (2000). *The social life of information.* Boston: Harvard Business School Press.

Cesari Lusso, V. (2001). *Quand le défi est appelé integration... Parcours de socialisation et de personnalisation de jeunes issus de la migration* [When integration is at stake... Socialization and personalization courses of young people of migrant origin]. Bern: Peter Lang.

Goodwin, C. (1995). The blackness of black: Color categories as situated practice. In L. B. Resnick, R. Saljo, C. Pontecorvo, & B. Burge (Eds.), *Discourse, tools, and reasoning: Situated cognition and technologically supported environments* (pp. 111–140). Berlin: Springer-Verlag.

Hamilton, S. F., & Hamilton, M. A. (Eds.). (in press). *Handbook of youth development.* Beverly Hills, CA: Sage.

Hutchins, E. (1993). Learning to navigate. In S. Chalkin & J. Lave (Eds.), *Understanding practice: Perspectives on activity and context* (pp. 35–63). Cambridge: Cambridge University Press.

Hutchins, E., & Palen, L. (1997). Constructing meanings from space, gesture, and speech. In L. B. Resnick, R. Saljo, C. Pontecorvo, & B. Burge (Eds.), *Discourse, tools, and reasoning: Situated cognition and technologically supported environments* (pp. 23–40). Berlin: Springer-Verlag.

Lave, J., & Wenger, E. (1991). *Situated learning. Legitimate peripheral participation.* Cambridge: Cambridge University Press.

Newman, K. S. (1999a). *Falling from grace: Downward mobility in the age of affluence* Berkeley: University of California Press.

Newman, K. S. (1999b). *No shame in my game: The working poor in the inner city.* New York: Alfred A. Knopf and the Russell Sage Foundation.

Orr, J. (1990). Sharing knowledge, celebrating identity: War stories and community memory in a service culture. In D. S. Middleton & D. Edwards (Eds.), *Collective remembering: Memory in society* (pp. 169–189). Beverley Hills, CA: Sage.

Palmonari, A. (1987). *Notes sur l'adolescence* (2nd ed.). Cousset and Fribourg, Switzerland: DelVal; and Dossiers de Psychologie, No 22. Neuchâtel, Switzerland: Université de Neuchâtel.

Perret, J.-F., & Perret-Clermont, A.-N. avec la participation de D. Golay Schilter, Claude Kaiser, & Luc-Olivier Pochon. (2001). *Apprendre un métier dans un contexte de mutations technologiques* [Learning a technical trade in a context of technological changes]. Fribourg, Switzerland: Editions Universitaires Fribourg.

Perret-Clermont, A.-N. (2000). Apprendre et enseigner avec efficience à l'école [Learning and teaching efficiently in school]. In U. P. Trier (Ed.), *Efficacité de la formation entre recherche et politique* [Efficiency of training between research and politics] (pp. 111–134). Zürich: Ruegger.

Perret-Clermont, A.-N., & Nicolet, M. (Eds.). (2001). *Interagir et connaître. Enjeux et régulations sociales dans le développement cognitif* [Interact and know: Rules and social regulations in cognitive development]. Paris: L'Harmattan.

Perret-Clermont, A.-N., & Zittoun, T. (2002). Esquisse d'une psychologie de la transition [Sketch of a psychology of transitions]. *Education Permanente, 1*, 12–14.

Resnick, L. B., Levine, J. M., & Teasley, S. D. (1991). *Socially shared cognition.* Washington, DC: American Psychological Association.

Schürch, D. (2002). *L'intégration des technologies de l'information et de la communication dans les projets de développement de régions enclavées* [The integration of information and communication technologies in the projects of development of isolated areas]. In T. Karsenti, D. Perays, & J. Viens (Eds.), *Revue des sciences de l'éducation, 28*(2), 435–358.

Schwarz, B. (1994). *Moderniser sans exclure* [Modernize without excluding]. Paris: Editions La Decouverte.

Suchman, L. (1995). Centers of coordination: A case and some themes. In L. B. Resnick, R. Saljo, C. Pontecorvo, & B. Burge (Eds.), *Discourse, tools, and reasoning: Situated cognition and technologically supported environments* (pp. 41–62). Berlin: Springer-Verlag.

Weber, M. (2001). *The Protestant ethic and the spirit of capitalism.* Los Angeles: Roxbury.

Wenger, E. (1998). *Communities of practice: Learning, meaning and identity.* Cambridge: Cambridge University Press.

Wilson, W. J. (1996). *When work disappears: The world of the new urban poor.* New York: Vintage Books.

Zemsky, R. (1997). Skills and the economy: An employer context for understanding the school-to-work transition. In A. Lesgold, M. J. Feuer, & A. B. Black (Eds.), *Transitions in work and learning: Implications for assessment* (pp. 34–61). Washington, DC: National Academy Press.

Zittoun, T. (2001). *Engendrements symboliques. Devinir parent: le choix du prénom* [Symbolic births. Becoming parents: Choosing a child's first name]. Unpublished doctoral dissertation, University of Neuchâtel, Switzerland.

3   Overview of the Volume

Tania Zittoun, Anne-Nelly Perret-Clermont,
and Clotilde Pontecorvo

The contributions of this book lead the way to a wide variety of questions related to young people moving toward adulthood in complex societies. Ideas such as youth, society, and adulthood are problematic; so is the nature of the move itself. In their opening chapters, Perret-Clermont and Resnick consider this period as a time of preparation or transition; but it can also be described in terms of socialization, of learning – and learning refers both to acquisition of skills in specific communities and to the ability to enter new social spaces – or of developing thinking abilities – for resolving problems or for reflecting on one's own trajectory. The authors included in this volume would all admit that young people neither learn nor think in isolation, and the authors would also assume the embeddedness of personal, intersubjective, group, and wider contextual dimensions, although their analyses focus on different levels.

In this dense landscape, the reader is invited to follow a spiral path, moving along these dimensions through different zones of social worlds. This path should provide some relief and some depth to this landscape. The book is organized in six parts. Parts II and III focus on communities of practice. Part II plunges us into *gray zones* of the social world. The study of these less known, more spontaneous spaces makes it possible to highlight tensions and challenges that young people face in transition periods in modern societies. Part III examines some more classical institutional learning settings in relation to nonformal spheres of life. Part IV focuses on an individual level of analysis, with special attention to discourse, before Part V shifts the focus to include interpersonal and, more particularly, intergenerational relationships in youth transition. Finally, Part VI returns to broader social and cultural determinations of transition pathways and shows at the end how such societal dimensions generate gray zones.

Part II: Youth-Constructed Socialization

The transition from childhood to adulthood is often considered primarily an interim period. During this time, the so-called young people are no longer children but are still not adults. As a consequence, on the social map, youth places tend to be identified as "out-places": for example, out-of-school, out-of-job, alternative leisure spaces. Furthermore, scientific approaches to skills transmission and elaboration generally focus on institutions such as school and workplaces. This part of the overview is based on the idea that noninstitutionalized spaces should be studied seriously, because young people may have good developmental reasons to invest their time and energy there with peers at the same developmental stage. Careful attention to social spaces emerging in gray zones, or *social interstices*, may increase our understanding of learning and developmental processes related to the transition to adulthood.

The four authors in this part describe different types of youth social spaces. These spaces are devoted to different kinds of activities within various socioeconomic contexts, but their structures, the way they work, and the kinds of skills they develop are very similar. They can all be described as socialization spaces in a particular culture, having their own rules and providing a place where each person can find or define his or her role. Activity is shared, and both practices and socialization processes enhance personal and collective skills, knowledge, and sense of identity.

Shirley Brice Heath argues that the youth-based organizations (YBOs) she has observed in the United States provide an institutional force to fill the voids left by lack of intergenerational communication, by nurturance breakdowns, and by an absence of meaningful work opportunities for youth in community and family life. She shows how the socialization models created there are not based on transmission but rather on the idea of putting younger and older people in an ongoing transitional movement centered on changing activities, resulting mainly in real performances or in concrete production works. In playing the roles requested in order to reach the organization's collective goals, members of those cross-aged YBOs establish and follow precise rules, take risks, and assume individual responsibilities.

Thus, in some cases, such YBOs occupy an intermediate space in society. Entering into them allows youth to build an identity and to construct cognitive and social competencies through collective activities. To some extent, these YBOs are peripheral communities of practice dealing with social uncertainty. Laurence Roulleau-Berger refers in her chapter to interstitial organizations as places with a *culture of uncertainty*. This emphasizes other features of youth organizations: the uncertainty of the individual and collective outcome of the socialization model and the kinds of competencies it fosters. Focusing on the adjustment between community-developed skills and results of the collective action and acknowledgment by their environment, Roulleau-Berger shows how intermediate or *interstitial spaces* lead, in some cases, to integration into the legitimate labor market and, in other cases, to social disaffection and marginalization.

These first two chapters of Part II give a complex view of the processes implied by a social activity oriented toward a collective, visible result. Feelings of belonging and out-group acknowledgment lead to agency and skill construction, which together can bring the group or the person closer to the official society, thus leaving marginal spaces. But not all youth groups present the features of the YBOs studied by Heath or the open, uncertain frames described by Roulleau-Berger. Some youngsters enter and stay in groups that offer far fewer developmental opportunities, provide fewer learning and creative activities, and increase the distance to official social spaces and institution. Why is this so?

In his chapter, Karsten Hundeide analyzes how particular youth-based groups with precise rules and role definitions may provide an extremely strong sense of belonging and responsibility to young people while also fostering antisocial, violent behavior. Such is the case with gangs and neo-Nazi groups. In developing a specific culture, therefore, some interstitial spaces seem to lead youngsters to deep marginalization and alienation. Using the notion of an *identity package*, Hundeide articulates specific group culture features, their potentially affective benefits for youth, and their related implied *life careers*. According to the attitudes and actions that an identity package promotes, or the sort of learning required, these life careers can be more or less oriented toward general societal integration. For instance, in the neo-Nazi group, Hundeide shows the dramatic consequences for individual thinking of a collective affiliation to an external, influential ideology offering the direct benefits of a sense of belonging.

Contributing to the understanding of a life-career concept, Alain Coulon gives a detailed view of one part of the path: the process of becoming a member of a specific group. He focuses on the positive consequences of learning the rules, both for identity development and for a possible transition in the societal space. The group he analyzes shares collective activities that result in neither performances nor visible products. Nevertheless, Coulon's discussion shows that rule-governed collective activities themselves enhance individual skills and positive identity feelings that can then help the young-sters find a way to be recognized and accepted in official institutional spaces.

One of the major challenges for scholars is understanding how and why shared activities in youth groups, placed in societal interstices, may lead to results that are the opposite of the evolving relationships their members will have with "official" society and the institutionalized world (including the educational sphere, the labor market, and the legal arena), and of their individual development.

From a social point of view, the youth groups described by Shirley Brice Heath and Laurence Roulleau-Berger are *open* to the social surrounding, allowing young people to be acknowledged individually or as a group by official institutions and to find ways to connect to official society. Some groups described by Hundeide are closed to others and cut off young people from official social activity, bringing them to full social alienation.

From a psychological point of view, constructive youth spaces are likely to help members define and construct their relationships with the outside world and contribute to a strong sense of self and to the ability to connect to others. Overall, they become *protected spaces* in which one can take the risk of thinking without threatening one's self-image or identity too much. They provide opportunities to risk ignorance or doubt, where proper thinking starts.

It seems that only interstitial spaces that offer opportunities for both socialization and thinking allow their members to be creative participants, open to external opinions and challenges, ready to accept new relational modes, to develop new skills, and to undertake a process of transition through different social spaces.

Part III: Personal Agency Through Collective Activity

Part II of this volume considers personal development within group dynam-ics in specific environments. Part III presents a different view of ongoing psychological processes occurring on an interpersonal or personal level. During shared activities related to learning and thinking processes, what happens to the individual's feeling of agency? How can the situation be meaningful for the learners or the novices? How does this meaning affect both the sense of identity and the thinking process? What is the place of the peer, the adult, or the more skilled person? And how do social and cultural environments influence personal meaning, the sense of self, and thinking processes?

The first two chapters in Part III provide a general theoretical orientation. Felice Carugati and John Rijsman present theoretical constructs articulating identity dynamics, meaning construction, and learning processes in contextualized sociocultural settings. The next chapter, by Tania Zittoun, presents specific cultural contexts or educational settings where articulations between learning and identity dynamics become particularly salient.

Carugati presents a new formulation of *joining society* as one of youths' learning challenges in modern societies. Those challenges can be seen as the paths to development of one's capacity to initiate new learning processes specific to new areas of activity required by today's conventional life. In modern societies, learning can be considered a collective process requiring partial rejection of the old organization of knowledge, and the development it fosters implies a horizontal movement (from one community of practice to another) rather than a vertical shift (from a novice to an expert position). Based on recent advances in sociocognitive psychology, Carugati's chapter emphasizes the deep embeddedness of cognition, social signification, and meaning-making challenges. Against this general theoretical background, learning interactive processes can only be considered by looking carefully at both their social frame, on the one hand, and their meaning for personal identity and self-esteem, on the other hand.

In the next chapter, Rijsman emphasizes the affective dimensions of meaning and identity that are related to learning processes. He proposes a model that shows the interdependence of self-image and coordination with other persons and with social objects. This model shows particularly the importance of the personal need to maintain a good sense of self in learning and thinking activities. From that perspective, Rijsman reinterprets the identity dynamics of school and family settings and some of the conditions of developing a positive sense of self, which brings him to new considerations of the process of becoming an adult.

These two chapters sketch a general framework based on the interrelations of social dynamics, cognitive processes, and personal affective implications, including *positive self-maintenance strategies.* This framework allows us to develop a complex understanding of group, intersubjective and personal youth actions, and of learning processes in their *social frames* and *cultural contexts* as they appear throughout this book and more specifically in the next chapter.

Tania Zittoun presents an example of a specific preapprenticeship school setting established to help adolescents who have failed in school prepare for further training as apprentices in the Swiss dual system. In this special program, adults try to work on improving youths' identity by helping them to acquire socialization skills and developing their cognitive competencies. Thanks to their engagement in this highly structured social space, young people can discover their own value and become able to confer new meaning on learning activities and on their own actions. Hence, they develop social and cognitive skills allowing their social transition to the labor market and the adult world.

Part IV: Learning in Practice and Discourse

Looking at different types of social and interactive frames, the first two parts of this volume show how learning presupposes socially shared activity and how it is embedded in personal identity and meaning-construction processes. Hence, learning can no longer be considered a simple transmission process. But what is it? And if learning is related to specific sociocultural settings, what happens when a person moves from one setting to another? How can one learn the way to enter new communities of practice? What competencies are transferable and how? Focused on communicative and shared practices, the authors in this part adopt different reflective positions that enable them to unpack the notions of learning and competencies and to think through the relations between formal educational settings, other everyday life social situations, and the role of communicative activities.

The chapter by Roger Säljö examines the discrepancy between the experience an adolescent can have in school versus that of everyday life. In order to analyze the origin of this gap, the author views formal education from a historical perspective, supposing the constitution of a specific body of knowledge, particular structures of communicative activities, and specific modes of thinking. Such a formal education has been justified by the necessity to conserve complex memories of knowledge that are not transmitted in everyday experience and produces a group of people who would conserve it. In democratic societies, where young people learn a lot outside of school and through media and new technologies, school has to redefine its function. History has produced a type of school knowledge, modes of thinking, and modes of communication that oblige students to make abstractions of their experience of the everyday world outside of school. This suggests that failing at school exercises or testing activities could be related to a student's inability to forget his or her knowledge of the real world. This also brings up the fact that school knowledge and its modes of communication are often irrelevant for everyday life and therefore may have no meaning for students. Säljö highlights the need to propose a new metaphor for learning that could help redefine school aims. He also points out the specificity of school, notably as a unique "context for systematic reflection on knowledge and for the production of a broad range of intellectual and practical skills."

Although not giving the same centrality to communication in learning and thinking activities, the next two chapters reduce the gap between school and other settings and challenge the idea of knowledge transfer. In his chapter, Jonathan Tudge argues that understanding processes should be seen as happening through complex practices, of which language is just one component. Rather than focusing on specific skills or bodies of knowledge, he looks at the *personal culture* that individuals establish throughout their life paths in several activity settings and communities of practice. Examining children's everyday lives, where they are involved in very different types of activities, in different contexts, and with different others, Tudge argues that they progressively become aware of the particular meaning some of these activities have for significant others in their lives. Children then seem to be willing to initiate similar activities in other contexts. Tudge proposes to consider *competence* as something that a person has acquired and practiced, and that he or she can display in various contexts. Viewed from that perspective, the difficulty of some adolescents to be considered competent in formal settings – especially girls from lower-income families – could be related to the fact that they were not, as children, encouraged to initiate communication practices within their families. From such a perspective, school can promote the development of transferable skills only if educational activities are understood in relation to other everyday interactive situations.

David Middleton situates his analysis on the level of *discursive activities*. This allows him to consider directly the articulation of the individual and the collective, because personal identity or individual learning can be considered as realized through the shared activity of communication. This perspective allows him to question the difference between formal and vernacular settings. In both cases, the "learnability" of a specific piece of knowledge or practice stems from its public visibility or its presence in discourse. This is the case for identity definition, meaning elaboration, or learning. But these settings are used to develop different cultures of discourse: What about conscious awareness, which, in Vygotskian terms, appears to be possible only in formal settings? Middleton questions this difference, because the discursive analysis of an everyday situation shows how complex thinking procedures are actualized as they are improvised in the games of argumentation and resistance. Such observation could be very beneficial for reflection on improving learning and thinking opportunities for young people.

In the last chapter in this part, Jacques Perriault looks at others' learning and thinking activities in shared practices, both discursive and concrete, which deal in another way with the question of knowledge transfer. This author focuses on cognitive operations required by new technologies in educational settings and questions the origin of their acquisition. At one level, Perriault shows the very important role of communicative activities in early family life for the acquisition of high-level cognitive abilities that are required for new learning technologies. For instance, a sense of timing or parallel processing ability is important for students to learn if they are to participate effectively in interactive videoconferences; several studies have suggested that such competencies are developed mainly through morning mother–child interaction. It seems that, once these cognitive abilities are acquired, they can be activated in other situations. But at another level, other culturally mediated skills that are required in order to benefit from a videoconference – such as taking notes and preparing questions – are developed in classical educational settings. Although these skills are familiar to students, they are not mobilized in these situations. Students seem to call upon two conflicting definitions of the situation: that the activity should be one of learning but the concrete situation should be an everyday experience, such as watching TV, which does not require these activities. Such an analysis of practice suggests that knowledge transfer is highly dependent on the way in which individuals interpret shared activities for only some types of complex cognitive processes.

More generally, the chapters in this part suggest that, in order to evolve and adapt to new societal challenges, educational settings should carefully take into account students' out-of-school experiences.

Part V: Intergenerational Sites for Thinking

Not only do youth groups and formal educational settings foster the development of young people's identities, communicative skills, and reasoning abilities, but so do families. More precisely, one of the important processes that occurs in youth is the evolution of one's position toward persons from preceding generations. This process implies interactions with adults. Intergenerational relationships imply negotiations, discussions, and sometimes conflicts. This part of the volume examines different types of youth–adult interactions and the nature and role of some of these relationships in the transition to adulthood.

The first two chapters in this part examine how, in familial intergenerational discussions, young people express new identities, develop strategies, and realize role changes in relation to older people. The first chapter, by Clotilde Pontecorvo, provides various examples of social settings involving middle-class Italian families during dinner table conversations. In these situations, children are usually asked to account for their behavior and to reason consequently, and adolescents often take the floor and challenge their parents with questions and issues that generally have social importance. By using conversational analysis, Pontecorvo shows that the family gathering, as well as schools, can provide a proper setting in which group conversations make it possible to share the difficulties of facing new problems and the pain of thinking and reasoning. Young children and adolescents become tuned to their family community of practice. Hence, they can develop good reasoning and thinking abilities: a critical competence for assuming responsibility of action and discourse that is necessary both for becoming adults and for developing the logical and scientific skills required in further education and work.

The families discussed by Pontecorvo seem to offer resources mainly for the transition to adulthood, whereas other studies show that families themselves are the sites of chief developmental struggles. Manfred Hofer is interested in parent–adolescent relationships and their modification in modern Germany. He considers discourse as a realized behavior that informs us about the adolescent's individuation process. First, speech acts mirror identity positions. Speech behavior and type of discourse are related to one's position in a symmetric or asymmetric relationship; they are highly sensitive to one's will to modify these respective roles or statuses. It is thus possible to observe changes in mother–adolescent speech behavior from early to late adolescence and to see how the individuation process is discursively realized. This brings Hofer to examine how adolescent speech acts are a means of modifying the nature of the relationship, the adolescent's role, and the parents' position toward them.

The two preceding chapters focus on discourse exchanges, but the next two chapters in this part examine intergenerational relationships as parts of wider dynamics on temporal and social levels. In her chapter, Ursula Staudinger adopts a life-span perspective. In such a paradigm, the role of a single interaction has to be understood as it happens at a specific moment in a life course, as it is related to former interaction, and as it has consequences for future situations. The meaning of similar interactions can change with the person's age, and it is highly dependent on wider historical and cultural circumstances. With an example taken from research on wisdom-related thinking, the author shows that social interactions should be understood not only as shared dialogic situations but also as symbolic, inner, or virtual ones. This sheds light on the fact that what develops during a situation of social interaction is often not visible in the interaction itself, but only through the person's action or thinking after a certain time, which is required for integration. Such a point may have consequences both for theory and for methodological approaches to learning in adolescence.

Claude Kaiser's chapter extends the notion of interaction to social and shared cultural contexts. Using a social-representation approach, he is interested in symbolic encounters between groups and the mismatches that can result from them. For instance, in studying a vocational school setting, he shows that the teachers' representations of the style of teaching provided in their innovative school and their expectations of the students' behavior were totally different from the students' representations of their own learning practices, which were very traditional. Looking at the effective actions of these students, Kaiser notes that their learning practices and interactions did not correspond to their discourse about these practices. Such remarks highlight the importance of the symbolic field in which intergroup relationships take place; ideologies and power games shape adults' and youths' representations of themselves and their relationships with each other in different ways. The consequences of such an analysis are two. First, one consequence for research is that a phenomenon such as youth has to be examined through a multimethod analysis: What is enacted is not what is said through discourse. Second, this could mean that young people's transition to adulthood requires the mastery of the symbolic game that structures the field of institutions, and that shapes discourse and practice, in order to move in this symbolic space.

Part VI: Pathways to Adulthood in National Context

The previous part of this volume suggests that young people's transition to adulthood may be related to knowledge, competencies, relationships, and specific social and cultural contexts. This final part looks at macrostructural determinations of this developmental path.

In the first chapter in this part, Annie Fouquet examines not individual but structural determination of the transitional pathway to adulthood. Although the unemployment rate has been the main indicator of youth's social insertion, recent societal evolutions call for deeper analysis. The duration and outcome of transitional pathways vary according to national school and vocational systems or the role of the family. Behind the relation between education/training and work that distributes youth into an occupational status, argues Fouquet, one should pay attention to the way labor markets are set up in each national economy. These different adjustments cause young people to develop new abilities to overcome difficulties addressed by national conditions; such abilities can be understood as responses to structural conditions.

Other difficulties arise in trying to give macrostructural views on transitions. In the next chapter, Paul Ryan analyzes some of the main indicators used to describe the youth school-to-work transition. Comparing France and the United States, he unpacks the notion of youth employment. Depending on whether or not military service, higher education, and voluntary inactivity are taken into account, youth employment rates vary drastically. All of these dimensions are important in enabling us to identify which resources young people may develop while not studying or working. The idea of the duration of the transition, which was examined by the Organization for Economic Cooperation and Development (OECD), can also be questioned. Considering the drastic changes in this transition in England between the 1950s and the 1980s, Ryan shows how measurement and calculation can reveal or hide the dynamics of school-leaving or entering the labor market, with or without formation. This approach emphasizes the variability and inertia of national and historical definitions of concepts related to youth and to becoming part of the labor market; it calls for clearer operational definitions.

The next three chapters examine some consequences of these national and societal structural situations, and especially some of the consequences of the economic and political breakdowns characterizing late modernity for youth development. They also shed some light on some of the bottom-up reaction against social fragmentation.

The national and historical variability of the notions of youth and transition to the labor market is highlighted in the chapter by Dragan Popadić, which refers to the situation in the former Yugoslavia after the war of the early 1990s. Because of Yugoslavia's isolation from other countries, its disintegration into five parts, and the decomposition of the national economic system and the labor market, youth transition here has a totally different meaning from that in other countries. Popadić nevertheless argues for the potentially integrative role of the educational system. Thanks to its resistance to change, the school system was the last institution that had maintained a memory of a traditional culture and of such prewar values as the importance of multiethnic and pluralistic communities. Thus, in this specific historical and cultural context, if it survives the changes, the school system may have an *integrative* function for youth and for the society in general.

The extreme situation in the former Yugoslavia reminds us that the school system not only offers a social setting in which young people can learn and develop but also provides the basis for the wider civic sphere while being highly sensitive to the evolution of society in general. Speaking about such evolution, the two next chapters explore some of the effects of political and economic liberalization on young people, their training, work opportunities, and means of action.

Another example of extreme social disintegration is the highly liberalized market that is characteristic of the United States and that generates new modes of work. In his chapter, Stuart Tannock examines recent typical youth workplaces in the United States, where a majority of working youth are employed in dead-end jobs, such as in fast-food restaurants or mall retail outlets, with turnover surpassing 100% per year. Although there is some policy dealing with this issue, education and special programs do little to change the conditions for most youth with low wages. Trade union leaders in both the United States and Canada have argued that an alternative response would be to organize youth service into unions, to benefit both youth and unions, which face a declining, aging membership. Tannock uses an ethnographic approach to explore how these youths position themselves with respect to their unions, coworkers, and employers and how they evaluate their work and union activity. He suggests that, if unions were to adopt a model of full membership and education for youth, it could potentially transform the cynicism created by dead-end service jobs into a positive motivation for learning and change. Here, then, resisting old institutions seems to offer a way to empower underskilled young people.

In the last chapter in this part, Saul Meghnagi brings together structural changes and the resources people can develop in order to survive in new social and work conditions, with special attention to the role of women. On one side, he examines the deinstitutionalization of life paths beginning in the 1990s in Italy after their institutionalization in the 1950s and 1960s. If the latter is characterized by the standardization of role definition according to age and gender, a strong social welfare emphasis, and, as a result of nonnormativity, a clear marginalization, the deinstitutionalization of the 1990s is less predictable. Behavior and roles are no longer related to gender or age; the welfare system is weak; and because norms are less clear, marginalization is hard to localize. Although women have been agents of this social change through their claims for new modes of social agency, they are still part of a fragile group in the new society. On the other side, Meghnagi identifies knowledge as an important resource for people to protect themselves in their fragile conditions created by social disintegration. This protective knowledge seems to be acquired primarily through lengthy, rich work experiences and supposes cross-context abilities.

This part closes the spiral path that we charted for this volume. Here we see how new, fragmented social conditions create new conditions for youth development. The lack of clear role definitions and social marks can handicap young people but can result in resourcefulness as well. Not only do young people belong to more than one social space, but they can also be active in different spheres, where different types of interaction allow them to develop specific kinds of knowledge. Finally, it appears that, in some new social spaces or gray zones generated by modern societies, young people create communities of practice, where they can be creatively and actively involved for a long time. Through such shared activities, they seem to develop competencies, reinforce their identities, and elaborate new means to move on to other social spheres.

II

YOUTH-CONSTRUCTED SOCIALIZATION

4 Risks, Rules, and Roles

Youth Perspectives on the Work of Learning for Community Development

Shirley Brice Heath

To give up obedience to the powerless is most difficult. . . .

Adorno

Institutional Voids

When institutions of society become unable to handle key changes in the rhythms and patterns of human behavior, new institutions need to emerge. Throughout human history, however, despite wars and major political changes, the emergence of our familiar institutions (e.g., family, religion, government, organized economies, and formal education) came slowly, silently, and in coordination with numerous shifts in key arrangements of daily patterns of existence and interaction among individuals.

Patterns of employment as well as leisure have drastically shifted family life and community cultures, and the need for new institutional arrangements to care for the young appears increasingly evident to certain decision makers. Acknowledged is the need to provide extended care for children from families with two working parents or a single parent who works outside the home in at least one job, often with extended hours (and in the United States, without health benefits). In addition, the fallout effect of pulling the best and the brightest out of failing impoverished communities is becoming ever evident. Since World War II, the United States, in particular, has stressed access to higher education for all.

A version of this chapter can also be found in Heath, S. B. (2000). Risk, rules, and roles: Youth perspective on the work of learning for community development. *Zeitschrift für Erzichung-swissenschaft, 1,* 67–80.

Consequently, as educational levels have risen, so has out-migration of the young from burdened rural and impoverished communities to either urban or suburban environments where jobs and promises of a comfortable middle-class life have beckoned. But as these middle-class parents have gone off to their jobs, their children have remained alone during out-of-school hours. Families can no longer manage the out-of-school time of their children. Schools in the United States now keep students occupied for only 26% of their day; traditional home chores as well as jobs in local small businesses cannot meet the demand for consumer goods and entertainment that fill teenage aspirations. Schools and policymakers increasingly stress the need for higher education in the form of 4 years of college or university life that should follow immediately the 4 years of high school. Yet at century's end, for the majority of postindustrial nations, the economy could not provide sufficient numbers of managerial jobs or professional slots commensurate with either the level of education or the financial expectations of the newly college/university educated. Fewer individuals, working with telecommunications and high technology, now do the jobs of more and more people, increasing the stress and responsibilities of the few while leaving many either underemployed or unemployed.

Such combinations of forces remind us that community life and intergenerational interactions as we have known them now exist primarily· in fantasies and memories. The exodus from rural areas and midsized towns in the second half of the twentieth century has overburdened urban zones, which have, in turn, been unable to provide self-sustaining neighborhoods for the poor and working class as urban centers have turned from industry to financial and governmental business. This chapter looks at the future of communities as learning ecologies for youth. The view here centers on a segment of young people within the United States who have responded to the absence of intimate transgenerational socialization and local work opportunities by finding places where they help set rules, take risks, and try out roles to prepare them to remain in their communities as assets. These young people resist continuing previous decades of brain drain from their poor communities – urban and rural. They perceive their own opportunities to achieve the dream of middle-class life as highly limited, and they choose now to focus on the social enterprise of community building through expanding their own learning in authentic ways. Social enterprise represents entrepreneurial efforts by neighborhoods to build responsible, aesthetic, locally grounded opportunities for resource development within impoverished communities. Simply put, those engaged in social enterprise efforts work to find ways to put local energies to work for the community without waiting for external educational, governmental, or multinational corporate forces. These efforts at work in postindustrial nations take much from grassroots microenterprise projects in Third World development programs: that key resources lie within local people, their ingenuity, social and moral values, and goals for rational approaches to intergenerational maintenance.

These efforts also reflect a new model of socialization that replaces that of *transmission*, whereby knowledge and skills are transmitted from the elder to the younger. *Transition* and *transformation* speak to the prefigurative culture that Margaret Mead introduced several decades ago by pointing out that, by century's end, we would be forced to acknowledge and adapt to the fact that the young would have to teach their parents and grandparents much. Carrying further her sense of this change, she noted that adults maintain cultural lag remnants of transmission and hold on to their own central stage position in this process, while simultaneously obliterating the respect, ruled relationships, and regularity for and with the young who for centuries have formed the base of transmission across cultures. In other words, adults, in clinging to their view that the central socialization frame is that of transmission – passing on the wisdom of the elder to the younger – continue to demand respect, obedience, and compliance with the rules and values they hand out without continuing many of the processes, learning opportunities, or relationships in work that previously carried transmission. In essence, although the ideal of transmission remains, with two working-parent households, single-parent households, and the relegation of elders to special care facilities, the infrastructure that provided long hours of side-by-side projects for children, youth, parents, grandparents, and even extended family members no longer remains.

Yet as the young are propelled forward through the changing circumstances of intimate associations in the early 21st century, they move to grasp and to create transitional and transformative contexts of socialization. In so doing, because their behaviors and attitudes have no match with what elders have known, youth lose the respect, understanding, faith, and often the affection of their elders. At the close-up level at which traditional cultural anthropologists and linguistic anthropologists work, we can see that they also lose details of interaction: eye contact, slow touch, sustained voice contact, shared rhythms of time, and opportunities for working together.

The transitional model of socialization centers the individual identity on the social, with room for a playing through of both. This model gives much attention to risk, taking its cue in part from the work of the German sociologist Ulrich Beck, as well as from other critics of politics, tradition, and aesthetics in the modern social order.[1] These critics illustrate something young people know all too well: Class solidarity has lost much of its former significance; trajectories of jobs and careers have lost their predictability. Currently, the main social issue for all is the distribution of hazards and dangers. Everyone is thereby likely to be engaged in transitions and transformations, changes that come on unexpectedly and for which transmission learning never prepares us. These transitions come about and test the ability of youth and adult to take risks, make new rules, find new social connections, and think of risk as inevitable.[2]

Young people know all of this and take this information into account as they watch adults push the ideal of transmission, behaviorism, and a trajectory of do-right-and-you-will-then-get-ahead. They note that their elders push these stories as empty shells without the accompanying work and discipline necessary to fill in the shells. They push these stories with none of the sense of reciprocity that operates in the ongoing work of youth organizations. Here adults and young people give and take, move in synchrony or in disharmony, but with reciprocity. The young know that their elders either will not or cannot follow reciprocal practices that place youth at risk, provide discipline and rules that they and the young must follow, or put young people and themselves to tests after adequate preparation. Under transmission as it exists today, adults run the gamut from the extreme of forbidding youth to take any risks to creating infantilizing safety nets of adult control to abandoning efforts at communication when their young seek out risks.[3]

---

[1] Although the writings of Beck focus on large societal issues and do not derive from the type of close field study reported here, his theories merit careful attention and carry possibilities for comparative framing. (See Beck, 1992, 1995; Beck, Giddens, & Lash, 1994.)

[2] We need to think here only of the thousands of middle- and high-level executives who have lost their jobs after years of loyalty and moving up in corporations (especially in the United States). They have done everything right, but something has gone wrong with the trajectory to which they were socialized. Events such as job loss, divorce, and early death of young people through acquired immune deficiency syndrome amount to transformations requiring new risks, new rules, new connections. The same may be said of the increasing number of young people in their 20s who now have incomes in excess of six figures because of their skills in computer programming, musical compositions, or sports. This pattern fits a trajectory not of transmission but of rapid transformation.

[3] In past eras, family, religion, and neighbors, as well as local economies, marked daily life and movement through known rituals and rites of passage. The young of today have little access to these key institutions and the joint work, sense of rhythm and pace, and sense of pride in group accomplishment that they provided earlier generations. Today, socializers come and go as strangers or nonintimates: the personnel of day-care programs, formal education,

Today, youth create risks and work for themselves in highly rule-governed youth-based organizations (YBOs) that center on the work of learning for and by youth. They work to support one another in cross-age transitional socialization groups, establishing rules, helping others find or know rules, and orienting newcomers who pass a few critical tests to the rules. Young people impose discipline on themselves and regulate themselves, even though the "discipline" they use often appears to adults as the exact opposite – unruliness, lack of control, and complete abandonment of self-discipline.

Some young people band together simply on the basis that they are different. They themselves want to be known as different, to dance to a different drummer, to hold a different beat in their heads. Some of these groups become primarily destructive to themselves through high-risk physical behaviors without adequate practice, experimentation with drugs and alcohol, and pushing the limits of police authority. Others become extraordinarily different but manage to walk in concert with forces large enough to protect them from higher-authority risks but also willing to exploit them for their own purposes. The recent revelations of the involvement of the Central Intelligence Agency in supplying drugs to gangs in Los Angeles during the 1980s is one of many examples of this kind of exaltation of difference, both with and without protection from these groups and with highly questionable moral notions of protection.

Transitions mean that individuals no longer look at themselves as being in waiting for adulthood or for a process of transmission to be complete. They see learning as ongoing and have a high level of distrust for any knowledge passed on to them that appears canned, untried, irrelevant, and lacking in relationships. In a manner of speaking, then, there are today no children or adults here; all are in transition, focused on unwanted side effects, general untrustworthiness, and celebrations of insignificance, because those of significance seem too broad, powerful, or threatening to try to overcome. Perched in such transitions, without guides or respect, rules or regularities, many adults have come to pay great attention to their own social and personal contexts, to draw on tacit knowledge, and to look in unpredictable ways to the

---

crime prevention, and juvenile detention. They work to fill the hours of youth with discrete, highly segmented, decontextualized tasks that must generally be executed and measured for individual, not group, achievement. Individual learners have few opportunities for real work done either individually or in collaboration with others. Thus, without opportunities for real work within households, communities, religious activities, and school, young people seek something to do that offers quick accomplishments that feel good and bring peer approval. Hence, too many move into early high-risk sexual and mind-altering behaviors, as well as peer-linked criminal activities.

warrantability of ideas and actions in which they see themselves as relatively powerless over the young, on whom they once placed their greatest hope.

This chapter outlines how some youngsters between the ages of 8 and 21 have responded to the failures of traditional fixed institutions in society to adapt to dilemmas presented by postindustrialism. Surrounding the efforts recounted here are concerns these youth have for media exploitation, heavy consumer and material forces on (especially) the working poor, and the empty promises educators make to link school achievement to guaranteed employment. The youth in this study feel the need to "do something different," to chart new means of accounting for self and meaningful connections, and to learn in new ways for purposes and goals not yet acknowledged by most adults.

Discovery of these organizations became analogous to finding a thriving ecological zone previously unknown in what was otherwise a dismal environment with little evidence of productive life from the young. Within the out-of-school ecological zone of learning provided by YBOs, the young develop a sense of themselves as learners within community contexts and pursue information, skills, and contacts in the course of high-risk work tightly governed by rules they themselves develop. Here seems to be a case of the young of the species enabling the building of youth organizations as an *institutional force* within a society greatly in need of some way to fill the gap left by contemporary demands of family, loss of social responsibility by religions and neighborhoods, and the shifting and encroaching demands of the labor market.

Youth-Based Organization

Working in 30 regional areas and about 120 youth-based organizations that hosted nearly 30,000 youngsters over a decade, a senior team of Milbrey W. McLaughlin, public policy analyst of Stanford University, and I, a linguistic anthropologist, headed a rotating group of young scholars acting as guerrilla anthropologists, living, working, and playing among the young people in various sites. The data for the results reported here came from a decade of study of YBOs in neighborhoods across the United States, including urban, rural, and midsized towns (25,000–100,000 people).[4] Data collected

---

[4] This study addressed the following questions:

1. What happens to the young during those hours when they are not in school? Where do they go, with whom, and, in particular, where do they find situations of learning that attract them?

included details of macroorganization, as well as audio recordings of the language used by the young people while in their youth organizations and numerous recordings of their leisure hours away from the organizations. In addition, many of the young people kept a variety of written forms of data, ranging from reflective journals to daily logs of activities, media usage, and transportation usage.

What Is Happening?

Neutral as this question sounds, it is the guide for most anthropologists who wish to capture the pace and substance of everyday life. The young people in this study sought out what they regarded as effective learning sites or, in their words, "places to be." These places ranged from grassroots organizations, such as tumbling teams or agricultural projects, to highly organized, nationally affiliated sports groups and community centers that sponsored programs in the visual arts, drama, video production, or disc jockeying. Some sites had fixed locations for coming together, such as urban performing arts centers, community center buildings, or athletic fields, but others moved about, finding space whenever and wherever it was available for their use. All groups had one or more adult leaders who served as the legal and fiscal agent(s) for the group. All groups organized their activities around *the work of learning* in order to produce peak performance by a certain deadline set for athletic playoffs, a show opening, or a production deadline. All groups went through a cycle from planning and preparation to intensive practice, followed by performance and evaluation. This cycle was in all cases followed by down time or time off before a new season or cycle began. All groups included considerable attention to play, lightheartedness, and rites of intensification that bonded group members through rituals

2. Early in the study, answers to question 1 indicated that many youth were drawn to YBOs that included high risk and stiff demands for organized work toward a performance or product of high quality. The question then became: What goes on in such programs, judged by young people themselves as highly effective learning environments? What makes risk and work so appealing in these contexts?
3. What features mark these organizations? What roles do young people play? How do the microorganizational and macroorganizational features of these sites connect and work together to sustain such organizations?
4. How does change come about in the structures, uses, and purposes of these YBOs? Where does the impetus for development come from? How adaptive or responsive to contextual shifts in their neighborhoods or in the broader youth populations can such organizations be? How do they integrate learning about work and leisure into their daily operations?

For full details on the methods and processes of the fieldwork, types of data collected, and analyses applied, see Heath (1996a, 1996b, 1998).

that looked much like family reunions, community fairs, or celebratory parties.

In all of these forms – plays, neighborhood cleanup campaigns, graffiti removal task forces, athletic games, or food cooperatives – the youth immerse themselves in high risk and hard work to revel in a strong present sense of what they are. Such "am-ness and are-ness" lie deeply encircled with a sense of efficacy in the self and in the group. Their work rarely celebrates the future as something distant for which they prepare; instead, the future is in the present, and the past starts right along with their present future. In that present future, these youngsters refuse to accept the grand narratives that adults push on them or that the public media promote: that of victim, culprit, perpetrator, or mastermind.

Three major categories of YBOs emerged: service-based learning, athletic/academic, and arts. Within each category, groups included those associated with large civic organizations (such as a performing arts center or community center) as well as grassroots groups. The number of meetings per week varied considerably, as did the groups' months of operation during the year; most met at least three times per week after school and/or on weekends, and most operated at least 9 months of the year. A majority provided few or no programs during periods marked by local major employers as vacation time. Of the three categories, athletic/academic groups tended to have the shortest seasons and service learning organizations the longest.

How Is It Happening?

Patterns and features of behavior of these organizations emerge slowly during long-term fieldwork. For many months, each site appears to be in utter chaos, with young people running in and out, talking all at once, laughing, and playing pranks on one another while being busily engaged in moving toward a time and product of final performance. Being within a YBO is not a *job*: that is, a series of tasks someone else directs.[5] Young people compare

---

[5] Here it is useful to make distinctions between *work*, on the one hand, and *jobs* or *chores*, on the other. Formal education is best characterized by the latter two rather than by the former. Consider that work has both positive and negative connotations, always carrying some promise of open involvement, connected tasks toward some end the worker can see and know. We tell ourselves, "I've got to work on listening better"; "I'll work on losing weight, exercising more, or spending more time with my children." When we talk of work, the elements of choice and outcome generally ring through our words. Jobs, however, appear in our thinking as both given and determined by others outside our own initiative and often beyond our will. The job of filling out government tax forms is given and defined by others,

the work of their YBOs with their outside jobs, where, in the words of one member, "No one is excited about it [their job], and no one is really upset about it, but they just kind of do it. Here [at the arts center], everyone's all, 'Yes, let's go work on this project.'" Youngsters remain keenly aware that authentic outside judges will assess their final performance, whether it is an athletic playoff among teams, or the mounting of a visual arts show in a gallery, or several weekends of play performances. Commitment to a final product before such assessors keeps the level of critique high within the group and between adult leaders and youngsters, especially through the final weeks of practice. Having a clear goal or direction toward which they must move, and knowing that their final judges will have no emotional attachment to them or their success or failure, provide high incentives for each individual to sustain commitment to the best possible performance for the benefit of the group as a whole. Competition exists first and foremost as an incentive for the group to work against its own best prior performance, as well as against high criteria or standards set by judging teams outside the YBO's immediate world.

These features give the work of learning within the organizations a definite cast of the real world. Each group mobilizes its own inner resources by seeing those who are outside or in the "world out there" as different, as judgmental, harsh, and demanding. In talking about how to get other youth involved in theater, one young member expressed his view this way: "What gets to kids [is] the real stuff... [what] really helps you find yourself when you do all the work. Because the minute you start doin' all the work, you feel as though it has to be a part of you." Another youth talked about the artwork of his YBO as a form of internal construction: "When you do something where you create, it builds something inside you that never really goes away." By their preparation within the group, individuals and groups see themselves as learning to face outsiders and the real world successfully. Those on the other side of the we–they dichotomy include school, "the streets," police officers, other teams or performance groups, authorities and judges in general, family members, and potential employers. Adult leaders often justify tough standards or harsh judgments within the YBO by explaining, "We've got to be tougher here so you'll be even more ready for what's out

as are jobs on a factory line. Chores come to all of us as those recurring, irritating tasks that march along with daily life and have to be done again and again, with no sense of complete and utter accomplishment ever lasting very long. The chores of taking out the garbage, keeping the garage clean, sorting paperwork, or mowing grass keep returning, despite our futile efforts on any one day or week to clear them away.

there waiting for you." Although very few rules mark the daily life of YBOs, those that exist embrace behaviors and attitudes broadly, and they must be followed. Refusal to follow these rules means expulsion from the YBO, a serious consequence, because the YBOs that are judged as "places you want to be" by local youth have long waiting lists and often can take in only a few new members during each cycle.

The overarching ethic of operation for all of these YBOs derives from seeing youth as resources and not as problems. For the work of the YBO to achieve a high standard of excellence, many resources are needed. Because finances, buildings, equipment, time, and involved adult personnel generally fall far short of needs, youth themselves become central resources for the maintenance of YBOs. This ethic behind the YBO reinforces the group conviction that "everyone has work – lots of it – to do here," and everyone takes responsibility for helping to teach others the skills and information needed to accomplish tasks. The group cannot afford any hint that learning benefits only single individuals, for whatever is learned is passed on, extended, and tested within group situations. Individuals therefore develop talents for teaching, facilitating, and demonstrating with others: newcomers, the less skilled, the resistant. Young people bond with one another and with their adult leaders; older, more experienced members move into positions of increasing responsibility to encourage and sustain within-group allegiance.

Critical to the group's cohesion are opportunities for young people to gain experience and expertise in order to achieve greater levels of responsibility, often accompanied by the awarding of a title and a slight change of uniform or a coveted piece of apparel, such as a hat or special T-shirt. Young people serve in nearly every capacity within their organizations, from board member and publicist to team manager or junior coach to receptionist or travel coordinator. Many, although not all, youth organizations have levels of membership, with transitional movement from a lower-skilled group to a group with recognized higher competence and often more frequent performances or a wider range of travel. YBOs judged by local youth to be effective learning sites are marked by some major aspects of organizational structure: primarily in the wide distribution of roles among the youth that keep them informed about rationale, philosophy, and ethics of the organization, as well as details critical to its ongoing maintenance and operation. Within this array of roles, as well as in working to move up through transitional positions that are available (e.g., from one level of a chorus to the next), young people find themselves needing certain literacy, numeracy, oral communication, and technological skills, as well as requiring assistance and information from those outside the YBO (e.g., insurance agents, travel agents, funders). The weaving from organizational need to individual competence impresses each member with the importance to the group of successful performance.[6]

Networking at the local level, as well as throughout the systems above that support YBOs, becomes critically important to sustaining learning and positive reinforcement for those young people who want to transform their learning into effective practices at the community level. In 1996, the International Youth Foundation took as its central theme the challenge of linking *scale* and *sustainability* with *effectiveness.* Although some YBOs work well in replicated form (e.g., the school club model expanded to over 250 locations by the German Children and Youth Foundation), others that may be closely coordinated with local social and cultural circumstances may not. It is necessary, therefore, to consider just what change means for YBOs and their youth and for intensifying youth involvement in community development.

How Do These Groups Change?

Institutional and organizational structures within families, corporations, governments, and many other groups familiar to adults generally change either gradually and relatively predictably or due to catastrophic circumstances, such as impending competitive threat. YBOs embody change within their ethos of operation, for adults know that keeping pace with young people's sense of "changing times" ensures continued youth interest. Closely linked to local circumstances as these affect young people, YBOs change some of their features with each new cycle or seasonal startup. Adult leaders,

---

[6] It is important to note that the International Youth Foundation, a group working to support many exceptional local efforts with youth worldwide, had surveyed YBOs in many other nations and found similar features that mark effective organizations. Through research with program practitioners, researchers, funders, international youth experts, and young people themselves, they have developed a consensus about the elements that improve young people's chances of being within a positive learning environment. These features include:

- a focus on holistic development
- development that engages character, competence, confidence, and connectedness to the community
- active involvement of youth in roles throughout the program
- active involvement of parents and community members
- coordination of program work with other agencies and institutions serving children
- approaches that are culturally relevant and developmentally appropriate (International Youth Foundation, 1997, p. 8)

with the help of young people who have been in the organization for several years, reexamine the group with each new cycle and reorganize responsibilities, reassign roles, and redesign times and means of operation as needed. Just as critique runs consistently through practice, performance, and evaluation of each product or performance, so members receive constant encouragement to think reflectively about the group as a whole. Adult leaders and youth members alike ask: Why is the group younger this year than last year? How is it that we are not attracting many of the kids out there who are over 14 years of age? Is it time we shifted from being a drama troupe to being a drama program that makes it clear how what we do here relates to job skills such as communication and responsible team building? Each season's opening brings a reassessment of rules, roles, and relationships of the group in the past season, with suggestions and questions tossed to young members for response, new ideas, and complaints. Hence, newcomers enter a group obviously committed to minding their own construction, for youth members shape the rules and roles by which they exist.

Here is social construction brought into the open and held up by adults and old-time youth members as open engagement and consistent calls for revision. In most YBOs, a meeting takes place at least once a week that opens with adults or older members asking, "Okay, how's it goin'? What's up? What's not goin' well and what's goin' okay? Any rules we need to change? Any thoughts on how the teams are workin'?" In some YBOs, journals and portfolios of work (e.g., visual arts, creative writing, schematic plays in a particular sport) supplement these public occasions. YBOs find every occasion to involve members in writing reflections, collecting and critiquing their work, and preparing portfolios for job interviews or for YBO visitors. A typical journal entry may range from recording the mundane details of practice to the moments of wonder and discovery. Two entries for a drum corps follow:

> We had to play for an hour, so that meant that we didn't have time to play and joke around. While we were setting up, I saw this girl. She was beautiful, so you know I had to flirt with her. I had to pause from flirting with her to go play [with the corps].

> We arrived at the school, and, you know, did our thing. We do the same thing every show. We unload, get everything inside, argue about who is doing what and why, get hollered at for arguing, set up our drums, then the bells, warm up, and then we get hollered at for warming up. . . . After we were done, the kids wouldn't let us get off stage so we played about

> three encores. . . . The show was over, and we did our other thing. Tear
> down the drums, reflect on how good we were, lay around, take the
> drums to the car, play around, get hollered at for playing around, and
> then after all of that we leave.

Changes that come with regrouping or sharing of journal entries and port-
folio components also occasion discussion of shifts in local circumstances:
open information about new gangs, realigned gang groups, turf changes,
school reorganization, reorganized community police units, or any other
circumstance that may affect the young people themselves.

Bringing into open discussion these issues that are often avoided or si-
lenced by adults in other circumstances is a key feature of organizations
that young people regard as effective. Every individual comes *as an expert in
something*; each person has different bodies of information, levels of competence in various skills, and a host of network affiliations on which the
youth group may need to call. "Let's make sure we all understand that this
group needs all the expertise we can get" means that every individual has
to assume a variety of roles to become as resourceful as possible for and
with the group. For one play of the year, an individual may be the technical
manager, whereas for several other plays, that individual's roles will vary
from scriptwriter to actor and from lighting crew to program designer.

But areas of expertise develop during their work within the YBO. Key
areas of development easily traceable for groups (and for individuals) are
language development, building social relationships, offering evidence and
gathering substantive information, strategy building through risk-taking,
and explication.

Language Development

As young children grow through the toddler years, a sure sign of their emergence as "little people" comes through their widening use of words, phrases,
and stances of performance that underscore different ways of using these
forms of communication. Although scholars rarely attend to language development as these toddlers grow older, the same pattern of linguistic development holds as individuals mature in widening networks. For many
young people who have not participated extensively at home or at school in
open discussions or small-group conversations about substantive matters,
and as planners and thinking partners, their facility with certain language
structures lies dormant. Conversations with peers to test and develop social
relationships only occasionally take speakers into roles that allow them to
play across a scale of adapted voices, strategic thinking, and listeners ever

ready to reinforce, substantiate, or add to the ideas of others. As young people come into their YBOs, we have been able to track both their linguistic development of certain syntactic structures and their ways of contributing to talk with their peers while working on a project or performance of the group (Heath, 1998).

Their language use with respect to narratives is particularly striking. They use very few narrative forms that we might term *stories*. Story as narrative appears to have fallen out of the language repertoire of older children and youth in connection with the dropping away of particular types of extended opportunities to engage with adults in performance and projects as learning opportunities. Within YBOs, language becomes central to the activity; and thus directives, questions, challenges, counterstatements, and thought completions account for the majority of utterances. Extended units of talk take place not by an individual (except adult coaches in art and athletics), but by the group collaborating. There is a high incidence of sentence completion with overlaps that tie meanings together rather than abort or contradict thought. Argument consists of firsthand experience, with abbreviated opinion being rebutted by secondhand reported experience and occasionally by direct citation of a referenced source (e.g., video, teacher, another youth group, referee). Stories appear at points of breach in social interactions or as special tests in order to see about bringing in someone else. Not talking about yourself, not telling stories, and not taking the floor as an individual operate as preferred forms of communication. Young people most often describe themselves as watchers and listeners.

Ritual and routine mark the groups' interactions, so that predictability reigns. Being on time, starting warm-ups, getting out paints or equipment, and then moving into what becomes an expected flow of rhythm and connection to the task and to group members takes over. Several key interactions in all the youth groups have well-known generic conventions. Examples include debriefing after a public embarrassment to the group, a weekly session with local corporate executives in which the youth talk about their work, the critic's circle, the daily opening eventcast that takes place in some groups, and talk after a show or game about where they are heading now, what's up at this moment, and occasionally snafus or high moments in the show or game. But otherwise, talk focuses on the work of the group, whether it is producing a script, getting philosophical about what the group means or is doing, or "dogging" one another to keep the pace and tenor of interpersonal relations out in the open. All of these actions except problem resolutions and debriefings are laced heavily with humor and play. All sit within an intense sense of group pride. The playfulness enters the work, sustains it, and accounts for much of its creativity. These youth repeatedly say that their work speaks for them.

In the opening weeks of each season, youngsters encounter hundreds of open-ended questions and hypotheticals ("what if?"; "what about?"; "if... then what?"), with plenty of time for answers, ideas, jokes, and exaggerated claims. During these weeks, a preponderance of such language forms is met by only rare directives or negatives on the part of adults and older youths in the group. As certain forms of language initially used by adults decrease in frequency, young members pick up these features and use them more frequently. During practice, young members put forward more and more hypotheticals (e.g., "If we do this, then how about...?") and offer more "what if?" queries and ideas that include modals (e.g., "It would be possible to cut that scene if Jenny could get that costume change cut down in time"). In the final weeks before the playoffs or the final performance, hypotheticals and "what if?" questions fall away as directives from adults reach a peak; everyone is frantically geared toward the final performance and the inevitable assessment.

Young people also participate in a widening range of oral and written genres. Many of these learning situations occur only at the draft stage, whereas others receive joint editing for final presentation. Group composition of written text often occurs on a computer, where individuals try to create a unified whole from their own journal notes or rough drafts of portions of the full piece from the group.

The cycle of YBOs allows a range of oral and written genres created by young people taking on various roles. Production of the YBO pamphlet has a completely different meaning for members of the public relations committee than it does for student representatives to the YBO board of trustees. The latter may consider themselves and the group's funders as the primary audience for the pamphlet, but the public relations committee may be thinking of distributing the pamphlet primarily to neighborhoods already sending their children to the YBO.

Although language use sits squarely within the ethos of these youth groups, the goal of all is to provide the best possible representation, performance, or product of the group. As the season end approaches, full engagement, including problem posing and problem solving by everyone concerned, helps ensure maximum achievement. *Full engagement* here means not only attendance but also cognitive and social interaction at the highest, most interactive levels. Even within athletic groups, mental state verbs such as *think, suppose,* and *consider* pelt young members throughout the practice phase. Young players have to explain how they decided to try a particular play, hold a bat in a certain way, or try to steal a base. "What are you thinking?" addressed to a youth group member serves a literal and not a rhetorical purpose.

Almost from the opening days of every season, adults address group members by name: their own, new nicknames, or names of the moment. A majority of statements of more than a few words come with a vocative or a call to a specific person, linguistic evidence that the adult is alert to what is going on and to how everyone is playing roles and is accountable and responsible.

Building Relations

Adults within these YBOs make it clear to the young members, as well as to us as researchers, that their goal is to enable members to take away from their group experience individual strategies for getting along in the world. Unlike schools, which tend to focus on the need for students to acquire skills and knowledge that may help them obtain jobs, YBOs focus on building relationships with colleagues and, in so doing, finding ways to work resourcefully with others.[7] Adults argue that core identities, such as family member, civic participant, and employee, depend in large part on being able to relate to others and to connect with them in ways that produce desired effects and outcomes. Conflict management, negotiation skills, self-presentation, problem posing and resolving, and clarification abilities lie behind much of the work of these youth groups.

Youngsters write scripts for their own plays and debate inclusion of particular lines, designation of roles, and set design. In taking on these tasks, they practice in authentic and meaningful contexts numerous communication skills that both sustain relationships and enable them to accomplish the work before them.

Here again, language provides evidence of just how individuals improve their relational skills as they talk together to accomplish the work of the group. A discourse analysis measure enables charting of the types and frequencies of relational skills of individual group members. For random tapings of small-group work and whole-group decision making, charts of

---

[7] Several theories of learning, ranging from those termed *communities of practice* to those known as *communities of learners* or *learning for understanding*, make similar points. Numerous publications by B. Rogoff (Rogoff, 1997; Rogoff & Chavajay, 1995; Rogoff, Matusov, & White, 1996; Rogoff, Radziszewska, & Masiello, 1995), as well as those of Brown (1994), Brown and Campione (1990), Bruner (1996), Chaiklin and Lave (1993), D'Andrade (1981), Lave and Wenger (1991), Palincsar and Brown (1984), and Salomon (1993), give only an initial indication of the several views that support a sociocognitive framework for learning.

specific language uses illustrate just how talk maintains relationships. Made from time to time of conversations that take place while the young people work, such charting of language use illustrates the extent to which individuals successfully complete the utterances of others, talk over the talk of another, with supportive and congruent ideas, and draw out shy or hesitant speakers. Often during planning sessions, as well as within actual work, the talk of individuals will swarm with multiple overlaps congruent in content and with a rapid pace showing common recognition and connection simultaneously. These occasions give strong evidence of common engagement.

Offering Evidence and Building Substantive Content

YBOs bring members together to accomplish goals, and the clear centrality of the goal supersedes attending to the needs of single individuals. Adults argue that this real-world feature of the work young members do moves beyond popular psychology approaches that support building self-esteem, strong identities, and "feel-good" approaches to tasks. Adults further argue that efficacy and extensive practice in demanding, risk-filled environments provide affective identity building, and that pursuing affective dimensions without the scaffold of work accomplished and performance demands explicated leads nowhere.

Curious to know whether and, if so, just how this philosophy might show up in hard data, we developed a charting rubric for content and confidence similar to that for relational communication. Our view was that, as young members came to know more and to recognize the need for sharing information and improving instruction regarding specific skills and resources, they would identify and help supply these needs. We analyzed key features used to chart each utterance of every individual, and to determine the density and distribution of substantive contributions within small-group discussions, especially those of planning and practice sessions. As individuals increasingly shared propositional knowledge, used technical or exclusive vocabulary, or expanded or clarified ideas of others, they exhibited their confidence and their incorporation of information into strategy building.

Adults working with these YBOs also surmised that, as young people grow in confidence because they know more about how to make projects or performances work, they will move away from relying on their own opinions or feelings to support ideas they suggest to the group. They will instead offer the sources of their ideas (e.g., from past rehearsals or other individuals engaged in similar work) or sources that can be verified and retrieved (e.g., videos, printed evidence, or known experts). In addition to analyzing those items that indicate substantive contributions, we analyzed items that also register the extent to which members move away from supporting ideas from their own personal experience to offering evidence that proposed ideas come from other sources that carry reputations relevant to the task at hand.

Cognitive Strategy Building Through Risk-Taking and Explication

Within the YBOs that young people regard as highly effective learning environments, ample opportunities come about that engage young people in forming strategies, rebuilding contexts, and identifying both problems and solutions. Most of these organizations operate with minimal and erratic financial support, within environments that rarely recognize their role as socializers of young people, and often through the determination of a few adults and the young people themselves. Hence, any need has to be met through strategies that call on the local resources of group members. To move beyond this group calls for other strategies that require negotiation, requests, and market-building, which are everyday aspects of the life of YBOs.

Young people, therefore, have to take risks from which their usual status of child, youth, or student may have heretofore protected them. One group has to decide on a particular travel plan for the basketball team and then determine costs, ways to raise funds, necessary expenditures, and methods of monitoring. Another has to make a last-minute decision on whether or not the theatrical troupe can go on with a show, even when they must play in a gymnasium with no raised stage and no adequate sound system. Does the group risk possible negative public relations by canceling the show, or does it go forward and risk complaints that the audience cannot see or hear the show? Such risks come in the form of situations that need analysis or as problems that may require a range of solutions. A general atmosphere of high risk surrounds YBOs, for every person must step forward and try something usually never before attempted, with high stakes and in front of many peers with whom he or she must continue to work if a project is to move to successful completion. The risks of "not measuring up," "making a fool of myself," or "messing up" come with high costs for young people, who are ever mindful of the importance of protecting themselves against their peers' insults, derision, or attack.

Explication of these risks runs throughout the language of YBOs. Technical explanations of how to work with the lighting board of a major performing arts center came from one older youth to his apprentice in statements interlaced with "If you mess up . . ." and "When you forget to do x, then y will happen, so don't forget." Groups develop numerous strategies for handling blame when something does go wrong. Some groups have a weekly debriefing session in which individuals can let off steam about the effects of the mistakes or goof-offs of others in the group; such occasions may also focus on the entire group for being in a "low funk" or for having taken on too much. Other groups create imaginary figures on whom everyone can blame snags, mistakes, and haunting errors that, once committed, cannot be corrected: a missed lighting cue in a final performance, a strikeout in the last inning of a championship game, or a failed free throw. Keeping groups cohesive and working does matter to all members; regardless of the strategy for allowing the group to move beyond problems, sustaining relationships and getting on with the work drive a sense that "We are all in this risky business together." One young man, a member of a drama club that produced original theater pieces written by its own members, talked of his risk taking: "There was this scene; it was a gang scene; it was called 'Tales from the Graveyard.' And when I did that, that and this monologue [the one I did today], I felt very powerful. I felt very, very powerful . . . because I figure now I can actually write other scenes like this. . . . It's the same thing that drives a man to get money and to own things and put things on." For him, as for the youth in the drum corps already noted, work had become "our thing." Young people often tell outsiders that, although they may have been involved in crime, drug trafficking, and street violence before their work in YBOs, the risks they formerly took bear little comparison to the high risks they face everyday within the work of a tight group of peers tied to a deadline and committed to excellence of performance and outcome before outside and often unfriendly audiences or assessors.

Does It Always Work?

Persistent questions addressed to this research on YBOs include: How representative are these youth? Aren't they self-selecting into these programs? What can this work tell us about the learning of youth in general? These questions miss the fact that it is in the decision of these youth to self-select that their resilience resides. These are needy youth whose needs are met by YBOs and acknowledged by young people as critically important. These youth select positive learning environments and do not choose to be somewhere else, even when they can do so. Using statistical data from the National Education Longitudinal Survey (NELS) survey, we compared our sample of 386 youth with a national sample of 10,000 students who responded to the survey in their school classrooms. A risk index developed from a collection of factors picked up by the survey (e.g., level of violence in the school and neighborhood, poverty and resources in the neighborhood, degree of parental support) shows that YBO youth with the highest risk index are most likely to select arts-based programs. This finding suggests that learning through the arts incorporates a host of cognitive, social, and linguistic features that have a strong positive impact on youth from the most needy environments.

Other types of YBOs also bring positive learning outcomes for youngsters, but the arts appear able to multiply these positive results because playing active roles (with an emphasis on the plural, *roles*) constitutes the arts. Art-based organizations also depend heavily on building competence in multiple symbol systems. Service-based learning and athletic/academic programs offer only a limited number of roles for youth. Moreover, service-based YBOs must *serve*; therefore, their pursuits cannot be as open-ended and allow as much youth planning as arts programs. Athletic/academic programs similarly feel the constraint of rules dictated by the game or sport, as well as by the relatively narrow range of possibilities open for academic pursuits in meaningful linkage with athletics. For example, a basketball team can spend 2 hours each day before practice working on physics and mathematics as they relate to the particular sport. But the contrivance that easily comes with going beyond these subjects to the humanities or social sciences will inevitably meet resistance from players, whose interest is most likely in playing the game and not learning about or through the sport itself.

Numerous theories of learning underscore why arts YBOs prove most fertile as ecologies of learning through risk-taking rules, and playing roles. These theories underscore as well the importance of ensuring that young people see themselves as remaining connected to their community. Such theories explain how learning that is ripe for transformation and extension occurs when macrostructural and microstructural features stay in sync to ensure that generative understandings and substantive knowledge receive active meaningful practice, reflection, and critique within a collaborative group of individual learners who recognize one another as necessary resourses to ensure excellence.

Research such as that reported here is greatly needed in learning ecologies outside formal schooling in other postindustrial nations. But such research requires a considerable risk for scholars and must depend on radical changes in approaches to youth development. Social scientists, particularly those who study education, have preferred to work within institutions familiar to them: classrooms, laboratories, and carefully controlled home settings. To branch out into work with youth appears to introduce too many variables and conditions that seem out of control. Furthermore, such work challenges given definitions of certain key concepts, such as community, family, and teaching, and calls for locally grounded definitions meaningful and translatable in specific ecologies.[8] Moreover, reflexive consideration of contradictions within society that highlight certain ecologies of learning while ignoring others makes evident just why residents of these latter sites distrust research and researchers. Young people carry an abundance of such distrust, along with a ready arsenal of tricks to hold questioners and onlookers at bay or to lead them astray.[9] Access to these learning ecologies and acceptance by their members come only with extraordinary care and over a long period of trust building; moreover, young people must themselves be brought in as coresearchers and data analysts. In addition, one can never feel completely grounded while deeply immersed in research on and with the young, because neither they nor society allows them sole control over their habitats. Shutdowns of YBOs by civic authorities, sudden family decisions to move out of the state, and arbitrary school transfers often discontinue and dislocate the work of learning in YBOs. Hence, the study of youth must always include the interdependent agents and institutions that seek to control young people who insist on managing their own lives. Researchers easily become caught in these crossfires.

An additional difficulty arises for social scientists who study youth in learning ecologies not dominated by the usual institutions of control for young people. Researchers have been relatively powerless in recent years to counter arguments that many policy prescriptions and corrective programs for youth do not work. A program that spends an extra thousand dollars per pupil to educate inner-city youth is cut by state or federal authorities because it has failed to raise reading scores by a specified amount. A program in a youth detention center is shut down because its recidivism rate is too high. These measures of success are linear, however, and learning is nonlinear. New epidemiological techniques for understanding societal change suggest that seemingly minor, remote, and isolated conditions or changes within or outside a system can have profound effects on it. A phenomenon is therefore best understood by examining the interrelationship of its various components rather than by repeated focus on one or a few components. As we come through cognitive psychology and cultural psychology to understand learning as a social pattern, we will also need to acknowledge that

[8] For a detailed analysis of shifting perspectives on *community* within the United States, see Heath (1996a).

[9] See Heath (1997) for a discussion of the hazards of long-term participant observation of young people outside schools and other sanctioned institutions of learning.

we can no longer accept linear assumptions about learning and teaching –
the expectation that every extra increment of effort will or should produce
a corresponding improvement in the result. Social behaviors are not linear;
improvement does not correspond directly to effort but rather to conditions
better thought of as *tipping points*: that is, those in which a situation shifts
perceptibly from one state to another. Jonathan Crane's work on the effects
of the number of role models in a community – professionals, managers,
teachers of high status – and their effects on the lives of teenagers illustrates
this idea. There is little difference in teen pregnancy rates or school dropout
rates in neighborhoods with between 5% and 40% of high-status workers. But when the percentage of professionals drops below 5%, the problems explode. For black school children, as the percentage of high-status
workers falls just 2.2 percentage points from 5.6% to 3.4%, the dropout
rate more than doubles. At the same tipping point, the rate of childbear-
ing for teenage girls, which moves hardly at all up to that point, nearly
doubles as well.

Preliminary analysis within our work suggests that, at the tipping point,
neighborhoods can be transformed overnight from wildly dysfunctional to
relatively functional. There is no steady increase, but a small change has a
huge effect. Our initial findings suggest that, for certain neighborhoods with
high rates of crime, truancy, and drug and alcohol abuse, as well as gang
activity, out-of-school effective sites to draw young people have to reach a
tipping point in drawing a percentage of the youth population; at that point,
positive changes become almost immediately evident in several other areas
of the community.

Hence, skimming off just a few community youth for positive learning
ecologies elsewhere will have little or no effect on general neighborhood
conditions. But planting effective YBOs within needy communities and
ensuring adequate space and opportunity for 10% to 13% of the local youth
may have a tipping effect that, in turn, enables other positive features of
community life to develop.

What Social Visibility Exists for Youths' Real Activities?

To the current array of institutions, ranging from the state to the family,
the view of youth that comes from effective YBOs remains largely invisible. In place of the portraits and other forms of evidence presented here
come images and perceptions of young people, especially teenagers, as being
threatening to parents and increasingly to society at large. Yet nations continue to pour funding and interest into infancy and early childhood, often

with the espoused hope of enabling children to avoid many of the pitfalls that have destroyed their older counterparts.

In the United States, many young people live in neighborhoods with few recreational facilities, no local meaningful work for adults or youth, limited transportation, and no appealing ways of spending the average 9 hours daily in which they are not attending school, eating, or sleeping. The majority of crimes committed by young people above the age of 8 take place in the 4 hours just after schools close, that is, while most parents remain at work and other out-of-school sites and activities are unavailable.

These occasions enable the young to plan behaviors that carry high risks and to do so by developing and executing what are often highly complex rule systems. The predominant view of postindustrial societies is that the young use their risk-taking and rule-making to carry out criminal or undesirable activities. Therefore, the young must be stopped through tougher controls.[10] Two perspectives justify this concept: that of the realists and that of the constructivists. The former point out what they see as the dire consequences for society from young people who turn more animal than human without institutions that provide them with caring, responsible frames for meaningful learning through work. Realists grounding the predictions for society speak of reports that only 40% of college/university graduates in Great Britain now obtain jobs commensurate with their educational preparation. Every mature follower of economic news knows that low-skilled jobs have either left or are leaving postindustrial nations, and that young people wishing to enter the labor market will need many competencies not now recognized or generated by formal schooling. Realists keep to a master narrative that rewards hard work in formal education with fitting employment and insists that development of individuals and societies moves from basics, standards, and predictability of phases that advance toward improvement. Such a narrative gives considerable impetus to increasing the powers of governmental forces not previously involved in institutions centrally concerned with youth.

Education, child care, and family services thus become the realm of bureaucracies, both state and regional, manned by employees who see themselves trying to reverse the disintegration of older institutional ways of schools and families. Public media provide reports of conditions that offer a

---

[10] Beginning in 1995, the United States, Great Britain, and some countries on the European continent became racked with uncertainties about what the media termed *child murderers*, whose violent crimes made newspaper headlines and television images. Judging these criminals as adults appears to be the judicial preference in the United States.

rationale for "protective" actions by institutions of government, while at the same time, those making decisions for such institutions often have little if any expert knowledge. The "facts" become those collected by public interest groups or evaluation centers whose "objective evidence" fuels pseudoscientific debates by the public media and self-aggrandizing reformers.

The realist view of youth is both unreflexive and unwilling to decenter away from adult self-interests, a mass-media collective consciousness, and the politics of interest groups. Such a posture receives unreflexive support from a long-standing faith in the interrelatedness of technology, heightened control, and rationally constructed production and discourse. This realist perspective further points to increased crime against youth and a growing range of forms of crime committed by young people, as well as their popular entertainment displays of disrespect for current forms of authority.

Postindustrial nations share a fear of repercussions that result when some contemporary youth endorse the authority of groups whose intentions and goals may turn decidedly antisocial. Such groups range from neo-Nazis to militia members who may inspire random terrorist acts and gangs that encourage fictive claims of territory and exert tight claims of control over local residents. The occasional media reports of their activities appear to stress tight discipline within the group, as well as the assumption of certain adult roles.[11]

---

[11] Policymakers, educators, parents, and social workers, along with juvenile crime authorities, respond to the unpredictability of young people and their dangerous risk-taking with punitive measures and medicalized solutions based on the belief that adults must control the young. Yet, given the loss of supportive control and necessary work formerly more available than now from families, schools, religions, and neighborhoods, contemporary youths seem unlikely to respond to imposed control outside contexts that acknowledge their capacity to take on some adult roles. Criminal gang life, unsafe sexual behaviors, and social activities that include alcohol and drugs offer adult roles. Many youngsters take these up in defiance of societal attempts to control their access to such behaviors and in a search for high-risk behaviors that generate peer respect as well as adult attention. Yet these often disastrous roles do not come with guided or facilitated planning, preparation, and thoughtful practice, and none carries clear outcomes, goals, or standards of performance generated through internal group negotiation. Relationships within gangs, for example, depend on given hierarchical structures (and often functions) that derive from corporate models and allow little room for negotiation, conflict management, and distribution of rewards and punishments for tasks accomplished well or poorly. Hence, many young people enter early adulthood having had few if any extended opportunities to engage with adults in joint work or collaborative enterprises that bring the linguistic, cognitive, relational, and informational payoffs that come in YBOs of the sort described earlier. Their views of what it means to be an adult therefore figure predominantly in activities of short-gain pleasures and relationships, high-risk escape efforts, and dangerous or at the least undesirable outcomes for society.

Positions that counter realist ways of grounding action have no central core of support, for these often seem mired in relativism and the jargon of social constructivists who talk of *discourse communities.* Slippery terms such as *culture, symbols, agency,* and *production* come into the discussion, and persons in different camps find little agreement among themselves in either identifying a problem or posing solutions that can go to scale or achieve replicability. To those who argue that the master narrative of societal development must attend to the role of culture, realists answer that culture is undefinable, lacking specificity and identifiability, and too easily falls prey to identity politics and concerns of highly segmented groups. Spokespersons for these groups often voice their preferences in strident public announcements, increasing the possibility that outsiders will perceive these groups as fractured and having little in common.

Meanwhile, young people themselves, many of whom go about busily creating their own authentic systems of meaning, remain invisible to adults unless they step out of line or until they point to flaws in the master narrative traditionally linking school and jobs. They construct as much of their own reality as they can possibly gain control of, and meanwhile they become intensely reflective about the contradictions between institutional claims regarding the need to control youth and prepare them for the future and any institutional realignments or innovations that would take into account in realistic terms the current local conditions of youth. They have little faith in any given institutions, as evidenced by the following essay submitted to a writing contest supported by a YBO and judged by outsiders:

> Every single person who enters this contest is going to write bullshit like going to college or getting good grades, stuff that sounds aspiring and pleasant. the kids who enter and tell you the truth risk everything. they may not be the ones with the pleasant stories and good grammar. they risk rejection of their personal aspirations and the exposure of the "monster in the closet": and for what? to spill their guts to someone who will feel sad or maybe even cry for a few a little while and then award prizes in order to make their egos feel better; and then you'll forget maybe you'll remember for a week a month or maybe even a year, but eventually you'll forget, meanwhile the kids who told you the truth can't forget . . . maybe you will show the one who tells the truth the way out – for a little while, and that's cruel. how can you expect them to go back after you've shown them the sun? you can not judge my hopes and fears. how can you expect to? this contest will exist year after year until one day maybe I'll be the one presuming things and trying to relate in order to

> fulfill my ego and giving awards for pleasant bullshit. that's what you
> want – isn't it? – me to tell you everything's going to be okay if I win. well
> it's not . . . one, two, tell me what's true, three, four, I don't know what's
> real anymore, five, six, I only write with bics, seven, eight, should I leave
> my life to fate, nine ten, am I going to be my parents all over again,
> thirteen, nineteen, who says life should be played clean, forty, one
> hundred, almost got enough words I can't think of anything that
> rhymes . . . the end.

Young people such as this writer owe their primary allegiance to groups they themselves either have a hand in forming or choose to join. Their depth of reflection and level of critique belie their chronological ages and speak to their high level of maturational development.

These youngsters care little for the long-term statistics that argue that greater economic benefits come to those with high school diplomas and college degrees, for their interests center on the young. They point out that going away to college or university not only costs money but also requires that money be spent; therefore, the loss of wages as well as the expenditure of funds may well deter young people who cannot depend on financial support for higher education from either their family or the state. Instead they set aside general material comfort and choose other means of pleasure and comfort. Some choose to remain in their home communities and to become highly entrepreneurial while looking for opportunities to study specific skills, obtain certificates, and, through courses taken at several types of institutions, collect credits or hours that may someday be used toward a degree. Others seek adventure through travel or exotic – often strongly ecologically based – lifestyles, often in remote areas or with groups of like-minded young people who eke out sufficient cash for bare necessities by doing local odd jobs.

Like the young writer just quoted, they adapt to life using their imaginations and often becoming self-consciously aesthetic and fueled by strong convictions and moral commitments. They demonstrate human agency and moral responsibility while exhibiting what is often an inconsistent, antimaterialist stance (e.g., they insist on recycling and "buying green," but they burn wood, a major source of air pollution, particularly in some parts of the world). They have often pushed through particular types of discursive politics and become convinced that their survival depends on flexibility and adaptability. Thus they create or find themselves drawn to organizations such as those that are youth-based. These organizations survive not by working through change in order to achieve a particular status, but by shifting in response to local constituents' needs and regional situations (e.g., a large influx of refugees from a part of the world currently almost unknown in the local community). Because YBOs operate with a skeletal staff of adults and often on marginal budgets, flexibility becomes the norm.

Other institutions traditionally believed to be committed primarily to youth, such as schools and families, cannot bear up under the need for constant adaptation. In many communities in the United States, for example, the major employer in a rural county may well be state governmental offices, including the schools, which may often be the largest single employer. That a major function of schools and their systems is to be a regional employer is a fact that often gets lost in rhetoric that asserts the need to put students at the center of these institutions. So long as many communities (particularly in the United States) depend to a great extent on rural schools to keep the local economy afloat, schools cannot respond flexibly to local constituents' needs. As employers of adults, schools must maintain a strong grip on routine, predictable methods, and borders that, if abandoned, would threaten – either immediately or in the long run – jobs held by local adults.[12]

Such forces help preserve the basics and argue for retaining the status quo within schools, giving them a license to ignore discussions of national labor market trends and stated ideals for potential employees of multinational corporations. These companies want individuals who can communicate well in their work within group tasks, recognize and solve problems, access information and other resources, and take pride in products and performances of high quality. But schools, the major institutions thought to be in charge of youth, cannot respond in wholesale ways or often in significant piecemeal fashion to these points, as often reported spokespersons from prominent corporations and regional businesses. Both cultural and time lags bind formal education to textbooks published several years ago and to

---

[12] In the United States, the same resistance noted here to fundamental alterations of institutions that serve primarily as employers for adults, while claiming to exist primarily to serve and to educate youth, also comes in response to calls for states and the federal government to shift somewhat the focus of public investments. Despite studies by economists showing that government support for the arts is a low-risk, high-yield economic investment, states and communities continue to see the arts as charity and as unnecessary frills. A report conducted for the New York State Council on the Arts by an independent research agency reported in the *New York Times* (July 16, 1997) that "More money should be spent on the arts because it is a sound way to spend the public's money, generating taxes, jobs and economic growth far in excess of the amounts invested."

assessments that favor rote learning and correct quantifiable solutions to given problems rather than to creative, open-ended explorations and information generation or problem identification. In the past two decades, many teachers and school change agents have pushed for some changes in these trends. Yet, for the most part, schools today retain a schedule of opening and closing hours that is over a century old and that fails to recognize the changed nature of family, neighborhood, and religious organizations. Moreover, their approach to the socialization of the young still emphasizes control, discipline, and punishment. Educational institutions, especially those under public control, have made little progress toward recognizing the risks taken and the rules made and remade by young people as central to learning for the present and the future. Work is still a condition held out as a future reward for successful learning in school and not as a key component of developmental learning both within and outside formal education.

Conclusions

What conclusions can be drawn from understanding the degree of risk-taking and rule-making that marks ecologies of learning valued by youth themselves? Foremost is the firm conclusion that macrostructural and microstructural features of effective YBOs operate interdependently and do so through three central linkages that hold between the macro and the micro: roles, rules, and risks. As young people move within and through roles and rules, they take risks that enable the macrostructural framework to continue and ensure that all the microstructural features work together to give each individual an understanding of "what this place is all about." *Visual* or marked aspects of membership include gestures (e.g., greetings, congratulatory signals), specific costumes (e.g., T-shirts, hats), and high valuation of several means of expression (e.g., dance, visual arts, logos, movement, talk). *Verbal* interactions that shift as the work moves from participation and planning to evaluation enable young members to see themselves as planners, thinkers, critics, agents, and instructors. They raise questions, propose problems and solutions, and offer evidence and substance in conversations that become increasingly relational as the group members come together in community throughout the cycle. *Performative stances* mark much of what goes on within the groups. Widely distributing roles within the YBO and reminding these role players of what they are and what is expected enables authentic practice. Being a group member means that one is *always* performing, not as the self but as a representative of something beyond the self, something that can be excellent only if constituted by members committed to such an outcome through performance.

Our research thus far has looked most closely at arts YBOs for high-risk youth and their communities. The infusion of art into the local learning ecology creates change in several components of individual lives and communities. What seems to happen is that, because of the tight linkage between macrostructural and microstructural components of arts in YBOs, the arts produce an onset of change that goes to a tipping point relatively rapidly because of the tightly interlinked structures and connections channeled through rules, roles, and risks within these organizations. The complicated interplay of these, along with macro and micro factors, makes chaos theory, with its model of complexity and randomness within systems, an ideal model for YBOs. These organizations retain complexity and constant states of change to challenge notions of status, linear causes and effects, as well as single-agent influence. They adapt constantly, and they require their members to do the same.

YBOs provide conditionality that is predictable. Patterns and orderings appear at first glance to be unpredictable and unique, but they are in fact highly predictable and yet complicated and interdependent in their underlying simplicities, principles, and regularities. The randomness of their pace and the shape of their processes fall into ordered patterns over time and in a conceptual frame that acknowledges them as learning environments filled with activities. These patterns are, so far as we can now tell, those that link together a discourse of inner states, an activity arena of conditionality and alternatives, and an interplay between a rhetoric of intentionality and the exercise of personal and group practice. These complicated interplays move along what are both routinized and highly stylistically open channels of risk, rule, and role. They bring together the macroorganizational and microorganizational levels that account for the effects on young people who are members of these chaotic systems.

What happens in YBOs, especially those in the arts, is that learners young and old claim agency and allegiance. At YBOs, youth know they can excel at the *work of learning*, which ensures that they have roles to play that distribute as expertise their talents, knowledge, and gifts of teaching, strategizing, and communicating. The diversity and nature of their roles in the work matters in these groups. These youth, in choosing to work in learning environments with multiple high demands, define possibilities for themselves in defiance of probabilities. In so doing, they elect to implant levels of self-awareness, positive possibilities of the future, and social entrepreneurship within their communities.

REFERENCES

Beck, U. (1992). *The risk society: Towards another modernity.* London: Sage.

Beck, U. (1995). *Ecological enlightenment: Essay on the politics of the risk society.* Atlantic Highlands, NJ: Humanities Press.

Beck, U., Giddens, A., & Lash, S. (1994). *Reflexive modernization.* Stanford, CA: Stanford University Press.

Brown, A. L. (1994). The advancement of learning. *Educational Researcher, 23*(8), 4–12.

Brown, A. L., & Campione, J. C. (1990). Communities of learning and thinking, or a context by any other name. *Human Development, 21,* 108–125.

Bruner, J. S. (1996). *The culture of education.* Cambridge, MA: Harvard University Press.

Chaiklin, S., & Lave, J. (Eds.). (1993). *Understanding practice.* New York: Cambridge University Press.

D'Andrade, R. G. (1981). The cultural part of cognition. *Cognitive Science, 5,* 179–195.

Heath, S. B. (1996a). Ethnography in communities: Learning the everyday life of America's subordinated youth. In J. A. Banks & C. A. Banks (Eds.), *Handbook of research on multicultural education* (pp. 114–128). New York: Macmillan.

Heath, S. B. (1996b). Post-epilogue. In *Ways with words: Language, life, and work in communities and classrooms* (pp. 343–369). New York: Cambridge University Press.

Heath, S. B. (1997). Culture: Contested realm in research on children and youth. *Journal of Applied Developmental Sciences, 1*(3), 113–123.

Heath, S. B. (1998). Working through language. In S. Hoyle & C. Adger (Eds.), *Kids talk: Strategic language use in later childhood* (pp. 217–240). New York: Oxford University Press.

International Youth Foundation. (1997). *Effectiveness, scale, sustainability* (Annual Report, 1996). Baltimore: Author.

Lave, J., & Wenger, E. (1991). *Situated learning: Legitimate peripheral participation.* New York: Cambridge University Press.

Palincsar, A. S., & Brown, A. L. (1984). Reciprocal teaching of comprehension-fostering and monitoring activities. *Cognition and Instruction, 1,* 117–175.

Rogoff, B. (1997). Evaluating development in the process of participation: Theory, methods, and practice building on each other. In E. Amsel & A. Renninger (Eds.), *Change and development: Issues of theory, application, and method* (pp. 217–240). Mawah, NJ: Erlbaum.

Rogoff, B., & Chavajay, P. (1995). What's become of research on the cultural basis of cognitive development? *American Psychologist, 50*(10), 859–877.

Rogoff, B., Matusov, E., & White, C. (1996). Models of teaching and learning: Participation in a community of learners. In D. Olson & N. Torrance (Eds.), *Handbook of education and human development: New models of learning, teaching, and schooling* (pp. 67–99). London: Basil Blackwell.

Rogoff, B., Radziszewska, B., & Masiello, T. (1995). Analysis of developmental processes in sociocultural activity. In L. Martin, K. Nelson, & E. Tobach (Eds.), *Sociocultural psychology: Theory and practice of doing and knowing* (pp. 125–149). Cambridge: Cambridge University Press.

Salomon, G. (Ed.). (1993). *Distributed cognition: Psychological and educational considerations.* New York: Cambridge University Press.

5   Youth Between Integration and Disaffiliation in French Cities

Laurence Roulleau-Berger

Contrary to accepted ideas, young people are not always passive in the face of risk and unemployment, nor are they merely the sum of their previous familial, educational, and social trajectories. Rather, they are coauthors of their own socialization, endowed with a capacity for interpretation and an ability to invent social roles, even in situations of constraint and great risk. Of course, when situations become intolerable, individuals' capacity for action diminishes almost to the vanishing point. At the same time, however, the socialization of young people is still a continuous and dynamic process that moves forward through a series of alterations, readjustments, and identity conflicts among those young people and the groups to which they belong. According to Becker and McCall (1990), "Nothing is fully determined. At every step of every unfolding event, something else might happen. To be sure, the balance of constraints and opportunities available to the actors, individual and collective, in a situation will lead many, perhaps most of them to do the same thing"(p. 6).

In the course of various research projects carried out in France since 1983, we have observed that, in socially vulnerable areas, interstitial spaces emerge between labor markets at the center and on the periphery of cities, where unemployment and employment alternate and are superimposed on one another. We call such spaces *intermediate spaces* in which cultures of uncertainty are produced (Roulleau-Berger, 1991). We define them as societal, spatial, and temporal spaces in which the individual and collective identities of young people living in precarious situations can be restored through a process of transitional socialization that may lead either to integration in the legitimate labor market or to social disaffection. The notion of an intermediate space forms part of an approach that seeks to find points of overlap and tension among social, urban, and economic centers and peripheries.

Social Forms of Intermediate Spaces

We have made a distinction between two types of intermediate spaces: *creative* and *reconstructive* (Roulleau-Berger, 1993, 1997a). In creative spaces, young people, mostly from the working and middle classes and with a range of educational attainment from levels VI to IV,[1] come together to set up neighborhood or cultural associations and to organize activities and events based on collective projects. These spaces exist at arm's length or may even be concealed from the authorities. Creative spaces vary in form with the urban context, depending on whether they are located in the center or on the periphery of the city and on the nature of the urban fabric. They usually become established in older districts or in marginal places such as empty garages or apartments on estates or in industrial wastelands. For some groups, the street is a fundamental element in their organization. As a result of economic changes occurring in the inner cities of Europe and the United States, young people who grow up in impoverished families in poor neighborhoods and young people from stable working-class families face uncertain futures; the groups help them to reinforce and define their social identity.

Reconstructive spaces emerge out of negotiated cooperation between young people with low educational attainment, usually living in working-class suburbs, and youth workers involved in the implementation of integration programs who are trying to help them bring their plans and projects to fruition. We have made a distinction between cultural reconstructive spaces, in which young people and community arts workers cooperate with each other, and social reconstructive spaces, in which young people and youth workers are engaged in a variety of programs. These spaces, which are socially visible rather than physical entities, have close ties with established social institutions. Public actors play an active role here in helping young people enter the labor market by distributing information about job vacancies that more or less accord with the young people's aspirations.

---

[1] Cf. the INSEE (French government statistical service) classification. Level VI: young people who have completed junior high school and 1 year of prevocational training courses; Level V: young people who have completed the final year of short vocational training courses but dropped out of senior high school before the final year; Level IV: senior high school students.

Intermediate spaces contain many different forms of exchange, both market and nonmarket, legal and illegal, that overlap with each other to the point where the distinction between them becomes blurred. How do people work in intermediate spaces? The young people involved in them are not in regular, continuous, paid employment but are never without work. Small groups of young people organize themselves around projects requiring them to work together to create collective experiences where all that is often expected is passivity. They define territories in which information on "little jobs" is exchanged, or they create their own employment, with or without the formal status of government-sponsored schemes such as the *employment-solidarity contracts* that occupy an intermediate position between training and regular employment. Group projects give rise to a micro-level system of work organization involving the definition of frameworks for action and of territories, the establishment of rules governing life in the group, and the distribution of roles (Sanchez-Jankowski, 1991). Here, a social process in group life creates and upholds the rules.

In intermediate spaces, different employment statuses and different types of activities are placed on the same level. While making plans, young people take advantage of the various forms of work that become available to them, including agency work, work in the informal economy, and subcontracting. They work and they produce. Intermediate spaces reveal the continuities that exist in clearly defined urban territories between forms of employment that are economically recognized and those that are not recognized. Intermediate spaces show that different forms of life in society merge and exist alongside each other: one based on work, one based on the social dimension, and one based on "getting by" (Laé, Madec, Joubert, & Murard, 1996). Collective competences emerge from the synthesis of these various forms of life in society, a synthesis that produces tangible and intangible work. It then becomes possible to talk of small-scale urban production that exploits the presence of invisible and renewable resources and is born of the coming together of autonomous and concealed forms of economic activity. The collective competences are constructed from a range of different employment statuses and types of activity. Intermediate spaces give rise to micro-level processes of regulation and adjustment within the urban economy.

The notion of intermediate space is an invitation to conceptualize work in all its diversity. Although the young people involved are not members of the wage-earning class, they do have a social identity and cannot be regarded as marginal, even though wage work is still a strong carrier of identity among the young.

Cultures of Uncertainty

Initially, intermediate spaces are born out of the experience of risk that is defined through alternating sequences of precarious work, work in the black market economy, and various other activities, as well as through the "stacking up" and superimposition of those same situations, in which the subjective feeling of riskiness and of the integrity of personal identity is particularly severely tested. Individual trajectories are punctuated by crises of identity in which the various selves become dissociated from each other, creating intense doubts about who the individual is and what he or she wants to do. These identity crises may be reflected in various forms of rupture with peers, close friends, relatives, and family. Risky situations reveal various aspects of individual identities, and management of these various aspects seems to be particularly complex (Nicole-Drancourt & Roulleau-Berger, 1995). Depending on the phase of the life cycle, the situation, and the sequences of experiences that constitute the individual trajectory, gaps develop between the objective and subjective identities (Goffman, 1963). Although the experience of risk includes situations of social distortion characterized by a significant disjunction between the subjective awareness of self and the identities assigned through suffering and the experience of destitution, it also includes situations in which identities are readjusted through adaptation (Goffman, 1961) and resistance.

Intermediate spaces then emerge as places in which identities can be reconciled and young people learn to resist precariousness. Young people feel safe in these spaces: The gaps between objective and subjective identities narrow; the various selves are harmonized; young people regain their self-confidence and self-esteem and learn to commit themselves once again to collective activities. Individual and collective identities react positively to each other and create bonds, mutual consideration, and exchanges.

Thus, the transitional processes of socialization that operate in these intermediate spaces produce cultures that come to diverge to a greater or lesser extent from the principles on which official institutions and the labor market operate. We call them *cultures of uncertainty* because they are based primarily on the management of pressing necessity and uncertainty and on the "right to hesitate," that is, the right to refuse a deskilling job. Such cultures arise out of the need, in situations of risk, to manage emergencies and uncertainty (Roulleau-Berger, 1997b). At the heart of these cultures is the ability to cope, to anticipate events while also remaining as true as possible to one's own identity. Such cultures take account of the task of managing damaged identities; what counts is being able to "face up to" situations (Pollak, 1990). These cultures of uncertainty threaten to disrupt an urban order based on market transactions and on the division of roles and social statuses; they have insinuated themselves into the interstices of social structures, institutions, and labor markets, where they lie, as it were, coiled like a snake in repose. They give rise to chains of economic and symbolic transactions in zones of insecurity. The circulation of resources among several members of a network is characterized by a positive state of debt in which the desire to give often gains the upper hand over obligation (Godbout, 1995).

Cultures of uncertainty are born out of these "skills in making do with very little," which are based on a variety of stratagems and a spirit of invention in dealing with everyday life. These cultures are constructed by individuals living in precarious situations who invert the state in which they find themselves by making a metaphor of it and forcing it to function on a different register without leaving it (De Certeau, 1980). Under no circumstances should cultures of uncertainty be thought of as marginal cultures; rather, they are cultures capable of bringing about social change and even innovations. They should also not be seen as transitional cultures that will disappear when strong economic growth returns; rather, they must be considered in their own terms. They might, however, develop into cultures of poverty or, conversely, lead to the creation of various forms of integration into the labor market.

Although intermediate spaces emerge as protective spaces in which identities can be restored, they are also places in which the self is put to the test. Involvement or commitment can turn to withdrawal at any time because precarious situations always weaken individual and collective identities. It may be, for example, that if young people suffer a lack of recognition in intermediate spaces, they will withdraw, and their identities will appear fragmented once again.

The Production of Collective and Individual Competences

Thus, cultures of uncertainty produce collective competences that play an active part in structuring individual identities and vice versa. Collective identities usually have a positive effect on the commitment and motivation of young people, who benefit from social recognition within that group that they have not always received elsewhere. Intermediate spaces emerge as spaces in which collective competences are constructed. For them to exist, there must be a zone of common intelligibility where the conditions under which individuals can cooperate with each other can be created.

The Construction of Collective Competences

The following discussion of competence is based on the definition put forward by B. Lepetit (1995):

We shall define competence as the capacity to recognise the plurality of normative spheres and to identify their respective contents, the ability to identify the characteristics of a situation and the qualities of the protagonists and, finally, the skill to insinuate oneself into the interstitial spaces that exist between the various rule-governed universes, to mobilise for one's own benefit the most appropriate norms and taxonomies and to use disparate rules and values to construct interpretations that organise the world differently. In none of these respects is there assumed to be equality between the actors. Their freedom varies in accordance with their current position, the multiplicity of worlds to which their life experiences have given them access and their inferential capacities. (p. 20)

The collective competences produced in intermediate spaces cannot be reduced to the sum of the individual competences that exist in those spaces and that are being permanently renegotiated. They depend on the types of interactions that are established between the competences of individuals who prove themselves able to cooperate, to share, to transmit knowledge, and to correct and adapt their actions. Interactions in these zones of riskiness are initially fragile. Individuals gain access to these spaces in complex ways that offer a wealth of multifarious experiences. These collective competences are constructed initially in situations characterized by uncertainty, instability, and urgency. Cultural, neighborhood, and familial solidarities establish ties in risky situations by creating the conditions under which young people can acquire knowledge of the world and a range of work-related skills through involvement in varied activities.

Work is not a given, however, but has to be constructed. For example, when young people set up a program of activities in a neighborhood abandoned by the public actors, this constitutes an enormous organizational task aimed at nothing less than the survival of an area inhabited by families that are very vulnerable socially, without work and suffering from multiple disadvantages. If the notion of complicity in the construction of collective competences is accepted (De Boterf, 1994), it can be said that that complicity is constructed differently in different intermediate spaces and that the elements of those collective competences vary from place to place.

Risk, Collective Competences, and Individual Knowledge

Collective competences activate and transform the individual knowledge and competences that acquire legitimation in the individual spaces. The diversity of superimposed situations in which they find themselves allows young people in risky situations to acquire more or less visible experiences, knowledge, and competences: urban competences, political competences, technical knowledge, artistic skills, communicative competences. These competences help to reestablish the social bond, with the knowledge and experience acquired emerging from a need to manage emergencies in which survival itself depends on the ability to devise rapid solutions.

Thus, individual knowledge and competences nourish collective competences. The ways in which places are appropriated and space is adapted and organized give rise to the development of collective urban competences. Intermediate spaces are also filled with a plurality of artistic competences. Various forms of technical competence develop in accordance with the nature of the projects. Finally, political competences are collectively defined on the basis of a critical analysis of institutions and of the forms of action taken by young people in order to defend their interests and convictions.

From Transitional Socialization to Socialization into the Urban Labor Market

The shift from transitional socialization to socialization into the urban labor market takes place when a provisional adjustment between job opportunities in the city and the individual or collective experiences of young people living in risky situations is realized. This adjustment is linked to the evolution of the labor market, the structure of the urban environment, and public policies on the one hand and, on the other hand, to the individual and collective resources of young people and their notions of work and employment. We also can begin to speak of socialization into the urban labor market when the range of roles adopted by young people is reduced and organized to fit in with the stock of roles available in the city, when young people transfer and decontextualize the skills mobilized and constructed during their precarious experience in order to recontextualize them for validation in the labor market.

When competences are transferred from intermediate spaces to the labor market and are legitimized, we describe them as *integrative* and indicative of the shift from transitional socialization to socialization into the labor market (Roulleau-Berger, 1999). In making the transition from intermediate spaces to the labor market, young people faced with a number of employment opportunities seek a highly regarded, desired, and desirable status. If, as H. S. Becker (1963) suggests, the normal trajectory of individuals within our society (and probably in all societies) can be regarded as an increasing series of ever deeper commitments to conventional norms and institutions, the question of commitment to the norm of wage work is raised when young people have an opportunity to enter the world of work.

There is a shift away from the multiplicity and diversity of roles that characterize the situations of young people in intermediate spaces toward a hierarchy and organization of those roles. Individuals move from a plurality of different roles to a social role (Goffmann, 1971) through the acquisition of a socially recognized status. Casual jobs are replaced by fixed-term or even permanent contracts. Access to a *social role* is created when social and communicative skills, experience, and urban competences are brought into play. These skills are structured and organized in accordance with the prevailing norms in the labor market. Although social and communicative skills are not radically changed, there is a change in the ways in which skills born of experience and urban competences are constructed.

The various activities through which experience was acquired are in a hierarchy that favors one central activity: that is, work of an economically recognized kind. Depending on whether or not young people obtain a job that they like, they will commit themselves to or remain distanced from the occupation in which they find themselves. In the process of transition from intermediate spaces to the labor market, young people's sense of commitment to work and employment changes and is structured in accordance with the roles to which they accede in the world of work. The roles developed in intermediate spaces begin to take on the characteristics of those expected in the labor market. Young people bring into play the social and communicative skills, the cognitive abilities, and the urban skills born of experience that were mobilized in the intermediate spaces, transferring and decontextualizing them in order to recontextualize them in the labor market. For socialization into the labor market to occur, however, these competences must be legitimized in that market, where they have to be standardized and recognized as economically useful. Public actors may intervene at this stage (Roulleau-Berger, 1994).

When young people obtain a job that meets their expectations, they gradually move away from the intermediate spaces, sometimes abandoning them altogether. When young people find a job that does not meet their expectations, they remain in close contact with certain places where they still enjoy social recognition. In some cases, however, young people legitimize their association in the labor market by, for example, transforming it into economic activity. In this case, work is seen as a collective experience that holds out the hope of a common future. Individuals in this situation reject stability and regularity of employment and commit themselves fully to the intermediate space.

The process of socialization into the labor market is not linear and is never completely stabilized. It is both individual and collective. When the transfer of skills seems to have taken place successfully, individuals' different selves become harmonized, with the private and objective identities merging to produce social recognition and a positive self-image linked to the way in which young people live in the city.

From Intermediate Spaces to Social Disaffection

When job opportunities do not arise for young people, they are unable to achieve their goals and do not acquire a highly regarded and desirable status, and socially recognized work seems to them to be inaccessible. The various roles they had created for themselves in the intermediate spaces fall apart, giving rise to a form of social isolation or a life of scuffling and getting by, involving a series of deals or activities of a more or less legitimate kind.

When this happens, the various skills and competences they possess become increasingly hidden from view because they are not socially recognized. In other words, some young people accumulate a range of experiences in intermediate spaces that fail to lead to success. Thus, although the skills acquired in intermediate spaces may become integrative, they may also become disintegrative, gradually becoming part of a process of disaffection that is the product of an accumulation of negative experiences. More generally, however, that process develops unexpectedly, in the sense that young people can string together a considerable amount of work experience without being able to gain a permanent foothold in the labor market. They continue to accumulate skills but become discouraged at the same time. Such trajectories may lead ultimately to long-term unemployment. At the individual level, it can be seen that private identities are experienced as increasingly negative. Repeated negative experiences make it very difficult to transfer the competences acquired in intermediate spaces to the urban labor market. Young people then fail to understand why their activities are not producing marketable skills and begin to doubt the group's collective ability. Collective identities dissolve and are no longer able to reinforce individual identities, continuing rather to change for the worse because young people are no longer able to invest in the group. Their competences become invisible because they no longer permit access to the labor market.

Young people then lose confidence in their ability to develop cooperative relationships with institutional actors. If they are not validated, collective competences may even go into reverse and become a stigma for individuals and groups. Young people in this situation become and feel themselves to be socially and spatially isolated, and the urban skills constructed and acquired in the intermediate spaces turn into an inability to move and find one's bearings within the city; they stay in their own district, feeling imprisoned and marginalized. The process of social disaffection (Castel, 1995) is triggered, urban segregation is further reinforced, and anomie rears its head. The skills and competences they have acquired are put into practice in the black economy, where they are validated.

The range of experience acquired in intermediate spaces could also be mobilized then to participate in the underground economy. The young people are no longer concerned with having a visible presence as far as official institutions are concerned; their identities are now constructed elsewhere, in a different world. Although they have no status in the official world, they do have one in the parallel world in which they now live; they have moved from the status of "galley slave" or "down-and-out" to that of gang leader. The various skills and competences that they have accumulated are completely individualized in order to help them survive or to assist their families.

When young people live in a parallel economic universe and gradually lose contact with the official worlds, they tend to gather in risky areas of the city, where social recognition is based on norms other than those that prevail in the official labor market. Here again, the process of social disaffection is triggered, and the city produces underground economies concealed from the official gaze (Sassen, 1998).

Thus, the evolution of collective and individual competences into disintegrative competences accounts for the process of urban disaffection. At this point, it becomes possible to speak of urban marginality. This process leads to a divergence between objective and private identities that is more or less marked from case to case. The process of disaffection, however, may turn into a process of integration; it is never irreversible, even when segregation is very pronounced.

Changing Perspectives

The crisis in thinking on work and employment makes young people living in risky situations in so-called developed societies appear to be the passive victims of circumstances beyond their control. Without distancing oneself from the Fordist model, the dynamics at work in the socialization of young people, the complexity of the process by which identities are constructed, and the forms of collective action that develop in situations of precariousness cannot be conceptualized. Thus, there is a need to challenge a theoretical perspective that leaves an empty intellectual space in which individuals find themselves stigmatized as the prisoners of images that have been thrust on them (Heath & MacLaughlin, 1993; Roulleau-Berger, 1996, 1999). So we have to change our theoretical perspectives. As Felice Carugati (this volume) says, "The new is a collective invention in the face of felt dilemmas or mismatches and contradictions that impede or constrain ongoing activities and imply movement and change." So we propose to conceptualize the process of socializing young people in terms of the notions of identity, commitment, and social world.

Plural Identities

The issue here is to understand the way in which young people construct their interpretation of their own situations and actions, by means of which or through which they perceive what they are. It is here that the concept of a negotiated social order constructed on the basis of structured actions and interactions becomes essential (Strauss, 1978).

As the gaps of varying size between themselves and the public authorities and the wage-earning class gradually grow, young people today are involved in the concerted creation of common norms that shape collective and individual identities made up of a multiplicity of selves. As a result, it is possible to speak of *embedded identities* (Heath & MacLaughlin, 1993). According to Becker and McCall (1990), "The stripped-down notion of the self recognizes people's ability to check their activity and reorient it on the basis of what's going on around them, rather than responding automatically to stimuli, impulses, or the dictates of a culture or social organization" (pp. 11–12).

Social Commitment and Work

Even if wage work in a stable job is still essentially a vector of integration and a source of social identity, it does not seem to be and is not always experienced as a source of social dignity, particularly for young people who enter the labor market in capacities that do not match their expectations or qualifications (Newman, 1999; Stack & Stein, 2001).

Young people commit themselves socially when they feel properly recognized, when confidence and consideration are combined. Even in risky jobs, young people generally seem willing to commit themselves; but when they are discredited, given little encouragement, or exploited, that commitment rapidly turns to disengagement and disaffection. It should not be inferred from this that the work ethic is on the wane. Rather, disengagement from work indicates that there was a high level of commitment but that it has not been given legitimacy.

Thus, it seems important to observe how young people's social commitment is constructed and legitimized in intermediate spaces, in the realization that under no circumstances can these spaces be regarded as alternative, residual, or marginal. Wage work is not the only sphere of social commitment (Ion, 1994; Rifkin, 1995), particularly when the work becomes too disqualifying. The question of the centrality of work is therefore misleading (Dubar, 1993), whereas the question of social commitment or involvement and the recognition thereof seems to be fundamental. Commitment is the feeling of belonging to a common society, and if there are no more spaces in which that commitment can be expressed, hatred and violence will seep out of all the pores in the social structure.

Social Worlds and the Socialization of Youth

The crisis of a social order based on wage work means that the stages that mark the life cycle are less clearly perceptible and are no longer arranged in a predictable sequence; consequently, the socialization of young people can no longer be regarded solely as an ineluctable progression toward adult status. The employment crisis has disrupted the established schedules based on the various phases of the life cycle: childhood, adolescence, maturity, old age. To speak of young people and work while retaining the definition of adulthood that has been used over the past 20 years – a definition based on the notion of virtually permanent stabilization in both the labor market and family life – seems to be anachronistic in a social order going through a period of radical change. What characterizes the young people of today is less the fact that the various thresholds on the road to adulthood are crossed at different times than the uncertainty of employment relationships, the reversibility of social status, and the overlapping of various forms of work (see Fouquet, this volume).

Thus, the process of socializing young people might be thought of as a sequence of transitions from one social world to another, some of them more visible than others, some more institutionalized than others. The concept of social worlds helps bridge the micro-meso-macro gap, which, according to Gilmore (1990, p. 152), "offers an alternative approach to social organization as well as relatively stable patterns of exchange and interaction. Social world research foci include issues of organization efficiency in addition to the meaning of structure and social processes." Here we consider the experiences and meanings of young people and the problematics of their social worlds. A social world is a more or less stable organization of collective activity. From this perspective, we also see the relations between different worlds. It provides us with a dynamic concept of the socialization of young people in which they cannot be the prisoners or victims of given social situations.

Conclusion

In this research, many points of convergence with the research of Heath and MacLaughlin (1993) have emerged on both empirical and theoretical levels. These researchers are interested in forms of postschool socialization among young people. In the United States, young people have also responded to the absence of transgenerational socialization and local work opportunities by finding places where they can set rules, take risks, and try out roles that will help them in becoming assets to their communities. Young people are not presented as victims or culprits but as authors of their own socialization. Here cross-age peers create an ecology of learning and produce cultures of risk.

Clearly, certain theoretical positions are more fruitful than others as a means of conceptualizing the process of socializing young people. It would be interesting to examine the epistemological and methodological aspects also and, above all, to develop international comparative perspectives around these notions of transitional socialization, cultures of uncertainty, and ecology of learning while also keeping at arm's length the very persistent social categorizations that still operate, even in societies based on wage work undergoing radical change.

REFERENCES

Becker, H. S. (1963). *Outsiders. Etudes de sociologie de la déviance* [Outsiders. Studies in the sociology of deviance]. Paris: Métailié.
Becker, H. S., & McCall, M. M. (Eds.). (1990). *Symbolic interaction and cultural studies.* Chicago: University of Chicago Press.
Castel, R. (1995). *Les métamorphoses de la question sociale* [The transformations of social debate]. Paris: Fayard.
De Boterf, G. (1994). *De la compétence* [About competence]. Paris: Les éditions d'organisation.
De Certeau, M. (1980). *L'invention du quotidien: Les arts de faire* [The invention of everyday nature: The art of doing things]. Paris: Flammarion.
Dubar, C. (1993). *Le travail, lieu et enjeu de construction identitaire* [Work, a stake of construction of identity]. Projet(236), 1993/1994.

Gilmore, S. (1990). Arts worlds: Developing the interactionist approach to social organization. In H. S. Becker & M. M. McCall (Eds.), *Symbolic interaction and cultural
studies* (pp. 148–178). Chicago: University of Chicago Press.

Godbout, J.-D., in collaboration with Caillé, A. (1995). *L'esprit du don* [The gift's mind].
Paris: La Découverte.

Goffman, E. (1961). *Asylums: Essays on the social situation of mental patients and other
inmates.* New York: Doubleday Anchor.

Goffman, E. (1963). *Stigma: Notes on the management of spoiled identity.* Englewood
Cliffs, NJ: Prentice-Hall.

Goffman, E. (1971). *Relations in public: Micro-studies of the public order.* New York: Basic
Books.

Heath, S. B., & MacLaughlin, M. W. (Eds.). (1993*). Identity and inner-city youth: Beyond
ethnicity and gender.* New York: Teachers College Press.

Ion, J. (1994). L'évolution des modes d'engagement dans l'espace public [The evolution
of commitments in the public sphere). In *L'engagement politique, déclin ou mutation*
[Political commitment, decline or mutation] (pp. 66–82). Paris: FNSP.

Laé, J. F., Madec, A., Joubert, M., & Murard, N. (1996). Economie de l'enclave [Economy
of the enclave]. In M. Peraldi & E. Perrin (Eds.), *Réseaux productifs et territoire ur-
bains* [Economic networks and urban territories] (pp. 265–281). Toulouse: Presses
Universitaires du Mirail.

Lepetit, B. (1995). *Les formes de l'expérience* [Forms of experience]. Paris: Albin Michel.

Newman, K. S. (1999). *No shame in my game: The working poor in the inner city.* New
York: Alfred A. Knopf/Russell Sage Foundation.

Nicole-Drancourt, C., & Roulleau-Berger, L. (1995). *L'insertion sociale des jeunes
en France* [Youth and social integration in France]. Paris: PUF.

Pollak, M. (1990). *L'identité blessée* [Wounded identity]. Paris: Métailié.

Rifkin, J. (1995). *The end of work: The decline of the global labor force and the dawn of
the post-market era.* New York: Jeremy P. Tarcher/G. P. Putman.

Roulleau-Berger, L. (1991). *La Ville-Intervalle. Jeunes entre centre et banlieue* [The interstitial city: Youth between center and periphery]. Paris: Méridiens Klincksieck.

Roulleau-Berger, L. (1993). La construction sociale des espaces intermédiaires: jeunes
en emploi précaire face aux politiques sociales [Social construction of intermediate
spaces; Poor young people and social policies]. *Sociétés Contemporaines, 14/15,* 191–
209.

Roulleau-Berger, L. (1994). Ordres et désordres locaux: des politiques d'insertion aux espaces intermédiaires [Local orders and disorders: From public policies to intermediate
spaces]. *Revue Française de Science Politique, 5,* 856–880.

Roulleau-Berger, L. (1996). Le sociologue, sa posture, ses méthodes face à la désaffiliation
social [The sociologist, his posture and methods about   dissafiliation]. *Pratiques
Psychologiques, 1,* 69–77.

Roulleau-Berger, L. (1997a). Espaces intermédiaires et cohésions urbaines [Intermediate
spaces and urban order]. In A. Martens & M. Vervaeke (Eds.), *Polarisation sociale des
villes européennes* [Social polarization in European cities] (pp. 71–89). Paris: Editions
Economica.

Roulleau-Berger, L. (1997b). L'expérience de la précarité juvénile dans les espaces intermédiaires [Youth and the experience of precariousness in intermediate spaces].
Formation/Emploi, 57, 3–15.

Roulleau-Berger, L. (1999). *Le travail en friche. Les mondes de la petite production urbaine* [Work lying fallow: The small-scale urban production]. La Tour d'Aigues, France: Editions de l'Aube.

Sanchez-Jankowski, M. (1991). *Islands in the street: Gangs and American urban society.* Berkeley: University of California Press.

Sassen, S. (1998). *Globalization and its discontents.* New York: New Press.

Stack, C., with Stein, E. (2001). *Tales of luck and pluck with fries.* New York: Russell Sage Foundation.

Strauss, A. (1978). *Negotiations: Varieties, processes, contexts, and social order.* San Francisco: Jossey-Bass.

6 A New Identity, A New Lifestyle

Karsten Hundeide

> Why are good people unable to achieve for good what bad people can achieve for bad?
>
> Tolstoy

It is tempting to raise the same question when it comes to intervention in relation to teenagers and other youngsters who have developed a negative and delinquent lifestyle: Why are parents, educators, and social workers unable to achieve for good that which extreme youth movements seem to be able to achieve, sometimes for bad?[1] Why do youngsters who are either unable to accept or opposed to normal codes of conduct and order sometimes become converts or get "snapped" into some extreme youth movement or sect where they seem to adapt and accept codes of conduct that can be far more demanding than the civil code they rejected earlier? Why are some of these movements successful in catching such youngsters psychologically, whereas the professional social and legal support systems very often seem to fail?

Some Examples of New Counterculture Youth Movements

What can we learn from studying these youth organizations? What do they offer that the professional social and educational support systems do not?

---

[1] The intent of this chapter is to present an argument and a theoretical point of view with some examples; it is not an empirical study of countercultural youth groups.

Before proceeding, let us look at an example of what an insider of the *house-culture* reports on what is special about *house parties*:

It is where the music functions best, the atmosphere is highest, where sound and light together create a massive feeling of energy.... You do not need to invite anybody for dancing because everybody dances; it does not matter who you are or how you look, the important thing is that we all join in.... It creates such an enormous feeling of being in the coolest place in the world.... For me it is the basic feeling, this spontaneous fearless joy of being together. The one beside me is going to support me in having more joy at the same time as I assist him – we push each other into this at the same time as the music regulates it all.... Some use dope to assist this (ecstasy), but for me it is the culture, the carelessness, so many people together experiencing this same feeling of energy and joy. (Grimshei, 1997, pp. 2–3)

The collective sharing of emotions seems to be the striking feature of this movement, which in many respects is similar to the hippie movement of the 1960s.

This example describes the innocent, ecstatic, emotional nature of a situation where positive emotions of joy, brotherhood, sharing, and participation are in the foreground. But other movements of a more militant, rebellious nature have emerged recently, including the war between different factions of the MC[2] movement in Scandinavia; Hells Angels against Bandidos, with members being killed on both sides; church burnings and murders connected with satanism; the new right-wing racist nationalist movements and their war against immigrants; and the antiracist skinheads against the new militant ethnic youth groups. Most of these militant movements have strict criteria of admission and internal discipline, and some of them, such as the new nationalists and the satanists, are more ideologically oriented.

The following selections describe a new ethnic youth gang who spend most of their time outside one of the big glasshouse shopping centers in central Oslo. Most of the members are school dropouts or unemployed.

The ideals and models of this militant ethnic group come from American films in which violence is the dominant feature. Their great hero is Rambo. They can identify with him because he is quite small. It is the guerrilla ideal they cultivate more than the strong musclemen. Another film figure whom they admire is Ice Cube; he is the ideal leader. He is brave, never afraid or cowardly; he faces any difficulty or challenge directly; if anybody attacks him or his gang, he reciprocates with the same measures.

---

[2] *MC* refers to *motocycle*. There are many MC organizations, some of which are highly organized, and some have criminal records (e.g., Hells Angels and Bandidos).

Admission to this gang is through appearance and style: They all have their heads shaved, except for a small clump of hair left on top. They wear college pullovers and tennis shoes of a particular brand or mark. In general they use loose clothing that gives them freedom of movement, which is important for fighting. (This is also an important difference from local drug addicts who use tight black trousers.)

Most of the participants in this ethnic group do not use drugs or much alcohol, particularly not when they go to fight. Most of them profess to be Muslims, but they do not practice the prayers and the rituals. Some of them sympathize with Black Muslim leader Malcolm X. (He represents an integration of Islamic devotion and militant opposition to the established American society.)

When it comes to group cohesion and belonging, the music-and-violence videos unite them. They play music from the films independently of the films; the texts usually have very violent content. It is sometimes called *gangster rap–hip-hop*. When these films and the music are taken away from them, as happens in institutions, it is as if "a part of himself is taken away," as one of them expressed it.

This group also cultivates fighting. They learn fighting techniques from observing films of kickboxing.

With regard to criminal actions, the excitement involved in a police chase is most important to them. In general, they are bored and looking for excitement and stimulation either through fighting with opposing gangs or through "making a break" in order to be chased by the police; if the police do not arrive, they feel disappointed

The basic code within this youth gang is never be a coward; be courageous and fight back when threatened, humiliated, or challenged; never leak information about others; support and help the other members when they are in difficulty; never touch another member's girl friend.

They feel that they are exposed to racism and humiliation and that their honor is challenged in Norwegian society. They tend to use the word *racism* for any prohibition that they do not like or accept.

Most of them have an extremely authoritarian orientation; many have had problems with their fathers, having been spanked and physically abused when they were younger. When they try to establish contact with their fathers, many report being rejected. (From police research files; Bjørnebekk, 1997)

These youngsters alternate between two cultures. They carry out their antisocial and violent actions against "racist groups" at the same time that they accept the traditional Islamic family code of taking responsibility for their mother and sisters as the oldest son in the family when the father is away (my summary from police research files; Bjørnebekk, 1997).

It is neither possible nor the intent of this chapter to give a comprehensive description of the variety of countercultural youth movements. The aim of this chapter is to use some examples to point out similarities between them and to explore what we can learn from that. Many of these movements seem to share their *countercultural expressive style,* not their ideologies. As Fangen (1995, p. 19) points out, "Members of a youth culture are identified by their special way of walking, speaking, acting and how they look. More than anything else, members of a youth culture can be recognized by their characteristic style of clothing, taste in music and also by the other youth organization they are in conflict with."

In many of these movements, the expressive style apparently appeals to the youth, and the ideological content is secondary to them, embedded in a stylistic pattern wherein clothes, marks and symbols, hairstyle, music, social activities (i.e., drinking beer together), genre of speech and of humor, rhetoric and expression of political opinions, and ritual actions form *one congruent stylistic pattern or image, a person-in-dialogue typification.* In the right-wing nationalist youth movement and among militant skinheads, for example, militant manliness, toughness, and aggressive "white rock music" may form *the expressive core or the ethos* with which all the other stylistic elements have to be in congruence, including political opinions.[3] In addition, many of these youngsters feel a togetherness and a sense of belonging and being accepted that they never have had before.

New Lifestyles[4] and Identity Alternatives

In the context that Giddens (1991) describes as late modernity, traditional recipes for making sense and finding existential meaning do not seem to work any longer; even the traditional and rational goal of modernism no longer has the same appeal to large groups of youngsters, despite their parents' pressure. As Giddens (1991, p. 9) says, "Personal meaninglessness – the feeling that life has nothing worthwhile to offer – becomes a fundamental psychic problem in the circumstances of late modernity. Existential isolation is not so much a separation of individuals from others as a separation

---

[3] It is important to notice that discourse topics, opinions, and ways of talking and discussing are part of this same "package" or image. I refer here to trendy, politically correct opinions and ideas that are part of the *presentational style* and part of being accepted into a group.

[4] *Lifestyle* as used in this chapter refers not only to "routinized practices and habits of dressing, eating, modes of acting and favored milieu for encountering others" (Giddens, 1991, p. 87) but also to the expressive style, the aesthetic pattern, and the rhythm that express a basic feeling of life.

from the moral resources necessary to live a full and satisfying existence."
From a different position, Bronfenbrenner arrived at a similar conclusion
in his well-known article "The Origins of Alienation" (Bronfenbrenner,
1975).

Under these circumstances, youngsters turn to available alternative
solutions. Idealistic ecology, human rights, and religious and political
movements seem to attract more educated youngsters, whereas the great
majority of less privileged youngsters seem to find their existential meaning
in less ideological movements: as football supporters, as skinheads, as MC
members, and as participants in the more stylistic-emotional youth cultural movements described earlier. The different countercultural groups or
movements vary from the more stylistic and emotional hip-hop and house
cultural groups on one side to the more ideological and militant groups on
the other. Table 6.1 summarizes some of the features or components that
are more or less present in some countercultural youth groups.[5]

As Table 6.1 shows, the New Nazi group rated high on most of these
indicators, whereas the House-Culture group rated high on style and emotional sharing but not on new identity, political activity, and aggressiveness
toward an enemy. The Heroin/Prostitution group was particularly low on
emotional sharing, whereas the Hare Krishna and the New Nazi groups were
high on most indicators except those linked to alcohol and dope, political
activity, and aggressiveness toward an enemy. For all these groups, listening
to particular music, using a particular genre of speech, and discussing new
values were important markers of participation. In Figure 6.1, an attempt is
made to relate these indicators in a theoretical model of a self-identity and
lifestyle package.[6]

At the core of this figure is what I call a *lifestyle package* (Berger, Berger,
& Kellner, 1974). This is a ready format or prescription for how to be, how
to present oneself, and how to participate as a member of a modern countercultural youth movement. Among the different elements in this package
is internal stylistic congruence, which results when elements fit together

---

[5] This was part of a student exercise in fieldwork where key informants and representatives
of the various groups were interviewed and their replies were rated on a Likert scale from 0
to 3. This table is a short version of the indicators used. Detailed causuistic interviews are
not included here.

[6] In this context, *self-identity* refers to the ways a person as a member of a group distinguishes
himself or herself from nonmembers of that group. This should not be confused with the
narrower concept of *personal identity* in which a person's unique biographical background
and memory are central (see Giddens, 1991; Goffman, 1968; Tajfel, 1982; Turner, Oakes,
Haslam, & McGarty, 1994).

Table 6.1 Summary of Some Style and Identity Markers of Various Countercultural Youth Groups (Average Values of Key Informants)

Identifying Qualities	Organizations/Groups/Cults			
	House-Culture	Heroin/ Prostitution	Hare Krishna	New Nazis
Style	**(9)**	**(5)**	**(9)**	**(8)**
Clothes	3	2	3	3
Hair	3	1	3	2
Ways of speaking	3	2	3	3
Emotional sharing	**(9)**	**(2)**	**(9)**	**(10)**
Joy, humor	3	1	3	2
Friendship	3	0	3	2
Images/symbols	2	0	2	3
Enemy image	1	1	1	3
Ideology	**(8)**	**(8)**	**(13)**	**(14)**
New definition of reality	2	3	3	3
Alternative society	2	0	3	3
New values	3	2	3	3
Redefining the past	1	2	3	2
Politically active	0	1	1	3
New identity	**(3)**	**(3)**	**(6)**	**(9)**
Emphasis on self-respect	1	2	2	3
Hero/leader identification	0	0	2	3
Collective emotional "we"	2	1	2	3
Shared activities, including asocial	**(14)**	**(11)**	**(9)**	**(15)**
Listening to special music	3	2	3	3
Dancing	3	0	3	3
Drinking beer together	3	2	0	3
Taking dope	3	3	0	0
Discussing insider topics	2	3	3	3
Bullying and fighting enemy	0	1	0	3

Note: How important is . . . among members of your group/movement?
0 = not present; 1 = present; 2 = important; 3 = very important.
Scores in parentheses summarize the category (in boldface).

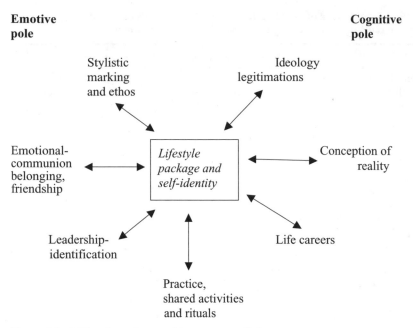

Emotive pole

Cognitive pole

Stylistic marking and ethos

Ideology legitimations

Emotional-communion belonging, friendship

Lifestyle package and self-identity

Conception of reality

Leadership-identification

Life careers

Practice, shared activities and rituals

Figure 6.1. A lifestyle package and its congruent links.

expressively as in a piece of art; elements that do not fit in will appear to be alien and incongruent.[7]

Look, for example, at House-Culture. These participants are clearly closest to the emotive pole, with a strong emphasis on emotional communion of "shared joy and energy." In the stylistic component, music is central, as is clothing style (although this movement is liberal in this respect). In the practice component, loud techno-music and dancing together in large halls are important. The House-Culture places little emphasis on ideology or leadership identification, and there seems to be no clear connection between participation in this movement and choice of life career.

At the other extreme, closer to the cognitive pole, are the more militant political and semireligious groups with strong ideological orientations and redefinition of their earlier lives and engagements. These groups also have strong stylistic codes with regard to "uniform" and marks; most of them are skinheads. They cultivate their special brand of heavy rock or techno-music, and this seems to be the common denominator of all countercultural groups. In the satanist groups, whose members usually have long hair, the

[7] This is not only congruence in the cognitive consistency sense (Festinger, 1957) but also consistency of a more Gestalt-like aesthetic and stylistic nature (Arnheim, 1986).

types of marks or symbols they bear also indicate their status in the group. In most of these groups, legitimizing ideologies give members some rational explanations for why it is reasonable to participate and fight: for a fair cause in a sick and unfair society.[8] The leadership is usually very authoritarian and strong, with a clear status hierarchy. A higher status can be achieved through so-called committing actions, in some cases with rituals, to which I return later. Their shared practices, beyond fighting, tend to be regular meetings to drink beer together in special pubs, discussing their aims and their enemies, and listening to music and dancing; some are also football supporters. In MC clubs, repairing motorcycles and planning new excursions to other clubs are the regular practice.

What Do Extreme Countercultural Groups Offer That Social Institutions Do Not?

What has just been described applies particularly to extreme groups that, in some cases, seem to offer a complete script for alternative living. For example, some of the important identity-sustaining qualities of a nationalist group are described by Fangen (1995), who did ethnographic field studies among Norwegian nationalists:

As a consequence of the new belonging, the member gets a new and very potent identity. He wakes up every morning with the knowledge: "I am a nationalist." He has acquired a new understanding of himself as a person, and this under-standing also implies that his inadequacies in other fields become less important. He is no longer going to fight for status inside the existing institutions, such as the school system and the employment market. He now has got the status he needs (however negatively it is defined by outsiders) by being a member of the nationalist group. (p. 20)

Combining the typical elements that we believe are operative in extreme movements that seem to attract youngsters may lead us to some conclusions or principles that inform us about what we, as psychologists and social workers, should pay more attention to in attempting to rehabili-tate youngsters who fall outside the normal range of development. These youngsters will vary in their needs and their search for meaning. The fol-lowing principles may therefore have a different relevance for different

---

[8] The discourse and construction of enemy images is central in some of these groups (Aho, 1994).

youngsters, but they summarize the attractive qualities that may characterize some of these groups:

1. Groups may provide a *feeling of belonging to a community* in which the youngsters are accepted as members. They are like an alternative family or home without the conflicts and problems that they have experienced in their real family. In some religious groups, the feelings of emotional communion and participation can be very strong; in other groups, the relationships are more like normal friendships. Still, protection against possible enemies plays an important role in extreme youth groups. Because the youngsters have cut all previous contacts, they have only the "family" left, which becomes a strong incentive not to leave the group.

2. As part of this new incentive, sometimes *a charismatic leader will evoke members' strong identification and emotional attachment,* serving as a model of adult identity and as a "guide into a new reality." Often it seems that the members of such groups need new adult models after many conflicts with parents. Combining the first two principles provides a script for liberation from childish dependency and conflicts with parents.

3. Such groups can provide members with *a new identity and a self-concept that invites self-respect and hope instead of self-degradation,* provided that the individual members are willing to commit themselves to the group's goals and activities. Members are offered a place within the new order and a new reality, which is confirmed by the other participants. In other words, "It is better to be a nationalist than to be nothing."

4. This new identity is usually further specified through *an alternative expressive style or lifestyle package with symbols and stylistic markers* that include a discourse style or genre marking the members' new identity and their belonging to a countercultural group. At the same time, this new "persona" expresses and symbolizes their deeper feelings – very often of frustration and hatred. In the case of some skinhead or satanist groups, this can become an expressive subculture of aggression and revenge in which their hatred can be legitimately expressed toward some symbolic or real enemy image.

5. In many cases, *a new ideology is offered that gives meaning and direction to members' existence.* New values and goals invite commitment and redefinition of their past and previous lives: "Earlier I thought . . . now I know. . . . " They are offered legitimations that attribute their failures not to themselves but to the "the system." A redefinition of reality is

offered that may help restore their self-respect and dignity. Instead of bestowing meaninglessness and alienation, the new ideology can offer "something worth living for" that mobilizes idealism and enthusiasm. This "something" may be a vision of a new world or a new order that requires collective participation for something bigger and more important: a revolutionary goal.

6. This vision also offers the possibility of *deep commitment and sacrifices, performing actions that may challenge members' courage and satisfy their need for danger and excitement.* Some of the more active group members seem to be high tension and danger seekers. In some cases, the level of commitment is also expressed in ritual forms, that is, rituals of entrance into political activity.

7. Finally, some groups provide members with the possibility of participating in *a new regime of order, internal discipline, and responsibility* in daily practice toward a shared goal, instead of goalless drifting and seeking of immediate pleasures and excitement (Jamieson, 1989).

In applying these seven principles to social and educational rehabilitation programs, we may ask: To what extent are these components present? How could they be included? For psychologists working to rehabilitate drug addicts, some of these principles are well known. Some therapeutic movements also include some of these components.[9]

The Appropriation of Lifestyles

According to the neo-Vygotskian school of psychology, children adopt or appropriate cultural forms beyond themselves through identification and *guided participation* with more mature models (Rogoff, 1990; Wertsch, 1985). This refers not only to linguistic forms, discourse style, and narratives that have been intensively studied and emphasized but also to the expressive lifestyle/identity markers that indicate to the apprentice and his or her social milieu the apprentice's identity and social category. Because such trends are appropriated and personalized (or internalized), they constitute key elements in the way modern identity is created.

But appropriation is not only a matter of simple copying or assuming stylistic patterns. It also has a practical, accommodative aspect wherein one's

[9] The new Australian therapeutic movement called Youth in Search is an example of *love bombing*, in which leadership identification and emotional participation (communion) are also explicitly used.

adopted patterns are personalized or *expropriated*, to use Bakhtin's term, "by forcing it to submit to one's own intentions and accents" through practice (Bakhtin & Holquist, 1981, pp. 293–294). The particular way in which this personalization of style takes place is also a way of marking one's unique identity. Like a jazz musician, the group member "plays" in a particular style, but his improvisations also reflect his particular personality, his personal expropriation of the style.

Becoming an Insider

Becoming an insider of extreme youth groups, therefore, is usually a matter not only of adopting the uniform and the stylistic markings but also of commitment to the group, which has to be substantiated through tests of participation in some shared practice, wherein ideological and expressive aspects are reciprocally confirmed through interaction, working together, drinking, and dancing, plus discussions – particularly in more ideological groups – of goals and strategies in relation to enemies and "what they hate together."

In more extreme groups with sharp boundaries (Barth, 1966), becoming a member may involve a slow process of negotiating through stages of initiation in which each step has to be earned through some sacrifice or committed action. In some cases, this may take place through rituals and ritual actions. Such groups are usually highly disciplined and have a clear hierarchical structure and leadership, as well as strong internal group pressure and control. This holds true for satanists, some militant right-wing nationalists, some MC clubs, and some fanatic religious charismatic groups. Leaving such groups may, in fact, be difficult for a member because of committed actions and the potential threat that the group's secret information might be leaked to the public and the police.

Other groups are more open, and some of them, such as the house culture and the more hippie, semireligious New Age brotherhoods and sisterhoods, are explicitly antiauthoritarian and equalitarian. They also demand a certain stylistic uniformity in order to be accepted, but that is usually more a part of a taken-for-granted laissez-faire lifestyle in which the group pressure toward sacrifice and personal commitment is less.[10]

The stages of becoming an insider of a deviant subcultural group (Becker, 1966) have been described by various researchers. The following paragraphs

---

[10] Note that a large number of youngsters regularly drift in and out of different youth groups, exploring different lifestyle alternatives. For example, 50% of those who joined the Hare Krishnas dropped out within 1 month (Bjørgo, 1997).

describe those for becoming an insider in a nationalist group, according to Fangen (1995) and Bjørgo (1997).

1. One must be labeled officially as an outsider or a deviant. In the nationalist milieu, this means to appear in public with the uniform or the identifying markers of a nationalist or to participate in fighting and being beaten up. According to Fangen (1995): "Being thoroughly beaten up at an early stage has a symbolic meaning to the group as well. If after such an experience the youth are still hanging on, they are considered loyal members" (p. 102).

2. A potential member will usually feel isolation and dissociation from existing social networks as a consequence of joining a stigmatized group. He or she may also lose a job, not be allowed in youth clubs or restaurants previously visited, or be expelled by the family:

   It did not take long before everyone knew that I had become a "neo-Nazi." Old friends suddenly shied away from me.... When my father heard that I had become a National Socialist, he kicked me out of the house and said that he did not want to see me again. Since this happened more than 25 years ago, I have not had any relationship with my family.... One of the things that kept us together was this shared feeling of being isolated. (Interview with Bjørgo, 1997, p. 169)

3. After going through this process, the person develops commitment through a strong feeling of belonging and a strong obligation of loyalty, like that in a family. This commitment also involves previous so-called committed actions that give a member an image to live up to. He or she is now bound by the group: "Having become one [a group member], you will never get out of it again. It is like a lifestyle, even a religion."

4. Finally, in this process of apprenticeship, the new members acquire a *legitimizing ideology* that provides a normalizing explanation for deviance: "Is being proud of one's native country no longer allowed?" According to Bjørgo (1997): "We just confirm each other's opinions all the time. We lived in a closed world, marginalized and isolated from others. Being at odds with society, stigmatized and under police surveillance gave us a feeling that what we did was secret, forbidden, important and exciting" (p. 169).

In addition to this gradual process of becoming an official member, with all its presentational markings and tests, there is a hidden insider socialization toward the tacit mentality and attitudes of the group's insiders. In some extreme groups, this is a socialization toward dehumanization, violence, and brutalization. The following excerpt is from an interview with a young female activist:

It is remarkable how fast I shifted my boundaries regarding violence. I used to be against violence, but now it does not cost me a penny to beat up and take out all my aggression against someone who represents what I hate. From being stunned and scared by seeing and experiencing violence, I have come to enjoy it. Due to all the pressure and stress I experience as an activist, I often get very tense in my neck. After I struck this girl in the face, I felt comfortably relaxed for days, having got rid of a whole lot of pent-up aggression. (Bjørgo, 1997, p. 168)

We find similar descriptions from child soldiers whose leaders have forced them to kill and to perform atrocities as committed action. After the initial reaction, killing became a matter of routine; some even expressed enjoyment of the power they experienced in connection with humiliation and killing (Hundeide, 2001). As Staub (1989, 1998) points out, *this change toward dehumanization seems to take place when the youngster starts performing dehumanized actions on victims face-to-face.* Indoctrination and ideology alone do not seem to be enough to cause this change. This violent and ugly face of extremism should not be overlooked.

Pilarzyk (1983) has noted the similarity between political and religious conversion and the recruitment to extreme youth cultural groups. A classic description of this can be found in Conway and Sigelman's (1978) study of how recruits are gradually converted and finally "snapped" into the belief system, and of the expressive style of religious and political movements. They describe the following five stages in this process (freely translated from Braaten, 1981, pp. 164–165):

The initial contact. This very often takes place during a period in which the recruit or novice is faced with a difficult situation and is seeking some solution for his or her existential problems. In this situation of openness, a positive approach from a "counselor" may be sufficient to convince the newcomer to embrace the new creed. Usually, however, the recruit or novice goes through further stages, such as those described next.

Love bombing. The novice is exposed to strong expressions of acknowledgment and warm, positive feelings of acceptance and togetherness before being invited to become part of a "family" or a sister/brotherhood. Compared with a cold or neutral existence outside the movement, this makes a strong impression.

Isolation. The novice is isolated as much as possible from relatives and friends, usually by traveling for a while. At the same time, the novice may encounter material obstacles to returning to a normal existence because the movement exhausted or took his or her funds.

Major commitment or committing action. The novice must commit himself to the group via an action that confirms an insider's status. Such an action must be carried out, even if it goes against the novice's existing system of beliefs and values.

Conversion or snapping. By the final stage, the novice has surrendered and has given up her or his previous identity, including bonds to family and friends, previous ways of understanding, values, and usually possessions, to the movement or to its charismatic leader. The conversion can be total and occur suddenly, as a strong emotional experience of having perceived the truth. From then on, the novice surrenders to strong internal discipline and the guidance of the leader. Personal sacrifice for the benefit of the movement is a general obligation.[11]

This scheme lacks reconstruction of one's conception of reality and identity, as described by Berger and Luckman (1967) and Berger et al. (1974). The recruit is invited to take on both a new lifestyle and a new worldview with new objectives. At the same time, the novice is provided with a redefinition of his or her past life in line with the new worldview. The novice is offered a place of acceptance and respect and is participating in a brother/sisterhood that confirms his or her new conceptions of self and the world. This redefinition also provides a recipe or a *legitimating apparatus* that gives sense and meaning to his or her life. In a period of isolation from society, as described earlier in Conway and Sigelman's scheme (1978), this process of indoctrination and redefinition of reality and self is essential in the more extreme ideologically oriented movements.

Contracts of Deep Commitment
To understand the powerful grip of an extreme organization on the lives of some youngsters, one has to look at the phenomenon of deep commitment. Deep commitment takes place when the negotiations of participation reach a level requiring sacrifices that involve adaptation or accommodations of the core of one's cognitive and motivational systems (Stryker & Serpe, 1994). Some research suggests that sacrificing something of central value in

[11] There are similar descriptions of people entering monastic life through a voluntary process of stagewise commitment (Hundeide, 1999).

one's life is an essential aspect of deep commitment (Bannister & Fransella, 1986; Festinger, 1957). The sacrifice can be anything ranging from deep attachments and family bonds to deep moral convictions and worldviews and personal possessions and money.

Committing actions represent another kind of sacrifice. Such actions express and confirm the recruit's status as an insider and often conflict with his or her previous values. These actions may involve taking a drug, participating in a criminal action against the recruit's previous code of morality, or simply taking on the style and extreme uniform of a youth movement and thus appearing in public with the other participants. Another example is tattooing, which symbolizes commitment for life. We know from studies of child soldiers that one way to guarantee their loyalty is to compel them to perform inhuman actions toward their own relatives or parents. Under such conditions it is impossible to return, both psychologically and physically, because afterward they are expelled from their village (Hundeide, 2001).

Members feel a deep commitment to the group leaders and to the organization. In fact, some of the more militant extreme youth organizations, such as the satanists, require a deep commitment of core members that usually involves sacrifices and committing actions. They believe that only persons who have been through those processes can be trusted and should have access to the group's secrets. This method of step-by-step commitment leaves no way of return without confronting conflicting actions and beliefs that may be impossible to face without a personal crisis (Festinger, 1957). In addition, if a member defects, he or she may need protection because such defectors may be considered a security risk for the group and therefore may be in serious danger. Having broken all contacts with previous friends, the defector has no one to turn to for protection (Bjørgo, 1997). This same process probably occurs in an involuntary way in the life of a criminal; after a series of committing actions, there is no way to return.

Possible Life Careers and the Lifestyle/Identity Package

In modern society it is no longer possible, as it was in traditional society, to predict life careers from a person's status and background at birth. Traditional social structures are no longer so definite and clear. Under certain conditions, however, there are some plausible links between social background, lifestyle packages, and life careers, especially when it comes to negative life cycles (Robins & Rutter, 1990; Rutter & Madge, 1976).

When a person adopts a certain lifestyle/identity package, certain life careers and activities, including acquisition of knowledge and skills, become relevant and plausible because they are *congruent with the style, ethos, or ideology of the package.* Therefore, in what could be described as a negative life cycle or career, there may be, implicitly, criminal actions that are stylistically relevant and congruent with this career. For example, a skinhead football supporter will have considerable knowledge about various football teams and stars. Such knowledge and related skills are congruent and relevant to the supporter's identity and lifestyle project. Traditional school knowledge, on the other hand, does not have the same appeal because it does not fit in. In fact, it may be incongruent with and irrelevant to his lifestyle/identity package or project. Looking on the acquisition of knowledge and skills in this way may have radical educational and therapeutic implications. In promoting a certain lifestyle/identity, for example, we also promote a relevance structure that may include or exclude the particular skill (or particular symptom, such as drug addiction) that we may wish to prevent or promote. This is shown in Figure 6.2.

In a certain "position" (i.e., by adopting a certain lifestyle and identity), a field of relevant activity is congruent with that style. From this field of activity, certain skills and knowledge become relevant and important because

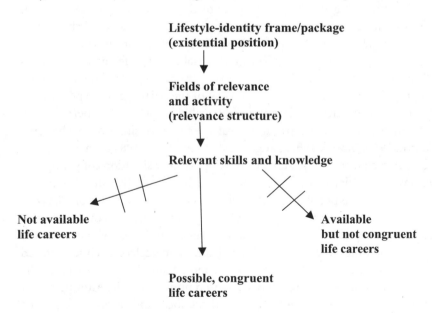

(Perception of one's opportunity situation)

Figure 6.2. A model of a psychological opportunity situation.

they sustain the image, style, and self-presentation of the adopted identity. It is relevant, for example, for a Viking skinhead to learn Nazi ideology and all the stylistic aspects of Nazi identity presentation, ranging from ways of talking, arguing, dressing, and behaving to preferred types of music and texts to which to listen. Such skills and knowledge become relevant and motivated because they are part of an identity presentational strategy (Goffman, 1968). I return to this important point for educative rehabilitation later.

Furthermore, for a person adopting a lifestyle/identity package, certain life careers appear possible as natural trajectories from his or her perceived field of relevant and congruent activity. The way this person perceives an *opportunity situation*[12] is very similar to what is psychologically relevant and plausible in relation to his or her habitual lifestyle and self-presentation. Thus, some life careers may be available, but they are incongruent with the style and, therefore, outside the person's psychological opportunity situation. Some life careers may not be available, because they are not available physically or they require qualifications that are far beyond those possible for that person. Participation in some of the more extreme youth movements may also block or jeopardize a future job or career (Bjørgo, 1997, p. 175).

The preceding model creates a bridge between the analysis of lifestyle/identity and possible life careers. In psychological research, the traditional approach to this problem has been correlative studies between certain personal qualities or background variables and life-career outcomes (Robins & Rutter, 1990). The alternative approach suggested here is a more biographical one from the point of view of the participant's experience of what is psychologically relevant and plausible at each step of personal development as his or her psychological opportunity situation is changing (Barth, 1966; Bjørgo, 1997; Fangen, 1995; Hundeide, 1989). An example of this emerged from a pilot study of the opportunity situations of youngsters who were associated with crime in a suburb of Oslo. By interviewing the youngsters, it was possible to map their social landscape of psychological opportunities. A strong polarity existed in this milieu between those who had a socially acceptable and school-adapted lifestyle and those who were on the outside – in other words, those who had failed and neglected school, showed no respect for the established codes of conduct, and had already taken the first steps toward a more rebellious countercultural lifestyle. Although most of these youngsters had not yet entered the local antisocial MC club and

---

[12] I use the concept of opportunity situtation to refer to the specific alternatives for choice and action that a person perceives as available, psychologically possible, and relevant (Barth, 1966).

drug milieu, this was still clearly within their field of relevance. They were strong candidates.

In this study, most of these youngsters' psychological opportunities within their social environment pointed in the direction of delinquency. A naive outsider might be tempted to moralize and ask why they did not join a local organization: a church, the scouts, or a sports club. Apparently, they had already taken too many steps in another direction; they had developed a beginning lifestyle/identity that was psychologically and stylistically at variance with a socially acceptable lifestyle alternative. The opportunities available to these youngsters at this point were different variants of criminal lifestyles/identities and life careers. This involves not only individual characteristics, such as criminal personalities, but also *institutionally established identities and life careers or packages* that these youngsters are adopting because they are more congruent and plausible in relation to their background experience and initial identity formation.

This type of analysis is similar to the analysis of the *message structure* of a text (Rommetveit, 1974), in which each move prepares plausibly for the next, at the same time as other moves become implausible and incongruent. The unfolding of life texts (Sarbin, 1986) seems to be regulated by the need to defend and sustain an identity presentation that is relevant and plausible within the person's social world. From this point of view, it becomes relevant to search for paths into and out of alternative lifestyles and countercultural movements.[13] In fact, this should be the key to intervention in this field (Hundeide, 1991).

Identity and the Acquisition of Knowledge and Skills

As noted earlier, the acquisition of knowledge and skills is often part of a self-identity presentation both to others and to oneself. Knowledge and skills of a certain kind become marks of who one is as a person. A well-known example of this is the acquisition of literacy in a largely illiterate society (Vittachi, 1990). According to some reports, those caregivers who acquired literacy as adults also started to change their lifestyles radically. They became more active, took better care of their children's health and of themselves, and tried to improve their lives. This effect was so strong that some health experts even suggested that, in a certain region, it would benefit

[13] Such plausibilities can be investigated and analyzed only in terms of a person's own experience. Bjørgo's recent doctoral thesis, *Racist and Right-Wing Violence in Scandinavia*, is an example of this approach (Bjørgo, 1997).

the children's physical health more to teach their mothers literacy than to set up a health clinic (Vittachi, 1990). In other words, by becoming literate, these mothers also seemed to acquire a new understanding of themselves as literate persons on a different level. In line with this new understanding, they adopted attitudes that were congruent with their expectation of how this new person should be.

A similar effect emerged from an early psychosocial intervention study conducted in a slum community in Indonesia (Hundeide & Setiono, 1995). We were surprised to find that our program seemed to attract more participants than did the other programs in the health field. By investigating what it meant for the mothers to participate in this program and how they categorized the knowledge conveyed, we noticed that they associated participation in this program with being modern and progressive. This quality seemed to attract them to the program. In other words, when we tried to teach competencies isolated from the cultural context, there was at the same time a cultural *meta-identification* of what kind of person we were trying to introduce, and the social meaning and attractiveness of this person became decisive for the outcome. The point is that people do not see isolated qualities and competencies; instead, they see whole persons. The same thing occurs when they see themselves.

But this principle can also operate in a negative way, as an obstacle to learning. Goodnow (1992) mentions one such example: Some aboriginal Australian children strongly resisted acquiring literacy skills because their parents considered literacy skills incongruent and in conflict with aboriginal identity. Similarly, when aboriginal students returned to their tribe after finishing school, they sometimes had to change their syntax to be in tune with the "broken" English style of the aborigine.

This is an important principle with implications for intervention. I will try, therefore, to formulate it in more general terms so that it can be adapted to new situations. Take, for example, a social intervention project intended to promote prosocial skills (x) among a group of violent youngsters through some educational activities. These youngsters have a violent, tough lifestyle and identity image (B), in clear opposition to the alternative lifestyle of, let us say, a socially well-adapted student (A). If the educational activities associated with the acquisition of x are meta-identified as belonging to A's lifestyle, there are reasons to believe that the acquisition of this skill would be inhibited and considered incongruent/irrelevant to their basic concerns.

This meta-identification, however, does not necessarily imply that x is incongruent with and irrelevant to the B lifestyle. In some cases, a new hero,

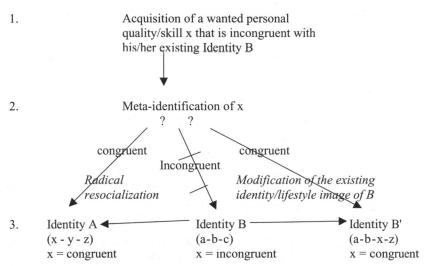

1. Acquisition of a wanted personal quality/skill x that is incongruent with his/her existing Identity B

2. Meta-identification of x

    congruent — Incongruent — congruent

    Radical resocialization — Modification of the existing identity/lifestyle image of B

3. Identity A ◄——— Identity B ———► Identity B'
    (x - y - z)   (a-b-c)   (a-b-x-z)
    x = congruent   x = incongruent x = congruent

Figure 6.3. Meta-identification of personal qualities/skills as congruent or incongruent with three identity/lifestyle images, and two solutions. The letters *x, y, z* indicate qualities that are part of and congruent with Identity A. The letters *a, b, c* are qualities congruent with Identity B. The letters *a, b, x, z* represent the qualities of a new, expanded Identity B' that can assimilate *x* (e.g., Malcolm X; see text).

such as Malcolm X, mediates a new and expanded tough image of B' with more human qualities (i.e., Black Muslims). This new image may open up the possibility for assimilating x as a relevant and congruent quality within the new and expanded version of the B' lifestyle. We refer to this solution as *modification of the existing identity/lifestyle image.* For the A lifestyle, there is no problem of assimilating x, because this is how it is usually meta-identified. In other words, it is inside the *relevance structure* of the A lifestyle.

In the context of intervention, however, we must ask if it is possible to change a person's identity/lifestyle from B to A so that x (i.e., prosocial skills) would be facilitated as a wanted and congruent quality of a new lifestyle. I refer to this solution as *radical resocialization,* because it involves a real change to an alternative and, in some respects, opposing identity and lifestyle (A) (Berger & Luckman, 1967). Such changes can be observed when drug addicts give up their addiction after joining a charismatic brotherhood in which a new identity and existential solution are offered.[14] This way of thinking raises an important question in relation to delinquent youth therapy or rehabilitation: Are we aiming at modifications of existing identity/lifestyle

[14] A similar analysis is possible for situational or communicative congruence, without involving lifestyle and identity.

images or are we aiming at radical resocialization? The answer will have fundamental implications for how intervention is organized.

Summary

In the case of marginalized youth groups and their symptoms, one has to adopt a similar perspective. In order to approach their problems of crime and violence, one must go beyond these symptoms, seeing them as part of a lifestyle/identity strategy that is partly established and codified as cultural scripts that they are adopting. For any radical change to take place, one must consider how alternative lifestyles and identity packages can be offered that do not contain these negative components or scripts.

A modest approach to this problem is to look for extensions that operate inside the same identity and lifestyle frame, such as joining a karate or martial arts club that cultivates similar stylistic and emotional ideals (Solution 1). A more radical solution is to bring these extensions into an opposite or conflicting lifestyle in a new community through conversion or *radical resocialization* (Solution 2). There are numerous examples of conversions within extreme religious sects and of "brainwashing" and resocialization to extreme youth movements where this strategy seems to have worked well "for bad." The question now is whether we can adopt such practices in a therapeutic and rehabilitative way "for good."

In more general terms, *a general principle of change of personal qualities, including the acquisition of various competencies, may be to help people to see and identify with new roles, identities, and life careers inside their culture, which contains the desired qualities as components.* The point is that most personal qualities or competencies are embedded or packaged within socially constituted roles and identity construction within a culture.[15] Thus, it is easier to approach the problem of change and relearning either through modification of a person's existing identity or by helping the person to take on or identify with a new role or identity that makes the object of learning more congruent and relevant. When learning takes place in this way, as part of a person's identification, it creates an inner need and a search for those qualities and competencies that are relevant and supportive of the new identity. This approach, of course, is very different from a narrow learning and instructional approach in which one tries to teach individual competencies without seeing them as embedded within social person and lifestyle typifications. Such approaches may be ineffective and unsustainable because

---

[15] Also activity or situational frames (Goffman, 1974).

they do not operate inside the existing person constructions available within the culture. Most learning approaches, when applied in a non-Western context, fall into this category.

REFERENCES

Aho, J. A. (1994). *This thing of darkness: A sociology of the enemy.* Seattle: University of Washington Press.

Arnheim, R. (1986). *New essays on psychology of art.* Berkeley: University of California Press.

Bakhtin, M. M., & Holquist, M. (1981). *Dialogic imagination: Four essays.* Austin: University of Texas Press.

Bannister, D., & Fransella, F. (1986). *Inquiring man.* Harmondsworth, England: Penguin Books.

Barth, F. (1966). *Models of social organizations* (Occasional paper 23). London: Royal Anthropological Institute.

Becker, H. J. (1966). *Outsiders. Studies in the sociology of deviance.* New York: Free Press.

Berger, P., Berger, B., & Kellner, H. (1974). *The homeless mind.* London: Penguin Education.

Berger, P., & Luckman, T. (1967). *The social construction of reality.* Garden City, NY: Doubleday.

Bjørnebekk, R. (1997). *Violence, identity and the media.* Lecture. Oslo: University of Oslo, Institute of Psychology.

Bjørgo, T. (1997). *Racist and right-wing violence in Scandinavia: Patterns, perpetrators and responses.* Unpublished doctoral dissertation, University of Leiden, the Netherlands.

Braaten, S. (1981). *Modeller av menneske og samfunn* [*Models of man and society*]. Oslo: Universitetsforlaget.

Bronfenbrenner, U. (1975). The origins of alienation. *Scientific American, 231*(2), 53–61.

Conway, F., & Sigelman, J. (1978). *Snapping: America's epidemic of sudden personality change.* Philadelphia: Lippincot.

Fangen, K. (1995). Skinheads i rødt, hvitt og blått. En sosiologisk studie fra "innsiden" [Skinheads in red, white and blue. A sociological study]. *Report UNGforsk, 4.* Oslo: Program for ungdomsforskning, Norges forskningsråd.

Festinger, H. (1957). *A theory of cognitive dissonance.* Palo Alto, CA: Stanford University Press.

Giddens, A. (1991). *Modernity and self-identity.* Cambridge: Polity Press.

Goffman, E. (1968). *Stigma: Notes on the management of spoiled identity.* Harmondsworth, England: Penguin Books.

Goffman, E. (1974). *Frame analysis.* New York: Harper & Row.

Goodnow, J. (1992) *Personal communication.* Lecture. Bergen: University of Bergen.

Grimshei, C. (1997). Notat om house-kultur og samfunnets premisser: media, pillekultur, urbanitet og identitet [Note on house-culture and society: Media, drugs and urbanity]. Oslo: University of Oslo, Institute of Psychology.

Hundeide, K. (1989). *Barns livsverden* [Children's lifeworlds]. Oslo: Cappelen Forlag.

Hundeide, K. (1991). *Helping disadvantaged children.* London. Jessica Kingsley.

Hundeide, K. (1999). *Becoming a committed nun.* Unpublished paper. Oslo: University of Oslo, Institute of Psychology.

Hundeide, K. (2001). Reactivation of cultural mediational practices. *Psychology and Developing Societies, 13*(1), 1–24.

Hundeide, K., & Setiono, K. (1995). *Psycho-social intervention in two poor communities in the Bandung area.* Unpublished paper. Oslo: University of Oslo, Institute of Psychology.

Jamieson, A. (1989). *Heart attacked: Terrorism and conflict in the Italian state.* London: Marion Boyars.

Pilarzyk, T. (1983). Conversion and alienation processes in youth culture: A comparative analysis of religious transformations. In D. G. Bromley & J. T. Richardson (Eds.), *The brainwashing/deprogramming controversy: Sociological, psychological, legal and historical perspectives* (pp. 61–62). New York: Edwin Mellen.

Robins, L. N., & Rutter, M. (1990). *Straight and devious pathways from childhood to adulthood.* Cambridge: Cambridge University Press.

Rogoff, B. (1990). *Apprenticeship in thinking: Cognitive development in social context.* New York: Oxford University Press.

Rommetveit, R. (1974). *On message structure.* London: Wiley.

Rutter, M., & Madge, N. (1976). *Cycles of disadvantage.* London: Heineman Educational Books.

Rydin, I. (1996). *Making sense of TV-narratives.* Unpublished doctoral dissertation. Linkøping: Linkøping University, Sweden.

Sarbin, T. R. (Ed.). (1986). *Narrative psychology: The storied nature of human conduct.* New York: Praeger.

Staub, E. (1989). *The roots of evil.* Cambridge: Cambridge University Press.

Staub, E. (1998). *Conditions releasing cruel actions.* Lecture. Oslo: University of Oslo.

Stryker, S., & Serpe, R. (1994). Commitment, identity salience and role behaviour. In W. Ickes & E. Knowles (Eds.), *Personality, roles and social behaviour* (pp. 149–150). New York: Springer-Verlag.

Tajfel, H. (1982). *Social identity and intergroup relations.* Cambridge: Cambridge University Press.

Turner, J. C., Oakes, P. J., Haslam, S. A., & McGarty, C. (1994). Self and collective: Cognition and social context. *Personality and Social Psychology Bulletin, 20*, 454–463.

Vittachi, A. (1990). *Stolen childhood: In search of the rights of the child.* Cambridge: Polity Press.

Wertsch, J. (1985). *Vygotsky and the social formation of mind.* Cambridge, MA: Harvard University Press.

7 Becoming a Member by Following the Rules

Alain Coulon

Karsten Hundeide's chapter (this volume) raises the questions of why and by which mechanisms – particularly psychological – some marginalized, delinquent young people are converted to sectarian, violent, or extremist groups that are much more demanding than is society in general. What can we learn from these ways of life, these alternative lifestyles? How can we think of rehabilitating the young people involved in a manner that could be congruent with their new identities?

For me, a sociologist of education and an ethnomethodologist, these questions raised two issues:

- What does it mean to be a member of a social group?
- What is involved in following a rule?

What Is Becoming a Member?

In the language of ethnomethodology, *being a member* is a technical term meaning sharing the language of the group in question. It means sharing a common world, common perspectives, and ways of categorizing reality. It conveys the impression of living in a unified and uniform culture when its members are at ease in the following senses: They have naturalized and incorporated the innumerable details of daily life, including minute details of behavior, clothing, and talk that allow the members to recognize each other instantly. This community of schemes of thought and action, which

I express my thanks to Jack Katz, Professor of Sociology at UCLA, for a close reading and a revision of this text.

Pierre Bourdieu (1987) calls *habitus*, generates nonreflective actions and always shapes agents' practices, but it can be discussed. In order to find that a person is a member of a group, we need not take the pessimistic view that he or she lacks the capacity to change or to develop in ways inconsistent with the group. Even with respect to his or her family *habitus*, the subject is not a prisoner but is capable of developing major changes, mainly through learning and training.

As Hundeide puts it, "Becoming an insider of extreme youth groups, therefore, is usually a matter not only of adopting the uniform and the stylistic markings but also of commitment to the group, which has to be substantiated through tests of participation in some shared practice . . . reciprocally confirmed." That is to say, perspectives are reciprocal. The novice who wants to enter a new world must learn to share the perspective of the other members of the group. Only when people have reciprocal perspectives can we speak of them as being members of the same social unit.

In education, becoming an insider is a process that we find every time we deal with someone who is entering a new institution, taking on a new status, or adopting a new role. This process is particularly significant in the education system; it occurs every time the student moves from one stage to another, such as entrance into first grade in elementary school or entrance into high school, college, or university. I call the process by which one joins a new group *affiliation*.

Van Gennep (1981) has distinguished and described the three stages of joining (*agrégation* to) a new group:

- The separation of the novice from his or her previous group.
- The liminal time when the subject is at the social margins, with neither past nor future.
- The membership stage, when the subject can live naturally in the new group because he or she has been initiated into the new world through a process of routinization. He or she has become, or is becoming, a member.

How does a novice move from novice status to member? That is the problem we must deal with when we are concerned with the way adolescents or young adults are caught in more or less marginal groups. Symbolic interactionism and ethnomethodology have studied how these processes occur.

For symbolic interactionism, social significance must be understood as "produced by the interacting activities of the actors" (Blumer, 1969, p. 5). We have to take into account the point of view of the actors under study because, through the meaning that they assign to objects, to people, and to the symbols that surround them, they build up their social worlds. The social significance of objects (other people, material things, or collective phenomena like those in a group) arises in the meaning that they take on in the course of our *interaction*. Even if some of these significances are stable over a period of time, they still have to be renegotiated at each new interaction. The world of social symbols can be defined as a negotiated, temporary, fragile order, one that has to be continually reconstructed as members interpret the world.

A good example of this theoretical point of view is provided in *labeling theory*. This theory holds that a social world is not given but is constructed here and now. Consider, for instance, the labeling of people as deviant. Deviance is not considered to be a quality, an inherent characteristic of the person, or something that is produced by the deviant. On the contrary, deviance is understood to be created by a group of instituted definitions, by the reaction of authority to more or less marginal acts: in short, as the outcome of a social judgment. As Howard Becker (1963) put it, "Deviance is *not* a quality of the act the person commits. . . . Deviant behavior is behavior that people so label" (p. 9).

An individual does not become a deviant only through the accomplishment of an act. Deviance is not an inherent part of behavior. A deviant is one who has been caught, defined, isolated, designated, and stigmatized. The social system, by labeling some persons as deviants, confirms them as being deviant because of the stigma attached to the label: People become what they are socially described to be.

Symbolic interactionism grew out of the University of Chicago's School of Sociology. For the Chicago School, all human groups, including violent groups, criminal groups, and gangs, must be studied in their particular habitats. For example, it is not possible to analyze a gang of young delinquents if we do not take into account, in a very precise and detailed manner, the living conditions of its members, their daily social practices, and their relationship to the rest of society. Empirical research as practiced by Chicago sociologists leads us to consider general *social disorganization* as part of the analysis, just as Durkheimian anomie is part of the analysis of suicide.

In this view, delinquents are not delinquents per se, even when they are very violent. Thrasher (1927/1963) noted that gangs were developing and living in an *interstitial zone* in Chicago not only in the geographic sense of the expression but also in the social sense. We can say that a sociological perspective has been taken in France since the beginning of the 1990s and has emerged in the form of efforts to explain delinquency by characterizing the way of life of youngsters living in a *banlieue* (suburban area) outside of big cities. The following characteristics, all noted by Thrasher, are also often noted now in explaining the French case: marginalization, pauperization, ghettoization of a young population, immigration, status as dropouts and as unemployed, a squalid environment, and a lack of constructive leisure activities. Youths living in these conditions form more or less well-organized and sometimes violent gangs; the gangs defy all real or potential authority and have well-defined markers such as language, clothing, graffiti (tags), and music (e.g., rap, break dancing).

These young people have a place in society that is interstitial and not one of legitimate right. Their delinquency can be considered as part of an individual and collective quest for identity. Young people become gang members because they have inside them, according to Thrasher, unemployed energy, energy that no social model compatible with a free society can control, energy that in gang activities is expressed freely and spontaneously.

Hundeide is right when he states that it is difficult and perhaps even useless to "teach competencies isolated from the cultural context. . . . People do not see isolated qualities and competencies; instead they see whole persons." I would rather say that they see members: that is, persons embedded in social life, persons who demonstrate to others that they are rational, persons who have reasonable behaviors and produce a social world congruently with others. Seen this way, young people are people in action, always acting or potentially acting.

We can consider that persons are, in fact, social members doing their job of being human. As Harold Garfinkel (1967) puts it, social reality is everywhere, always, only, exactly, and entirely a matter of members' work. The consequence of this statement is to change our conception of social facts. Whatever social world we consider, it is for its actors rational, organized, and commonsensical (Katz, 1988). The outsider, often a sociologist, psychologist, or anthropologist, defines these worlds as marginal, strange, disorganized, irrational, and so on.

Following Rules

For several years, I have been conducting research on first-year students at the University of Paris 8 at Saint-Denis (Coulon, 1997). Paris 8 is an interesting site for several reasons. It has a tradition of pedagogic innovation. Located some miles to the north of Paris, it operates in a "difficult" suburb, a *banlieue* culture. About one-third of new students come from first-generation immigrant families in which parents have had and known a different school career from the familiar one at the university. With respect to the standard criteria of university culture, these students' initial outlook can be considered culturally oppressed.

The French university system is extremely demanding during the first year; in general, students experience difficulties in surviving the first year. Becoming part of university life is always difficult for new students because they are attempting to enter a new world, one with its own rules and stages. Learning new rules, learning how to learn new rules, and acquiring a sense of the purpose of the enterprise are the main challenges.

Learning the rules is probably the most important challenge when we think of how adolescents or young adults in general enter a new world. For instance, university rules are numerous and complex, and it is not sufficient to learn the rules as if the point of the learning process is to create a stock of knowledge.

When I was doing fieldwork at the university during the first weeks of a new academic year, I heard new students every day endlessly talking about and commenting on the rules of their new world. Their common problem was to verify reciprocally the correctness of their understanding of the rules of the curriculum and of their future intellectual work. Their questions, which included the following, were always very practical: "How many courses do I have to attend each semester, each week, each day?" "Is there a chronological order in which to take them?" "What are the consequences for my possible future choices if I take this course instead of that one?" "How many hours of work must I invest in each course?" "How many pages of work will I have to do next month?" "What does the professor mean when he asks us to write an 'abstract' of this book?" "Of what length?" and so on. As in the "Agnes case" (Garfinkel, 1967), learning the ethnomethods of the group in which one wants to live implies doing the work of a detective. Hundreds of small questions are exchanged among students about the innumerable rules of their new *métier*: They have to learn the "job" of being a student.

Even in an intellectual world, a rule is, before and above all, a practical matter. To understand a rule is useless unless you can practice it. A rule is meaningless for one who does not practice it, who does not perceive what it indicates about what one should do. The subject constructs a relationship to institutions and to knowledge by understanding the practicalities of rules. In that manner, the subject acquires competence as an affiliated member. This incorporated competence is acknowledged by others, particularly teachers, as a sign that the subject is on the way to becoming a competent student.

Understanding the rules is crucial. Following a rule is not a mechanical process. This topic opens up an immense domain of external contingencies and a wide scope of interpretation. Long before the ethnomethodologists arrived, Wittgenstein had already found this to be true about rules of grammar: For him, a rule is not the faithful reflection of preexisting contents of meaning.

In the following example, *I* represents instructions in general, including rules, prescriptions, guidelines, directives, orders, and norms, and *A* refers to the corresponding action. To refer to an action that is not any action but the "instructed" action, we use A_i:

This represents a pair, $(I\ A_i)$, which Garfinkel (1967) calls a *Lebenswelt pair*.

I call the analysis of the space between I and A_i, the *strong program of ethnomethodology*. I mean that the analysis of the space that is opened when a rule is applied (e.g., sports but, even more commonly, any action realizing the pair: instructions/instructed actions) reveals the properties of the social action implied by the rule. Those properties can be specific to some actions; others – such as sequentiality, temporality, rationality, and a sense of action – are common to all rules.[1]

A rule must always be interpreted because its use is never contained in itself. The meaning is not already there; it is always built up by a subsequent action. The meaning is not given beforehand; one must do the work of interpretation at every occurrence of an event, even if one already knows the rule. The interpretation is *crystallized* in the code, but the practice, not the code, reveals the interpretation. The practicality of the rules exists and appears only through the work of interpretation by the subject. Along with the ethnomethodologists, therefore, we have to consider social reality as an ongoing practical achievement (and not as a *thing*, according to Durkheim's aphorism) in which people are constantly surveying and objectifying the common daily world that each of us knows so well.

We have a tendency to believe that young delinquents do not follow the social rules because *we* regard rules as being ready-made. That is not so for at least two reasons. First, between an instruction and its corresponding action, there resides an immense domain of contingency that always turns up unexpected outcomes (i.e., events that could not be anticipated from and are not contained in the instructions). Second, there is always a process of interpretation, even when people follow simple instructions, such as assembling a table bought in a kit, following a map in response to a friend's

---

[1] For that reason, I consider that ethnomethodology is theoretically related to and should be practically linked to the fields of ergonomics, microsociology, conversation analysis, cognition, connectionism, computer science, and the robot and space industries. My notion of the strong program includes several aspects of the complexity of a pair.

invitation, or following a recipe. And third, when we consider more complex social rules, we must take into account the effects of personal interests and both individual and collective strategies. A rule is never completely ready-made, even when it has already become familiar and been applied for a long time.

Don H. Zimmerman (1970) has shown that the employees of a public social work agency were systematically ignorant of the practical use of the rules on which their work was founded: What they could say about the rules was of a different order of reality than what they could do with the rules in practice. The employees regarded the rules as idealizations that have stable meanings and exist independently of their use in various situations, as existing distinct from the practical interests of the actors involved, from their perspectives and their interpretations. But the way they acted in their daily affairs demonstrated just the opposite of this conception of rules: They were analyzing their files case by case and examining exceptions to the rules, not the rules themselves. In brief, they were continuously engaged in a process of interpreting the current situation.

Between an instruction and an action, between a rule and its application, a space resides that has not been analyzed by classical sociology, wherein exists a zone of contingencies and the world of interpretation by the subject. Some essential properties of the practice appear if we analyze work that consists of following instructions, rules, norms, or prescriptions in general. These properties include sequentiality, temporality of action, how people define the situation, their cognitive orientation, and the membership categorization devices (Sacks, 1992) they use.

This way of analyzing the process of learning the rules can be transposed to the issue of a social remedy for delinquency. For instance, learning a sport is sometimes considered a "social therapy" for young people. If sport activity is interesting, it is not only because of the virtues of a shared social and corporal activity, but mainly because young people, when learning the game or the sport activity, are learning the rules and the practicalities of the rules. They discover *in situ* the open space that they will fill in with their inventive and ingenious practices; their focus will be on what happens between a rule and its open-ended concrete application. The sport does not "cure" the delinquent; the use and comprehension of the rule does.

Think of the karate example offered by Hundeide. I agree that karate can be an interesting activity because it fits with young delinquents' culture; they tend to be fascinated with fighting sports. But it is not because of a sort of sociocultural proximity that karate may be a pedagogical and integrative activity. Instead, it is because one cannot practice karate without considering tacit questions about the instructions, how to understand them, and the process of their endless interpretation and application, the last being a matter that opens an immense domain of contingency that the subject must reduce if he wants to continue his practice. Young delinquents or predelinquents practicing karate all know this aspect of the sport: After a stage of imitation that can last several months or several years, they begin to perceive that the interpretations of their instructor's indications vary from one situation to another and can be variously applied, even though the same set of instructions is concerned. They discover that the use is not contained in the rule, that the rule does not "contain" its significations. These will be constructed by the social use of the rule, by its application in practice. The rule indicates to us that two of its applications are identical. The rule creates the similarity. The rule puts together different occurrences. The essence of the rule is to abolish the distinction between old and new cases. The very first function of the rule is to allow repetition and, consequently, the possibility of deviation. In that sense, karate practice can be considered an integrative and curative social activity.

Learning the code means being able to transpose the code to other situations, to innovate, to create new variations and significations for the code. When the subject, for whom the density of life was first residing in the present, discovers these strange properties of the rule, he becomes able to project himself into the future.

REFERENCES

Becker, H. (1963). *Outsiders: Studies in the sociology of deviance.* New York: Free Press.
Blumer, H. (1969). *Symbolic interactionism. Perspective and method.* Englewood Cliffs, NJ: Prentice-Hall.
Bourdieu, P. (1987). *Choses dites* [*In other words: Essays toward a reflexive sociology*]. (M. Adamson, Trans.). Paris: Minuit.
Coulon, A. (1997). *Le métier d'étudiant. L'entrée dans la vie universitaire.* [The job of being a student: Enrolling at a university]. Paris: PUF.
Garfinkel, H. (1967). *Studies in ethnomethodology.* Englewood Cliffs, NJ: Prentice-Hall.
Katz, J. (1988). *Seductions of crime: Moral and sensual attractions in doing evil.* New York: Basic Books.
Sacks, H. (1992). *Lectures on conversation* (Vol. 1). Cambridge, MA: Blackwell.
Thrasher, F. (1963). *The gang: A study of 1313 gangs in Chicago* (2nd ed., shortened). Chicago: University of Chicago Press. (Original work published in 1927)
Van Gennep, A. (1981). *Les rites de passage* [The rites of passage]. (M. B. Vizedom & G. L. Caffee, Trans.). Paris: Picard. (Original work published in 1909)
Zimmerman, D. H. (1970). The practicalities of rule use. In J. D. Douglas (Ed.), *Understanding everyday life* (pp. 221–238). London: Routledge and Kegan Paul.

III

PERSONAL AGENCY THROUGH COLLECTIVE ACTIVITY

8   Learning and Thinking in Adolescence and Youth

How to Inhabit New Provinces of Meaning

Felice Carugati

More than 50 years ago, Kurt Lewin was very conscious of the tremendous task of approaching the multifaceted phenomenon of adolescence and transitions to adulthood. According to Lewin (1951), "The problem of adolescence shows clearly that a way must be found to treat changes, shifts in ideology and group-belongingness within one realm of scientific language in a single realm of discourse or concepts. How can this be done?" (p. 133).

Lewin tried to conceptualize, within the framework of his field theory, some characteristics of this transitional period of life. Instead of treating the issue from an Aristotelian point of view, Lewin proposed (from a Galileian perspective) to engage in a study of situations and instances that show the so-called typical difficulties of adolescent behavior (1951, p. 135). Thus, the transition from childhood to adulthood could be seen as a change in group affiliations, particularly salient in social contexts in which the separation between children's and adults' worlds becomes a crucial feature of the modernity of societies. Moreover, the transition to adulthood can also be considered a situation unfamiliar to adolescents, a region of experience for which they are requested to build up adequate cognitive, social, and emotional tools; a region in which salient questions must be answered: for example, What kind of person does society require me to become? What kind of person would I like to become? What kind of conflict or contradiction arises when coping with these two major questions? In addition, the widening of spatial, temporal, emotional, and social regions, as well as of future perspectives (expectations, fears, hopes, projects); the new interests in social

The preparation and writing of this chapter was supported by grants from the Italian Ministry of University and Scientific and Technological Research (1995, 1998, 1999).

groups and gender-marked interpersonal relations; and the coping with ideologies, organizations, bureaucracies, and institutions, (i.e., coping with the social distribution of power, social conflicts, and social inequalities) – all these characteristics of adolescents' lives could lead to a conceptualization of the transition to adolescence and youth as a major phenomenon in *secondary socialization* (Berger & Luckmann, 1966). During that socialization, contradictions, conflicting viewpoints (i.e., the multiple social realities and, in a sense, the eventual incompatibility between different life trajectories and perspectives), and personal and societal requests have to be negotiated, and new decisions, new trajectories, and reorganization of perspectives, beliefs, and opinions have to be produced. The analogy between adolescence and marginal groups proposed by Lewin seems very appropriate to describe the intriguing task of adolescents joining society.

By no means can the transition to adulthood be seen as entering a stable, unchangeable period. In this sense, Lewin, unlike most of his contemporaries (e.g., Erikson, 1950, and the mainstream of structuralist-functionalist sociology of the 1950s and 1960s; cf. Havighurst, 1952, and his notion of *developmental tasks*), anticipated perhaps the most crucial aspect of modern societies and cultures: adulthood as a period in which career and job are unstable and social integration is far from being ensured. Moreover, achieving adult identity is not a mere consequence of attaining a stable job, and the developmental task of learning should become a lifelong adventure. Recurrent experience of unemployment; life crises; and turning points in individual, interpersonal, and societal trajectories due to economic, political, and ideological transformations have been questioning the major issue or illusion in social sciences and particularly in psychology: that is, a shared representation of all the grand theories of adulthood as a teleological point from which the plenitude of development – cognitive, emotional, social – could and should be regarded and admired.

In an almost unknown, marginal paper, Piaget (1972) writes about the major point in our discussion in the following terms:

The period from 15 to 20 years marks the beginning of professional specialization and consequently also the construction of a life program corresponding to the aptitudes of the individual. We now ask the following question: Can one demonstrate, at this level of development as at the previous level, cognitive structures common to all individuals which will however be applied or used by each person according to his/her particular activities? The essence of the logic of cultured adults and the basis for elementary scientific thought are thereby provided. The rate at which a child progresses through developmental succession may vary, especially from one culture to another. Different children also vary in terms of the areas of functioning to which they apply formal operations, according to their aptitudes and their professional specialization. *Thus, although formal operations are logically independent of the reality to which they are applied, it is best to test the young person in a field which is relevant to his/her career and interests.* (p. 1; emphasis added)

Learning, Thinking, and Social Practices: A Dialogue Among Three Partners

The state of the art of the wonderful illusion held by almost all prominent scholars in psychology (e.g., Erikson, Piaget) should be carefully discussed in order to see what *joining society* means and implies for present and future adolescents. The main point here is that the teleological (i.e., ideological) view of development should be questioned so that we may better understand the inextricability and the interpenetration of societal, intergroup, interindividual, and individual changes, as well as the different degrees of influence these levels of analysis have on each other.

Three major challenges to most developmental and learning theories could be addressed (cf. Engeström, 1996). Learning may be viewed as a partially destructive rejection of old ways and old organizations of knowledge and as a matter of (normative) majority influence instead of being a benign, automatic, information processing-like achievement of mastery of new (taken-for-granted), positive knowledge. Learning may be viewed (at least partially) as collective transformation instead of just individual transformation. Learning may be viewed (at least partially) as collective transformation instead of just vertical movement across levels.

The next three paragraphs provide comments on these three challenges. With regard to the first challenge, one might ask if the increasing number of school dropouts in modern countries is a mere consequence of a generational decline of cognitive capital due to some biological degeneration of individual DNA or if this fact challenges any learning theories to account for possible socially negative or even destructive phenomena. If we realize, for instance, that in some European regions the level of economic development (what we might call *microeconomic rich niches*) in a sense pushes young people to abandon school to enter these rich niches, then the very meaning of the dropout phenomenon needs a careful reexamination. According to Lewin's insightful assumption, what seems very similar at the phenotypic level does not automatically imply the same genotypic understanding.

As for the second challenge, almost all learning theories are about individuals. In the course of this chapter, we will moderate this assumption, but even Vygotsky, a champion of the social and cultural explanation in developmental and learning psychology, did not conceptualize development and learning as the transformation of human collectives. There is evidence both in empirical research and in novel literature (Høeg, 1994), however, that development and learning means changing one's course of life, as far as rejection of the old ways of thinking and reasoning is concerned, as well as changing them together with significant others in the process of constructing a collective. Thus, the challenge to learning theories is to account for such processes of formation of new (even provisional) collectives. Note the echo here of Berger and Luckmann's (1966) claim that major transformations during secondary socialization are more likely to occur when the dynamics of conversion take place.

As for the third challenge, learning theories are about climbing learning ladders. In some theories, ladders are well known and fixed; in others, they are more locally and culturally contingent. But learning happens along a vertical or at least oblique dimension, from immaturity of the novice (or apprenticeship) toward maturity and expertise. In other words, exclusive concentration on the vertical dimension requires closed boundaries, with elimination of horizontal movement across social worlds. The issue of boundary crossing (again echoing Lewin's perspective) is of particular interest for this discussion: Is joining society only a matter of triumphal ascension from novice to expert?

As we turn to the whole set of challenges, an image arises of adolescence and youth as not merely a set of developmental tasks assigned by society and accomplished conformistically by every new adolescent generation, but also a complex interplay of facing and struggling with contradictions. At least some of these contradictions could be conceptualized as simultaneously practical double binds and intellectual dilemmas. Contradictions have played an important role in developmental and learning literature: for instance, in Piaget's work, although his perspective is radically individualistic. In his conception of the environment or the real world, objects and systems are not contradictory in themselves; thus, contradictions can be resolved by means of individual cognitive reorganization. But objects and systems in the social world and in organizations (families and school systems not excluded) are frequently internally contradictory. To develop and to learn means, in these cases, to tackle and negotiate those real contradictions in both everyday life and culturally well-established knowledge.

A central issue in learning during secondary socialization is the asymmetry both between social roles and in the social distribution of knowledge. Several metaphors have been used to describe the latter phenomenon:

apprenticeship (Rogoff, 1990); *expert-based knowledge; situated learning* and *legitimate peripheral participation* (Lave & Wenger, 1991); and *distributed cognition* (Salomon, 1993). The novelty of these metaphors is undeniable as far as they have moderated the dominant vertical and teleological architecture of developmental and learning models. Nevertheless, the fundamental social nature of contradictions between competing definitions of reality (or other worlds), and consequently the nature of knowledge and a fortiori of learning, still needs careful integration in these models through a dialectical approach. They seem to share a functionalist vision of knowledge as either a more or less unitary and asymmetrical transmission of knowledge from various kinds of experts to various kinds of novices/apprentices or a vision of a peaceful, symmetrical/horizontal echoing of knowledge. They do all that in a historical period in which different cultures, with a tremendously asymmetrical distribution of power, meet, collide, fight, and merge. We should again avoid the fundamental sociocentric error, persistently reproduced in the history of psychology, of extending models of modern societies' development and learning to other worlds. We should be aware here of the fundamental difficulty (or even inability) of ever understanding people who inhabit other worlds (Berger & Luckmann, 1966). Nevertheless, Kramsch (1993) proposed the concept of *contact zone* to describe important learning and development that occur as people and ideas from different cultures (not groups) meet, collide, and merge. In the same vein, Gutierrez and her coauthors (1995) have suggested the concept of a *third space* to account for similar events in classroom discourse where the seemingly self-sufficient teachers' and students' worlds occasionally meet and interact to form new meanings that go beyond the evident limits of both.

Traditionally, the study of cognitive processes, cognitive development, and the cultivation of educationally desirable skills and competencies has treated everything cognitive as being possessed and residing in the heads of individuals: Social, cultural, and technical factors have been relegated to the role of backdrops or external sources of stimulation. This perception is fine as far as it goes, allowing us to examine in great detail some specific mechanisms of information processing or problem solving and learning. But once human behavior is examined in real-life problem-solving situations and in other encounters with social and technological surrounds, a different phenomenon emerges: People appear to think in conjunction or partnership with others and with the help of culturally provided tools and implements. Almost any form of human cognition requires one to deal productively and imaginatively with some technology: To attempt to characterize intelligence independently of those technologies seems to be a fundamental error. Some authors have brilliantly summarized these points underlying the shift from a person-solo cognitive approach to a person-plus one approach (Perkins, 1993).

If we agree in general terms with this major argument, some complementary questions should be addressed. The first one concerns the necessity to consider a theory of distributed cognition that includes individual participation. At least four reasons could be given for this. First, daily observations and experiences provide us with ample cases in which cognition is not distributed. Second, there may be several classes of cognition, higher-order knowledge, and even processes, skills, and operations that might not be distributable. Third, even in the most radical formulations of activity-in-setting, there is no way to get around the role played by individual representations. Finally, the total dismissal of individual cognition in favor of situated and distributed cognition provides only frozen pictures of states that neither develop nor grow. Moreover, a radical formulation seems to prevent an understanding of which conditions block individuals' actions, thinking, and learning (development).

A second question concerns the possible interaction between individuals' and distributed cognition. In exploring this issue, we should avoid both a holistic and a totally independent view of this dualistic position. A genuine European social-psychological approach to cognition has been developed (Carugati & Gilly, 1993; Doise & Palmonari, 1984; Moscovici, 1990; Perret-Clermont & Nicolet, 1988) in which cognitive development has been studied as a tripolar dialogue between social interactants and the knowledge at their disposal, to which they have to give meaning in order to build new cognitive tools. Thus, a proposed conception of spiral development has also been agreed on by some ethnographers of everyday life (Corsaro, 1993). This conception has served as a theoretical guideline for a research program that illustrates the importance of studying both the level of joint performances and individual progress in appropriating cognitive tools (cf. Carugati & Gilly, 1993). Borrowing conceptual and methodological tools from experimental social psychology, the social-psychological approach to cognitive functioning has drawn attention to (a) the dynamics of peer–peer and expert–novice interaction; (b) the structure of the task (chosen by the expert); and (c) the representation and meaning of the task that novices build during the interaction, plus its relation to the task structure. Two main conceptual models have been proposed in accordance with the empirical evidence that has been gathered: *sociocognitive conflict* and *social marking*.

With the first notion, sociocognitive conflict, we conceive of the negotiation between partners having different points of view of the same task, which means different representations and meanings of it. The second notion, social marking, means the homology between the organization of social relations in the interaction (e.g., social symmetry between peers, asymmetry between novice and expert) and cognitive relations between objects that constitute the task. A case in point is a task on conservation of spatial relations that is built on a representation of a classroom (with teacher's and pupils' desks) versus a representation of a village. The classroom representation is shown to be more effective than that of the village if we use them with dyads of nonconservers and if we compare individual performances. Here, with a careful experimental procedure, we have been giving evidence of the inextricability of communication and negotiation of meaning at both interindividual and intraindividual levels. Further evidence has been offered by research that focuses on school tasks instead of more classical Piagetian-like ones: for example, the ways in which novices construe mathematical symbols when asked to communicate them to partners. In general terms, this line of research shows, with experimental procedure, the positive effects (i.e., a more abstract formalistic coding) of both interaction between peers and the necessity of communication with absent partners. Following the same line is research on the construction of scientific concepts or formal operations (Flieller, 1986; Gilly & Roux, 1984; for a careful review of these topics, see Carugati & Gilly, 1993).

Learning and New Technologies

The situations of distributed cognition should be regarded not only as ends in themselves but also as means for improving mastery of individual cognitive tools. Pragmatic considerations suggest that, in a rapidly changing world, we ought to equip students with cognitive tools that will allow them to operate intelligently outside of situations of distributed cognition and activities. Normative considerations suggest that descriptions of performances situated in distributed cognition are no educational guide: They do not always provide desirable educational guidelines. Moreover, situations of distributed cognition (particularly those that entail reliance on intelligent technologies) should be designed to promote or scaffold rather than to limit the cultivation of individuals' cognitive tools. Partnerships with powerful tools that are characterized mainly by cognitive offloading may improve (joint) performance, and even redefine intellectual tasks, but they may prevent the appropriation of useful cognitive skills. Note that, in research on the influence of interindividual interaction among peers for solving a cognitive task (cf. Carugati & Gilly, 1993), different dynamics have been shown of coping with the asymmetry in mastering cognitive differences. Particularly when the partner is perceived to be much higher in cognitive level, the dynamic of social compliance leads the inferior to accept the better or even correct solution imposed by the superior; the performance is better or correct, but both partners do not progress in mastering higher-level cognitive tools.

In the same vein, Dillenbourg and Self (1992) point out that, among both human and artificial learners, learning effects are generated, provided that the discussion is intensive: that is, provided that many arguments are brought into the dialogue. In some sense, the major issue is a conceptualization of distributed cognition as a case of collaboration among individuals who have to cope with a *savoir* partly shared, but that they have to co-construct in joint action. During collaboration, each peer is often requested by a partner to explain why he or she suggested or performed some action. This higher-order knowledge, which one party implicitly used to regulate self actions, is then made explicit to regulate and negotiate the joint action. In a broader sense, higher-order cognitive tools could be seen as the appropriation of mutual regulation and negotiation skills. In a sense, it is ironic that some artificial intelligence researchers have been studying how social processes influence the confirmation bias: that is, the fact that subjects tend to discard empirical evidence contradicting their hypothesis (Hutchins, 1991). Thus, higher-order cognitive tools should be regarded as the most sophisticated tools whereby adult subjects negotiate and regulate social interaction in which different partners possess relational and cognitively different points of view about the definition of a situation.

Further evidence of a role played by the new technologies in influencing adolescent and adult learning is provided by the computer-mediated collaborative approach to learning (in this case, language learning; cf. Warschauer, 1996). From this review of research, it is puzzling that the notion of *situated learning*, largely implemented in here-and-now research designs, becomes far more complex and enlarged, thanks to new cultural tools such as the World Wide Web and e-mail, which enable long-distance collaborative exchanges that also bring about a more macro-level situated learning. The ability to access and interpret information from around the world in collaboration with people from various cultures will be a critical skill for success in the new jobs of the 21st century. Collaborative exchange via the Web is thus seen not only as an opportunity for situated language learning practice but also as a context for developing broader skills of importance to students' and workers' futures. The special features of online communication – that it is text-based and computer-mediated, many-to-many, time-and-place independent, and distributed via hypermedia links – provide an impressive array of new ways to link learners with a potentially large age range.

When evaluating computer-assisted learning, however, it is important to distinguish potential from reality. Research to date on the topic has been thin and has largely consisted of innovators reporting on the outcomes of their own teaching. A broad research agenda is called for to gain a better understanding of the social, affective, motivational, long-term processes involved.

In summary, plenty of evidence shows that, given specific sociocognitive conditions, adolescents and adults are able to learn and reason using higher-order cognitive tools; but transferring their use from situation to situation and from one domain of knowledge to another seems far from self-evident, unlikely to happen, or at least in need of specific scaffolding and specific sociocultural tools. Moreover, future research must consider how deeply new technological tools affect learners' long-term motivation and identity and how far gender, ethnic, linguistic, and cultural differences reproduce themselves online, both within a learning or a work context and in long-distance exchanges. The main caveat concerns the risk of substituting the wonderful illusion of a universal, formally reasoning young adult with a more subtle and modern illusion of a universally computer-dependent young virtual adult.

Abilities of Learning and Dropout Outcomes: A Challenge to Modern Societies

One of the puzzling issues at this point is that learning is possible but school failure and dropouts are of sociological, economic, and emotional relevance for modern societies, families, and individuals. Where, when, and what kinds of processes are likely to be suitable for a tentative understanding of this web of phenomena? We propose to approach this web by considering that, for decades, dominant grand theories – developmental, cognitive, and psycho-analytic – have mainly described the compulsory school period through conceptualizations such as *latency* and *concrete operations* (i.e., in the form of *lack of, invisibility,* or *moratorium*), waiting, in a sense, for several kinds of Godots, be they puberty, S*turm und Drang*, turmoil, upheaval, or formal thought. Some of these Godots have been shown to be necessary but not sufficient, and others never appear, but adult life is still possible. Consequently, the schooling period should be approached not merely as "invisible" years but also as a laboratory wherein transitions are set to be experienced. The focus on the invisible years – with their foregoing of adolescence and youth – as the site of spiraling dynamics among social demands, individual changes (or perspectives), and school systems should be emphasized here as possible dynamics of both spiral download or upload that leads adolescents to different school – work trajectories and to varied swinging between school and job experiences. Specific studies that integrate students' characteristics and school systems (or curricula) are needed. In particular, European countries still differ greatly about what compulsory school and transitions to high school mean and about how they are organized: that is, how deeply European school systems scaffold the different transition periods between different grades within compulsory school and the transition from school to work.

European empirical evidence on this topic is far from exhaustive. Several studies have focused on the social-psychological impact of school selection and failure (Bell & Perret-Clermont, 1985) and on correlates of low academic attainment, self-esteem, and identity (Robinson, Tayler, & Piolat, 1990). Further evidence from U.S. research on the transition from elementary to junior high school highlights how strongly students' and teachers' perspectives, attitudes, and trajectories make the difference in transition experiences of success, failure, and dropout (Eccles & Midgely, 1990). Early adolescent years mark the beginning of a downward spiral that leads a huge part of adolescent cohorts to academic failure. Furthermore, the magnitude of this decline is predictive of subsequent school failure and dropout. Although the high school transition effects are not so extreme for most adolescents, there is evidence of a gradual decline in various indicators of academic behavior, motivation, and self-perception during the adolescent years.

Various explanations have been advanced, mostly at the intraindividual level: the coincidence of the timing transition with pubertal development (puberty as a biological, morphological, and social stressor). The quality of the school environment is probably the most powerful explanation for those declines. Drawing upon constructivist and interactionist views of development, junior high school cannot provide a developmentally appropriate educational environment; motivation and mental health can best be understood by examining the fit between the characteristics brought by individuals to their social environments and the characteristics of these social environments. More specifically, there could be a mismatch between the developing needs and motivational orientation of the individuals, social demands of socioeconomic niches, and the typical demands and characteristics of the new transitional environments.

It would be interesting to have a careful updating on European school systems in terms of Silberman's (1970) judgment that "[U.S.] junior high school, by almost unanimous agreement, is the wasteland – one is tempted to say cesspool – of American education; what is likely to happen when we put developing adolescents into wastelands?" (p. 324). Developmental changes outlined in the literature are especially marked in conjunction with the junior high school transition: for example, the discontinuity in the rate of change in attitudes toward math between Grade 6 and Grade 7, when U.S. children move from elementary to junior high school. There is a dramatic drop in these adolescents' confidence in their math abilities and in their interest in learning mathematics. There is a sharp drop in students' preferences for challenging work, as opposed to easy work, and for independent mastery, as opposed to getting good grades between sixth and seventh grades, before and after the transition to junior high school.

There is clear evidence of school transition effects: In general, girls seem more at risk than boys for the negative consequences (for self-esteem) of the junior high school transition. The main point here is that the timing of the transition results in more disruption to individuals already feeling the stress associated with puberty than would a similar transition a few years later, after the individual has developed a more mature sense of who he or she is. If timing seems to be a critical factor, when and why is the timing good or bad and for whom? Even if findings are inconsistent for when (some studies are concerned only with students in the same school, whereas other studies focus on school transitions), why seems to be related to the fact that these studies do not take into account what is going on in the classroom and in the school before and after the transition: Do pupils in one study move into a less facilitative (e.g., increase in competition or in ability assessment, or a laissez-faire attitude) environment than pupils in another study? Does the transition imply a broader move from traditional to more innovative programs or vice versa? Then the nature of transitions as well as the timing must be considered; this means being attentive to changes in both the school environment and the classroom environment.

General Environmental Influences. Research has documented the impact of various classroom and school environmental characteristics on motivation. For example, the big-school/small-school literature has demonstrated the motivational advantages of small schools, especially for marginal students. Similarly, the teacher efficacy literature has documented the positive student motivational consequences of high teacher efficacy. Finally, organizational psychology has demonstrated the importance of participatory work structure on workers' motivation. The main point here is that there may be systematic differences between typical elementary classrooms and their schools and typical junior high classrooms and their schools, and that these differences may account for some of the declines in indicators of academic motivation and performances. Thus, some of the changes we attribute to stagelike developmental processes may instead reflect systematic changes in the microsocial cultures that we provide for pupils as they grow up.

We propose integrating the zone of proximal development approach with the person–environment fit approach for a better understanding of classroom dynamics and sociocognitive construction of cultural tools. Maintaining a developmental perspective becomes very important, because a teacher should take into account not only students' contemporaneous needs, by providing whatever structure they currently require, but also their present need for structure on a developmental continuum, along which growth toward independence and less need for structure is the long-term goal. Teachers should provide the optimal level of structure for pupils' current levels of abilities while also providing a sufficiently challenging environment to pull pupils along a developmental path toward higher levels of cognitive and social maturity. A consequence of that approach is that some changes in educational environments may be especially inappropriate, particularly if they afford the pupils fewer opportunities for continued growth than did previous environments. Thus, at certain stages of development or for specific groups of children, such environments could be developmentally regressive transitions from richer to poorer environments that could lead to a particularly poor person–environment fit, and this lack of fit could account for some of the declines in motivation.

Some Classes of Empirical Indicators of Environmental Changes. First, junior high school classrooms are characterized by a greater emphasis on teacher control and discipline, by a less personal and less positive teacher–student relationship, and by fewer opportunities for student decision making, choice, and self-management. Second, they show an increase in practices such as whole-class task organization, ability grouping between classrooms, and public evaluation of work accuracy, each of which may encourage the use of social comparison and ability self-assessment. Third, during the first year of junior high school, there is evidence that the classwork requires lower-level cognitive skill (or a sharp change in level) than did classwork in the elementary school. Fourth, junior high school teachers feel less effective as teachers, especially for low-ability students (this may be an extension of a perceived decrease in influence that adults have on adolescent behavior [Goodnow, 1981]). Fifth, junior high school teachers appear to use a higher standard in judging students' competence and in grading their performances than do elementary school teachers.

Such school environmental changes may be particularly harmful in early adolescence, given what is well known about (classical) psychological development during this stage of life: desire for autonomy, peer orientation, self-focus and self-consciousness, salience of identity issues, concern over heterosexual relationships, and capacity for abstract cognitive activities. It could be argued that adolescents need a reasonably safe, intellectually challenging environment to adapt to these shifts – an environment that provides a zone of comfort as well as a zone of proximal development with challenging new opportunities for growth. This shift in judgments seems especially harmful in that it emphasizes competition, social comparison, and ability self-assessment at a time of heightened self-focus. Moreover, all five shifts could be harmful as far as they decrease decision making and choice at a time when pupils/adolescents desire to control their personal growth. They emphasize lower-level cognitive strategies at a time when the ability to use higher-level strategies is increasing, and they disrupt social networks at a time when adolescents are especially concerned with peer relationships and may especially need close adult relationships outside the home. Thus, the nature of these changes, coupled with the normal course of individual development, results in a developmental mismatch, so that the fit between the pupil/adolescent and the classroom environment could be particularly poor, increasing the risk of negative motivational outcomes, especially for pupils/adolescents who are having difficulty succeeding at school.

Teachers' Beliefs and Self-Efficacy About Specific School and Classroom Issues, and Pupils' Motives, Values, Beliefs, and Behavior. High school teachers more than elementary school teachers believe that students need to be disciplined and controlled; moreover, high school teachers feel themselves less efficacious than do elementary teachers. Students' and observers' perceptions of the quality of the student–teacher relationship before and after the transition are similar. For example, seventh-grade posttransition math teachers are seen as less supportive, friendly, and fair than sixth-grade pretransition teachers by observers and students (Feldlaufer, Midgley, & Eccles, 1988). Although the relation between teacher efficacy and student beliefs and attitudes has yet to be firmly established, when schools are used as a unit of analysis, negative correlations have been shown between teachers' sense of academic futility and students' self-concept of ability and self-reliance. In summary, convergent results show that low teacher expectations for these students undermine students' motivation and performance.

Teacher–Student Relationships. The differences in perceived teacher support before and after the transition influence the value that students attach
to school subjects – for instance, mathematics. When students move from
teachers whom they perceive to be low in support to teachers perceived to be
high in support, the value students attach to math is enhanced. In contrast,
students' transition from teachers whom they perceive to be high in support
to teachers perceived to be low in support lowers the value that they attach to
math. Again, there is evidence that low-achieving students are particularly
at risk when they move to less facilitative classroom environments. Thus, the
decline in motivational orientation to school subjects followed by the low
streaming or dropping out (as an individual life trajectory) is not inevitable.

Actual and Preferred Decision-Making Opportunities in the Classroom.
The desire for more input into decision making as a product of the transition to high school could be seen as a sign of development. Unfortunately,
students and teachers report that students have fewer decision-making opportunities after the transition than before; thus, there is a growing lack of
congruence between students' desires and the opportunities afforded by the
school environment. In fact, students who perceive that their first year of
high school math puts greater constraints on their preferred level of participation in classroom decision making than did their previous year of school
math show larger and more consistent declines in their interest in math
than do their peers who do not perceive such constraints. Thus, the increase
in unmet desire for input in classroom decision making at the moment of
transition seems to be a major issue in understanding the decline of interest
in school subjects, particularly math.

Toward Late Adolescence and Youth: Becoming Workers?
Planning and preparing for a vocation has been considered an important
turning point or transition in the life trajectories of adolescents. As adolescents move toward appropriate vocational years, schools and families are
prodigals in teaching work values and beliefs, charting maps of the labor
market, and assessing their abilities or skills, interests or aptitudes. The adolescents' older counterpart again has to negotiate among these teaching and
assessing tools and a more personal interpretive reproduction of them in
terms of professional identities, personal decision making, and awareness of
abilities and interests. In this sense, choosing a job or a vocation and achieving an occupational identity could be significant outcomes of adolescent socialization. Thus, the socialization processes are by no means accomplished
within formal education: Work entry experiences should be conceived of

as a further transition that needs new negotiations that, once more, may activate a spiral between perceived opportunities, desires, projects, and economic characteristics of the labor market. The dominant literature (role theory oriented) on work socialization overemphasizes organizational features influencing first-job novices and describing work entry as a predictably passive or reactive transfer of a student force (or dropout force) from school or family to industries, offices, or bureaucracies.

The process of becoming a worker should be understood as a lifelong process in which at least two key features can be distinguished. The first feature is new role-related learning, which requires individuals to appropriate specific skills; to establish new interpersonal relationships with coworkers and superiors; to give their work role an acceptable meaning; to appropriate beliefs, values, and behaviors that are shared and rewarded within the organization; and to evaluate and accept the perspective of the work career. The second feature concerns leaving the past and building up the new and the future. Høeg's novel (1994) reminds us that entering a job will not be without effect and will not be an automatic information processing-like achievement involving mastery of new skills. In other words, entering a job may be viewed as a partially destructive rejection of old ways and old organizations of knowledge and a matter of (normative) majority influence. Instead of being just an individual transformation, entering a job may be viewed, at least partially, as a collective transformation with significant conovices; instead of just vertical movement across skills, entering a job may be viewed as horizontal movement across borders (Engeström, 1996). Again, the decision-making opportunities, the congruence between students' (or dropouts') desires, and the opportunities afforded by the work environment seem to be relevant. As in the case of within-school transitions, the school-work transition could imply possibly increasing mismatches between personal trajectories and work opportunities or constraints, with a variety of back-and-forth experiences between school and work that characterize some specific categories of young people, such as low achievers or dropouts.

In the preceding section, we highlighted the importance of the transition from elementary to junior high school as a possible downward spiral between personal trajectories and environmental requests. In the same vein, one could consider the possible effects that school ethos and organization might have on adolescents and young people during their work entry. West and Newton (1984) documented these effects in a study of two schools in England that differed remarkably in their organizational structure. One school adopted a banding system in which roughly half of the students, those considered more academically able, were assigned to the A band, and the other students, considered academically less able, were assigned to the B band. The second school was run along mixed ability lines, with a mixture of ability levels in classes being the general rule. That streaming in schools has an effect on school organization and on the attitudes of pupils is a matter of some evidence, but the effects on the school-work transition could be of particular relevance.

Defining *transition* as stretching from about 6 months prior to the date of leaving school to 30 months after the date of leaving, West and Newton interviewed about 150 boys and girls. The streamed students in the first school were significantly less positive in their attitudes toward teachers and their schools than were the students who were not streamed. Streamed students were also most likely to choose a job of higher status than were nonstreamed students; of the streamed students, A band students were much less likely to have a job by the time they left school than were B band students. Students from the streamed school also secured jobs, on average, of significantly lower status than those they hoped for originally.

Differences in attitudes toward training for jobs also emerged. Streamed students, having left school, found their jobs less interesting than did workers who had attended the nonstreamed school. Streamed workers saw their jobs as offering them less in the way of promotion prospects, pay, useful learning, or even social contacts; they were also less settled in their jobs and more likely to be considering a job change.

Interestingly, workers from the unstreamed school were more likely to describe their coworkers as very easy to get along with than were those from the streamed school; they were also more likely to choose items describing favorable characteristics of supervisors. The latter finding is of considerable interest when taken in conjunction with the finding that they also had more favorable attitudes (on the same scales) toward their teachers. Given that the kinds of jobs taken by the young people from the two schools did not differ in any significant way (because of the economic characteristics of the labor market in the area), these results suggest that differences between supervisors did not produce differences in attitudes. It appears more likely that attitudes toward authority figures, engendered at school, persisted into working life.

Another difference between the two schools was the emphasis on academic values and the stress laid on the rewards of hard work in the streamed school. The covert propaganda within this school may have given credence to the idea that if one worked hard at school, one's working life would be better. The effect of this propaganda might then have been to raise students' expectations about working life throughout the school, with even B band students being affected by the optimism of A band students. West and Newton's finding that streamed students had to take jobs of significantly lower status than they had originally aimed at suggests that, by some means, expectations of working life were raised more among streamed students than they were among unstreamed students. Clearly, some aspects of the organization and ethos of the schools affected subsequent choices and attitudes toward work and the work hierarchy. West and Newton (1984) also found gender differences in attitudes toward teachers, with girls' evaluations being significantly less favorable than those of boys. There is some evidence that even if preadolescent girls' academic achievements are higher than those of boys, and even if girls perform better and are more likely than boys to work to their full ability in school, from early adolescence on a proportion of girls begins to decline in achievement; thus, it is possible to argue that, during adolescence, girls experience a critical role conflict that is responsible for differences in their attitudes toward teachers. Moreover, it could still be plausible to maintain that, throughout childhood, girls are socialized to be dependent and at the same time to be competitive, individualistic, and achievement-oriented as far as they follow the school curriculum during adolescence. Studies in adolescent self-concept have indicated that gender-role identity is important to self-definition during adolescence and that gender-linked interests and goals influence adolescents' behavior. Consequently, achievement-oriented, competitive, individualistic behavior could cause more conflict in defining girls' social identity, because it could be less gender-linked, and it is less central to gender-role social definition (i.e., stereotypes) of females, particularly in cyclical expanding and recessing opportunities of the female labor market.

Such social-psychological dynamics may be the underlying cause of girls' less favorable attitudes toward teachers and toward work, two crucial findings in West and Newton's research. The gender-related conflict in school and the objectively worse training conditions for work and employment for girls, could be seen as factors responsible for their more conflicting and troublesome life trajectories during adolescence and youth (i.e., during the transition from school to work). The societal and economic counterpart is that participation of women in the labor force tends to be intermittent because of attitudes and policies of employers themselves, and that jobs requiring training entail a perceived risk for the employers, who see jobs requiring little training as better alternatives for women.

The usefulness of longitudinal studies charting the job entry and various experiences of leaving and reentering in the transition from school to work has been well documented in a 10-year research program at the University of Bremen (Heinz, 1996). In a sample of Italian young people (18 to 21 years of age), the social-psychological processes of the school-to-work transition have been studied (Depolo, Fraccaroli, & Sarchielli, 1993). Topics such as the following were explored: how young people choose sources of support and information for future occupations; the representations of future work held before and after school leaving; and the mismatch between prior expectations and work experiences when people were at work. Results showed that the degree of clarity concerning personal projects influences both the representations of environmental resources and the ways they are used. To the extent that young people better perceive (before leaving school) specific job requirements (e.g., linguistic and communicative skills, technical skills, counting skills), they evaluate their personal skills more accurately, and they are more satisfied with their job after work entry.

A complementary confirmation of the critical role played by the interpretation that job entrants produce about their work environment during the first 2 years of job experience is provided by the European research project WOSY (Work Socialization of Youth; cf. Gamberale & Hagström, 1994). As part of this project, Depolo, Fraccaroli, and Sarchielli (1994) interviewed a sample of Italian late adolescents and young adults (younger than 24 years old; operators of office technology and machine operators) about their psychological well-being as an important outcome of occupational socialization. The main finding was that the psychological well-being felt by young people entering organizations depends more heavily on their cognitive appreciation of the organizational context feature than on objective features per se. What matters most seems to be the new job entrants' interpretations of the work context (e.g., what they have to learn and what social skills are needed to cope with peers and superiors). The role of the help provided to beginning workers by superiors in the first phase of job entrance seems to be of major importance for the evaluation of personal well-being 18 months later. Work entry, which is generally assumed to be a phase of greater difficulty and confusion, requires the new worker to learn how to behave in a new technical and social environment; but it also requires the young worker to perform, and it assesses him or her according to the results. According to the Italian study, the support of direct supervisor(s) may be crucial, because that person provides an important point of reference at both the cognitive and social-emotional levels. These results are worth noting because the mainstream in transition literature emphasizes that transitions can be harmful to psychological health. We refer to this literature for a complementary reason: The issues of well-being, stress, psychological risk, and resilience during transitions should be regarded as nontrivial in learning and in life course socialization. They are issues that are also prominent in the developmental psychology approach to the life course (Rolf, Masten, Cicchetti, Neuchterlein, & Weintraub, 1990).

Conclusions

The long journey within adolescence, from Lewin and Piaget through new and different provinces of meaning, peels away a monolithic, linear, and teleological understanding of adolescence and leaves a complex interplay of transitions between and within institutions, groups, and relationships that constitute everyday practices and what learning nowadays is intended to be by an increasing community of scholars. My interest in merging information from school and work and from phenomena of transition was inspired by attempts to introduce a discussion about the relations between learning and everyday practices: learning as cultural and social products provided by modern societies. It could be useful to shift from terms such as *learning* (given its traditionally narrow connotations) to concepts more akin to *understanding, participating in,* and *interpreting ongoing activities.* In brief, I have tried to illustrate that learning during adolescence (the same argument may be appropriate for the life course) is not only a matter of transferring or internalizing a fixed stock of existing knowledge but also of inventing new knowledge in different practices – which may be the most critical feature of the modern labor market and of modern society. The fundamental imprint of interested parties, multiple activities, and different goals and circumstances on what constitutes knowing on a given occasion or across a multitude of interrelated events should be acknowledged. Becoming a worker or entering a university implies that one is learning (often collectively) to do things that have not been done before. Once more, the zone of proximal development notion could be at least partially conceived of as a collective rather than an individual or interindividual phenomenon. The "new" is at least partially a collective invention in the face of felt dilemmas, mismatches, and contradictions that impede or place constraints on activities and impel movement and change.

Modern economic conditions also call for educational strategies aimed at helping people develop skills for learning, even when optimal instruction is not available. Such strategies are essential to prepare people to function well, even when breakdowns in the customary structures of activities occur. Unexpected changes, mismatches, or difficulties that render the routine way of doing things inadequate can result from equipment failures, changes in staffing patterns at a work site, new weather or economic conditions in a region (Capecchi, 1993), and the like. Such occurrences should be treated as normally recurring features of technologically and economically complex modern societies. When breakdowns occur, people have to do exactly what machines cannot: Step outside the system and reason about it. People using various mechanized and computerized systems need to be equipped to recognize breakdowns, to work around them temporarily, to repair them, and ultimately to design better systems. For safety and efficiency in work (all kinds of work, including those at social work sites), these capabilities cannot be limited to those at the top, that is, to the traditional decision makers. Productive responses should be possible everywhere in an organization.

Transitions between environments also require capabilities beyond (or different from) those that can be acquired in situation-specific learning. This argument could serve as a way of understanding the transition or breakdown between compulsory education and the subsequent experiences of entering work or continuing education (university). I have already discussed the dynamics of dropout versus a negative spiral of download of motivation, gender marked (either as positive or negative), and its amplitude at the macro level of cohorts. Few authors (Capecchi, 1993) acknowledge that the download of the positive meaning of schooling (and culture) could be partially due to the influence of opportunities to make money quickly in specific niches of the labor market (i.e., in some specific European regions such as northeastern Italy and Emilia Romagna, where the textile and ceramics industries are well developed). Some other European regions (e.g., Bayern, the Ruhr) could be explored, searching for such social dynamics to understand this side of the dropout phenomenon. Conversely, the other side is the socioeconomic necessity of getting money as soon as possible for young workers' families, whose future allows few chances for the "luxury" of higher education for their adolescents and other youngsters. Several European regions are candidates for confirming the Italian patterns.

The 1995 "White Book" of the Commission of European Communities (1995), entitled *Teaching and Learning: Towards a Cognitive Society,* testifies to the importance of the issues discussed in this volume for future goals of European countries. In this sense, these issues are at the core of the *Zeitgeist* of the European Community's contradictions, conflicts, fears, uncertainties, dilemmas, mismatches, social demands, and hopes. This is a provisional list of feelings, opinions, beliefs, and intentions that are not so different from those of adolescents and young people.

We close with a quotation from Høeg: "Understanding is something one does best when one is on the borderline" (1994, p. 37).

REFERENCES

Bell, N., & Perret-Clermont, A.-N. (1985). The socio-psychological impact of school selection and failure. *International Review of Applied Psychology, 34,* 149–160.

Berger, P., & Luckmann, T. (1966). *The social construction of reality.* New York: Anchor.

Capecchi, V. (1993). L'Emilia Romagna. In V. Scardigli (Ed.), *L'Europe de la diversité: la dynamique des identités régionales* [Europe of diversity: Dynamics of regional identities] (pp. 129–150). Paris: CNRS Editions.

Carugati, F., & Gilly, M. (1993). The multiple sides of the same tool: Cognitive development as a matter of social construction of meaning. In F. Carugati & M. Gilly (Eds.), *Everyday life, social meanings and cognitive functioning* [special issue]. *European Journal of Psychology of Education, 8*(4), 345–353.

Commission of European Communities. (1995). *Teaching and learning: Towards a cognitive society* (number of catalog CB-CO-95-658-IT-C). Luxembourg: Bureau of Official Publications of European Communities.

Corsaro, W. A. (1993). Interpretive reproduction in the *Scuola Materna*. In F. Carugati & M. Gilly (Eds.), *Everyday life, social meanings and cognitive functioning* [special issue]. *European Journal of Psychology of Education, 8* (4), 357–374.

Depolo, M., Fraccaroli, F., & Sarchielli, G. (1993). Tactiques d'insertion professionnelle pendant la transition de l'école au travail [Strategies of becoming a worker during school-to-work transition]. *L'Orientation scolaire et professionnelle, 22*(4), 305–316.

Depolo, M., Fraccaroli, F., & Sarchielli, G. (1994). Psychological well-being in early work socialisation. *Arbete och Hälsa, 33,* 19–34.

Dillenbourg, P., & Self, J. A. (1992). A computational approach to socially distributed cognition. *European Journal of Psychology of Education, 8*(4), 353–372.

Doise, W., & Palmonari, A. (1984). *Social interaction in individual development.* Cambridge: Cambridge University Press.

Eccles, J. S., & Midgley, C. (1990). Changes in academic motivation and self-perception during early adolescence. In R. Montemayor, G. R. Adams, & T. P. Gullotta (Eds.), *From childhood to adolescence* (pp. 138–152). London: Sage.

Engeström, Y. (1996). Development as breaking away and opening up: A challenge to Vygotsky and Piaget. *Swiss Journal of Psychology, 55*(2/3), 126–132.

Erikson, E. (1950). *Childhood and society.* New York: Norton.

Feldlaufer, H., Midgley, C., & Eccles, J. S. (1988). Student, teacher, and observer perceptions of the classroom environment before and after the transition to junior high school. *Journal of Early Adolescence, 8,* 133–156.

Flieller, A. (1986). *La coéducation de l'intelligence* [The co-education of intelligence]. Nancy, France: Presses Universitaires de Nancy.

Gamberale, F., & Hagström, T. (Eds.). (1994). Young people and work [special issue]. *Arbete och Hälsa, 33,* 1–88.

Gilly, M., & Roux, J.-P. (1984). Efficacité comparée du travail individuel et du travail en interaction socio-cognitive dans l'appropriation et la mise en oeuvre de règles de résolution chez des enfants de 11–12 ans [*Differential efficacy of individual and interpersonal ways of solving cognitive tasks in 11- to 12-year-old children*]. *Cahiers de Psychologie Cognitive, 4*(2), 171–188.

Goodnow, J. (1981). Everyday ideas about cognitive development. In J. Forgas (Ed.), *Social cognition* (pp. 181–194). London: Academic Press.

Gutierrez, K., Rymes, B., & Larson, J. (1995). Script, counterscript, and underlife in the classroom. *Harvard Educational Review, 65,* 445–471.

Havighurst, R. J. (1952). *Developmental tasks and education.* New York: Davis McKay.

Heinz, W. R. (1996). *Job entry patterns in a life course perspective.* Unpublished manuscript.

Høeg, P. (1994). *Borderliners.* New York: Farrar, Straus and Giroux.

Hutchins, E. (1991). The social organization of distributed cognition. In L. B. Resnick, J. M. Levine, & S. D. Teasley (Eds.), *Perspectives on socially shared cognition* (pp. 283–391). Washington, DC: American Psychological Association.

Kramsch, C. (1993). *Context and culture in language teaching.* Oxford: Oxford University Press.

Lave, J., & Wenger, E. (1991). *Situated learning: Legitimate peripheral participation.* New York: Cambridge University Press.

Lewin, K. (1951). *Field theory in social science.* New York: Harper.

Moscovici, S. (1990). Social psychology and developmental psychology: Extending the conversation. In G. Duveen & B. Lloyd (Eds.), *Social representations and the development of knowledge* (pp. 164–185). Cambridge: Cambridge University Press.

Perkins, D. N. (1993). Person-plus: A distributed view of thinking and learning. In G. Salomon (Ed.), *Distributed cognition* (pp. 280–295). Cambridge: Cambridge University Press.

Perret-Clermont, A.-N., & Nicolet, M. (1988). *Interagir et connaître* [Interact and know]. Cousset, Switzerland: DelVal.

Piaget, J. (1972). Intellectual evolution from adolescence to adulthood. *Human Development, 15,* 1–12.

Robinson, P., Tayler, C. A., & Piolat, M. (1990). School attainment, self-esteem, and identity: France and England. *European Journal of Social Psychology, 20,* 387–403.

Rogoff, B. (1990). *Apprenticeship in thinking: Cognitive development in social contexts.* Oxford: Oxford University Press.

Rolf, J., Masten, A. S., Cicchetti, D., Neuchterlein, K. H., & Weintraub, S. (1990). *Risk and protective factors in the development of psychopathology.* Cambridge: Cambridge University Press.

Salomon, G. (Ed.). (1993). *Distributed cognition.* Cambridge: Cambridge University Press.

Silberman, C. E. (1970). *Crisis in the classroom.* New York: Random House.

Warschauer, M. (1996). *Computer-mediated collaborative learning: Theory and practice.* (Research Note #17). Honolulu: University of Hawaii, Second Language Teaching and Curriculum Center.

West, M. A., & Newton, P. (1984). Social interaction in adolescent development: Schools, sex roles, and entry to work. In W. Doise & A. Palmonari (Eds.), *Social interaction in individual development* (pp. 249–260). Cambridge: Cambridge University Press.

9 From the Provinces of Meaning to the Capital of a Good Self

Some Reflections on Learning and Thinking in the Process of Growing Adult in Society

John B. Rijsman

We can, crudely speaking, distinguish between two basically different episte-mologies in social psychology: one in which the primary source of meaning is the individual subject, and in which intersubjectivity is considered a con-sequence of that condition; and another one in which intersubjectivity is taken as the primary source of meaning and the individual subject only as a derivative of that condition (e.g., Rijsman, 1990, 1996; Rijsman & Stroebe, 1989). Classic experimental social psychology, which emerged from general experimental psychology early in the 20th century, is clearly an example of the first epistemology, whereas social constructionism (e.g., Gergen, 1985, 1994) and sociogenetic constructivism (e.g., Doise, 1989; Perret-Clermont & Nicolet, 1988) are examples of the second epistemology. In addition, con-cepts discussed in chapters in the present volume (e.g., Carugati's *provinces of meaning* and Pontercorvo's *thinking with others*, as well as papers that triggered several of my comments in this chapter) are examples of the sec-ond epistemology. Therefore, I begin this chapter with a short outline of the intersubjective construction of meaning and then use the fruits of this outline to deal with the issue of growing adult in society.

The Social (in the Sense of the Intersubjective) Construction of Meaning

Once we realize that understandable meaning cannot be autistic, but by its very definition must be social, we also realize that meaning has to be a prod-uct of the coordinated interaction between subjects and that the apparently individual discovery of meaning must be a quasi-individual reproduction of that coordinated interaction. To make this clear, take the example of the meaning of a *stone*. By definition, this meaning is a product of a specific coordination between subjects (in this case, a stonelike coordination) that has been internalized in our concept of stone and that we reproduce quasi-individually: that is, as if it were an individual discovery of an a priori meaning in nature each time we recognize an object as a stone and/or refer to it by words. Of course, once we can refer to internalized meaning by words, we can also go on with constructing meaning by verbal coordinations, and this is what leads to the discursive construction of reality.

The notion that meaning is socially constructed instead of individually discovered also implies that the *perceptual features* of meaning are socially constructed as well. For instance, when we recognize in the round and glittering stimuli of an object the perceptual features of a boulder, this is not because the object emits this inherent meaning to us via these cues, but because we ourselves project the social coordinations of a boulder-meaning (e.g., pick it up to throw it or cut it in pieces to make instruments) in what we see. If we had been raised in another culture (e.g., one in which we never coordinated our activities in a boulderlike way but in which we worshipped the sun), the same round and glittering cues would not be seen as perceptual features of a boulder, but as something like a child of the divine sun; and we would probably pray and dance for it, or for the social coordinations of a divine meaning, instead of cutting it into pieces to make instruments. This is no problem as long as we live in our own culture, for the meaning of what we perceive simply reproduces, virtually or factually, the cultural coordinations that led to that meaning. But when we have to interact with alien cultures (i.e., alien communities of coordinated interaction), we obviously get into trouble, for then we have to interact with people who seem to pray for a boulder or who seem to cut a child of the divine sun into pieces. The latter is called not only false or crazy but also sacrilege. Truth or reality problems of that kind are typically resolved in an orthodox way: that is, either by colonization (e.g., by forcing the weaker party to adopt our coordinations) or by excommunication, not only physically (e.g., expulsion or even killing) but also symbolically (e.g., by laughing at them, calling them crazy, or, in one word, *psychologization*). But when both parties are about equally powerful and cannot or do not want to break their interaction (typical in experiments on the social development of intelligence in which an experimenter does not allow children to use power or break the interaction), new social coordinations or new meanings may emerge that did not exist on either side before. Thus, by the constructive resolution of sociocognitive conflicts of coordination, people constantly create new meaning, which they internalize not only in their private minds (e.g., their concepts and thoughts) but also in their public minds (e.g., their rituals, books, institutions), and which they obviously use again later for the more or less orthodox socialization of newcomers in society.

The Social Construction of Self

What holds for meaning in general obviously also holds for the meaning of Self; in other words, it is a product of the coordinated interaction between subjects. The only question is which subjects and what coordinated interaction? The answer to that question is very simple (at least in a formal sense; in a concrete sense, it can be quite complex): The subjects are by definition the Ego and the Alters (the Ego being the owner-subject of Self and the Alters being the other subjects with whom Ego coordinates the meaning of Self), and the interaction must by definition differentiate Ego's ownership of Self from Ego's nonownership of comparable Others. This is symbolically expressed in Figure 9.1.

To the left in Figure 9.1, we see the Ego/Alter coordination that leads to the Self/Other meaning, and to the right we see the resulting meaning of Self and Other, with the formally necessary integration (large circle) and differentiation (smaller circles) of both concepts. This integration and differentiation is a formal necessity because obviously, without integration, Self and Other cannot be comprehended as *socii* (that is, as comparable cognitions in the same category of meaning); and without differentiation, Self cannot be

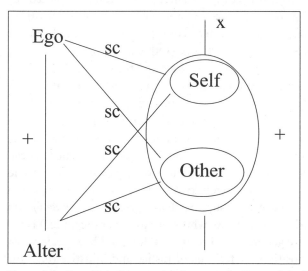

Figure 9.1. Coordinated interaction between the Ego and the Alters.

comprehended as a unique socius, namely the only one owned by Ego. Because Self refers to the only socius owned by Ego, however, the differentiation from Other is a preference (because a preference is by definition a differentiation in which the subject construes a stronger appropriative relation with one of the differentiated elements, as in the preference for this stone instead of for that one). This necessary "preference for Self," in the psychologically valid differentiation from Other, is symbolically expressed by the + to the right in Figure 9.1, and the vertical axis, X, is a symbol of any dimension on which this preference is projected. Thus, X is a value or literally a dimension in terms of which Ego, together with Alters, construes the basic preference for Self, from which all other preferences, as forms of appropriation to Self, are necessarily derived.

The other +, to the left in Figure 9.1, symbolizes the cooperation between Ego and Alters that is necessary to coordinate the preference for Self. This cooperation has two basic features: altruistic and commercial. By *altruistic*, we mean the Alter's preference for Ego's Self for reasons of identification (which means that the Alter treats Ego's Self as if it were his or her own Self). The prototype of this altruistic kind of preference is the symbiosis between mother and child during pregnancy. Clearly, the womb gives priority not to children outside the womb but instead to the fetus inside; if not, the fetus would simply not survive and, by implication, would never become a conscious Ego with a conscious Self. Immediately after birth, this altruism goes on for a while (but it is negotiated behaviorally instead of symbiotically). Very soon, however, it is complemented, if not totally replaced, by more commercial forms of preference or preferences that derive not from identification but instead from other needs of the Alter, which can be better satisfied by Ego's own Self than by competing Others. Thus, Self-realization is always cooperative and competitive at the same time: cooperative with cooperating Alters (altruistic and commercial ones) and competitive with competing Others (those competing for altruism and those competing for commercial preference). We can, of course, also express the fundamental need for cooperation and competitive success in terms of its opposite: that is, by Ego's rejection of those Alters who seem to prefer the Other instead of Ego's own Self (which implies that we put two negative signs, left and right in Figure 9.1, instead of the current two positive ones). This attraction to positive Alters (e.g., those who support Ego's preference for Self) and rejection of negative Alters (e.g., those who seem to prefer the Other) is the generic basis of what we generally call reciprocal love and hate, reciprocity of friendship and opposition, or feelings of justice and injustice (e.g., the feeling that Alters differentiate Self from Other in a right or wrong way), and even of Self-justification (e.g., Ego's explicit attempts to create a more preferred Self for Alters by, for instance, invoking external justification for failure).

The other symbols in Figure 9.1, namely, the intermediate social cues (sc) and the corresponding horizontal lines, are symbols of the perceptions that, due to the specific coordinations between Ego and Alters, turn in social cues of Self and Other, or literally cues that refer to the meaning of socii (the reason that we identify these cues as social instead of merely cues). In principle these social cues can be anything, but they can sensibly be divided into four major categories: (a) body (not only the exteroceptive signals of the body but, for Self, also the interoceptive ones); (b) behavior (words and deeds); (c) possessions (anything Self and Other have); (d) groups (the social groups or categories with which Self and Other are identified and from which their meaning as persons is inferred). The last type of social cues, groups, is generally called the *social identity of persons* (e.g., Tajfel, 1982); but clearly, any identity of Self and Other is to some extent social, namely, in the sense of being socially constructed and in the sense of being based on the discrimination between Self and Other (e.g., Rijsman, 1997).

Processes of Change in the Service of the Maintenance of Self

In our previous publications concerning the social construction of Self (e.g., Rijsman, 1983), we have usually referred to the *intersubjective* Ego/Alter coordination as *social validation,* the use of *intermediate* social cues as social *attribution,* and the *interobjective* Self/Other comparison as *social comparison.* We have also identified six processes of change by which Ego can construe and maintain a positive Self as specified in Figure 9.1. In that figure, these processes of change are, from left to right, a change of Alter; a change in the perception of the social cues (the lines to the left of sc); a change in the social cues themselves; a change in the attribution of the social cues to persons (the lines to the right of sc); a change of Other; and a change in the dimension of comparison, X (and any possible combination of these six processes).

To make this clear, let us take a simple example. Imagine that a pupil, A, is told by a teacher, T, that his score in mathematics is inferior to that of another pupil, B. How, according to the model, can A react to this situation in order to maintain a positive sense of Self? To deal with that question, we should imagine A as Ego, T as Alter, B as Other, the feedback on the score as the perception of the social cues, the inference of ability from the score as social attribution, and mathematics as X. Now, A can escape from a negative Self, for instance by rejecting T as a valid Alter and by invoking other Alters (i.e., other teachers or friends) who use other criteria, namely, those resulting in a positive Self for A. Another possibility is to change the perception of the score, for example by perceptual biases or by asking T to revise the score. One other possibility is to change the attribution of the score to ability, for instance by invoking fatigue or by suggesting that B has cheated. Still another possibility is to invoke for comparison another, less accomplished pupil, C, instead of B. And still another possibility is to reject mathematics as a valid dimension for comparison and to choose sports or art or another ability as a more valid dimension. A very constructive method is for A to work harder and make sure that, on the next occasion, his own score is better than that of B (the third method in the preceding list of processes of change).

In our own research on social comparison (Rijsman, 1983), we have often chosen the latter method as operationalization of the constructive work of Ego, not because it is the only method or the most important one psychologically, but because it is clearly the most visible and most measurable one in practical research. Monteil's work on social comparison in educational settings (Carugati, this volume) generally used objective changes in performance as indicators of the constructive work of pupils (e.g., Monteil, 1989, 1993). According to his remarkable finding, which also appeared in our own research, the effect of feedback on performance depends very much on whether it is personal or categorical. Concretely, subjects, told that they scored better than the Other, generally performed less well afterward than those who were told that they scored equal or worse. However, subjects who were told that they "belonged to a category of people" who scored better than the "category of the Other" reacted in just the opposite way. Those subjects who were told that they belonged to a superior category generally performed better afterward (instead of worse) than those who were told that their category was equal or inferior. These two patterns are factually opposite but theoretically identical, in the sense that they both illustrate the need for Ego to associate the Self with social cues of superiority, either by performing better when their own performance is not yet superior or by performing better when it can help to make the Self identical to a social cue, namely, their own group, which is already superior. This observation is obviously very important for education, because it shows the power of projecting positive expectations on pupils by means of positive categorization.

Of course, we can develop an understanding of many other concrete phenomena in social life by simply using the structure and dynamics outlined in Figure 9.1. For instance, it is immediately clear that two subjects, say

A and B, cannot function as positive Alter and as negative Other for each other's Self on the same dimension of comparison because, in order to validate their partner's Self, they must accept their own inferiority, which is against the fundamental preference for Self. This is the well-known conflict of identity in which two subjects want to receive from their partner a social validation that they cannot give themselves. The need for mutual social validation, however, which makes it impossible to cooperate in the case of a single dimension of comparison, becomes the very source of cooperation in the case of two or more complementary dimensions of comparison. For instance, imagine that A and B want to reach K but that A is blind and B is lame. In that case, A and B must cooperate, and their cooperation is instrumental not only to reach K but also to attain and maintain identity. A and B will each value their partner's ability, namely, A's walking and B's seeing, and they will not only accept but even strongly want their partner to be superior in that ability. Thus, they both give what they want for themselves. This also makes clear why A and B will reject technical innovations that take over their roles, such as a wheelchair for walking and a radar system for seeing. These innovations certainly make it easier to reach K, but they take away A's and B's identities. The famous "resistance to change" is therefore not really a resistance to change but a resistance against the loss of identity. In fact, people change continuously, and they even want to change, but only in the sense of making changes that are needed to attain and maintain identity (see the six processes of change discussed earlier).

This is very important in understanding the dynamics of a learning organization. Once we understand that changes are motivated by the social construction of Self, we also understand that the best system to make people learn offers a project of positive identity in which things that need to be learned are defined as contributions to Self. It is amazing how loving parents do this almost by instinct. When a child needs to learn something, the parents go "down" to the child's proximal level of development (see Carugati's reference in this volume, to Vygotsky's zone of proximal development) and "pull" the child up until he or she reaches the required skill level. Parents do not consider this as making their own Self inferior; on the contrary, they regard it as contributing to the continuation of their own identity in the future skills of their child.

This differs dramatically from the behavior of managers who blame their employees for lacking the required skills and even threaten them with firing in the hope of inspiring them to loyal cooperation. Of course, the opposite results; the manager gets the employees' external compliance from fear of being fired, but the employees inwardly reject the whole system. The fear of losing a job is a threat, but the fear of losing identity is worse; we call it *anxiety*. In Freud's language, neurotic anxiety is simply Ego's desperate resistance against the reentry of repressed sexual and aggressive impulses into consciousness. In our language, it is the desperate resistance against an explicit social construction of a negative Self. Thus, in our language, consciousness is not a place in Ego's brain that can open or close; it is a matter of communicability with Alters. In case Ego's relevant Alters accept or even validate the impulses, there is a sense of pride but not of anxiety. By definition then, anxiety is community-bound, and when Ego has to live in different communities with conflicting values, the vice in one becomes the virtue in the other or vice versa (the pun on *vice*, in this case, is obvious). Therefore, a postmodern society in which electronic communication and physical mobility make it virtually impossible to monopolize truth and value is also a dangerous place to maintain Self. It may well lead to mental reconstructions of islands of truth (e.g., the rebirth of orthodoxy) as well as to hypertexts of meaning (e.g., the apparently immoral "anything goes"). This is not immoral at all, because it recognizes that truth and value are not the voice of nature, or God if you wish, but are the voice of communities in which people socially construct their viable meaning of Self. Needless to say, this insight into the social background of the meaning of Self is also crucial for our conception of any system of professional help, such as therapy and organizational consulting, because it clearly can no longer be the enforcing of orthodox truth on people; it must become the facilitation of *texts on Self* that help to find Ego a valid place in relevant communities (e.g., McNamee & Gergen, 1992).

Various Provinces of Thinking with Alters on the Meaning of Self

We are now ready to read several chapters in this volume from a new perspective: for instance, those of Carugati and Pontecorvo, on the issue of becoming an adult in society, because this clearly boils down to what we have called a socially valid construction of Self. Pontecorvo's close analysis of conversations at the dinner table in Italian families, called *thinking with others* (*others* should clearly be taken as Alters in our terminology), is a perfect illustration of the importance of *supportive niches* (I deliberately use the same term that Tania Zittoun uses in her chapter [this volume] dealing with the *construction of the person*) in the social construction of Self. We can clearly see the incisive power of these conversations in the textual construction of the identity of children and parents. The language in these conversations is not mitigated; it is often very direct but never destructive.

This reminds us of the difference between shame and guilt that is often used to qualify cultures. (I do not want to go into the validity of that qualification here; it is used only as a basis for reflection.) In using the term *shame-culture*, we generally understand a culture to mean "like a family," which means that the Alter supports Ego's Self on a basis of altruistic identification. Ego's Self is therefore not replaceable by some Other, and the Ego/Alter conflicts, although rough sometimes, do not break the relation but keep Self on board until some positive effect is achieved.

This stands in sharp contrast with a *guilt-culture*, in which the Alter preference is based on the commercial superiority of Ego's services or goods in comparison with those of some Other. In principle, then, Ego's Self is not person-based but can be exchanged by any Other that produces the same goods and services equally well or better (see our differentiation between altruistic preference and commercial preference in the paragraph preceding Figure 9.1). The latter is often used as a managerial tool in business to create learning and enhance the development of employees. But when we look at the immense educational success of supportive family niches (by far the most successful learning organizations in human history, and the place where billions of people have been raised from relatively incompetent babies to relatively competent adults without being fired), we wonder if we could not better use some of the shame rules ("You should be ashamed for not doing the good things you are capable of") as managerial tools for learning and development in business as well.

In any case, in societies that put a high financial cost on firing, the generative or family-type attitude toward employees might prove to be less costly macroeconomically than the guilt-oriented one. Because aging is an invariant property of human existence, it might be wise to remember this in the philosophy of "life at work" as well, with the necessity of performing in different roles: for example, executive performance in an early stage and mentoring or coaching in a later stage. The valuing of coaching, which implies a redefinition of identity along the way (see our analysis of complementarity in the example of the lame and the blind becoming the seer and the walker), would not lose the fruits of older generations at the expense of paid exclusion from the process of economic coproduction (e.g., Rijsman, 1997).

Carugati's chapter (this volume) is a continuous illustration of the crucial role of social practices in learning and development and of the central role of Self in that endeavor. His first pages challenge the classic, more individualistic epistemology in (social) psychology, to which we referred at the beginning of the chapter: Can we conceive of human understanding and, by implication, human learning as a growing (or decline, in the negative case) of the individual intellect into the grown-up intellect of the adults who are already supposed to have learned to understand nature as it is and thereby deserve to be recognized as experts? Carugati's answer clearly is no. His arguments are very similar to those we used in describing meaning as a collective product in principle. But Carugati also warns us against a sociotropic error as much as against the error of individualism, because social practices involve not only interaction but also those who interact and something to interact about. As a result, Carugati immediately recognizes the central role of Self and identity in the collective construction of meaning. He draws our attention to this by asking simple but incisive questions about the identity effects of dropping out, about the effects of social comparison (using mostly Monteil and Huguet's work to illustrate), and about the effects of social marking.

The meaning of the latter can easily be illustrated by one of our own experiments in this regard. Imagine that we ask two children – a conserving one, C, and a nonconserving one, NC – to distribute lemonade equally between them; in one condition, the NC child is given a broad glass and the C child a thin one, and vice versa in the second condition. If C pours a lower level into the broad glass than into the thin one, NC will regard it as harming in the former condition and as helping in the latter one. The question, then, is, does this make a difference for the child's learning of conservation? The answer is yes, but in a complex way: Helping fosters learning more than harming in case the final test is a neutral one (e.g., the glasses are detached from ownership); in case the final test is not neutral (e.g., the glasses are again defined as owned by the child and the experimenter), the effect is the opposite, that is, harming does better than helping (e.g., Rijsman, 1988). This shows that social marking is important not only during the learning stage (e.g., the kind of ownership of the glass during the children's interaction) but also afterward, during the so-called testing (which is another type of interaction). This is also what Carugati implies when referring to learning as "shifts in the communities" that sustain the validity of meaning rather than as a purely individual shift of the subject alone.

Carugati uses a truly remarkable illustration of this idea: the negative effect of positive streaming in school on after-school work. Apparently, the good Self that is sustained in one context, school, causes trouble in new contexts, with new players, who use different criteria of validation. The most astounding result to which Carugati specifically refers, however, is the positive effect of the self-confidence of teachers, specifically their own belief in their capacity to be good teachers, on their realistic success as teachers. Apparently, Alters (to use our words) who are confident in their cooperative capacity with Ego are most effective in construing a communal world of valid meaning. The educational strategy of going down to the zone of proximal development of Ego acquires a special meaning in this regard. As we said earlier, this strategy is typical of loving parents who do not exclude the learning Ego from their cooperation by a momentary difference, but instead use the difference as an invitation to a strategy of a step-by-step pull toward their own community of adult practice, thereby influencing not only Ego's activities but also their own. This is immensely different from the strategy of arrogant and impatient expertise, which looks at difference as an invitation to almost immediate exclusion, justified by the notion of the impossibility of creating a communal world of meaning. Again, the remarkable thing is that the latter attitude is often used as a model for learning in commercial settings, whereas the family model, with its proven educational capacity, is probably more effective.

Epilogue

When trust in our own capacity to educate other people is an important determinant of our success as educators, any attempt to form good educators should transfer not only abstract knowledge but also that kind of trust. In a sense, then, forming educators is like creating a cascade of the capacity for constructive inclusion rather than skills for effective exclusion. Of course, this requires communities of practice (to use Lauren Resnick's term, this volume) that walk their talk. This leads to an intriguing question: Can the initial reservoir of trust, from which the cascade starts, be created or must it be found? In any case, there is a hidden reservoir of this kind of capacity (hidden not because it is beneath the surface of the earth, but because it is such a vast lake that we hardly recognize it as a reservoir): the millions of families without formal education, who have formed, generation after generation, trustful specialists of constructive inclusion, using the zone of proximal development as their powerful tool. What can we learn from these outstanding practitioners, and how can we include their tacit knowledge in our formal system of education? This is not an abstract question but a concrete one about the ways in which we interact with our own students and appreciate their voices in our communal definition of what is valid.

REFERENCES

Doise, W. (1989). Constructivism in social psychology. *European Journal of Social Psychology, 19*, 389–400.

Gergen, K. (1985). The social constructionist movement in modern psychology. *American Psychologist, 40*, 266–275.

Gergen, K. (1994). *Realities and relationships.* Cambridge, MA: Harvard University Press.

McNamee, S., and Gergen, K. (1992). *Therapy as social construction.* London: Sage.

Monteil, J.-M. (1989). *Eduquer et former. Perspectives* psychosociales [Educate and form. Social psychological perspectives]. Grenoble, France: Presses Universitaires de Grenoble.

Monteil, J.-M. (1993). *Soi et le Contexte* [Self and the Context]. Paris: Armand Colling.

Perret-Clermont, A.-N., & Nicolet, M. (1988). *Interagir et connâitre* [Interact and know]. Fribourg, Switzerland: Delval.

Rijsman, J. (1983). The dynamics of social comparison in personal and categorical comparison situations. In W. Doise & S. Moscovici (Eds.), *Current issues in European social psychology* (pp. 279–312). Paris/New York: Maison des Sciences de l'Homme/Cambridge University Press.

Rijsman, J. (1988). Partages et norme d'équité: recherches sur le développement social de l'intelligence [Distribution and norms of equity: Research in the social development of intelligence]. In A.-N. Perret-Clermont & M. Nicolet (Eds.), *Interagir et connâitre* (pp. 123–137). Fribourg, Switzerland: Delval.

Rijsman, J. (1990). How European is social psychology in Europe? In P. Drenth, J. Sergeant, & R. Takens (Eds.), *European perspectives in psychology* (pp. 1269–1281). Chichester, England: Wiley.

Rijsman, J. (1996). Le panorama intellectuel et technologique de la scene Piagetienne [The intellectual and technological *Zeitgeist* of Piaget's work]. In J.-M. Barrelet & A.-N. Perret-Clermont (Eds.), *Piaget et Neuchâtel* (pp. 145–164). Lausanne: Editions Payot.

Rijsman, J. (1997). Social diversity: A social psychological analysis and some implications for groups and organizations. *European Journal of Work and Organizational Psychology, 6*(2), 139–152.

Rijsman, J., & Stroebe, W. (Eds.). (1989). Controversies in the social explanation of psychological behavior. *European Journal of Social Psychology* [special issue], *19*, 339–489.

Tajfel, H. (1982). *Social identity and intergroup relations.* Cambridge: Cambridge University Press.

10 Preapprenticeship

A Transitional Space

Tania Zittoun

The process in which young people make the transition to adulthood may be considered a developmental process with at least two aspects. On the one hand, such a process necessitates a newly mature sense of one's own identity, which in turn entails a redefinition of the roles one plays socially, particularly with regard to new social groups. On the other hand, adulthood means acquiring new skills, knowledge, and know-how, all of which the young adult will need in order to play new social and professional roles. These two aspects of becoming an adult have traditionally been studied separately: School, the place where skills are acquired, is the focus in some studies; and social groups, wherein young people develop their sense of identity and social skills, are the focus in other studies. Some innovative studies have addressed both issues concurrently, however, showing that socialization and the construction of identity may also take place at school (Coulon, this

The work presented here (Zittoun, 1996, forthcoming) was done for two reasons. The first was a request from the creators and administrators of the training program itself – J.-C. Gindroz, general director of the CPLN; J.-C. Gosteli, assistant director of the CPLN and the Ecole des Arts et Métiers (EAM) and now the director of the EAM; J.-F. Graf, coordinator of the preapprenticeship section and current dean of the section within the EAM – and of C. de Castro, student counselor at the CPLN. (In addition to a job-training school that includes the preapprenticeship section discussed here, CPLN includes eight other technical and professional schools that accept students at age 15.) The second reason was the relevance of the training program to a study undertaken by the Psychology Seminar at the University of Neuchâtel, supported by the Swiss National Program of Research (PNR 33, Efficiency of Our Training Programs, Grant Number 4033-30846 to A.-N. Perret-Clermont). I would like to thank all of those mentioned, as well as the teachers and students, for their help during this study. Finally, I thank David Jemielity, lecturer at the University of Neuchâtel, for his translation.

volume) and that social groups often allow young people to acquire certain complex skills (Heath, Hundeide, this volume).

These two different spaces often function in complementary ways for young people. There is a direct link between the way in which a person gets involved in an activity and the way he or she makes sense of that action. This is particularly true of the social visibility of that action and the identity-related benefits he or she might procure via that action (Carugati, Rijsman, this volume). People need to have self-esteem and a sense of their own competence in order to act and think. Otherwise, a young person whose school experience is not welcoming, motivating, or reassuring, or who is too alienated in his or her social interactions at school, may turn to other sorts of activities. In such situations, participating in peer groups (e.g., sports, music, or friends) may help a youngster to experience himself or herself as a competent person, one who is valued by others and who functions within a satisfactory, active relational space. Multiple affiliations or changes from one group to another allow young people to change the evaluation dimensions of their identity (Palmonari, 1993).

Understandably, a young person who has been defined in exclusively negative terms at school (e.g., bad student, discipline problem) may wish to be judged by others on something other than school-related skills. Such negative definitions are generally internalized, however, and those internalizations can have a profound effect, vitiating a person's sense of self-worth or ability to act meaningfully. This sort of wound can end up affecting the way in which a person sees and makes sense of the world, and it can influence the decision to act or not act. With this in mind, is it then sufficient to change one's group affiliations in order finally to feel competent and valued? Is it not possible to imagine a school in which it might be possible to feel valued for nonacademic reasons?

To put the question another way, rather than divide social spaces into two distinct types – spaces that are good for scholarly children and spaces that are good for less scholarly ones – might it not be possible to conceive of a school context that can be interpreted more flexibly? Such a space might have therapeutic benefits by allowing students to experience themselves as valued individuals. In addition, such a space might function as a transition toward life as a socially and professionally integrated adult. In this chapter, we describe a "mixed" program: It is set within the school but designed for less scholarly students. We describe the complex ways in which such a space can allow students to make a transition in both the psychological and social senses of that term.

An Institutional Context for the Case Study

In Switzerland, education is obligatory until the student is 15 years old, that is, after 9 years of school. At this point, students can move on to college preparatory programs, professional schools, or apprenticeships in various sorts of companies. A small number of young people reach the end of their compulsory education without managing to get any type of qualification and without a chance for further training. Their only choice is to enter the labor market as unqualified labor; otherwise, they are quickly placed on the dole and socially marginalized. In such cases, no real affective or social maturity is possible for them. In some Swiss cantons, a make-up year (i.e., a 10th year of obligatory education) has been established for these students, but the 10th year does not necessarily allow them to attain acceptable levels of personal development or professional skills; in any case, not all of those who fail at the end of the 9th year are admitted.

The Centre Professionnel du Littoral Neuchâtelois (CPLN), a professional training school in the canton of Neuchâtel, has developed a preapprenticeship training program for these students, which has produced good results. For example, 80% of participants manage to begin a job apprenticeship or another long-term training program and to complete it after a year-long program that is split between classes and on-the-job experience (60% and 40%, respectively). This program has been successful for various reasons, which are explored in this chapter.

An ethnomethodological approach seems most appropriate in this effort, because it allows us to compare different kinds of data: interviews with the persons responsible for this training program, as well as with students or former students; examination of the archives and other school documents; and direct observation of classes and of the school in general. (Here we were influenced by Carugati, Emiliani, & Palmonari, 1981, and by Woods, 1990.)

Our initial contacts with the preapprenticeship teachers provided us with two hypotheses to start from as we observed and analyzed the data. One of the first things we observed was the teachers' concern for the history of their section of the school and their desire for the entire community to become aware of the existence and success of their program. What needs and what realities do their discourse make manifest? Our first hypothesis, linking the concrete success of the program with the political action of its teachers, suggests that the program's fate depends directly on the relations the teachers are able to build and maintain with the socioeconomic milieu and with national political representatives.

Our second hypothesis relates directly to the specific academic situation of the students in question. Admission into the preapprenticeship section presupposes a long personal history of failure in school and, therefore, also entails a severe lack of self-esteem and a feeling of academic incompetence. Our hypothesis is that any successful transition to an apprenticeship is contingent on repairing these young people psychologically and emotionally.

In the following sections, we examine the actions taken by the teachers in terms of these two approaches, attempting to use them in order to see how the trainers help students to develop the skills that will eventually lead to recognition and approval in the context of a future apprenticeship.

The Socioeconomic Context of the Program: Making Links

In Switzerland, to receive federal and cantonal subsidies, a training program has to fulfill specific structural criteria. For example, specific guidelines regulate the number of hours that students devote both to classroom work and to on-site practical job experience. The educators responsible for the creation of the preapprenticeship section of the CPLN during the 1970s were influenced by the new ideas of the post-1960s ideological ethos. They suggested that the section offer courses in artistic creation and dance, for example, in order to give participants a chance to express themselves and feel personally fulfilled. This training program was a failure. Those responsible for running it maintain that its failure was directly related to the local employers' and politicians' misunderstanding of the novel educational approach used in the section. (This obviously caused serious problems, because the local employers would hire – or not hire – participants after their preapprenticeship.) There was a widespread feeling within the local community, which was not particularly sensitive to or enthusiastic about the new post-1960s ideologies, that the participants had spent their year dancing, painting, and generally having fun. Those students were not taken seriously on the job market, and the training program quickly ran into trouble.

The current section managers have taken account of their predecessors' experiences without abandoning the original underlying philosophy of the section (i.e., giving the participants the chance to get the training that fits their personal choice). This has entailed a sort of "reality testing" in which those responsible for the program must weigh the desire for personal development against more practical considerations, such as making sure the program has some concrete value in terms of participants getting employment afterward. This does not mean that the concern for personal development that imbued the original creators' conception has been dropped;

rather, it has been placed within a set of guidelines; concern for personal fulfillment is still very strong in the section. (How this works is detailed later.)

As mentioned, another major concern is the program's credibility with future employers. It is essential that, in addition to whatever they learn in the classroom, the participants get hired by local enterprises, at first temporarily for job-training programs, and later on as apprentices. If this does not happen, the section cannot attain its goals; getting hired is not an easy task in light of the low educational level and multiple school failures of many of the section's students. This is why the section's managers market the program so intensely, using their own networks to publicize the work of the school, speaking to local business groups, using the media, or taking advantage of the more informal methods particular to Neuchâtel: for example, a convivial aperitif warmed up by a few glasses of Neuchâtel white wine. This admirable public relations campaign seems to have worked, and local bosses are willing to give these young people a chance.

The structural conditions necessary to establish a program allowing people to make a transition are, therefore, all in place: The redesigned curriculum makes those indispensable federal subsidies possible, and the networking undertaken within the local economy allows graduates to get their foot in the door of the Neuchâtel job market. How young people end up in the section remains to be explored.

The Student Body of the Preapprenticeship Program: Damaged Identities

Generally, the young people who sign up for the preapprenticeship program have suffered serious damage to their self-esteem. For one thing, most have continually failed in school and are thus marginalized within the school. Another factor is the families of many of the participants, who often come from difficult social and economic backgrounds. The participants' sense of identity is thus generally negative, and many have chosen to give up on activities in which they have been subjected to too much denigration and marginalization. A good example of such an activity is education.

This painful situation often leads to defensiveness on their part. For example, some of them systematically hide behind the statement "I don't get it," which may be interpreted to mean not just "I don't understand" but also "The teachers don't know how to make/help me understand." Certain phenomena illustrate this very weak sense of personal identity coupled with a tendency to attribute their problems to external causes. This is reminiscent of observations made by Dubois and Trognon (1989) about adults excluded from the job market who tend to attribute it to external causes. For example, participants have trouble arguing a position or using the word *I*. These are some of the signs of a fragile sense of identity (Charlot, Bautier, & Rochex, 1992; Heath, this volume).

Such a weak sense of one's identity can have serious adverse effects. Developmentally speaking, it can complicate the processes of cognitive, affective, and identity-related maturity that take place at adolescence (Tap & Malewska-Peyre, 1992). From a more specifically sociocognitive perspective, such a feeling of incompetence can inhibit the desire to learn things and thus diminish efforts at school: Of what use is school to me if *I* am not there?

Generally speaking, the affective, cognitive, and identity-related aspects of this question are intimately linked to each other. Once one realizes this, it becomes possible to identify several processes that contribute to the problems these students have in learning, problems that are all linked in one way or another to the fact that their sense of personal identity has been damaged.

In fact, it is clear that in order to learn, to acquire skills, and to make the jumps in status that a successfully completed school experience necessarily entails, one needs a sufficiently solid sense of self.[1] All of these aspects of development presuppose that the person abandons things he or she has accepted as givens: things known, things one is certain of, things one feels instinctively, the unvoiced but deeply felt feeling of one's own incompetence. At issue here is giving up what one knows for the unknown (Aumont & Mesnier, 1992; Carugati, Rijsman, this volume). Giving up on these "givens" means taking a risk. One is temporarily cast adrift, both cognitively and emotionally: cognitively, because my old knowledge is not valid anymore and I can no longer take for granted what I did before; and affectively, because my very identity is at stake. This temporary state of cognitive and emotional flux is both inherent in and necessary for any type of learning experience. Therefore, taking such a risk is possible only for those whose sense of self is sufficiently strong. Otherwise, giving up on all one takes for granted, all the elements that consolidate one's sense of self, can jeopardize

---

[1] Although we have stressed personal identity here, other identity-related factors are also linked to learning capacity. For example, the children of immigrants are often caught up in conflicts of group loyalty when what they have to learn within the school represents a betrayal of their origins (see especially Cesari-Lusso, 1997; Gretler, Hurny, Perret-Clermont, & Poglia, 1981). Similarly, unemployed parents or parents who work in unskilled jobs can cause students to reject schooling.

the tenuous psychological unity of the person. In such cases, the learning experience is rejected, because it is psychologically intolerable (Paín, 1989).

A relatively fragile sense of identity can also affect the processes of knowledge-related negotiations involving others, including those who might or might not prove to be helpful in the learning process. For example, group working situations in which differing points of view come up against each other can induce the subject to construct new representations and skills, as long as these negotiations remain centered on the subject at hand and not on the respective status of those involved (i.e., the negotiation must occur on a cognitive level; see Perret-Clermont, Perret, & Bell, 1991; Zittoun, Perret-Clermont, & Carugati, 1997, on sociocognitive conflict). It is not certain that a person with a very fragile sense of identity will be able to engage in a productive negotiation if that person's ideas are at stake: Such a person may well be incapable of isolating the cognitive from the affective and identity-related issues he or she links with the strictly cognitive.

On a more fundamental level, if the weakness of a person's self-image, a weakness that is often linked to the internalization of uncomplimentary external discourse, prevents that person from learning new skills, this is because the ability to think is itself undermined. Here *ability to think* refers to the ability to conceive of and bestow a symbolizable form on the real and imaginary events lived by a person at the emotional, cognitive, and corporeal levels. This process allows the person to achieve a certain distance from what is immediately at hand; to act on it; to transform it with words, action, or thought; and in so doing, to integrate it within the internal narrative we each develop for ourselves. In this way, mere events are transformed into experience and become part of our definition of ourselves.

If such a definition of the difficulties linked to learning is accepted, much is at stake during the preapprenticeship year. How can the trainers possibly change a participant's self-image in only 1 year? Yet they must succeed in allowing the desire to learn to return; in making the risk of thinking once again an acceptable risk; in short, in making possible these apprenticeships that are so important for the participants' careers.[2]

---

[2] If the ability to think autonomously, with the feeling of coherence this necessarily entails, develops during very early childhood, a bad family situation or other negative circumstances can undermine this initial psychological development. Certain studies in psychology have shown that even when this early development has been hindered, specific forms of group organization can restore the development of the psychological conditions needed for thinking, developing a sense of personal coherence and psychological independence (Emiliani & Bastianoni, 1992; Grossen & Perret-Clermont, 1992; Kaës, 1993). The idea explored here is that the preapprenticeship program, like some other youth-based organizations (Heath,

The Structure and Organization of the Preapprenticeship Program

Motivated by the stakes and the urgency of their participants' plight, the program's teachers set up a syllabus that attempts to engage participants in a process of complex development while also getting integrated into a useful sociorelational network.

The program begins with three events that are meant to "shake up" the participants enough to provoke a few doubts about themselves and, ideally, a solid commitment to the program. The first thing required of the students is that they find themselves a temporary work-experience job-training program position before the preapprenticeship program even starts. Here the participants' parents often get involved, and in many cases it is the first time the parents have played a role in their child's schooling. The participants and their parents benefit from the preparatory work the program's teachers have undertaken with the local employers. If a participant is unable to find a post, the school helps out with the search. This first requirement obliges the young people to face the possibility of getting turned down by prospective employers; and these experiences are discussed in class once school starts, as we see later.

In the next event, when school actually starts, the program staff "talk tough" to the students: This year will be their last chance, and it is going to be intense and difficult. Note that the only people accepted into the program are those whose results at school absolutely preclude any other training program. Furthermore, as the program coordinator has said, "If up till now the teachers have limited themselves to telling these people that they're not very 'good at school,' now the stakes have changed; it's up to the students to show the teachers what, indeed, they are 'good for.'" Such discourse allows these teachers to set up a process of change in the dimensions of identity-related evaluations.[3] The last of the three events is actually a nonevent. No mention is made of past school performances, because the teachers ignore

---

Rolleau-Berger, this volume), helps young people to acquire the ability to think and to develop a sense of personal coherence and psychic autonomy, even if they have not been developed earlier in other contexts. Such open-ended spaces allow the participants to develop personally and to move on in the direction of social integration. We must then distinguish such spaces from "closed" ones that do not lead to personal autonomy (Hundeide, this volume).

[3] Such changes also happen naturally. For example, when a young person is negatively judged in a dimension that defines him, such as school ability, he can restore a positive self-image by appealing to another dimension, one in which he may be positively evaluated, such as sports. The need here is to define a "school space" sufficiently different from the old one so that the participant can redefine a positive sense of identity *related to learning* within it.

them. Individual school files have not been opened, and all judgements will be based on present acts and not on past history.

Thanks to these measures, the participants can avoid feeling as though they are prisoners of their school records and of their status as "bad students." They can thus reasonably hope to be able to construct a sense of identity linked to their future experiences as preapprentices. Note that the three salient characteristics of this first step – a prerequisite commitment, the creation of a sense of urgency and challenge, and a voluntary forgetfulness regarding the past history of participants – recall the processes of conversion and/or initiation typical of some traditional societies (Nathan, 1988/1993b; Hundeide, this volume).[4] In this way a clear break with the past, joined with a real commitment, is the prelude to reconstructing a sense of identity adapted to new rules and a new situation.

Life at school is very strict: Limited spaces, schedules, rules, deadlines, and punishments are facts of daily life in the preapprenticeship program.[5] Despite this atmosphere, a relational space of very high quality develops that will play a key role in the affective and cognitive development of the participants. This is made possible through both the structures and organizational modes of the preapprenticeship program and the enthusiastic involvement of the teachers.

Within this highly structured framework is a solid network tying together all those involved – the program coordinator, the teachers, the psychologist, and the counselor for people outside the program, such as the parents and the employers – with students in temporary work-experience programs. The program coordinator, for instance, knows all of his "preapps" because he teaches a course on "Preparing for Professional Life," keeps up links between the preapprenticeship program and the outside world, and represents authority within the school by making sure that its strict rules are respected. He keeps track of each preapp's progress, particularly the search for an apprenticeship at the end of the year. Every program participant ends up developing a relation of mutual confidence with either the coordinator or one or more of the teachers, all of whom have been chosen for their interest

---

[4] These processes of conversion are particularly relevant to entering an authoritarian or a sectarian type of group. Here, a very strong emotional link ensures the group's unity, and psychic independence is banished, while individuality is structured by a "prefabricated" ideology. Later we attempt to show just how the preapprenticeship program is distinct from this sort of group.

[5] For example, almost every day, the instructors remind students of how much time remains before the end of the year, and constantly urge them to find an apprenticeship post and do other relevant work.

in and commitment to this type of young person. The psychologist plays the role of counselor and also has contact with all students in the program. Those who need someone to talk with or, more often, to listen to them frequently turn to the psychologist. Finally, each class has a *maître de classe*, the equivalent of a homeroom teacher in an American high school or a moral tutor in some British universities. This teacher is personally responsible for the members of a given class, even if he or she only teaches them one discipline daily. The teacher also maintains contact by both letter and telephone with the employers and parents of each student in the group. Of course, the parents are also involved with the professional integration of their child.

The high-quality relational space such a network presupposes is made possible through a series of concrete measures: telephone lines in the classrooms, schedules that put the students in contact with the adults tracking their progress, architecture facilitating informal conversations between participants and staff, meetings and other events where everyone sees each other, and recreational activities that build group cohesion and a sense of team spirit. In such an environment, a young person can have emotionally significant experiences.

The quality of this relational space also depends on the working principles that govern it. One such principle, called the *frankness policy*, calls for complete and open sharing of information about each student among the staff members. This applies to both signs of progress and signs of trouble regarding the student. In this way, the staff can react rapidly and in an informed manner to any problems encountered by students on both practical and emotional levels. The frankness policy also includes the students themselves: The staff is very open with each student about any problems he or she might be causing the teachers, and staff members also freely refer to what other staff members have told them about a given student when talking with that student. The students themselves gradually adopt the same frank and open attitude during the course of the year. Generally speaking, this policy leads to a more personalized teaching atmosphere, and the students themselves become aware of this through the conversations they have with the staff during the year, conversations that make it clear to each student that the teachers really do know a lot and care about him or her.

The students thus find themselves within a space that is both forbiddingly structured and comfortingly social. They are, after all, at the heart of a network of exchanges. They are conscious of being the center of the teachers' attention and efforts. The various aspects of this experience – in school, in the temporary work program, and at home – come together in the image of themselves offered to them by the teachers. (This is reminiscent of the "good enough" mother described by Winnicott [1975, 1988], who looks at the child, thus showing the child that he or she exists in the mother's gaze and therefore that he or she exists.) For what may be the first time, these young people have the impression that they are being taken seriously within this relational space, that they are seen as being worth the trouble, and that they are considered personally responsible. In addition, thanks to the roles given to links among family, professional activities, and school, the program also tries to resocialize these often socially marginalized young people.

A Framework for Developing the Skills Needed to Integrate

Any training program is judged on its results, essentially on what the outside world thinks of the student's acquired skills. Exactly what skills have been acquired within this program for academically unmotivated adolescents, and how are these skills taught?

In the core academic subjects such as math, German, and French, minimal grades are necessary if one wants to be able to begin an apprenticeship. In the preapprenticeship program, the teachers do not have time to make up for the lost years completely, and thus they opt for a strategy of efficiency. This involves a heavy emphasis on test-taking and problem-solving strategies and lots of work on problem sets and drills. The content of each course is custom-made according to the professional orientation of each class. During free time, the students are guided in individual work on social or cultural themes that interest them. The teaching staff believes that these students do not get much out of group work or workshop pedagogical formats and therefore have chosen more traditional teacher-to-entire-class methods.

Certain classes have been created, however, to take up the specific problems linked to moving into work life. Within these courses, topics include the work experiences the students are undertaking, the job interviews they will be going through, and other aspects specifically linked to their particular situations. The teachers designed this course themselves, based on personal observation and professional experience. For example, in conceiving the part of the course that would cover job interviews, the teachers made two observations. First, even if an employer officially hires people based on their school report cards, often other ingredients, such as a young person's inventiveness, enthusiasm, or ability to project the impression that he or she will simply get the job done, actually determine the employer's decision. Such intangibles quickly become part of the image that a young, would-be apprentice takes on in the mind of a prospective employer. This image is also partially determined by respect for certain social codes that everyone, including employers, wants to be respected: being polite, on time, and decently dressed. Infractions can adversely affect the image of a participant in the mind of his or her boss. Second, and closely related to these codes, is the observation that, because of their specific familial, cultural, and academic trajectory, some of these young people simply do not have access to these implicit codes. Often, such a participant will end up almost immediately, but innocently, marginalized: He or she will have no idea of the rules being broken, but unfortunately the negative image in the mind of the prospective employer is already taking shape. The course "Preparing for Professional Life" addresses this two-fold problem, as does the "Office Techniques" course.

To teach the young people to project a "can-do" image, the teachers begin with the idea that people are often judged in offices simply on things such as how they go about fixing the photocopier or making coffee. Therefore, specialists in photocopiers and coffee machines take part in these courses. As a result, the students receive very favorable reviews from their bosses. Such courses seem to prepare a young person to deal with tests of self-identity, because he or she can feel competent during these situations, be they interviews or on-the-job training experiences. In addition, these courses allow the students to see that other people accept them as skilled, useful, and potentially attractive coworkers. When the judgments made later on are favorable, these courses have given participants more than just the practical benefit of getting into an on-the-job-training program: The benefits are also there on the level of their very sense of identity.

Second, the teachers observe the need for and set up specific courses, as well as one-on-one sessions, to make students fully conscious of and finally internalize the implicit social codes just discussed. (By *implicit social codes*, we mean gestures, expressions, modalities, and attitudes that the other person tacitly expects in any situation of social interaction in a given sociocultural context.) As we will see, these exchanges are also the occasion for important identity-related work.

"Preparing for Professional Life," taught by the coordinator, plays a key role. Near the beginning of the year, the students are invited to tell the class about their work experiences, job interviews, and other contacts with the business world. For many participants, this is the first time that these events, be they successes or humiliations, become the object of discourse. As narrative, they become shareable, comparable with the narratives of other students. Collective analyses and judgments can be formulated with the help of the teacher. Such collective narratives can confer on these experiences the status of an example: A positive experience can serve as a metaphor for interpreting a new situation, whereas a negative one can be "reread" and used as a basis for anticipating future situations.

This course also contains a section on getting ready for the "test," that is, the job interview. Using evaluative and projective tests, the teacher attempts to raise the consciousness of the students in terms of their own tastes, qualities, desires, aptitudes – indeed, their own rich and variegated identity. Role-playing games are also used to simulate job interviews. Thus, the unknowns are considerably reduced, but this is just one benefit. What is really at stake is that the young person is put before the gaze of another in an atmosphere of mutual confidence. Thus, the participants become aware of the image other people have of them. The teacher attempts to make the participants aware of their own positive sides, particularly the socially positive sides of certain gestures or words used during these mock interviews. During the course of the year, the participants gradually discover their own ability to express themselves, to think about themselves, and finally, to speak for themselves. They acquire not self-consciousness, but consciousness of themselves as independent entities possessed of an *I*.

The one-on-one sessions play an important role in developing participants' skills and sense of identity. Often, in anticipation of an impending meeting with a potential employer, the coordinator meets with a student or has a class discussion about an upcoming concrete situation. During their dialogue, the coordinator guides the student's anticipation of the various stages of the situation. Together, they imagine the possibilities, break them down, and set up step-by-step strategies, including presenting themselves upon arrival, greeting someone, and deciding what to wear. Here, the implicit social codes may be rendered explicit: For example, do not chew gum during the interview. Other unknowns – for instance, how to make sure the student is on time – are also taken up in this context. Finally, an attempt at confidence building is made. Note that the type of thinking required by this discourse is hypothetical, strategic, and fundamentally decentered (e.g., What do I do if x happens? How should I respond if that question comes up?). This entails imagining points of view other than one's own and representing the unknown to oneself, which presupposes not only certain cognitive skills but also the psychological coherence needed to take such cognitive risks and to deal with the uneasiness they may provoke. What makes all this possible? For one thing, mutual respect does, because the teacher recognizes the cultural and personal specificity of the young person and addresses him or her in the formal *vous* form that French adults use when speaking to each other, rather than in the informal *tu* form that teachers use with students in grammar school, and the student respects the school's rules as represented by the coordinator. Another essential element is the mere presence of the coordinator and the cognitive and affective support he provides.

A Space for Personal Reconstruction

These various exchanges – in class, with schoolmates, and during one-on-one sessions – all contribute to the construction of a sense of self as conscious and competent. In class, this starts when the young person first feels that he or she is being taken seriously, and it continues with the cognitive and affective exchanges among class members that allow each student to reappropriate his or her own experience and to recognize the instructive value of each person's experience for the members of the group as a whole. This construction is also linked to the way in which the program facilitates the acquisition of a personal point of view and one's own voice.[6] The construction of a sense of self is then inscribed in a sense of duration, by the progressive reappropriation of elements of one's personal history, by an open and favorable present in which a feeling of personal existence has become possible, and by thought experiments involving a future in some other place. Finally, other factors contribute to the preapps' commitment to the program: their teachers' expectations, the "last chance" atmosphere, and the climate of mutual confidence and recognition. All of this helps participants take the necessary risks for success in the business world, with its interviews, job searches, apprenticeships, and the like.

Structures such as the preapprenticeship program or that discussed by Heath (1994), involving a group of young people open to and directed toward the outside world, act on different types of processes that are strongly interdependent. First, the process of identity consolidation and the reinforcement of the feeling of having one's own voice and a certain amount of self-confidence allow a person not only to risk not knowing, to suspend his

---

[6] The group can facilitate the digestion and development of experience in its cognitive and affective aspects. Events that a person has undergone, that have prevented him or her from conceiving an individual personal experience (Tisseron, 1998), can be shared with a group as long as that group has a sufficiently open attitude; in this way the subject can deal with those events (Kaës, 1993, 1994). The group permits a collective approach to dealing with the narrative and multiple points of view, a form of shared thinking that makes individual integration easier. This way of working one's thought, which has been used in therapeutic contexts (Nathan, 1993a), also takes place in class: A group activity can be individually assimilated and individually remobilized later (Lipman, 1996; Pontecorvo, Amendola, & Fasulo, 1994; Portecorvo & Girardet, 1993).

or her certainties, and to tolerate the idea of being in error, but also to project himself or herself toward a future, even if that future is still ill-defined and quietly terrifying. Thus, the conditions for moving toward and engaging in an apprenticeship are fulfilled. Second, preapprenticeship, seen as "groups of young people," represents social integration and the development of social skills (the implicit codes), interpretive skills (e.g., resolving problems, anticipating), and practical as well as professional know-how. Such skills allow students to obtain recognition from others and to consolidate their own feelings of self-value and identity. Third, thanks to this consolidation and these skills, the young people can start making projects for their future and can initiate actions linked to getting a job and the like. Here, they are constructing a future in the outside world in which they will be socially and professionally recognized. Finally, all experiences linked with confronting this outside world contribute either to consolidating the sense of identity or to making it fragile; those experiences either jump-start or inhibit the desire to learn and the commitment to the apprenticeship process.

Conditions for Maintaining the Framework Section

Having described the structures and functional modes of the preapprenticeship program, we now discuss some of the internal conditions necessary for maintaining it. Here we emphasize the roles of the teachers, particularly their ability to decenter themselves, to serve as protector and maintainer of the framework, and to mediate between two social spheres. But note that a personal obstacle can cause problems for the program: The program objectives require the teachers to do something that goes against their training. They must encourage the students to find an apprenticeship above all else, including learning academic material. To facilitate getting an apprenticeship, the teachers have to promote the development of nonscholarly aptitudes in their students. The orientation is practical, not theoretical, as is normally the case in school. Often they must discourage students from considering longer programs of study.[7] Remember that all of the teachers have had serious intellectual training and, therefore, might have certain prejudices concerning young people who prefer practical occupations to theoretical studies or intellectual curiosity. Nevertheless, the teachers/trainers must transmit a sense of their own worth to the young participants, as well as the feeling that manual training can lead to satisfaction and success despite the discourse traditionally dominant in school and society. These teachers, then, can play

---

[7] But this is not always the case. Some students end up in preuniversity programs.

their role only if they are capable of valuing choices contrary to their own and of giving up the "democratic ideal" (which may be democratic but is certainly also sociocentric) that everyone should study during youth to prepare for higher education. Their pedagogical and relational role requires them to decenter themselves from their personal histories and their own points of reference. This entails recognizing otherness.

The teachers' role must not be considered to be simply one of creating a warm, cozy space for "damaged" young people. Although their role involves some therapeutic reparation, it is mainly characterized by transmission, guided by clearly defined goals. These teachers play a role in maintaining the program framework by establishing a set of rules. The ideology of a program or of a group, or *second-order rules* (Heath, 1996), plays an essential role here, providing the overall orientation for work within the program, defining the sorts of actions taken by the teachers, and imposing certain types of rules. In Neuchâtel, this ideology is at times explicitly enunciated, as in the following statement by the program coordinator:

> My dream is that one day I can see a young person and say, "That is a preapp" – you can't explain it, you just know it. Because he's able to take the initiative, to work, to help the team, to be in a good mood, to be a leader. . . . Concretely, when he walks in the door, ten minutes later you know he's a preapp, just by the way he acts while he's in there, the way he shows that he's already figured out how it all works – but not intellectually. For example, he'll say, "Look, the copier's out of paper." He'll say that, but the difference is then he'll go get some!

This ideology is clearly oriented toward the social integration of the participants. The second-order rules have two indirect functions. They contribute to creating a microculture with a specific group identity complete with its own emblems, rituals, and memory. And they have practical effects on the organization of daily life, such as following schedules, respecting rules of personal hygiene and appropriate dress, and being polite. All of these issues, which are often heard during the school day, help students to prepare for life outside the school. These rules allow the students to overcome their social handicap by acquiring skills that are both useful and a source of recognition within the institutional environment. In this way, the rules define the group ethos that the adults, especially the teachers, are in charge of maintaining (see Hundeide, this volume). In this way, the adults play the role of *framework protector* (Grossen & Perret-Clermont, 1992): Rather than repeating the rules, they concretely regulate daily pedagogical and social interactions.

As we have seen, the teachers play the role of cognitive models, particularly in linguistic exchanges (Heath, 1996), and they also facilitate the recognition and constitution of the young person as a subject. But they also have a clear function as *mediators*: The teaching team mediates the group of young people in the direction of the outside world. This role as a mediator has two aspects. One is related to identity: The older teacher knows how to be recognized in two worlds, that of the young people and of the school and also that of the outside world. When students identify with their teachers, as is often the case, they can imagine themselves being recognized in the outside world, too. The other aspect is cultural: Young people who have encountered failure at school or who come from socially marginalized groups do not have access to the codes and languages of the social groups they wish to join. The mediator, by belonging to both groups, transmits these codes of social behavior but also calls on "meta" skills, such as the ability to translate the social codes of the target group into the language of his students, through such devices as metaphors or catch phrases.

In such transitional spaces and programs, it is important for the teachers to be fully aware of where their students are coming from, that is, the world constituting their students' frame of reference, to which, at times, they may return. The teachers need to know how this world works and what its rules are; they need to be able to relate to their students' world. The mediators also appear to be conscious of their role in the construction of a specific social framework, with rules to uphold, a space to maintain, and individual processes of thought to facilitate.

Frameworks and Spaces: Building Conformity or Independence?

The program described here resembles in some respects various groups of young people in interstitial situations. It constitutes a framework within which young persons can socialize themselves, as well as a space within which relational development, allowing these persons to become aware of some of their personal qualities and skills, may take place. On another level, the program sets up a bridge to the professional world: This once impossible goal becomes possible, thanks to the contacts between teachers and the outside world, the ideological commitment of the teachers in their role as mediators, and the content of the courses, which give the students the skills to use the bridge. With all this taken into account, it is clear that a person's identity can be deeply changed.

Two questions arise: What makes this socialization based on specific relational modes something other than a form of indoctrination? And what makes this preparation for the business world anything other than a type of alienation?

The first question leads us to socialization spaces similar to that provided by the preapprenticeship program, which also develop a microculture, a complex system of rules, and a requirement that, to enter the group, the person must break with the past, particularly the school-related aspects of the past; in addition, the relational space proposed is open to the young person. In religious or political groups such as those described by Hundeide (this volume), a young person will frequently give up a personal identity to become one with his or her cohorts. At the very least, the young person can totally conform to the role assigned by the hierarchy. At times, the emotional payoff and recognition provided by the group induce the young person to assume the group's ideology and whatever actions it promotes. Unlike in these organizations, however, in the preapprenticeship program, the group is not concerned solely with its own survival but concentrates primarily on the students' futures, which are *independent of the group*.[8] The group attempts to develop every member's skills and thus allows for personal recognition, rather than taking as its goal victory over some other group, as is the case with gangs.[9] The program may not be reduced simply to its therapeutic function or to its identity-related function because of this openness and this status as a temporary space of transition.

The second question, about alienation, relates to the necessity of students to conform to market laws. Students who have encountered failure in school have a tendency to reject any responsibility for their situation and to adopt a *discourse of external attribution*. This becomes a problem, because most employers adopt the dominant ideology, which prefers an affirmative personality that takes the initiative and manifests an internal attribution of responsibility. A training program that is intended to make its participants more hireable could develop a set of superficial devices, a manual of ways to present a self-image that conforms to expectations of internality. A training program that tried to design only a set of social masks in this way would just reinforce the identity-related feelings of uselessness that plague these young people, whose sense of self is already very fragile. They would

---

[8] Tarcena (1994) suggests distinguishing groups based on this criterion as open and closed groups.

[9] More precisely, young preapps going on job interviews know they are competing with other students from more highly regarded schools and programs. The benefits of their success will, of course, go to the group in the form of gratitude to the teachers, higher status for the program, and a social triumph; but they will also go to the individual students whose own future, not that of the school, is taking shape.

then become totally alienated. On the other hand, within the preapprenticeship program, such activities represent only a small, superficial part of a human organization that aims to take in these young people, help them to understand their experiences, and allow them to gain consciousness of themselves, their relations with other people, and their ability to reflect on what happens to them and the actions they take. As we have explained, the initial goals of the program are the affective and cognitive development of the person, the reconstitution of the *I*, and the transition to psychological autonomy. All the program's rules and structures are a function of these essential goals.

The preapprenticeship program is not one of indoctrination and does not alienate its participants. This is due to its double transitional function. As an open social space, it allows the participants to make a social transition: from the margins of society to a possible occupational integration. As a transitional space, it provides participants with a space for thinking in which they can become conscious of themselves and develop psychological autonomy.

REFERENCES

Aumont, B., & Mesnier, P.-M. (1992). *L'acte d'apprendre* [The learning act]. Paris: Presses Universitaires de France.

Carugati, F., Emiliani, F., & Palmonari, A. (1981). *Tenter le possible* [Trying the possible]. Berne, Switzerland: Peter Lang.

Cesari-Lusso, V. (1997). *Quando la sfida viene chiamata integrazione... Percorsi di socializzazione e di personalizzazione di giovani, "figli di immigrati"* [When the challenge can be called integration...]. Rome: La Nuova Italia Scientifica.

Charlot, B., Bautier, E., & Rochex, J.-Y. (1992). *École et savoir dans les banlieues et ailleurs* [School and knowledge in the suburbs and elsewhere]. Paris: Armand Colin.

Dubois, N., & Trognon, A. (1989). L'apport de la notion de norme d'internalité à l'approche des pratiques de formation [The contribution of the notion of *internality norm* in educational practices]. In J. L. Beauvois, R. V. Joule, & J. M. Monteil (Eds.), *Perspectives cognitives et conduites sociales* [Cognitive perspectives and social behavior] (pp. 213–224). Cousset, Switzerland: Delval.

Emiliani, F., & Bastianoni, P. (1992). La vie quotidienne comme thérapie [Everyday life as therapy]. In M. Grossen & A.-N. Perret-Clermont (Eds.), *L'espace thérapeutique: Cadres et contextes* [The therapeutic space: Frames and contexts] (pp. 63–90). Neuchâtel, Switzerland/Paris: Delachaux et Niestlé.

Gretler, A., Hurny, R., Perret-Clermont, A.-N., & Poglia, E. (1981). *Etre Migrant. Approches des questions socioculturelles et linguistiques relatives aux enfants migrants en Suisse* (2nd ed.) [Being a Migrant. Approaches to sociocultural and linguistics questions related to migrant children in Switzerland]. Berne, Switzerland: Peter Lang.

Grossen, M., & Perret-Clermont, A.-N. (Eds.). (1992). *L'espace thérapeutique: Cadres et contextes* [The therapeutic space: Frames and contexts]. Neuchâtel, Switzerland/Paris: Delachaux et Niestlé.

Heath, S. B. (1994). The project of learning from the inner-city youth perspective. *New Directions for Child Development, 63,* 25–34.

Heath, S. B. (1996). Ruling places: Adaptation in development by inner-city youth. In R. Jessor, A. Colby, & R. A. Shweder (Eds.), *Ethnography and human development: Context and meaning in social inquiry* (pp. 225–251). Chicago: University of Chicago Press.

Kaës, R. (1993). *Le groupe et le sujet du groupe* [The group and the group's subject]. Paris: Dunod.

Kaës, R. (1994). *La parole et le lien* [The word and the bond]. Paris: Dunod.

Lipman, M. (1996). *Natasha: Vygotskian dialogues.* New York: Teachers College Press.

Nathan, T. (1993a). *... fier de n'avoir ni pays, ni amis, quelle sottise c'était* [... proud to have neither country, nor friends; how foolish it was]. Grenoble, France: La Pensée Sauvage.

Nathan, T. (1993b). *Le sperme du diable, éléments d'ethnopsychothérapie* [The devil's sperm: Insights in ethnopsychotherapy]. Paris: Presses Universitaires de France. (Original work published 1988)

Paín, S. (1989). *La fonction de l'ignorance* [The function of ignorance]. Berne, Switzerland: Peter Lang.

Palmonari, A. (1993). *Psicologia dell'adolescenza* [Psychology of adolescence]. Bologna, Italy: Il Mulino.

Perret-Clermont, A.-N., Perret, J.-F., & Bell, N. (1991). The social construction of meaning and cognitive activity in elementary school children. In L. B. Resnick, J. M. Levine, & S. D. Teasley (Eds.), *Perspectives on socially shared cognition* (pp. 41–62). Washington, DC: American Psychological Association.

Pontecorvo, C., Amendola, S., & Fasulo, A. (1994). Storie in famiglia [Family stories]. *Età Evolutiva, 47,* 14–29.

Pontecorvo, C., & Girardet, H. (1993). Arguing and reasoning in understanding historical topics. *Cognition and Instruction, 3–4,* 365–395.

Tap, P., & Malewska-Peyre, H. (Eds.). (1992). *Marginalisation et troubles de la socialisation* [Marginalization and socialization troubles]. Paris: Presses Universitaires de France.

Tarcena, E. (1994). La construction psychique de l'enfant sous l'influence de modèles identitaires différents [The psychic construction of the child under the influence of various identity models]. In C. Labat & G. Vermes (Eds.), *Cultures ouvertes, sociétés interculturelles* [Open cultures, intercultural societies] (Vol. 2, pp. 165–175). Paris: L'Hamattan.

Tisseron, S. (1998). *Y a-t-il un pilote dans l'image?* [Is there a pilot in the picture?] Paris: L'Aubier.

Winnicott, D. W. (1975). *Jeu et réalité* [Playing and reality]. Paris: Gallimard.

Winnicott, D. W. (1988). *Conversations ordinaires* [Everyday conversation]. Paris: Gallimard.

Woods, P. (1990). *L'ethnographie de l'école* [Ethnography of the school] (P. Berthier & L. Legrand, Trans.). Paris: Armand Colin. (Translated and reprinted from *Inside Schools: Ethnography in Educational Research* [1986]. London/New York: Routledge/ and Kegan Paul.)

Zittoun, T. (1996). L'envie devant soi. Étude monographique d'un secteur de préapprentissage [Monographic study of a preapprenticeship school department]. *Dossiers de Psychologie, 46*. Neuchâtel, Switzerland: Université de Neuchâtel.

Zittoun, T. (forthcoming). *Insertions. Étude monographique du secteur de préapprentissage du centre professionnel du littoral neuchâtelois* [Insertions. Monograph on the preapprenticeship section of the Neuchâtel Pre-professional School]. Berne, Switzerland: Peter Lang.

Zittoun, T., Perret-Clermont, A.-N., & Carugati, F. (1997). Développement social de l'intelligence [Social development of intelligence]. In H. Bloch (Ed.), *Dictionnaire Fondamental de Psychologie* [Basic Dictionary of Psychology] (pp. 649–650). Paris: Larousse.

IV

LEARNING IN PRACTICE AND DISCOURSE

11 From Learning Lessons to Living Knowledge

Instructional Discourse and Life Experiences of Youth in Complex Society

Roger Säljö

In public debates today, it is easy to agree that knowledge is one of the most important assets of a society and its population in a global economy. Belief in education as a tool for the advancement of life conditions and for economic prosperity has never been stronger than it is now. The knowledge economy seems to require an endless influx of well-educated people who can contribute to further development by using their skills to expand dynamic sectors of society. The official policies of most countries reflect these assumptions. This means so far, so good for formal education. But in the midst of this emphasis on knowledge and skill, educational systems are also suffering what seems to be a crisis caused by an increasing lack of confidence. Young people in many countries appear far less enthusiastic about what education has to offer than is reflected in official policies. They seem less committed than previous generations to accept the challenges of schooling as central to their own concerns and aspirations. The manner in which formal schooling is organized does not connect to the life experiences of young people, and many explore other contexts for investing their energy, as exemplified in this volume.

The traditional functions of schools – providing information, knowledge, and skills – are being challenged by other actors. Schools have lost their position as the dominant source of information. Media and information technology that young people encounter in their everyday activities have a different agenda than do schools, and they also communicate experiences in a radically different manner. Their immanent pedagogy is not grounded

The work reported here was financed by the Swedish Council for Research in the Humanities and Social Sciences (HSFR).

on the same set of assumptions as is traditional education. Thus, although young people at some level are better informed and more knowledgeable about the world than any previous generation has been, there is a growing misfit between everyday experiences and the approaches to understanding the world that are offered by formal schooling. In this chapter, I explore some features of the origin of the traditions of communicating that dominate schooling as an activity system in order to contribute to a discussion of the challenges facing modern education when it comes to resonate with the interests of youth. We need to ask serious questions about how it can be changed to accommodate and connect to the priorities and aspirations of youth.

In addressing such an issue, one should remember that this problem is not new. Almost 100 years ago, John Dewey (1916/1966) pointed out that as "formal teaching and training grow in extent, there is the danger of creating an undesirable split between the experience gained in more direct associations and what is acquired in school." Dewey also adds that this "danger was never greater than at the present time, on account of the rapid growth in the last few centuries of knowledge and technical modes of skill" (p. 9). Considering what has happened in terms of knowledge and technology since Dewey issued his warning, the problem about the interface between schools and youth seems well worth further consideration.

Learning, Pedagogy, and the Emergence of Formal Schooling

Every society has to make sure that its most important collective insights and skills survive generational shifts. This is a fundamental condition of organized social life. Collective forgetting is too expensive. Even our predecessor among the hominids, *Homo erectus*, knew several hundred thousand years ago (Donald, 1991; Mithen, 1996) how to control and deliberately set fire, how to make tools, and how to cook. Obviously, the skills needed for such activities required learning in a sociocultural sense (Wertsch, 1991). Most likely, the reproduction of such skills also relied on explicit instruction to some extent (even though we cannot be certain about the role of verbal language as we go far back). Some kind of "guided participation" (Rogoff, 1990) and cooperation between adults and young people would have been necessary when learning how to manage such complex, skill-dependent activities as those involved in preparing food; hunting and fishing; collecting berries, mushrooms, and whatever nature offered; and learning how to manufacture increasingly sophisticated stone tools.

In a traditional society with a low division of labor and few technical innovations, learning is not separated from life in general. Even if instruction is necessary to master some skills, it is integrated into the activities themselves. Young people learn the central skills of a community while involved in adult activities, and they do so by taking the position of a novice who is tolerated in the activity but who initially plays no major role in it. Observation and imitation of adult behaviors are essential ingredients in the induction into adult practices. In such a society, it was and still is highly unusual to arrange situations with the specific purpose of teaching a skill. The pedagogy was largely invisible, and most likely people were not able to think in terms of teaching and learning as we conceive such phenomena.

Literacy was one of the first cognitive and communicative skills that was so complex that it had to be acquired through explicit instruction and in a specifically arranged social setting. As early as in the famous city-states in what the Greeks referred to as Mesopotamia, in present-day Iraq, where the predecessors of our alphabetic script originated some 5,000 years ago (Coulmas, 1989; Foley, 1997), schoollike learning sessions were organized to teach the scribes who were urgently needed in the administration of a society growing in complexity. In the differentiated economy that followed the transition to life in permanent settlements, recordkeeping was an important element in business, taxation, regulation of land ownership, and many other social activities. Some knowledge of mathematics was also necessary when keeping records of taxes and duties (Walker, 1990, pp. 43ff). From an analytical perspective, this emergence of contexts specializing in teaching specific skills can be seen as the beginning of secondary socialization (Berger & Luckmann, 1966) of human beings. In contrast to the primary socialization that takes place in the family and local community and that is firmly grounded in direct experience, as Dewey put it, secondary socialization is a very different process that relies on mediated experiences and some kind of explicit pedagogy.

Secondary socialization is a process through which the broader society and its priorities begin to intervene in a very concrete sense in a young person's life. The manner in which it is organized does not take into full account the individual experiences and interests of each person. Rather, it presents people with knowledge, skills, and communicative experiences that are grounded in rationalities that may not be immediately relevant to each individual involved.

Throughout history, the period of secondary socialization has become longer, and successively larger proportions of each generation have been enrolled. Both of these factors are essential when considering the transformation of schools from elite to mass institutions providing for the majority of a population. During the Greek and Roman periods, schooling gained in importance, and what was to be learned was organized in terms of academic subjects. Such subjects represented new and rather abstract manners of contextualizing knowledge and of conceptualizing intellectual skills. The curricula built on the subjects of the *quadrivium* (arithmetic, geometry, astronomy, and music) and *trivium* (grammar, rhetoric, and logic). These areas were important for running the state and for cultivating aesthetic and intellectual skills among the ruling elite, the so-called free men. Slaves and women engaged in physical labor and were not considered to be in need of cultivating their *ratio* (i.e., mind). The distinction between theory and practice as we know it today is rooted in a division of labor in a very concrete sense. These subjects, what the Romans called *artes liberales*, in turn, shaped schooling throughout the medieval period and into our time.

Discourse Formats and the Institutionalization of Learning

In order to understand modern education and its conceptions of knowledge and learning, it is essential to keep in mind its communicative traditions, which I will limit myself to discussing. Through institutionalization, a social activity such as education (or religion, the legal system, bureaucracy, health care, and so on) becomes visible as a social practice, establishes its raison d'être, and defines its modus operandi. Institutionalization is an important element of social continuity and change. "Institutions do the culture's serious business," as Bruner (1996, p. 30) puts it, and they tend to cultivate social practices that eventually may become so natural that they invisibly determine ideas and communicative patterns as well as physical resources such as buildings.

The development of schooling as an institutional activity per se is an illustration of an increasing complexity and division of labor in society. When the skills needed in society cannot be easily acquired in the family or in an informal setting, pedagogy has to be explicit and organized systematically, as I have already pointed out. Skills in literacy, numeracy, bookkeeping, and foreign languages take some time to master, and they require some kinds of curricula. At the same time, institutional forms of pedagogy, when doing the culture's serious business in Bruner's terms, operate with ambiguities and mixed messages. Teaching, rather than learning, became the organizing principle of schooling, and the latter was seen to follow more or less automatically from the former. Although one supposedly learns for life rather than for school, learning in the institutional setting very much became a matter of mastering forms of communication that were local and culturally very specific. The relation between this type of knowledge and everyday cultural practices turned very complex and largely indirect; as a consequence, schooling became abstract.

Institutions to some extent thus define their own realities. What counts as learning in schools is different from what counts as learning in other spheres of life. The goals of an institution that has learning as an overarching principle are different from those that characterize other activity systems – in the Vygotskian sense (Vygotsky, 1934/1986) – in society. Communication is based on the systematic learning of concepts and skills, and information is organized in terms of academic disciplines. As a consequence, the interactional patterns and individual actions differ from those that characterize other social settings. As an activity system, schools do business in a particular manner. Concepts such as *learning* and *knowledge* are highly metaphorical, but once they are given institutional definitions, their meanings have very concrete consequences.

In formal schooling, the *conduit metaphor*, or pipeline model, of communication (Reddy, 1979) has played a decisive role in determining how communication has been organized. In fact, it has served almost as a root metaphor (Lakoff & Johnson, 1980), invisibly regulating the roles of teachers and students. This metaphor implies that information and knowledge are transferred between people in a very concrete sense. As one person speaks, he or she encodes information and sends it to the receiver through a medium. The latter, in turn, decodes it. This metaphorical construction is grounded in a parallel with the technology of broadcasting. As Reddy points out, even the terms are the same: *sender, receiver,* and *medium.* The belief that information and knowledge pass from the teacher as he or she speaks to the student who listens has been foundational for schooling, and there are several elements of this metaphor that make up a coherent whole. The role of the learner is primarily one of receiving information and committing it to memory. This implies that learning is conceived as essentially passive, an activity that implies listening rather than participating, receiving rather than producing. Those are the basic expectations for the learner. The material that is to be acquired by the learner consists of a discrete piece of information that exists by itself as an independent, prepackaged fact or, alternatively, as a well-defined skill.

From a historical perspective, the wider social background of such an attitude to learning is not difficult to understand. The origins of the communicative practices that characterize formal schooling go back to a society in which information had to be committed to memory if it were to survive.

This was also a society in which information was scarce, and whatever new could be learned was channeled through the school and a small elite associated with such institutions. When schools begin to serve a broader group of citizens, however, this pattern of communicating implies that the agenda and the daily interactional patterns end up rather far away from the interests and backgrounds of many of those involved.

Historically, the separation of schools from other sectors of society is apparent both at a general level and in terms of the definitions of what was to be learned and the nature of the communication that became dominant. An obvious example of this is that Latin maintained a strong position in schools and other institutions of learning for centuries. Mastery of Latin has been seen as an essential part of the training of an educated person, even though its relevance in most other social sectors has been drastically reduced, to put it mildly. In the ideology of formal schooling, learning Latin syntax and vocabulary was not only a matter of acquiring an ancient language but was also construed as a way of exercising your mind in some general sense. The ideology of privileging Latin as the language of knowledge and social prestige could be maintained through the independence and relative isolation of schools from the rest of social life. An interesting observation in this context has been made by the Swedish historian of education Ödman (1995), who points out that the Protestant Reformation resulted in a rather swift change from using Latin in church to using the local language. This was a very important pedagogical revolution in many respects, because it made it possible for the public to participate in religious practices in a completely new manner. Although Latin was abolished in sermons and other church practices in the 16th century in Sweden, it did not lose its status in society. On the contrary, Ödman argues, it seems to have gained an even stronger position as the language of religious and secular knowledge and as a vehicle for cultivating one's mind. But the institution in which it survived after losing its position in Protestant religion was the school. One consequence of this was that schooling came to be separated even further from life in general, because there were no other contexts in which this language could be used for communicative purposes. Learning Latin, even more clearly than before, became an end in itself and an important element in the career of the chosen few who went on to study. But what was said and done during these lessons had very little relevance to the young boys of the time. Students read texts in Latin over and over again during lessons, and they practiced grammar and regurgitated quotations and long excerpts. But, very likely, they were not able to connect this activity to their social life in general; the ritual was in itself means and ends.

This preference for increasingly abstract forms of communication is one of the most significant features of education, even though Latin is perhaps an extreme example. The communicative traditions of education serve as resources through which new activities and content areas are adapted to fit institutional patterns; educational activities imply communicating about the world rather than acting in it. An interesting case in point, which clearly illustrates the firm traditions of how teaching in institutional settings should be carried out, has been given by the Swedish historian of literature Thavenius (1981) in his analysis of how Swedish was introduced as a subject in school after the Protestant Reformation in the 16th century. The very idea of teaching Swedish in school was revolutionary, and it presented the established school system with a concrete problem: What and how do you teach when you try to teach someone his or her own language, an area of knowledge and skill where people already have considerable expertise? This is a fascinating question. Those faced with this intriguing dilemma made choices that reflect assumptions indicative of an institutional definition of what learning in this particular setting was about. One element of the approach taken implied that the new subject was based on a normative conception of language. Teachers assumed the role of guardians of High Swedish, a language norm grounded in the written version of the language that, at the time, was available to only a small elite. They spent considerable time and energy correcting their students' use of language. The everyday spoken vernacular was considered inferior, sometimes even morally defective, and it had to be consistently monitored and corrected.

Even more interesting from the point of view of institutional definitions of learning is that the teaching process was modeled entirely on the tradition of Latin. The teaching of Swedish placed heavy emphasis on grammar, spelling, and the formal aspects of language. Students had to learn about the inflection of verbs, conjugations of adjectives, construction of passive forms, and the different tenses. And they had essentially the same difficulties with these grammatical features as they had always had in learning Latin. Being good at Swedish in this institutional definition meant knowing one's own language in a particular way and more or less as a foreign language. This is a very interesting historical instance of a tradition of teaching that is still very influential; knowing a language results from mastery of its grammar. And the focus on grammar, which can be conceived as a particular kind of meta-language about the structures of natural languages, represents a clear sign of the institutional inclination toward abstraction. In communicative terms, discourse about language in language teaching must be considered extremely abstract (which can be readily discovered in the kinds of learning difficulties pupils have in language teaching; Gustavsson, Linell, & Säljö, 1993). Such discourse requires that students distance themselves from their own everyday attitude toward language in order to view it as an autonomous system of symbols.

As learning activities became institutionalized, the nature of these activities changed. In the school setting, learning is very much a communicative activity; studying, as a sociocultural practice, implies that people learn largely through talking, reading, and writing. The almost exclusive reliance on language and the indirect relations to other social activities make learning abstract. One learns about objects and events that are not present but are introduced through spoken and written language and are organized in terms of academic subjects. One has to master concepts, rules, and formulas that are encountered as texts. The link to the outside world is often implicit and hard to establish. As Bruner (1996, p. 28) points out, the "chief subject matter of school, viewed culturally, is school itself." This is a dilemma of modern schooling; it introduces modes of communicating that cause what we have come to recognize as learning problems.

Although rare, historical studies of communication in school settings reveal the manner in which such demands began to cause problems for young people. In particular, these difficulties in adapting to new discursive practices became obvious when schools in the 19th century began to enroll children from diverse cultural and social backgrounds and school was made mandatory in many countries. A thorough analysis of the relation between institutional teaching and learning on the one hand, and student difficulties on the other, has been conducted by the historian D. Calhoun in his book entitled *The Intelligence of a People* (1973). Calhoun, who analyzed reports from school inspectors in the United States, found ample evidence of problems that had to do with students' inability to relate to the information they were learning in school in a meaningful manner. According to reports from the inspectors, during reading lessons, children were found "to read without expression, in a 'hum-drum' or 'sing-song' tone. Their manner was 'unnatural' and 'mechanical.' Pupils rarely succeeded in reading 'understandingly and effectively'" (p. 79). In a similar vein, pupils "could rattle through their reading lessons, but could not talk about what they had read" (p. 80), the inspectors noted. A report by a New York State superintendent in 1871 concluded that "children go hurriedly through their books, grasping a few disconnected points in a rote-like manner, and when brought to a test, fail in showing any knowledge of the principles that underlie the subject" (p. 80). The evidence convincingly demonstrates that pupils were dragged into intellectual territories where their frames of reference were no longer sufficient for keeping them in control of what they had to acquire.

These difficulties of coping with the abstract discourse practices that came to dominate schools became especially obvious for children and youth who were conceived of as slow learners. In a historical analysis of children and youth with more or less clearly defined learning problems and mental handicaps, Trent (1994) illustrated how children who could otherwise manage most aspects of their daily lives in the community without great difficulties were transformed into what he referred to as "six-hour retarded children." That is, their problems became visible as they were exposed to, and when they had to contribute to, such abstract institutional discursive practices as those dominating schools of the time.

In recent years, this issue of contrasting performances in everyday settings with school contexts has received considerable attention. As a matter of fact, the realization of the situatedness of human knowledge and skill is currently shaking the foundations of the psychology of learning field. In their much-acclaimed study of the mathematics of street vendors in Brazil, Carraher, Carraher, and Schliemann (1985) illustrated how almost perfect performance in transactions that involved buying and selling dropped considerably when mathematically identical items were introduced as school tasks. This was one of several studies that have helped raise awareness of this problem of the local nature of knowing, which had been sensed by many but never surfaced as a major issue in the previous intellectual paradigms.

The context of elementary mathematics learning is an interesting arena for illustrating the peculiar manner in which the discursive traditions of formal schooling present problems for children that do not appear elsewhere in their social lives. In 1997, the Swiss scholars Reusser and Stebler published a study of mathematics achievements among 10- to 12-year-old students that included the following items:

A boat sails at a speed of 45 km/h. How long does it take this boat to sail 180 km?

John's best time to run 100 m is 17 seconds. How long will it take him to run 1 km?

This pair of problems and many similar ones have been used in several studies (De Corte, Verschaffel, Lasure, Borghart, & Yoshida, 1999) over the past two decades. What is interesting about them is the dramatic difference in how children manage to handle these mathematically isomorphic problems successfully. In the study by Reusser and Stebler (1997) and that by Verschaffel, De Corte, and Lasure (1994), the first problem was correctly solved by 85% to 90% of the participants. Viewed as an instance of mathematical reasoning, and disregarding for the moment the referential problem of what was said in the text, the second problem was solved by an even higher percentage of students. The only catch was that the response was a simple multiplication of 10 by 17. Only a tiny fraction of the students in these empirical studies, 4.5% and 2.5%, respectively, indicated that there was something problematic about the second item.

Interestingly, the kind of mistake that children make on the second item illustrates the text-based nature of school activities. The multiplication, 10×17, is a natural response to a piece of text that is presented as a mathematics task. Unless you handle it in this manner, the problem is impossible to deal with as a mathematics task (a remark made by some thoughtful children on why they multiplied in this manner). My mathematician colleague, Jan Wyndhamn, and I conducted a study in the mid-1980s (Säljö & Wyndhamn, 1988) in which we attended to the same problem of how students interpret word problems. We asked the same age groups the following pair of questions:

> *A cow produces 18 liters of milk per day. How much milk does the cow produce during one week?*

> *Lisa goes to school and she has 6 lessons per day on the average. How many lessons does she have per week?*

Again, the first item is essentially unproblematic. About 90% of the students performed the multiplication: 7×18. In the second case, the situation turned out very differently. Among low achievers in mathematics, for instance, only about 40% managed to solve this problem because they realized that the reference to the concept of week in this case (in Sweden and many other countries but not everywhere) means 5 days.

In my opinion, these two studies illustrate something fundamental about institutionalized communication: that is, the manner in which we talk and write in school. The difficulties that these text-based traditions of communication present for children (and adults) can be understood in terms of their indirectness in relation to a lived reality. The exercises in elementary mathematics imply that children have to learn to *take meaning* – to use Olson's (1994) expression – from texts in a very particular manner. They have to be aware of the relation between what is assumed and what is claimed about the world in the text. When the world appears as an illustration in an exercise, it is there for a very specific purpose. It is not meant to be acted on in a direct manner. Rather, it serves as an illustration and a background of an institutional practice, which in this case is that of doing elementary mathematics. In substantive terms, the text could be about anything that produces the same kinds of arithmetic operations. And the results obtained in studies in this area (Greer, 1997) convincingly demonstrate how sensitive learners are to the traditions of designing test items and exercises. As soon as the tasks deviate from the standard version (as in the case of John running 1 kilometer), performance drops dramatically. Doing mathematics tasks is a matter of relating given figures to each other in specific patterns, not about considering what the world is like in an empirical sense.

The *exercise* can be seen as a prototypical element of the communicative practices that make up institutionalized schooling. It represents a particular form of contextualization (Linell, 1992) of the world that is specific to the educational system. The exercise represents a mode of organizing information so that, when attending to it, the reader qua learner will build up a set of skills that ideally will take him or her through such problems with success. When doing grammar or word problems, learners are assumed to acquire sets of skills that emerge as a consequence of being taken through these exercises. In this sense, the word problem in mathematics, as Lave (1992) points out, and the grammatical exercise represent a theory of learning. A cognitive skill is the outcome of consistent practice on items that share some defining features. Once acquired, the skill is there and can be used in relevant settings. In a similar manner, the *testing* of knowledge in schools is carried out within the same conception of knowledge. Knowledge and skills are tested as if they were discrete entities stored within the individual. In most cases, students are not allowed to use the tools and resources available to them in other settings. Thus, in a language test, they are not allowed to use a dictionary, and for mathematics tests, the presence of a calculator is often a problem.

The manner in which modern education requires that people alienate themselves from their personal, everyday experiences is readily visible in textbooks. Consider, for instance, the following excerpt from an introductory textbook in material physics written for A-level students in the United Kingdom:

1.2 Bonding

If an electron from one atom is shared with or transferred to other atoms, electrostatic forces come into play, and the atoms are strongly attracted towards one another. A primary bond is formed between the atoms. They are joined together to form individual molecules such as gaseous oxygen O_2, or three-dimensional structures such as sodium chloride, diamond or copper.

It is apparent however that, as the electrically neutral molecules which form oxygen can be cooled to form a liquid or solid, other attractive forces must also act when uncharged molecules come very close together and have little kinetic energy. These weaker – secondary – bonds arise from the redistribution of electrons *within* a particle. In a polymeric material such as polyethene, primary bonds join adjacent carbon atoms to form a molecular chain. Primary bonds also join the carbon and hydrogen atoms together. However, as polyethene is a solid at room temperature, other forces must attract the chains together. These are the weaker secondary bonds. (Cooke & Sang, 1986, p. 17)

To understand a text of this kind is a matter of being able to connect claims and statements within a very abstract discourse. There are no obvious links to a lived experience or to any kind of social action that is available for the student. The contextualization is specific to the particular practice of formal schooling. The text gives an account of what the world allegedly is like, and the reader is assumed to be interested in this. In historical terms, this is an extremely abstract type of discourse in form as well as content. It is written in a neutral third-person voice and presents a set of claims about physical entities that are true. The text is circular in the sense that it moves completely within a specific social language – in Bahktinian terms (Wertsch, 1998, pp. 76ff.) – in which the concepts are defined and the conclusions are drawn. The contrast between this type of text and texts that the majority of youth of this age will encounter when having a choice is probably striking. Learning to talk science (Lemke, 1990) involves appropriating and moving within very specific social languages in which the expressive registers probably appear highly constrained for young people.

Institutional Forms of Learning and Dialoguing with the Young

The traditional modes of communicating in schools rest on the assumption that schools had control over the information that would reach young people. As late as a few decades ago, the reading of a geography or history textbook was for many students their first contact with foreign countries, foreign peoples, and their lifestyles. School books in biology served as introductions to nature and to a world of more or less exotic animals and thought-provoking phenomena that students would not encounter in any other contexts. There were many stories to be told that the new generation had not heard. Today, this situation has changed dramatically. People encounter a wealth of information through other media, and the textbook is a genre that has considerable problems in staying up-to-date. Its status is being seriously challenged by other media in the modern classroom but primarily through the information channels that are available in everyday settings.

In a similar vein, modern education builds on the old tradition of assuming that knowledge and skills are stored in academic subjects. And these subjects form an important element of the administration and practice of schooling as we know it. But the academic subject is an abstract construction that organizes knowledge in a manner that is different from the way people encounter the world. The manner in which it contextualizes the world is often not immediately relevant to young people. The hidden curriculum of modern media is very different from this.

Institutions are conservative, often for a good reason. The continuities in teaching and learning practices over the past 150 years are impressive. The limited impact of new technologies in schools (Cuban, 1986) illustrates how strong the communicative traditions are. Suspicion and resistance have been the response to cultural innovations such as radio, television, the VCR, minicalculators, and, more recently, computers. But the pipeline model of communication will have to yield to other metaphors of knowledge and learning. In a democratic society, learning practices have to be accepted by those concerned, and they have to be relevant to their needs. Schools are no longer the only institutions producing knowledge and skills in society, but their role is still unique, and their curriculum is very different from that of the media. Schools serve as the most important context for systematic reflection on knowledge and for the production of a broad range of intellectual and practical skills that are more important than ever. It is interesting, however, to see to what extent the communicative practices of schooling can overcome the temptation to resort to abstractions when dealing with the wealth of information (mostly useless) produced. This is a formidable challenge that will put to the test many of our basic assumptions of what knowledge is like. The image of the isolated individual operating without resources other than what is in his or her head is still the dominant metaphor of learning. But this is no longer a valid model. Our competencies are much more sophisticated and distributed in artifacts and intellectual tools. The challenge for schools is to accommodate to a world in which their traditional conception of knowledge, neatly packaged into subjects, is no longer sufficient. The trick is to focus on what happens outside the school itself, to learn from other activity systems, and yet to maintain autonomy in terms of the ambitions to cultivate "a culture of reason, analysis, and reflection, based on certain shared knowledge" (Resnick, 1987, p. 14). No other institution in society is equipped to take responsibility for this important task.

The communicative traditions of formal schooling have their origin in an authoritarian society where information was scarce and hard to come by. There were few, if any, rival information sources on the scene to compete with the teacher and the textbook, and education was a privilege. The form and contents of education in general served the purpose of subordinating young people to a particular ideology in which they were taught to fear religious and secular elites. The questions and answers were provided by the institution, and the sole responsibility of the student was to connect the two. The transformation to a democratic society implies that socialization now is to be based on a voluntary commitment to learning knowledge and skills. Such a system requires that young people be given the opportunity to express themselves and their own interests in formal settings, and that the manner in which the activities of schools are negotiated is grounded in respect for the worldviews and priorities of youth. Education is a particular kind of ongoing conversation that society has with itself, a dialogue between generations. A democratic ideal assumes that the partners share the rights and responsibilities for keeping the dialogue going. For this to be success-ful, both sides have to be genuinely interested. Considering the origin of the communicative traditions of schooling, the transformation to such a situation will be quite a challenge.

REFERENCES

Berger, P., & Luckmann, T. (1966). *The social construction of reality.* New York: Doubleday.
Bruner, J. (1996). *The culture of education.* Cambridge, MA: Harvard University Press.
Calhoun, D. (1973). *The intelligence of a people.* Princeton, NJ: Princeton University Press.
Carraher, T. N., Carraher, D. W., & Schliemann, A. D. (1985). Mathematics in the streets and in schools. *British Journal of Developmental Psychology, 3,* 21–29.
Cooke, B., & Sang, D. (1986). *Physics of materials for A-level students.* Leeds, England: University of Leeds Press.
Coulmas, F. (1989). *The writing systems of the world.* Oxford: Blackwell.
Cuban, L. (1986). *Teachers and machines: The classroom use of technology.* New York: Teachers College Press.
De Corte, E., Verschaffel, L., Lasure, S., Borghart, I., & Yoshida, H. (1999). Real-world knowledge and mathematical problem-solving in upper primary school children. In J. Bliss, R. Säljö, & P. Light (Eds.), *Learning sites. Social and technological resources for learning* (pp. 61–79). Oxford: Pergamon Press.
Dewey, J. (1966). *Democracy and education.* New York: Free Press. (Original work published 1916)

Donald, M. (1991). *Origins of the modern mind. Three stages in the evolution of culture and cognition.* Cambridge, MA: Harvard University Press.

Foley, W. A. (1997). *Anthropological linguistics. An introduction.* Oxford: Blackwell.

Greer, B. (Ed.). (1997). Modelling reality in mathematics classrooms [special issue]. *Learning and Instruction, 7*(4), 293–397.

Gustavsson, L., Linell, P., & Säljö, R. (1993). Discourse in language and discourse on language. *International Journal of Educational Research, 19*(3), 265–276.

Lakoff, G., & Johnson, M. (1980). *Metaphors we live by.* Chicago: University of Chicago Press.

Lave, J. (1992). Word problems: A microcosm of theories of learning. In P. Light & G. Butterworth (Eds.), *Context and cognition. Ways of learning and ways of knowing* (pp. 74–92). New York: Harvester/Wheatsheaf.

Lemke, J. L. (1990). *Talking science: Language, learning, and values.* Norwood, NJ: Ablex.

Linell, P. (1992). The embeddedness of decontextualization in the context of social practices. In A. Heen Wold (Ed.), *The dialogical alternative. Towards a theory of language and mind* (pp. 253–272). Oslo: Scandinavian University Press.

Mithen, S. (1996). *The prehistory of the mind. A search for the origins of art, religion and science.* London: Phoenix.

Ödman, P.-J. (1995). *Kontrasternas spel 1–2: En svensk mentalitets-och pedagogikhistoria* [Play of contrasts 1–2: A Swedish history of mentality and pedagogy]. Stockholm: Norstedts.

Olson, D. (1994). *The world on paper.* Cambridge: Cambridge University Press.

Reddy, M. (1979). The conduit metaphor: A case of frame conflict in our language about language. In A. Ortony (Ed.), *Metaphor and thought* (pp. 284–324). Cambridge: Cambridge University Press.

Resnick, L. B. (1987). Learning in school and out. *Educational Researcher, 16*(9), 13–20.

Reusser, K., & Stebler, R. (1997). Every word problem has a solution: The social rationality of mathematical modeling in the school. *Learning and Instruction, 7*(4), 309–327.

Rogoff, B. (1990). *Apprenticeship in thinking.* New York: Oxford University Press.

Säljö, R., & Wyndhamn, J. (1988). A week has seven days. Or does it? On bridging linguistic openness and mathematical precision. *For the Learning of Mathematics, 8*(3), 16–19.

Thavenius, J. (1981, October). *Modersmål och fadersarv: svenskämnets traditioner i historien och nuetK* [Mother tongue and the inheritance of our fathers: Traditions of Swedish teaching in history and at present]. Järfälla, Sweden: Symposion Förlag.

Trent, J. W. (1994). *Inventing the feeble mind: A history of mental retardation in the United States.* Berkeley: University of California Press.

Verschaffel, L., De Corte, E., & Lasure, S. (1994). Realistic considerations in mathematical modeling in the elementary school. *Learning and Instruction, 4,* 273–294.

Vygotsky, L. S. (1986). *Thought and language* (A. Kozulin, Trans.). Cambridge, MA: Harvard University Press. (Original work published 1934)

Walker, C. B. F. (1990). Cuneiform. In J. T. Hooker (Ed.), *Reading the past* (pp. 15–74). London: British Museum Press.

Wertsch, J. V. (1991). *Voices of the mind: A sociocultural approach to mediated action.* Cambridge, MA: Harvard University Press.

Wertsch, J. V. (1998). *Mind as action.* Cambridge, MA: Harvard University Press.

12 Practice and Discourse as the Intersection of Individual and Social in Human Development

Jonathan Tudge

My goal in this chapter is to show how a focus on everyday practices, including discourse, allows us to understand the interpenetration of individual and social in the course of human development. A practice-based approach does not seek to explain development by reference only to individual factors, without simultaneous consideration of the social context within which the individual is acting, or to social factors, without examining the ways in which the social world is experienced differently by the different individuals inhabiting it. Such an approach is in keeping with the ideas of Vygotsky and Piaget, both of whom (albeit in different ways) eschewed the dichotomy of individual and social (Smith, 1996; Tudge & Scrimsher, 2003; Tudge & Winterhoff, 1993). The difficulties inherent in this more systemic approach, however, stem from the fact that most scholars interested in development have not been trained to think systemically but rather in terms of causal models inspired by the positivist tradition (Guba & Lincoln, 1994).

I would like initially to illustrate the issue by referring to Roger Säljö's recent article (2000), based on his presentation at the 1997 Johann Jacobs Foundation conference on social interaction. The session in which Säljö's talk took place appeared under the heading "How Knowledge Is Transmitted. . . ." In his article, Säljö rejected the use of this implicitly unidirectional formulation that has knowledge being transmitted from one (presumably more competent) individual or group to a (presumably less competent) receiver. Instead, he spoke about *appropriation*, a term that necessarily involves active participation by the learner. That change in terminology was helpful, given that Säljö's aim was to lead us toward an understanding of understanding that is not an individual construct but instead is rooted in social and discursive practices (see also Säljö, 1999).

His argument drew on sociocultural and discourse theory and the work of others in the sociocultural tradition to show that "psychological functioning [is] situationally intimately intertwined with social interaction" (2000, p. 35). Rather than thinking in terms of individual competencies (someone "possesses" some cognitive attribute or some knowledge of a concept), Säljö (2000) argued that learning is primarily about how individuals come to appropriate and use concepts in specific situations (*discursive practices*). Säljö placed himself squarely in opposition to a mentalist view of concepts that has them "residing inside individuals as abstract copies of an outside reality" (2000, pp. 36–37). Säljö's position was that one understands something in a specific context with no guarantee that the same understanding will be in evidence once the context is changed or the thing to be understood is in any way different. This is something that traditional cognitive researchers have had difficulty with for years, the problem of transfer, which is a problem only if we take an approach that has the individual owning some competence.

To this point, Säljö's (2000) argument was clearly in accord with the systemic perspective mentioned earlier. However, he also used wording that implied a more dualistic position and took an almost socially deterministic position, arguing that meaning is "to a significant extent determined by factors that lie outside the mental apparatus of the student" (2000, p. 35). If one takes seriously the position that knowledge does not lie within the skull of the individual but in the spaces between individual and other, it makes little sense to speak of inside the head and outside; it is while engaging in some practice or activity (being in a social situation) that one is able to succeed at some task (perhaps with help) or to show understanding of some concept, with no guarantee that one will be able to have the same success or understanding in a different context.

Elsewhere in the article, by contrast, Säljö seemed to want to retain the view that an individual possesses knowledge or competence. His statement that "Even a student sitting [alone with a book] cannot be conceived as involved in an activity that is entirely private and internal" (2000, p. 35) seems to suggest that the activity is *somewhat* private and internal, rather than being necessarily social, simply because the activity involves at least one social other (the author of the text). Säljö also stated: "The assumption that knowledge forms part of discourses leads to the scrutiny *not only of individual competencies* but also to an interest in the concrete conditions under which people act, and the constraints and affordances that are built into these situations" (2000, p. 38; emphasis added).

It is perhaps not surprising that this apparently dualist position (emphasizing at one time social determinants of cognition and at another time individual competencies) appeared in an article that sought to take a constitutive approach to cognition. The relations between individual and social are complex, and even among those who take what has been termed a *socio-genetic* perspective, there is debate about whether the epistemic individual, the active, thinking, planning individual, exists at all. Lightfoot and Cox (1997), reviewing recent writing on this topic, distinguished between different ways of conceptualizing the boundaries between self and other:

By one version, the child is understood to be part of a larger social or cultural whole; by the other, the child is seen as an ensemble of social relations. The first of these encourages a dissolution of boundaries, whereas the other insists on their centrality. (p. 7)

My view is that we do not want to lose sight of the individual, with his or her unique perspectives; but at the same time, we must acknowledge that individuals are socially created. We are all well aware of our own particular ways of making sense of the world. These ways are unique to us, our *personal culture* in Valsiner's (1989) term. As I have written elsewhere (Tudge, 1997), in one sense it is clear that I am writing this chapter (no one else has ever written exactly what appears before you) and that the ideas being expressed "are at one and the same time my own and a social product – the ideas of others, half-forgotten, combined, transformed, and reconstructed in their own peculiar way by me" (p. 129). Moreover, they are ideas that were highly influenced by Säljö's (2000) article or at least my interpretation of it. The trick is to understand that these ideas are at one and the same time individual *and* social, an interpenetration of individual and social, which is essentially the argument that Säljö is making. As Säljö expressed it:

I will not . . . regard understanding as an internal . . . psychological quality characteristic of a particular class of experiences. Even though I myself truly enjoy the feeling of understanding, I will consider the psychological dimension as a derivative of my participation in collective social practices. (2000, p. 36)

Does this mean, echoing Packer (1993), that, although individuals are social *in origin*, they are independent, autonomous beings as a result of their prior social experiences? I think not, for with every engagement in any practice (including reading a book in solitude or thinking), the individual is actively playing a part in a social world.

In the remainder of this chapter, I present some of the ways in which I would take Säljö's (2000) argument a little further, first placing his article into a broader metatheoretical framework and, second, moving away from a focus on discourse to activities more generally.

As Winegar (1997) has argued, it is helpful to place the theories that we find useful into their broader metatheoretical framework. As Säljö (2000) has pointed out, there is a crucial distinction between idealist and realist positions, on the one hand, and situated practices, on the other. The distinction is, I think, redolent of a broader shift that has been taking place in developmental psychology over the past few years, away from an individualistic and unidirectional approach to developmental issues. Increasingly, scholars are taking an approach to development that is more systemic, co-constructive, and dialectical, an approach that stresses the interrelatedness of social and individual aspects of development. This approach is by no means new; echoes are found in the writings of Baldwin, Dewey, Janet, Lewin, Mead, Piaget, Vygotsky, and others writing a century ago and into the 1930s (Cole & Engeström, 1993; Tudge, Gray, & Hogan, 1997; Van der Veer & Valsiner, 1991). The ideas may not be new, but perhaps the time is right for them to be taken seriously.

This is the argument that has been made by Guba and Lincoln (1994) in their discussion of competing metatheoretical paradigms. They contrasted positivist and postpositivist paradigms with the postmodern paradigms of critical theory and constructivism. Distinctions between them can be drawn in terms of ontology (the form and nature of reality), epistemology (the relation between the knower or would-be knower and what can be known), and methodology. The first two paradigms can be characterized by their essentially realist (naive or critical) ontological position, whereas the two postmodern paradigms may be characterized by a view of reality that is shaped both historically and at the local situated level. In terms of epistemology, the positivist and postpositivist positions reflect a dualist position in which the investigator and "subject" are separable entities, although this separation may be obtainable only through strict experimental control. By contrast, proponents of the postmodern paradigms argue that the relation is transactional, with no separation between investigator and participant in the study. As might be expected from these epistemological stances, positivist methodology relies on experimental and manipulative methods, whereas postmodern methodology involves dialogue and a dialectical stance (at least if the methodology is related to the underlying theoretical assumptions, something that is not always the case).

Another way in which it is possible to take Säljö's (2000) argument a little further is to place his ideas in the broader context of situated practice rather than simply in that of discourse, which, in Säljö's article, was involved in the process of trying to find out what someone knows in the course of interviews. This is not to argue that discourse is unimportant – far from it – but rather to point out that this type of interview may be an unusual type of practice in which to engage. As Säljö pointed out, children who are perfectly well aware of the number of days they go to school in a week can still be fooled by the nature and context of a question about days in a week. Similarly (using another example that Säljö incorporated into his paper), ice hockey players know precisely how hard to hit the puck to ensure that it begins to slow down before officials halt play for icing, and yet they may have great difficulty with a question that requires thinking about force and friction. Their understanding of these concepts may thus be more related to their everyday use of skills in one context (a specific type of practice) than to discourse. What may be more beneficial than interviewing participants in our studies about some concept or activity would be observing them and having them talk about the same things in the context of the relevant activity itself. Of course, this involves far more trouble for psychologists, which is why so many choose to engage in lab research or to interview in a context far removed from the setting in which the relevant activity typically takes place. Ethnographic studies of discourse, or of language development, allow us to see the ways in which children come to appropriate the concepts that are relevant in their cultural groups in the course of engaging in relevant activities and participating in discourse (see, e.g., Goodwin, 1990; Heath, 1983; Ochs, 1988; Schieffelin, 1990). Greater familiarity with and exposure to concepts or skills in a variety of contexts and practices may help children to appropriate them, to make them "their own" in the sense that they are able to show their understanding of the concept or their competent, skillful performance in a variety of different contexts (see also the study by Schoultz, Säljö, & Wyndhamn, 2001, of how children required to use an artifact, a globe, can successfully master conceptual structures that they otherwise could not). This does not imply, of course, that there will be no contexts in which the child fails to show understanding.

In fact, if we are truly interested in understanding the process of understanding, maybe we should move beyond situated discourse and focus instead on practices, practices that often feature language (interpersonal or intrapersonal). The work of Jean Lave (1988; Lave & Wenger, 1991) illustrates nicely the interpenetration of individual and social in the context of engaging in everyday activities, as does the research of those who have examined the ways in which mathematics is learned in school and on the streets (Nunes, Schliemann, & Carraher, 1993; Saxe, 1991) and the work of Cole and his colleagues in the area of reading (Cole & Engeström, 1993).

Other authors in this volume make very similar arguments about the necessity to study activities. Not surprisingly, given her earlier work (e.g.,

Heath, 1983), Shirley Brice Heath (this volume) is particularly interested in analyzing the discourse of the adolescents who participated in the youth-based organizations that she has studied. As one of her informants pointed out, however, "When you do something where you create, it builds something inside you that never really goes away" (p. 49). Analysis of discourse may well be an effective way to understand how adolescents become drawn into, change, and are changed by an activity, but it is by *engaging* in that activity (not simply by talking about such engagement) that one changes and is most changed. Discourse is relevant to change, of course, and Heath provides nice examples of the ways in which her adolescent participants use language to help refine their understandings of the rules of the organization, the roles that they are learning to fulfill, and so on. Nonetheless, participation in the activities in every way, including linguistically, is key. Discourse without practice would signify little.

Karsten Hundeide's work (this volume) dealing with counterculture youth movements, rather than with the more socially acceptable groups that Heath studies, illustrates the same basic point: that discourse is but one aspect of a broader range of activities in which people engage in the process of becoming a part of the group. Hundeide discusses the roles played by actions that "express and confirm the recruit's status as an insider and often conflict with one's previous values. These actions may involve taking some drug, participating in some criminal action against the recruit's previous code of morality, or simply taking on the style and extreme uniform of a youth movement and thus appearing in public with the other participants."

My own recent research (Tudge, Hogan, & Etz, 1999a; Tudge et al., 1999b; Tudge & Putnam, 1997) is also focused on the ways in which individuals appropriate an understanding of their culture's concepts, skills, and practices in the course of participating in their everyday activities. This work does not relate to adolescents but rather to young children as they move from the preschool years and enter formal schooling. The points that I wish to make are generally applicable, however, and not relevant only to young children's development.

I would argue that the best way in which to understand this process is to observe it in action, focusing on the types of commonplace activities in which people often engage. I illustrate this with some details from my research. My colleagues and I have collected a great deal of observational data (20 hours per child, spread over the course of 1 week in order to encompass a complete waking day) on preschoolers in a single medium-sized city in each of various countries, including the United States, Russia, Estonia, Finland, Korea, and Kenya. The children were observed wherever they were situated:

at home, with friends or relatives, in a preschool center, and so on. We focused on the activities going on around the children (those that were potentially available to them), the activities in which the children engaged, how those activities started and how the children became involved, partners in those activities, and the roles taken by participants in the activities in which the children were involved. Those who were around the children (i.e., teachers, parents, friends, and others who played important roles in their lives) made activities available to their children in various ways. They engaged in those activities themselves (e.g., cleaning house, watching television, reading a newspaper, playing) and encouraged or discouraged their children from engaging in those activities. They made available to their children objects that they wished their children to engage with (e.g., books, television, toys, at least in industrialized, wealthy societies) and talked to their children about things they deemed interesting and important. At the same time, the children themselves were actively involved in the process of participation in the activities that were available, trying to engage in some activities that those around tried to discourage them from, and initiating new activities and trying to recruit others to join in with them.

Because the project is designed to be longitudinal, with data collected again once the children have entered school, our first publications have focused on those activities that may be most apropos to school-related competencies. These activities are lessons that relate to literacy or numeracy (academic lessons); lessons about how to do things or about the workings of the natural world (skill/nature lessons); looking at a book or using school-relevant materials, but without an explicit lesson being involved (play with academic objects); and being involved in conversation with one or more adults (conversation). In each of the cities, children whose parents are well educated by the standards of the society and whose occupations are professional (i.e., middle class) engage more in these types of activities than do children whose parents do not have higher education and whose jobs are not professional (i.e., working class). It could be that the reason for this differential involvement is simply that the middle-class parents think that it is more important for their children to engage in these activities than do working-class parents. If this is so, the former make such activities more available to their children (a unidirectional, culturally transmitted view of the process of development). It is particularly striking, however, that at least some differences in engagement between middle-class and working-class children result from the former being more likely to initiate those activities themselves. In other words, the children actively involve themselves in activities that those around them deem important.

What are some of the consequences of inhabiting social systems that encourage different types of activities? I am trying to argue not that, by engaging in lessons or talking with adults, children simply learn more, but that they come to understand that these activities are considered important by significant others in their lives. They come to have meaning beyond the specific lesson that is or is not being learned in the course of interaction. What is being appropriated by the children is revealed in their willingness to initiate similar types of experiences, asking questions, or trying to engage adults in conversation. To put this in clearer focus, it is worthwhile to look at a different type of lesson that we coded: interpersonal lessons, or lessons about how to behave well with others. Our U.S. data show that middle-class children (particularly boys) engaged in more academic lessons, whereas working-class children (particularly girls) engaged in more interpersonal lessons. When looking at these gender differences, the inferences that can be drawn are striking: Middle-class boys inhabit a social world in which things academic are viewed as important (by adults and children alike), whereas working-class girls are learning that what is important is knowing how to behave appropriately with others. Subsequent encounters with the social world are then influenced by what these children have come to see as appropriate and what they have made their own through their earlier participation in practices with others.

In some sense, of course, this is the essence of the sociocultural approach: to show that, through engagement in activities, children come to be drawn into the social world and to learn, through participation with others who are more competent, the skills and concepts deemed relevant and important in that culture. However, this point is complicated by the fact that cultures are not homogeneous entities. It is one thing to argue that different cultural groups value different competencies, whether for all children or further differentiated for boys and girls within the group. But the situation is more complex when the cultural groups can be thought of as subcultures within a larger culture. In such a case, one subculture's competencies may well occupy a more privileged position than do others. For example, in the United States at present, academic competence is valued more highly than interpersonal competence. What are the long-term consequences of engaging in and initiating these types of academically relevant activities, as opposed to spending more time learning interpersonal lessons? The data suggest (Tudge, Odero, Hogan, & Etz, 2003) that there is a moderate relation between these types of academically related activities and teachers' perceptions of their academic competence approximately 4 years later, when the children are ages 7 and 8, both in terms of initiation of these activities ($r = .24$) and for engagement in them ($r = .40$). It is necessary to point out that these children are for the most part in different schools and have different teachers, so the teachers are not comparing middle-class and working-class children within the same classroom. The story is thus more complex than simply that middle-class children in the United States engage in more of these activities and are viewed as more academically competent by their teachers than are working-class children.

At this point, it may seem that I have focused too much on practice in general and excluded discourse as one example of practice. There is more of a connection, however, than might be apparent. Of the four activities (academic lessons, skill/nature lessons, play with academic objects, and conversation with adults) that I have discussed so far, one was far more related to teachers' perceptions of academic competence than were the others: namely, conversation with one or more adults. The correlation between preschoolers' initiation of conversation with an adult and perceived competence 4 years later at school was a remarkable .67, and engagement in conversation was also highly correlated ($r = .59$). Moreover, the one activity that was not at all predictive of later academic competence was play with academic objects. Of the four activities of interest, this was the only one that did not necessarily involve some discourse. It is thus apparent that, through participation with others in everyday activities (particularly discursive activities), individuals come to be perceived as competent. Those perceived to be more competent in any domain are likely to be treated differently (often better) from those perceived to be less competent, thereby continuing to illustrate the interrelations of psychological functioning and social interaction, as Säljö (2000) argued in his article.

It is worth emphasizing that these processes are by no means limited to children's development. Adolescents and adults, like children, engage in myriad activities in which discourse may play a large role, a small role, or no role at all. By engaging in activities, often in conjunction with others, we all (no matter what age) become more competent at those activities. We do so sometimes because we engage with others who are more competent. Examples include children engaging with an adult in work or play, as well as adolescents becoming involved in a youth organization with others who are already members. However, we also become more competent as we engage with others who are less competent; for example, professors often understand concepts at a higher level after teaching them to students. It would thus be a mistake to think that such interactions are simply *scaffolding*, or a more competent partner providing the necessary assistance to enable the less competent partner to learn or become more skilled. The process is dynamic and dialectical, not unidirectional. What is done and said by any one person in any interaction depends in part on what the other is doing and saying. What each of the participants appropriates from the interaction is different, because the sense or meaning of the interaction is different for each and is understood differently because of prior experiences and understandings. As teachers, we know that, no matter what concept we try to "transmit," we can guarantee that there will be as many new understandings as there are students, each of whom will transform what is said in light of his or her previous understanding of the concept. There can thus be no simple transmission from one to the other: Instead there is a transactional relationship in which what each appropriates from the interaction is socially constructed and individually transformed.

The more that individuals engage in different practices, discursive or otherwise, with different people in different settings, the more they come to be seen as being competent at those practices. Indeed, we may consider people to be competent or to have understanding when they can display it in a variety of settings rather than in just one specific setting. Competence or understanding is then deemed an individual attribute: What has been appropriated from multiple engagements in practice is part of the individual's personal culture and will be part of what the individual brings to subsequent encounters with the social world. Competence or understanding is thus simultaneously entirely individual and entirely social.

REFERENCES

Cole, M., & Engeström, Y. (1993). A cultural-historical approach to distributed cognition. In G. Salomon (Ed.), *Distributed cognitions: Psychological and educational considerations* (pp. 1–46). New York: Cambridge University Press.

Goodwin, M. H. (1990). *He-said – she-said: Talk as social organization among black children.* Bloomington: Indiana University Press.

Guba, E. G., & Lincoln, Y. S. (1994). Competing paradigms in qualitative research. In N. K. Denzin & Y. S. Lincoln (Eds.), *Handbook of qualitative research* (pp. 105–117). Thousand Oaks, CA: Sage.

Heath, S. B. (1983). *Ways with words: Language, life, and work communities and classrooms.* New York: Cambridge University Press.

Lave, J. (1988). *Cognition in practice: Mind, mathematics, and culture in everyday life.* New York: Cambridge University Press.

Lave, J., & Wenger, E. (1991). *Situated learning: Legitimate peripheral participation.* New York: Cambridge University Press.

Lightfoot, C., & Cox, B. D. (1997). Locating competence: The sociogenesis of mind and the problem of internalization. In C. Lightfoot & B. D. Cox (Eds.), *Sociogenetic perspectives on internalization* (pp. 1–21). Mahwah, NJ: Erlbaum.

Nunes, T., Schliemann, A. D., & Carraher, D. W. (1993). *Street mathematics and school mathematics.* New York: Cambridge University Press.

Ochs, E. (1988). *Culture and language development: Language acquisition and language socialization in a Samoan village.* New York: Cambridge University Press.

Packer, M. J. (1993). Away from internalization. In E. A. Forman, N. Minick, & C. A. Stone (Eds.), *Contexts for learning: Sociocultural dynamics in children's development* (pp. 254–265). New York: Oxford University Press.

Säljö, R. (1997, November). *Concepts, learning, and the constitution of objects and events in discursive practices.* Invited presentation, "Joining Society: Social Interaction and Learning in Adolescence and Youth." Johann Jacobs Foundation Communication Center, Marbach Castle, Germany.

Säljö, R. (1999). Concepts, cognition and discourse: From mental structures to discursive tools. In W. Schnotz, S. Vosniadou, & M. Carretero (Eds.), *New perspectives on conceptual change* (pp. 81–90). Oxford: Pergamon.

Säljö, R. (2000). Concepts, learning, and the constitution of objects and events in discursive practices. *Cahiers de Psychologie,* No. 46, Université de Neuchâtel, 35–46.

Saxe, G. B. (1991). *Culture and cognitive development: Studies in mathematical understanding.* Hillsdale, NJ: Erlbaum.

Schieffelin, B. B. (1990). *The give and take of everyday life: Language socialization of Kaluli children.* New York: Cambridge University Press.

Schoultz, J., Säljö, R., & Wyndhamn, J. (2001). Heavenly talk: Discourse, artifacts and children's understanding of elementary astronomy. *Human Development, 44,* 103–118.

Smith, L. (1996). The social construction of rational understanding. In A. Tryphon & J. Vonèche (Eds.), *Piaget-Vygotsky: The social genesis of thought* (pp. 107–123). Hove, England: Psychology Press.

Tudge, J. R. H. (1997). Internalization, externalization, and joint-carving: Comments from an ecological perspective. In B. Cox & C. Lightfoot (Eds.), *Sociogenetic perspectives on internalization* (pp. 119–131). Mahwah, NJ: Erlbaum.

Tudge, J. R. H., Gray, J., & Hogan, D. (1997). Ecological perspectives in human development: A comparison of Gibson and Bronfenbrenner. In J. Tudge, M. Shanahan, & J. Valsiner (Eds.), *Comparisons in human development: Understanding time and context* (pp. 72–105). New York: Cambridge University Press.

Tudge, J. R. H., Hogan, D. M., & Etz, K. E. (1999a). Using naturalistic observations as a window into children's everyday lives: An ecological approach. In C. Shehan (vol. ed.) & F. M. Berardo (series ed.), *Contemporary perspectives on family research, Vol. 1: Through the eyes of the child: Re-visioning children as active agents of family life* (pp. 109–132). Greenwich, CT: JAI Press.

Tudge, J. R. H., Hogan, D. M., Lee, S., Meltsas, M., Tammeveski, P., Kulakova, N. N., Snezhkova, I. A., & Putnam, S. A. (1999b). Cultural heterogeneity: Parental values and beliefs and their preschoolers' activities in the United States, South Korea, Russia, and Estonia. In A. Göncü (Ed.), *Children's engagement in the world* (pp. 62–96). New York: Cambridge University Press.

Tudge, J. R. H., Odero, D. A., Hogan, D. M., & Etz, K. E. (2003). *Relations between the everyday activities of preschoolers and their teachers' perceptions of their competence in the first years of school.* Early Childhood Research Quarterly, 18, 42–64.

Tudge, J. R. H., & Putnam, S. A. (1997). The everyday experiences of North American preschoolers in two cultural communities: A cross-disciplinary and cross-level analysis. In J. Tudge, M. Shanahan, & J. Valsiner (Eds.), *Comparisons in human development: Understanding time and context* (pp. 252–281). New York: Cambridge University Press.

Tudge, J. R. H., & Scrimsher, S. (2003). Lev S. Vygotsky on education: A cultural-historical, interpersonal, and individual approach to development. In B. J. Zimmerman & D. H. Schunk (Eds.), *Educational psychology: A century of contributions* (pp. 207–228). Mahwah, NJ: Erlbaum.

Tudge, J. R. H., & Winterhoff, P. A. (1993). Vygotsky, Piaget, and Bandura: Perspectives on the relations between the social world and cognitive development. *Human Development, 36,* 61–81.

Valsiner, J. (1989). *Human development and culture: The social nature of personality and its study.* Lexington, MA: Lexington Books.

Van der Veer, R., & Valsiner, J. (1991). *Understanding Vygotsky: A quest for synthesis.* Oxford: Blackwell.

Winegar, L. T. (1997). Developmental research and comparative perspectives: Applications to developmental science. In J. Tudge, M. Shanahan, & J. Valsiner (Eds.), *Comparisons in human development: Understanding time and context* (pp. 13–33). New York: Cambridge University Press.

13 Talking Matters

Studying the Use of Interdependencies of Individual and Collective Action in Youthful Learning

David Middleton

Although my research is not directly focused on issues of learning and interaction in youth and adolescence, there are implications for the sort of research agenda that might be pursued in that area. My work examines how, in our interactions with others, we identify and use past experience, and in particular how we establish continuity and change in the social organization of our lives in social groupings and organizational settings. I am particularly interested in how we use interdependencies of experience as both individually and collectively relevant. For example, projects concerned with multiprofessional teamwork in hospital settings (Middleton, 1996) and with families talking about the significance of holiday photographs (Middleton & Edwards, 1990) examined what it is to be a "team" or a "family." Such studies are both occasioned and made relevant in designating and claiming experience as individually and collectively accountable. Such an approach can be applied to a consideration of social interactions and learning in adolescence and youth. For example, we can examine how what-it-is-to-be-young is used as a conceptual resource in communicative activity concerning social interaction and learning in adolescence and youth. We do not need to describe a priori the conditions that define what it is like to be young. We can study how joining society is accomplished in terms of talk in which the topic of concern is what-it-is-to-be-young. We can examine possibilities of experience that may or may not be attributed to such a category. The argument is that you cannot separate the condition of being young from the ways in which what-it-is-to-be-young discursively resources the very practices in which youthful membership is sought and accomplished. Analysts (i.e., researchers interested in these issues) and participants (i.e., young people who are the subject of their own actions and the actions of others)

204

have positions in the very issues that are at stake in being a young person. Similarly, what-it-is-to-join and how notions of what constitutes society are accomplished and studiable in communicative action concern boundaries of participation and nonparticipation.

Does joining imply some inevitable disjunction between youth and those they might join as they move into adulthood? Others have written extensively on whether it is possible to define a special category of being and attendant issues bounded by some notion of youth and adolescence (e.g., A. K. Cohen, 1955; P. Cohen, 1997; S. Cohen, 1973; Furlong & Cartmel, 1997; Garratt, Roche, & Tucker, 1997; Griffin, 1993; Hall, 1908; Hall & Jefferson, 1976; Hebdige, 1979). One of the important implications of a discursive approach to learning in interaction is that debates defining the status of what-it-is-to-be-young are not just the province of researchers. They resource the communicative action of those who would define themselves as young. An examination of communication as social action places interdependencies of individual and collective action at the center of any research agenda on discursive practices of learning. This is a key issue if we are to unpack issues concerning the interdependencies of learning and interaction in terms of interdependencies in individual and societal action.

In Roger Säljö's presentation to the 1997 Johann Jacob Foundation conference on "Joining Society: Social Interaction and Learning in Adolescence and Youth," it is possible to identify three interdependencies of individual and collective action (see also Jonathan Tudge's discussion of Säljö's work, this volume). These include interdependencies between the objects of learning and the social practices of learning; between the discursively realized identities of the learner and the objects of learning; and between the individual appropriation of modes of reasoning and the rhetorical organization of institutional practices of learning. My initial concern with these interdependencies is threefold. Conceptually, they provide a means of avoiding forms of social reductionism in discursive studies of human action, where the interactional and social merely displace the individual as the central analytical and theoretical concern (cf. Valsiner, 1994). Then I would argue that interdependencies of individual and social action are precisely where the action is, both as analysts and as participants. For example, as I have already indicated with respect to my own work, interdependencies of experience as both individually and collectively relevant are attended to in the sequential organization conversation in organized settings of work and family experience. Finally, examining interrelations of individual and social action resources a research agenda on learning and social interaction in youth and adolescence that has at its center interdependencies of theory and need. The point is that talking matters, and the matter of talk as constituted in the interdependencies of individual and social action collapses the divide between research and practice. The main thrust of my discussion is to identify a number of interdependencies that are worth further research attention in discursive studies of learning and interaction in youth and adolescence.

Objects of Learning and the Social Practices of Learning

In the field of learning, it is possible to separate out what is being learned from the flow of activities and situated practices in which learning occurs. This is more than a plea to examine the ecology of learning. More than that is at stake. The key point is that we cannot assume in advance just which activities and what practices of learning are relevant (Dunne, 1993). These are established in communicative action. In addition, such action always involves people in adopting some position on what is at hand. We are inevitably drawn into taking a stand on the communicative reality that is being made relevant or foregrounded.

Discursively Realized Identities of the Learner and the Objects of Learning

There are also crucial interdependencies between the discursive identities of someone who is positioned as a learner and what are taken to be objects of learning. In adopting a discursive position on learning, however, we are confronted with a number of key questions. Is it just that the contents of mind may be social? In other words, we face challenges to our competence and understanding in relation to issues set by others, whereas the intellectual processes of our minds (their organization and how we do it) remain essentially our individual property. Or does the social basis of mind go deeper than this into the very processes of reasoning and feelings of competence and incompetence? If we take up a discursive agenda, is it no more than the study of learning as realized in and through various forms of joint action, be they with peers or adults? Or is the discursive position capable of supporting stronger claims in which what develops is familiarity with modes of reasoning that are the tools for reasoning in new realms of practice?

Modes of Reasoning and the Rhetorical Organization of Institutional Practices of Learning

This brings me to the third interdependency, between the individual appropriation of modes of reasoning and the rhetorical organization of

institutional practices of learning. In such a view, the relation between institutional forms of reasoning and learning is crucial. The privileging and
perspectivization of knowledge and understanding within modes of dis
cursive action are crucial resources in the constitution of what it is to be a
member or not of domains of practice that have cultural relevance.

Dickens (1854/1970) graphically illustrated the link between the power
of knowledge and the knowledge of power in his cryptic parody of Victorian
education in *Hard Times*:

"Bitzer," said Thomas Gradgrind, "Your definition of a horse."
"Quadruped. Graminivorous. Forty teeth, namely twenty-four grinders, four
eye-teeth and twelve incisive. Sheds coat in the spring; in marshy countries sheds
hoofs too. Hoofs hard, but requiring to be shod with iron. Age known by marks
in mouth." Thus (and much more) Bitzer.
"Now girl number twenty," said Gradgrind. "You know what a horse is."
(p. 6)

We may pride ourselves that such iconoclastic domination of the tutorial
process is no longer a property of contemporary educational practices. For
girl number twenty to thrive in Gradgrind's world, she must learn to know
what it is to know in terms of discursively mediated performances that
Gradgrind marks as institutionally relevant. What is it to find your footing
in terms of such practices? Dickens was an astute observer. The government
inspector compounds just what is discursively relevant in his subsequent
exchange with the class.

"Very well," said this gentleman, briskly smiling, and folding his arms. "That's
a horse. Now, let me ask you, girls and boys, Would you paper a room with
representations of horses?"
After a pause, one half of the children cried in chorus, "Yes sir!" Upon which
the other, seeing in the gentleman's face that Yes was wrong, cried out in chorus,
"No, sir!" – as the custom is, in these examinations.
"Of course, No. Why wouldn't you?"
A pause. One corpulent slow boy, with a wheezy manner of breathing, ven-
tured the answer. Because he wouldn't paper a room at all, but would paint it.
"You must paper it" said the gentleman, rather warmly.
"You must paper it," said Thomas Gradgrind, "whether you like it or not.
Don't tell us you wouldn't paper it. What do you mean, boy?" (p. 7)

Individual and collective formulations of understanding are interdependent. The power of knowledge and the knowledge of power are interrelated. Such uncertainties of relevance are precisely what vexes contemporary
sensibility. Finding some sure footing in the discursive practices of learning

is constitutive of what goes for understanding in both formal and informal settings. The final implication of the discursive argument is that we should look to the rhetoric of privileging that occurs in such practices where understanding is grounded and formulated in terms of interdependencies of individual action and institutionally mediated practices.

Such arguments provide a context for discussing four other interdependencies of learning as both an individual and a collective enterprise: interdependencies between visibility and learning; vernacular and institutional learning; improvisation and reasoning; and uncertainty and certainty of being ordinary. My argument is that the discursive formulations of such interdependencies are also key resources in the constitution of what is at stake and to be established in discursive practices of youthful learning.

Visibility and Learning

Jerome Bruner (1990) argues that it is "by virtue of participation in culture, that meaning is rendered public and shared.... We live publicly by public meanings and shared procedures of interpretation and negotiation" (pp. 12–13). Derek Edwards (1997) concludes that "The 'learnability' of discursive and other cultural practices stems from their visibility, or public nature" (p. 296). The implication of this is that the problem of learning is not treated as a matter of conceptualization, where people with minds and experience must have communicated to them in one form or another those forms of wisdom to which other cultural members are already parties. The focus of discursive analysis is the way in which "psychological states, actions, events, beliefs, dispositions, motives and so on, are conceptualized, invoked, and talked of" (Edwards, 1997, p. 296). Within this view, we do not learn concepts that allow us to move into public spheres of debate and practice. Rather, the issue is how "psychological discourse is possible, learnable and works as an element of public practices" (p. 296). As Edwards points out, this position is not new. It draws from debates in "ordinary language philosophy" outlined by Ryle (1949) and Wittgenstein (1958) and, in addition, from the writings of C. Wright Mills (1940) on situated actions and vocabularies of motive:

Motives are imputed by others before they are avowed by self. The mother controls the child: "Do not do that, it is greedy." Not only does the child learn what to do, what not to do, but he is given standardised motives which promote prescribed actions and dissuade those proscribed. Along with rules and norms of action for various situations, we learn vocabularies of motives appropriate to them. (p. 907)

My work on how people in families and other groups conceive of their pasts and display both understandings and the resources for taking meaning from such cultural artifacts as photographs is one attempt to follow the interdependencies of visibility and learning (e.g., Buchanan & Middleton, 1996; Edwards & Middleton, 1988; Middleton & Edwards, 1990). For example, viewing family photographs not only provides an opportunity to invoke various interpretations and changes of family membership, relationships, and identities but also makes visible the very processes that enable children to justify plausible claims to experience. Children have demonstrated both what it is to make experience claims in relation to what may or may not be depicted and how it is that they can make such claims stick as part of any rhetoric of justification. If we turn, for example, to the problematics of learning in adolescence, we can identify equivalent issues. Making analytically visible those cultural practices that derive meaning and form from argument and justification is just one way of developing the discursive agenda of research into the linkages between social interaction and learning.

Widdicombe and Wooffitt's (1995) study of identity talk and authenticity of membership in youth culture provides an example of this type of research. Their work examines how people build authentic memberships in terms of how they discursively manage, in the sequencing of their talk, their own position and identity of subgroups. Widdicombe and Wooffitt focus on youth culture, but their approach is equally suited to any issue that relates to the nature of inclusion and identity of membership. Identities are demonstrated as part of personal stories that attend to motive and accountability.

Economou's (1994) work also provides a detailed example of how young persons' participation in microcultures of musical performance makes visible interdependencies of these practices as both leisure and possible work. His analysis explores music making as youth subculture and how such practices are both penetrated by and afford the possibility of participation beyond the organized settings of "youth clubs" and in the institutional setting, where making music is, or could be, taken as a form of work. Such research examines how young people succeed and fail in constituting their actions in ways that work the boundaries between leisure and work. The challenge is to build analytical bridges between settings that carry with them an orientation to learning and accomplishments as visible enterprises (e.g., worlds of fashion and music making) and settings (e.g., the youth clubs in Economou's study or the youth-based organizations in Shirley Brice Heath's work, this volume) that display equivalent yet "invisible" accomplishments.

Making analytically visible those cultural practices that derive meaning and form from argument and justification is just one way of developing the discursive agenda of research into the linkages between social interaction and learning. Bruner (1990) puts it in the following way: "Narrative becomes an instrument for telling not only what happens but also why it justified the action recounted" (pp. 86–87). We should note, however, that the rhetorical crafting of accounts finds voice in both vernacular and institutional settings.

Vernacular and Institutional Learning

One of the implications of Economou's work is that, from a discursive perspective, it makes little sense to separate the vernacular/informal from the institutional. The challenge is to understand the interdependencies of motive and accountability that permeate and are deployed in settings, however we choose to designate them. Clearly, in institutional settings such as formal schooling and higher education, certain forms of reasoning are given premium value. As Vygotsky's work on scientific concepts reminds us, however, it would be foolish to lose analytical sight of the interdependencies of understanding across vernacular and formal settings. Rhetorical practices of claim and counterclaim are common to both.

For Vygotsky (1934/1987), the achievement of conscious awareness (the capacity to turn around on the objects of consciousness; cf. Bartlett, 1932) was through the "gate opened by scientific concepts" (p. 193). Such concepts relate to systems of knowledge that are the product of cultural invention. According to Vygotsky, we do not develop as independent learners within everyday activity but through the agency of other members of that culture within the context of instruction. Through exposure to scientific concepts, concepts that presuppose a system of knowledge grounded within social practices of cultural institutions such as schools, the potential for conscious awareness and reflective thinking is brought about.

In Vygotsky's (1934/1987) terms, conscious awareness is the hallmark of the voluntary exercise of "higher mental functions." At the same time, scientific concepts are not independent of children's everyday concepts because they are the very things that "become the objects of conscious awareness and systematisation" (p. 217). The term *zone of proximal development* was coined and the importance of social interactions was emphasized as a way of linking these two strands of situated thinking. Vygotsky describes scientific concepts as growing "downwards through everyday concepts, while everyday concepts move upward through the scientific" (p. 220). Thus, the notion of the zone of proximal development was a theoretical construct for bridging two domains of conceptual activity: those to be found in formal settings and the product of forms of instructive activity and those that are the spontaneous product of the child's everyday activity in vernacular settings. The essential point for Vygotsky was that scientific concepts were seen as outstripping the development of everyday concepts, because, in a sense, they are precoordinated with one another and reflect higher-order relationships that have already been worked on and incorporated into the domain of discourse that mediates and within which the child is introduced to them.

Whether the distinction drawn between everyday and scientific concepts can be maintained in the form that Vygotsky outlined is certainly a matter for further debate. His arguments do, however, address the interdependencies of mindful practices in vernacular and institutional settings. The discursive agenda can be seen as one way in which this semiotic analysis can be taken forward. Certainly the challenge of understanding the demands placed on young persons in formal settings remains a worthy topic of concern. How they achieve full-fledged membership in communities of practice that depend on the achievement of what Vygotsky referred to as *concrete abstractions* (e.g., any conceptual discourse in which the objects of concern are the interdependencies of conceptual objects) is one issue that can be tackled through the discursive approach to learning. However, interdependencies of discursively accomplished reasoning in vernacular and institutional settings are resourced in terms of another important interdependency: the interdependency between improvisation and learning.

Improvisation and Reasoning

In a discussion of Bakhtin and Vygotsky, Caryl Emerson (1983) argued that crucial to the accomplishment of reasoning

is the presence of a challenging verbal environment. The descriptive "monologue" of which egocentric speech is composed can be internalised creatively only if questioned and challenged by outside voices. In this way alone is intelligence possible, intelligence defined not as an accumulation of already-mastered skills, but a dialogue with one's own future and an address to the external world. (p. 11)

Such a view implicates the improvisational design of situated reasoning. Reasoning should be conceived of not only as the presentation of inner logic but also as a dialogic based in the improvisational accomplishment of reasoning in communicative action. This would imply that settings that are subversive of formalization, where fun and irony are the topic of concern, are also worthy topics of analytic attention. Subversive play is resourced in terms of that which is being subverted.

The improvisational sequencing of articulate resistance is as much a resource for learning as is compliant engagement. Within this view, it may well be a more powerful resource. Resistance engages witcraft of argument, be it in the street culture of ritual insults (see, e.g., Marjorie Goodwin, 1990) or in the rejection of knowledge claims in classroom discourse. The improvisational nature of such argument richly resources reasoning as a situated accomplishment and is another area for the focus of research into youthful learning. Such improvisation is also resourced by uncertainty. This brings me to the final interdependency that I wish to highlight: the interdependency of certainty and uncertainty on the nature of ordinariness.

Uncertainty and Certainty of Being Ordinary

Harvey Sacks (1970/1992) argued that what it is to be an ordinary person cannot be taken for granted. Being ordinary is something we work at in our communicative relationships with others. Ordinariness is not an inevitable product of being an ordinary person. Rather, we accomplish, in our communicative relationships with others, that our lived experience of life can be taken as being the experience of an ordinary person. Interdependencies of certainty and uncertainty over what it is to be ordinary also resource learning as a discursive practice. The rhetoric of achievement, educational attainment, and economic inclusion so favored in political discourse on young people challenges the status of talents as the projectable property of persons who claim their experience as ordinary. The dilemmatic status of talent provides for crucial tensions between the certainties of achieving ordinary talents for understanding in contrast to the uncertainties and fragilities of "being talented." By the same token, how problems are positioned as peculiar to you and how you do things can be contrasted with problems as a routine property of a particular domain of action. How we manage such interdependent contrasts in the discursive working up of memberships based in culturally loaded competencies is another area of research interests and practice in the interactive study of learning.

Concluding Remarks

These interdependencies were formulated in the context of relating a discursive approach to learning to the conference topic "Joining Society: Social

Interaction and Learning in Adolescence and Youth." Establishing a research agenda on social interaction and learning involves examining interdependencies of individual and collective action. I have outlined how such interdependencies are featured in Säljö's work on discursive approaches to learning. In addition, I have identified other ways in which the interdependencies of individual and collective action are realized in the context of youthful learning. We can draw some further implications concerning interdependencies of theory and need from that conference title. For example, concepts of youth and adolescence are not just the property of academic research, policymakers, and those who work and live with younger people, be they teachers, social workers, or parents. Like all concepts, *youth* and *adolescence* are terms freely available for all to use in their claims concerning lived experience by the old or the young (see, e.g., Garratt, et al., 1997). If we take up arguments concerning learning as a discursive practice, the very notion of what-it-is-to-be-a-youth and adolescence are usable as conceptual resources, in contrast to de facto descriptions of stages of being from childhood to adulthood. In this view, the relevance of these terms goes beyond some putative description, mundane or otherwise, of a period in life. Such concepts are part of, and resource, the very activities associated with what it is to be designated as a young person.

Thus, any designation of youth need not necessarily be defined in terms of fixed attributes of people. What it is to be designated as young is more likely to be defined in terms of interdependencies of persons and their social actions. As a son-in-law, I may be attributed understanding of experience fitting that of a youth. As a father, however, I am frequently denied youthful understanding. Both attributions resource communicative actions that make relevant interdependencies of position, experience, and understanding in forms of reasoning that make up interpersonal relations in families and other social groupings. Social memberships and identities are thus formulated in communicative action.

In the field of learning, it is impossible to separate out what is being learned from the flow of activities that are made relevant as part of the situated practices in which the learning is taken to occur. Communicative action is central to this, and once any process of engagement or resistance is in progress, it is impossible to ask a question without first adopting some position on what is at hand. We are inevitably drawn into taking some stand on the communicative reality that is being made relevant or foregrounded. Talking matters, and the matter of talk frames and gives voice to research and practice. Where theory and need meet are interdependent concerns.

REFERENCES

Bartlett, F. C. (1932). *Remembering: A study in experimental and social psychology.* Cambridge: Cambridge University Press.

Bruner, J. S. (1990). *Acts of meaning.* Cambridge, MA: Harvard University Press.

Buchanan, K., & Middleton, D. (1996). Voices of experience: Talk and identity in reminiscence groups. *Ageing and Society, 15,* 457–491.

Cohen, A. K. (1955). *Delinquent boys: The culture of the gang.* London: Free Press.

Cohen, P. (1997). *Rethinking the youth question: Education, labour and cultural studies.* London: Macmillan.

Cohen, S. (1973). *Folk devils and moral panics.* St. Albans, England: Paladin.

Dickens, C. (1970). *Hard times.* Harlow: Longman. (Original work published 1854)

Dunne, J. (1993). *Back to the rough ground: Practical judgment and the lure of technique.* South Bend, IN: University of Notre Dame Press.

Economou, K. (1994). *Making music work: Culturing youth in an institutional setting.* Linköping, Sweden: University of Linköping, Team K.

Edwards, D. (1997). *Discourse and cognition.* London: Sage.

Edwards, D., & Middleton, D. (1988). Conversational remembering and family relationships: How children learn to remember. *Journal of Social and Personal Relationships, 5,* 3–25.

Emerson, C. (1983). Bakhtin and Vygotsky on internalization and language. *The Quarterly Newsletter of the Laboratory of Comparative Human Cognition, 5*(1), 9–12.

Furlong, A., & Cartmel, F. (1997). *Young people and social change: Individualization and risk in late modernity.* Buckingham, England: Open University Press.

Garratt, D., Roche, J., & Tucker, S. (1997). *Changing experiences of youth.* London: Sage.

Goodwin, M. H. (1990). *He-said–she-said: Talk as social organisation among young black children.* Bloomington: Indiana University Press.

Griffin, C. (1993). *Representations of youth: The study of youth and adolescence in Britain and America.* Cambridge: Polity Press.

Hall, G. S. (1908). *Adolescence, its psychology and its relation to psychology, anthropology, sociology, sex, crime, religion and education.* New York: Appleton.

Hall, S., & Jefferson, T. (1976). *Resistance through rituals.* London: Hutchinson.

Hebdige, D. (1979). *Subculture: The meaning of style.* London: Methuen.

Middleton, D. (1996). Talking work: Argument, common knowledge, and improvisation in teamwork. In Y. Engeström & D. Middleton (Eds.), *Cognition and communication at work* (pp. 233–256). Cambridge: Cambridge University Press.

Middleton, D. (1997). The social organisation of conversational remembering: Experience as individual and collective concerns. *Mind, Culture and Activity: An International Journal, 4*(2), 71–85.

Middleton, D., & Edwards, D. (1990). *Collective remembering.* London: Sage.

Mills, C. W. (1940). Situated actions and vocabularies of motive. *American Sociological Review, 5,* 904–913.

Ryle, G. (1949). *The concept of mind.* London: Hutchinson.

Sacks, H. (1992). Doing "being ordinary." In G. Jefferson (Ed.), *Harvey Sacks lectures on conversation* (Vol. 2, pp. 215–221). Oxford: Blackwell. (Original work published 1970).

Säljö, R. (1997). *Concepts, learning and the constitution of objects and events in discursive practices.* Paper presented at "Joining Society: Social Interaction and Learning in Adolescence and Youth," Johann Jacobs Foundation Conference, Marbach Castle, Germany.

Valsiner, J. (1994). Co-constructionism: What is (and is not) in a name. In P. van Geert & L. Mos (Eds.), *Annals of theoretical psychology* (pp. 1–15). New York: Plenum Press.

Vygotsky, L. S. (1987). *Thinking and speech* (N. Minnick, Trans.). London: Plenum Press. (Original work published 1934)

Widdicombe, S., & Wooffitt, R. (1995). *The language of youth subcultures: Social identity in action.* Hemel Hempstead, England: Harvester Wheatsheaf.

Wittgenstein, L. (1958). *Philosophical investigations* (2nd ed.). Oxford: Blackwell.

14 Young People's Use of Information and Communication Technologies
The Role of Sociocultural Abilities

Jacques Perriault

Observing students building knowledge with digital media leads us to assert that some sociocognitive abilities that are trained within family life and more generally in social life can play an unexpected role in enabling youngsters to use media for accessing knowledge. Focusing attention on students' representations and behaviors when using media definitely shows that the usual vision of electronic tools always enforcing transmission of knowledge is nothing but a technician's illusion (Perriault, 1989; Pochon & Grossen, 1994). Our observations of young people using telecommunication and computer devices, including interactive videoconference equipment (Jaecklé & Perriault, 1998) and video games (Perriault, 1996), for entertainment or education show the prominent role of specific abilities that are hidden by the global notion of interactivity that is commonly used to describe such activities (Perret, 1996; Perriault, 1996, 1998). The abilities stressed here are both metacognitive abilities (Lowyck, Elen, Proost, & Buena, 1995) – namely, time management, parallel processing, and multi-level analysis of communication devices – and social abilities in collaborative study.

Sociocognitive Abilities

Time Management by Students
We have observed the use of telecommunications facilities that link students with teachers or experts at a distance through interactive videoconferences and Internet forums (Jaecklé & Perriault, 1998). For interactive videoconferencing, a panel of experts, teachers, and students were gathered in a studio on the broadcasting site. The duration of the session was strictly fixed: one and

a half hours. The broadcast was received on TV screens viewed by groups of tutors and students at universities. Viewers were allowed to raise questions via telephone or fax. An appropriate person at the broadcast site selected those deemed most significant and transmitted them to the expert panel. A moderator on the set managed the whole broadcasting time. Surprised by the contrasting attitudes of students, we felt obliged to advance a hypothesis in order to understand these discrepancies.

Contrasted Behaviors in Time Management

Our observations related to time management by teachers and students at the reception site can be summarized as follows:

- More than half of the group followed both expert speeches and consecutive interactions with some delay.
- Some students viewed in a group, whereas others did so individually. Students working in a group managed time constraints more effectively than did those working alone.

For many students, the effective challenge of such a session was not to acquire knowledge but to manage time in a retrospective way (Arnaud et al., 1996). When synchronous media are used for learning purposes, conflicts appear between performing a complex task and practicing time management. Success implies an ability to perform many tasks at the same time.

Parallel Processing Abilities

During broadcast sessions, students were forced to perform the following unusual tasks at the same time:

- Identify which level of the communication system was actually concerned: teachers, experts, students at the broadcast site, another university group at a distance, or their local group.
- Take notes while simultaneously looking at the screen (which traditional TV viewing does not require).
- Ask neighbors for information and make comments *mezzo voce* (which the French school model does not allow).

Various media, such as video games and computers, frequently require the user to observe simultaneous evolutions of icons, data links, and so forth on a screen and to make correlative decisions that have to be implemented. Video games, particularly arcade games, are a good example: The player has to shoot many vessels attacking him or her at the same time from different areas on the screen. This implies an ability to interrupt one task because another one suddenly has a higher priority; to perform and to close the second task; and then to come back to the previous task and complete it (Perriault, 1996). Computer scientists know how to manage these embedded structures with a pushdown storage automaton, but many people encounter difficulties in parallel processing. This has to be stressed because digital media require more and more such ability.

Management of time and the parallel processing of simultaneous tasks appear to constitute one hindering factor when media are being used to build knowledge. Beneath this factor lies the risk of increasing the digital divide between students and more generally between users and nonusers of computers.

Conflicting Reference Models
The observed students behaved as if they were alternatively referring to two reference models that conflict in this process of accessing knowledge. One of these is a traditional teaching model that produces a continuous flow of ideas delivered by the teacher, an exchange of questions and answers, and a flexible allocation of time. The other is a mass media model in which attention is focused on events, whatever their contents. Unlike the teaching model, however, the flow here is discontinuous. It is a string of changes and breaks regulated by a rigid technical inner timer. Students felt – correctly – that there was no place to negotiate on time allowance. Although they did not clearly perceive these as conflicting models, students tried to manage and to balance them. After each video session, they were required to look at the videocassette recording of it. They were reluctant to have the teacher interrupt their viewing of the video, even for good pedagogical reasons. They all seemed to want to hear a continuous flow (pedagogical model) after a disrupted one (mass media model; Jaecklé & Perriault, 1998). Remember that many students had difficulty correctly identifying the structure of the communication system.

Ability to Discern Levels of Information Processing
In this study, there were at least two levels of information processing and interaction: local reception sites and a global broadcast system. The first or local level relates to how the group handled the educational message. Performing at this level implies the ability to identify the type of a given sequence, for example, dialogue at a distance between the panel and dispersed groups and exchanges among experts on the panel versus dialogue between experts and student panelists. Some students were unable to discern the

student panelists from the experts for various reasons, including the use of a foreign language and mass media stereotypes such as the assumption that if a given person is a TV panelist, then he or she must be an expert. Performance at this level also implies the ability to separate data from comments, which is all the more difficult because experts themselves frequently mix the two kinds of messages. For instance, an expert presented ecological data concerning two conceptions of *ecology* – one "natural," the other "cultural" – without explaining that this distinction was based on his personal opinion.

The second level concerns the global structure of the communication device. Performance at this level implies an ability to understand the protocol and to build an inner spatial representation of the whole architecture and the information flow. Many students encountered difficulty understanding specific functions of the system, such as the possibility of querying from a distance, which implies time anticipation for suggesting a project to others, being admitted to the group, and sending a question to the broadcast site. Students also had difficulty understanding that this communication device permitted only very short, precise questions and that often the answer was also very short and required close attention. Several times when the group succeeded in having a query admitted to the broadcast site ahead of others from various universities in Europe, the situation resembled a sports competition more than an educational exchange. The group was so excited when they were successful that they hardly paid attention to the answer. Here the mass media model takes the place of the educational one because of the competitive process.

In such communication situations, time anticipation, collaborative work, and the ability to interact at a distance play a prominent role. Thus, we may assume that mastering new technologies of communication is related to social abilities much more than has been acknowledged.

Social Abilities

In our field of interest, the role of the family appears to be very significant. Our investigations have been concerned with cultural and relational abilities inherited from the family.

Sociocultural Abilities
Where does the ability to process information in a parallel way come from? Youngsters playing video games or learning at a distance show contrasting attitudes and performances. Some studies on cultural inheritance have allowed us to generate interesting hypotheses about this issue (Fouquet,

Haicault, & Boffety, 1991). They suggest that the ability to manage two processes at the same time is developed at an early age by interactions between mother and child. From direct observations of mothers and their children at home between breakfast time and their departure for school, the authors emphasize the role of what they call the *morning time sequence*. According to their research, this sequence trains children to manage *social times*. They have identified contrasting mothers' attitudes in terms of time management skills, characterized by the types of orders given to the children, namely:

- Mode of transmission, for example, imitation and repetition, maieutics, or didactics. The distinction between the authoritarian mode and the substitutive one is of particular interest to us. The first one imposes a rigid sequence of tasks – "to wash, then to have breakfast, and if it is not yet ready, to wait." The second one, however, allows permutations of order such as "If breakfast is not yet ready, do something else."
- Formulated anticipation (or lack thereof) of the time schedule for home activities, such as "You have ten minutes for breakfast," and school-oriented activities.
- Autonomy partially or totally granted to children to perform these tasks.
- Homology between home timing and school timing.

Further investigations should explore how the ability to embed tasks evolves in adolescence. Looking at how waiters and waitresses do or do not gather orders and bring dishes one by one or several at the same time shows clearly that this ability is not used actively by everyone.

Relational Abilities

Another ability that enables people to master the use of computers relates to the management of social relationships. About 15 years ago, we performed a 2-year investigation into the effective practices of new technologies by young people in the 13th district of Paris. We wanted to study how noninstitutional groups were set up to practice technologies and how technologies favored their cohesion. We were interested in a particular concept developed by Jacques Ellul (1980): that of the *communiel*. For Ellul, the notion of communion – understood as an active symbolic linking inside a community, in the religious sense – is applicable to technical artifacts, which also generate communities: "The technician system . . . implies and generates communion relationships under different forms" (p. 148). We stated the relevance of this concept, as we observed for 2 years two groups playing rock music and another group developing activities with electronic technologies, on the radio and on the computer, respectively (Boudinot, Boffety, Daphy, Descolonges, & Perriault, 1985). This study drew our attention to the social abilities of these young people facilitating their mastering of digital devices, for rock music as well as for computer applications.

During our 2 years of contact, the members of the electronic group shared an interest in discovering broadcast and computer techniques and made up an affinity group of three to five persons (boys only). They understood that electronic techniques are very complex and imply working in a cooperative way. At the beginning, the electronic group was motivated by a conflict between one of its members and a teacher at the *lycée* where he studied. When we first met them, they were testing radio communication through walkie-talkies between the teacher's room inside the school and outdoors, trying to hear what the teachers had decided about their friend's future. Then they decided to retaliate by replacing the shape of a space vessel in a video game that they enjoyed with the shape of the teacher; this made it possible to explode the teacher's shape when they shot at it. To carry out this project in which they were strongly invested, the students succeeded in dumping the computer program, identifying the routine relative to the vessel, and building up the other one. Around 1984, that was still relatively possible, because the game they diverted was not as sophisticated as games are today (Boudinot et al., 1985).

The members of the electronic group did not aim to own a computer but thought that they could use the machines located in places such as computer shops and schools as a potential park. It was obvious to them that such machines quickly became obsolete, a fact that most adults had not yet come to understand. Their social ability to negotiate access to machines in diverse locations has to be considered one of the abilities that are useful in learning technology by oneself.

The rock music groups that we followed were particularly good in such interactions. These youngsters were experienced at social networking because there were either militants or musicians in their families. In both cases, networking is imperative, either for political or economic reasons.

Conclusion

As we have observed, young people are very sensitive to change provoked by new technologies of information and communication in their management of time and their development of knowledge. Such change reveals deficiencies in various abilities. As a further hypothesis, we can assert that abilities such as parallel processing of information, multilevel analysis of a device, collaborative work, and social networking help them to master the use of these digital technologies. The family culture plays a significant role in transmitting or not transmitting the ability to engage in parallel processing of information, collaborative work, and social networking. The assumption, then, is that social marking and social links play roles that may be decisive in mastering the digital culture.

It is highly probable that teachers and students in the future will learn to improve their management of such communication devices. But the risk of being a dropout still threatens young people who lack the appropriate abilities to meet the requirements of such technologies.

REFERENCES

Arnaud, M., Dubois, H., Fualdès, V., Jaecklé, L., Misseri, M., Perret-Clermont, A.-N., Perriault, J., & Porte, L. (1996). *Project humanities. Work package 4. Research and evaluation* (Final Draft). Poitiers: Centre National d'Enseignement à Distance, Laboratoire de recherche sur l'industrie de la connaissance.

Boudinot, J. F., Boffety, B., Daphy, E., Descolonges, M., & Perriault, J. (1985). *Rock ou micro-informatique. Enquête sur des adolescents du 13ème arrondissement de Paris* [Rock music or computing? An investigation of teenagers in the 13th district of Paris] (Collection Rapports de Recherche, No. 1). Paris: Institut National de la Recherche Pédagogique.

Ellul, J. (1980). *L'empire du non-sens* [Empire of nonsense]. Paris: Presses Universitaires de France.

Fouquet, A., Haicault, M., & Boffety, B. (1991). Production domestique des acteurs sociaux. Apprentissage des temps sociaux liés à l'école [Domestic production of social actors: Learning social times related to school]. In Programme *Héritage du quotidien* [Inheritance from everyday life] (Final Report, pp. 125–149). Paris: CNRS/IRESCO.

Jaecklé, L., & Perriault, J. (1998). Synchronous communication as a disturbing element of a university curriculum. In *Research perspectives on open distance learning: A collection of research papers from four projects supported by the European Union. Joint action on open distance learning* (pp. 145–159). Bologna: Scienter.

Lowyck, J., Elen, J., Proost, K., & Buena, G. (1995). *Telematics in open and distance learning. Research methodology handbook.* Leuven, Belgium: European Open University Network.

Perret, J. F. (1996). Un enseignement universitaire par vidéotranmission: *Comment les étudiants interprètent-ils la situation de formation?* [University instruction by videoconference: How do students understand the training situation?]. Unpublished manuscript, University of Neuchâtel, Switzerland.

Perriault, J. (1989). La logique de l'usage. Essai sur les machines à communiquer [The logic of use: Essays on communicating machines]. Paris: Flammarion.

Perriault, J. (1996). *La communication du savoir à distance* [Communication of knowledge at a distance]. Paris: L'Harmattan.

Perriault, J. (1998). Le temps dans la construction des savoirs à l'aide des médias [Time in knowledge building with media]. *Revue Européenne des Sciences Sociales, 36*(111), 109–118.

Pochon, L. O., & Grossen, M. (1994). Définition d'un espace interactif pour aborder l'étude de l'utilisation d'un ordinateur [Definition of an interactive space for studying computer use]. *Cahiers de Psychologie de l'Université de Neuchâtel, 31*, 27–47.

V

INTERGENERATIONAL SITES FOR THINKING

15 Thinking with Others

The Social Dimension of Learning in Families and Schools

Clotilde Pontecorvo

My primary research effort over the past 10 years has been devoted to quasi-ethnographic studies of verbal interactions in schools (Pontecorvo, 1992) and families (Ochs, Pontecorvo, & Fasulo, 1996). That research contributes to the issues raised in this volume by throwing light on conditions that can facilitate cognitive and social elaborations in children and adolescents during their complex socialization process in society.

This research interest began while I was studying curriculum implementation in innovative school settings with an interdisciplinary group of researchers. I was particularly struck by the collective development of reasoning through arguing and opposition, which could easily be observed when primary and secondary schoolchildren had the right to speak freely, as in a normal conversation (Pontecorvo, 1987). In social settings such as autonomous or teacher-guided groups, students were allowed and requested to say what they actually thought about a physical or biological phenomenon, a social event, a historical document, a literary text, an everyday issue, and so on: in other words, about something that was really questionable and problematic for them and that they wanted to understand thoroughly. As shown by scholars such as Barnes (1976; Barnes & Todd, 1977), it is possible to create the proper motivation to think and learn in children when interacting and speaking in a group within the context of primary or secondary schools.

In this chapter, I address four related issues.

1. Group interaction is not only a communicative facilitator but also a means of sharing the pain of thinking and reasoning and the difficulties of facing new problems (Pontecorvo & Ajello, 1994). Such interaction is a strong facilitator of thinking, because these pains and difficulties associated with learning can be shared in a process of cooperative thinking.

Interlocutors can co-construct, even at the level of sentence production, a phenomenon that developmental researchers had found in early verbal interaction between mother and child, particularly in first language acquisition.

We observed that this collective thinking activity was facilitated by classroom discussion guided by an attentive teacher (see Castiglia, Pontecorvo, & Stilli, 1987; Pontecorvo, 1984, 1988, 1989, 1993; Pontecorvo, Ajello, & Zucchermaglio, 1991; Pontecorvo, Castiglia, & Zucchermaglio, 1983). We identified and checked the relevance of certain features of the teacher's guide as a variable linked to children's more elaborated discourse (Orsolini & Pontecorvo, 1992b). Teachers can be trained to facilitate students' interactions through a guided collective analysis of their taped interactions with children.

2. It is critical that teachers mirror or rephrase what children have said so that they can elaborate on their discourse. Requests for information or explanation were not very effective in having children produce more elaborate answers. With strong oppositive sequences between children, the teacher's verbal behavior was less relevant.

We also found – at least in Italian culture, in which arguing and verbal dispute are acceptable ways of interacting (as shown by other researchers, such as Corsaro, 1990) – that contrast and opposition provide a natural spurt for productive communication between peers: Disputes on cognitive topics concerning both story reconstruction and the world of physical objects can easily be produced between 4- and 5-year-old children in preschool settings (Orsolini & Pontecorvo, 1992a).

Our research group, based at the University of Rome and composed of researchers and expert teachers, began to experiment with different settings of small-group interactions in both science education (Pontecorvo et al., 1991) and history teaching (Fasulo, Girardet, & Pontecorvo, 1998; Pontecorvo & Girardet, 1993). We discovered the depth of the students' analyses when the natural conditions of conversations were (re)established within the classroom and students could advance and check their hypotheses. Such situations include the possibility of mistakes, as in any other learning and thinking activity. The fear of error may be a remnant of the operant conditioning theory or of an older school tradition that abhors errors. Agreeing with the old Italian dictum *sbagliando si impara* (one learns by making mistakes), I strongly maintain that school – compared with the everyday world of work and training – is still one of the few places where children and students are allowed to make mistakes.

This may present a paradox. In a sense, school, operating as a useful tool to facilitate children's "joining" society, has to make it possible for students to practice in natural conditions of interaction (as in other communities of practice) in which autonomy and responsibility are progressively attributed to all members of the group. It is a serious limitation, however, when other conditions of learning (e.g., vocational or further training settings) are made too similar to schools in their formal aspects. Similarly, focusing too much on the role of school learning and achievement for designing future work careers must be avoided.

3. Formal and informal educational institutions must make it possible for learners and apprentices to try other routes, to take unexpected turns, to find their way while risking making mistakes. Schools (and families) are socialization places in which it is possible to practice skills rather freely, without undue negative practical consequences.

In another study, carried out with Castiglia, Di Chiara, and Tavanti (in preparation), we focused on 10-year-olds' conceptions of air pressure in studying both the interaction processes within children's groups (starting from amazing simple experiments about air and water) and the pretest and posttest results of individual conceptions of air pressure (investigated in individual interviews). Although we found an evolution of children's conceptions as measured by the interviews, we began to reflect more deeply (see also Pontecorvo & Girardet, 1993; Resnick, Säljö, Pontecorvo, & Burge, 1997) on whether we should consider learning as only the change in the individual answers (and in the management of the interview, as Perret-Clermont, 1993, said) or as what the children had learned to practice by interacting with the materials and by speaking, in a semantically contingent way, among themselves: in other words, by learning to participate in a social exploratory activity, as some researchers have also emphasized (Matusov, 1996; Rogoff, 1990).

4. Consequently, a significant change in the traditional concept of learning is needed. Learning is not just a change in the skills and/or in the conceptual structure of an individual mind. An important part of learning is critical for adult life concerns, including ways of behaving, of interacting and working with others, of facing problems, of practicing diverse scientific or technical methods, and of actively participating in communities of practice, which all have a cultural, normative background. This is evident in any professional training, be it that of the musician or the mechanic: Learning a job is not only technical training but also a complex process of cultural and professional socialization.

Based on this point of view and with a research interest in what happens in formal educational institutions, we began to study family interaction by observing particular Italian families during dinner table conversations, with three main aims:

- To determine whether family discourse, as a multiparty natural conversation, can be considered as the prototype of an asymmetrical participation structure in which parents and older children take the lead and the younger ones participate in a progressively more competent and active way.
- To determine whether it was possible to see via family discourse how children (and parents qua parents) practice thinking and reasoning and how much these cognitive activities are discursively based.
- To determine how much the genesis of the argumentative skills of children could be seen in family discourse, particularly in conflictual sequences.

After collecting an adequate number of dinner conversations and carefully transcribing them (we now have almost 70 protocols from more than 20 families living mainly in Rome and Naples), we found a new world of natural interactions open to us.

We discovered how complex discourse was in families with children who entered into it through the right conversational rules of topic drift (Sterponi & Pontecorvo, 1996a); how everyday events and stories were conarrated as much by the protagonist as by the other participants (Pontecorvo, Amendola, & Fasulo, 1994); and how children were challenged by parents and had to respond to requests for recounts and accounts (Pontecorvo & Fasulo, 1997). Accountablity is always present in families and concerns all members at any age (Pontecorvo, 1996b), although parents seem to concentrate their more demanding requests in the period between ages 5 and 9. They are much more cautious with younger children (in our sample between ages 3 and 5), who still have "to learn how to speak for accounting," and with preadolescent or adolescent children, who are less problematized by parents (Sterponi & Pontecorvo, 1996b), perhaps because older children counterargue, often strongly and in elaborated ways, as we show later in this chapter. These older children are very keen to reveal parents' contradictions between what they say and what they do.

As might be expected, discourse about rules and values is common in family conversations. Parents want to teach their children how to behave properly and to be convinced of the need for doing so; but when topics are complex (e.g., sexual and genre education, relationships with other people, conflicts about rules), parents sometimes cannot solve their children's problems (Pontecorvo & Pirchio, 1997). In general, there appears to be a clear difference when problematic discourse concerns children's breaking rules: Parents frequently announce possible negative consequences if children do not comply with parental rules. In this parental behavior, we detect the genesis of the typical forms of argument previously found in young children (Orsolini, 1991; Pontecorvo, 1995; Pontecorvo & Sterponi, 2001), which contradict other speakers by showing the negative or false consequences of what has been stated.

When knowledge of the world is at stake, the child, frequently the oldest one, initiates a problematization or "a request to be taught" that is addressed to the parents, sometimes even with some insistence (Pontecorvo & Sterponi, 1997). From a series of different families, we have determined that parents learn to be parents through the active mediation of their younger and older children (Pontecorvo, Fasulo, & Sterponi, 2001).

Aimed at understanding the ontogenesis of learning and thinking in families, our study of family dinner talk taught us that learning is, in most cases, embedded in larger socialization practices in which both children and parents are thinking, learning, and defining their identities reciprocally.

If we consider learning as a process of becoming tuned to diverse communities of practice by children and students (Resnick et al., 1997), the discursive practice of children and parents in the family arena is a relevant activity setting for developing reasoning skills that can then be used in diverse social endeavors and not just in school. The request for accountability, which is present in any family conversation, can be a route to taking responsibility for action and discourse that is considered typical of any adult activity and is often considered difficult to implement and practice in formal school settings.

It would be helpful to have a better understanding of how the formal learning of teachers and other skilled professionals can be implemented in an apprenticeship setting. Clearly, important questions concerning identities and selves would be at stake when issues of learning both a tradition and an attitude to change are considered.

We have looked at families with children between $3\frac{1}{2}$ and $5\frac{1}{2}$ years of age and at older siblings ranging in age from 7 to 14 years. This chapter concludes with some excerpts of family conversation showing the complexity and difficulty of interactions between parents and older children. Younger children are always more protected and excused, whereas more is asked of older ones. The parents, more or less consciously, are using the principle of diversity according to the different ages and personalities of their children, although the children are eager to be treated in the same way and seek equality between themselves.

Excerpt 1

Nacchi Family. Mother asks 14-year-old Ludovica to help 3½-year-old Antonia; Ludovica reacts negatively, requesting that Dad also participate in the family management. Emotional tension increases in the family and is probably decreased somewhat by the TV, which is purposively turned up loud:

1. Mum: Ludovica per piacere vai a.
               Ludovica please go.

(Ludovica imitates the voice of an orangutan pointing to the other speakers, one after the other)

2. Antonia: mamma no # quella di Biancaneve [= la mela]
               Mummy, no. I want Snow White's apple.

3. Mum: e questa non è di Biancaneve?
               and this is not Snow White's.

4. Antonia: **no** [whining].

5. Mum: e la vuoi andare a scegliere tu <nel frigorifero>?
               And do you want to choose it by yourself in the fridge?

6. Antonia: <è tutta verde>
               it's all green

7. Mum: e vabbè (:va bene) d'accordo allora questa me la prendo io
               Vai a scegliere tu nel frigorifero
               All right, okay, then I'll take this one for myself;
               go and choose one yourself in the fridge
               e poi vattela a lavare subito da Ludovica lavale
               la mela che sceglie per piacere
               and then have it washed by Ludovica, the apple that you
               chose.

8. Ludovica: mamma mi scoccio
               Mummy, I am annoyed

9. Mum: e gliela lavi lo stesso Ludo(vica).
               and you wash it for her too, Ludovica.

10. Ludovica: no gliela lava papà.
               no, Daddy has to wash it for her

11. Mum: forza muoviti.
               go on, quickly

12. Ludovica: vabbè però papà sparecchia.
               all right, but Daddy will have to clean off the table

13. Mum: siccome lo stai facendo tu ogni giorno
               as if you do it every day (*ironically*)

14. Ludovica: ohh
15. Mum: Ludovica smettila di fare l'imbecille
                Ludovica, stop being the stupid girl
16. Papà: <tanto lo sappiamo giè>
                we already know it
17. Mum: <che lo sei>
                that you are so
18. Ludovica: ohh.
19. Mum: stai zitta imbecille sta zitta!
                shut up, stupid, shut up!
20. Ludovica: ohh

(Silence follows).

This excerpt makes it immediately clear that the adolescent, Ludovica, has a difficult role in the family. Although the problem is triggered by the younger girl, Antonia (who wants a particular apple), the solution falls on the shoulders of the older girl, who reacts negatively (8) to her mother's request to help her younger sister wash the new apple, and tries to have the task done by the father (10) or, alternatively, to have the father share some other domestic chore (12). This proposal leads both parents to a very negative evaluation of Ludovica as a stupid girl (which is really insulting). Both parents have lost their control of Ludovica.

Excerpt 2

Traverso Family

Dad: Gino; Mum: Gianna; Daughters: Carla, 11; Federica, 4.11
Carla, the older daughter, questions both parents: first the father, for his lack of attention, then the mother, for her lack of justice.
(Dad points to Carla because he wants her to stop telling a joke about a teacher)

Carla: papà guarda ogni cosa che faccio io.dopo trenta secondi che l'ho
         detta "e no ma dai <mi dà fastidio>"
         **Daddy, look anything I do, after thirty seconds of my beginning
         to say it, says "eh no, stop it; I am bothered"**
Dad: <so(no) dieci minuti>
         For ten minutes
         che stai insistendo <con (que)sta storia>
         you have been insisting on telling this story
Carla: <se' [: sì] dieci minuti> #
         <yeaah, ten minutes>

senti se non ti diverti dì "senti scusa"
listen if you aren't amusing yourself, you say "excuse me"
appena apro bocca dici "Carla non parlare".
as soon as I open my mouth; "Carla don't speak"

Mum: senti Carla ma la professoressa di
listen Carla but your teacher

Carla: no papà si è scocciato di sentirmi mamma
no, Daddy is annoyed to hear me, Mummy

Dad: Carla ti sto solo dicendo di non esagerare
Carla I am only saying not to exaggerate

Carla: non sto esagerando
I am not exaggerating
(*Father gestures signaling resignation*)
(common silence)

Carla: e vabbè [: va bene] per te sto esagerando ma per me no tu sei il padrone
e tu decidi quindi io mi sto zitta
All right, I am exaggerating according to you, but according to me
you are the boss and you decide, then I'll be silent

Mum: così è il fatto tu sei il padrone
that's it, you are the boss (with a smiling tone)

Dad: <non ti sto dicendo di stare>
I am not saying that

Carla: <tanto la democrazia in questi giorni non esiste più>
so democracy doesn't exist anymore

Mum: <ahh no>?

Carla: <no>

Dad: <non ti sto dicendo di stare zitta
I am not telling you to be silent
<ti sto solo dicendo>
I am only telling you

Mum: <e perché non esiste più>?
and why doesn't it exist anymore
aspetta Fru Fru[addresses the younger child with a diminutive]
wait Fru Fru

Carla: c'è il fascismo
That's fascism

Dad: sto solo dicendo <se per piacere non esageri>
I am only saying (speaking aloud) **please don't exaggerate**

Mum: <c'è il fascismo>
That's fascism (with a smiling tone)
Dad: non di stare zitta questo c'è una differenza fondamentale
I am not saying shut up; there is a fundamental difference

Here Carla uses the arguing strategy of exaggerating what the father is asking of her: that is, to stop joking about a teacher. The father asks her not to exaggerate, but that is exactly what the daughter does so that she can accuse him of being authoritarian and thus declare that fascistic ideas still exist in their family.

Excerpt 3
Traverso Family. This excerpt is taken from a period later in the same dinner. Carla starts discussing the same topic, this time referring to her mother's behavior:

Carla: fascismo metto una bella striscia
fascism I put a nice poster
davanti a casa. venite il fascismo.
in front of the house: come to fascism
Dad: tu i fascisti non li conosci proprio Carla.
the fascists, you don't really know them Carla
Carla: però é meglio la democrazia.
but democracy is better.
guarda la legge é uguale per tutti.
Look, law is the same for all.
mamma ha istituito la sua nuova legge.
Mum has established her new law.
chi fa il cattivo, chi da le botte,
the one who is naughty, who hits,
chi è arrabbiata con lei anche l'altra è arrabbiata.
who gets her angry, but that makes the other child angry too
Mum: (*smiling*)
Carla: così tu hai detto non lo negare.
this is what you said, don't deny it
perché è vero.
because that's true
Mum: cioè che ho detto?
What did I say?
Carla: cioé praticamente se Federica faceva male a me,
essentially that, if Federica hit me

se Federica- se Federica gridava.
if Federica if Federica screamed
tu le davi le botte e le davi anche a me.
you will hit her and me too
quando io non avevo fatto niente.
even though I didn't do anything

Mum: ah si questo è vero cioè siccome siete sempre
           oh yes this is true since you are always

Carla: e questo non è giusto non è giusto non è giusto.
           and this isn't fair, isn't fair, isn't fair

Mum: siccome siete sempre complici.
           since you're always partners in crime.

Carla: non è vero non siamo mai complici.
           this isn't true; we never are partners in crime

Here Carla complains about her mother's unjust treatment of her and her sister. In rhetorically developing her complaint, the older daughter reveals both the ad hoc nature of her mother's rule construction and the situation-related code application. This is a good example of how aware older children are of the work on rule construction that their parents discursively accomplish. Carla unmasks and threatens her mother's rhetorically designed rule by arguing about the way in which her mother treats the misbehavior of the two daughters. Carla even categorizes her mother's rule enactment as "fascist," revealing that the law established by her mother is "the same for all" in a new sense: She also punishes the older daughter when only the younger one is guilty. In this case, the deployment of a competing version of the norm leads to a joint reformulation of the rule "for another first time," when the mother is involved unwillingly and is obliged to justify her behavior.

Apart from the differences between the two settings, the three excerpts show how much the family contributes to triggering and supporting – although through opposition against enactment of the parental rules – the thinking activity of the adolescent children, who argue against any possible silent compliance. In a sense, these children are actively using with their parents a general rule of any Italian middle-class family interaction: Everyone has to be accountable, even parents, for their action and talk (Pontecorvo, 1996a). This familiar framework, a particularly fruitful ground for cultivating children's reasoning, constitutes a thinking space for adolescence. It is a protected area in which errors are admitted and behaviors can be negotiatied. The family unit, to which all members contribute, must be maintained not only through their actions but also through shared and accountable talk.

In concluding, we return to the four points presented earlier.

1. Family interaction is a type of multiparty conversation that reduces youngsters' "pain of thinking" about rules and norms; it is particularly important because of the great familiarity of the interactants and the embedded relational asymmetry, which necessarily trigger opposition, debate, and a range of diverse justifications from all participants.
2. In family conversations, as we have shown, adults stucture adolescents' talk by asking for conscious and convincing compliance and not for mere obedience of rules. Parents' requests for information or explanation require adolescents to elaborate on their discourse.
3. Families offer a space in which mistakes are more accepted, because parents need those mistakes in order to formulate and exemplify parental rules (Pontecorvo et al., 2001). Apprentices also try other routes and take unexpected directions to find their way while risking making mistakes. Families (and schools) are socialization places where one can practice skills rather freely and make mistakes that can be negotiated and corrected without serious negative consequences.
4. Family interaction exemplifies how much learning is a process of participation in communities of practice (Pontecorvo, 1994).

Parents and children experience many learning and reasoning activities in family conversations. Such activities are important in socializing children to further specialized cognitive and social practices. At any age, at least in the middle-class Italian families we have observed, children are continually practicing the rules of accountable talk and action during family conversation. At the same time, they practice some of the logical and scientific skills required in formal education, training, and work. Even when just recounting stories about their everyday life, they have to be precise, linking causes and effects correctly.

Our research on Italian family interactions, studied via conversational analysis, also has an important implication that is shared by much of the ethnographic research on youth groups and organizations: that is, the need for studying learning and socialization in their naturally occurring contexts. This could be done more frequently in the other settings that are considered relevant experiences of youth development, and in learning to provide a better understanding of what is really occurring and to promote adequate socialization activities.

REFERENCES

Barnes, D. (1976). *From communication to curriculum.* Harmondsworth, England: Penguin.

Barnes, D., & Todd, F. (1977). *Communication and learning in small groups.* London: Routledge and Kegan Paul.

Castiglia, D., Di Chiara, E., & Tavanti, V. (in preparation). *Air and water pressure in children's representations.*

Castiglia, D., Pontecorvo, C., & Stilli, R. (1987). Fare e parlare a scuola su alcune cose che stanno "in su l'acqua" [Doing and talking at school about things that are "on the water"]. *Scuola e Città, 34,* 199–213.

Corsaro, W. (1990). Disputes in the peer culture of American and Italian nursery school children. In A. D. Grimshaw (Ed.), *Conflict talk* (pp. 21–66). Cambridge: Cambridge University Press.

Fasulo, A., Girardet, H., & Pontecorvo, C. (1998). Seeing the past: Children's use of historical iconographic sources. In J. F. Voss & M. Carretero (Eds.), *Learning and reasoning in history, Volume 2: International review of history education* (pp. 132–153). Portland, OR: Wolburn Press.

Matusov, E. (1996, April). *When solo activity is not privileged: Participation and internalization models of development.* Paper presented at the annual meeting of the American Educational Research Association, New York.

Ochs, E., Pontecorvo, C., & Fasulo, A. (1996). Socializing taste. *Ethnos, 61*(1–2), 7–46.

Orsolini, M. (1991). Oralità e scrittura nella costruzione del testo [Orality and literacy in text construction]. In M. Orsolini & C. Pontecorvo (Eds.), *La costruzione del testo scritto nei bambini* [Children's written text construction] (pp. 5–26). Florence: La Nuova Italia.

Orsolini, M., & Pontecorvo, C. (1992a). Children's talk in classroom discussions. *Cognition and Instruction, 9*(2), 113–136.

Orsolini, M., & Pontecorvo, C. (1992b). When the teacher tries to make children discuss and compare their points of views. *Verbum, 15*(1), 33–51.

Perret-Clermont, A.-N. (1993). What is it that develops? *Cognition and Instruction, 11*(3–4), 197–205.

Pontecorvo, C. (1984). Children's science, children's thinking: What about it? In D. Hadary & M. Vicentini (Eds.), *Proceedings of U.S.–Italy joint seminar on science education for elementary school children* (pp. 11–19). Washington, DC: American University Press.

Pontecorvo, C. (1987). Discussing for reasoning: The role of argument in knowledge construction. In E. De Corte, H. Lodewijks, R. Parmentier, & P. Span (Eds.), *Learning and instruction* (pp. 71–82). Oxford/Leuven: Pergamon Press/Leuven University Press.

Pontecorvo, C. (1988). I bambini parlano per fare scienza: la formazione del linguaggio scientifico nella discussione in classe [Children's talk in doing science: Scientific language in classroom discussions]. In A. R. Guerriero (Ed.), *L'educazione linguistica e i linguaggi delle scienze* [Linguistic education and scientific languages] (pp. 85–110). Florence: La Nuova Italia.

Pontecorvo, C. (1989). Recherches sur l'éducation scientifique à l'école primaire Italienne [Issues on scientific education at Italian primary school]. In A. Giordan, A. Henriques,

& V. Bang (Eds.), *Psychologie génétique et didactique des sciences* [Genetic psychology and science teaching] (pp. 189–209). Bern, Switzerland: Peter Lang.

Pontecorvo, C. (1992). Instructional talk in the classroom: A discursive strategy for a lesson. *Verbum, 15*(1), 82–85.

Pontecorvo, C. (1993). Forms of discourse and shared thinking. *Cognition and Instruction, 11*(3–4), 189–196.

Pontecorvo, C. (1994). Rethinking learning processes and products. *Behavioral and Brain Sciences, 17*(4), 580–581.

Pontecorvo, C. (1995). L'apprendimento tra culture e contesti [Learning in cultures and contexts]. In C. Pontecorvo, A. M. Ajello, & C. Zucchermaglio (Eds.), *I contesti sociali dell'apprendimento. Acquisire conoscenze a scuola, nel lavoro, nella vita quotidiana* [Social contexts of learning: Acquiring knowledge at school, at work, and in everyday life] (pp. 13–42). Milan: LED Edizioni.

Pontecorvo, C. (1996a). Argumentation et compétence linguistique des jeunes enfants [Argumentation and linguistic competence of young children]. In S. Rayna, M. Delau, & C. Laezers (Eds.), *Quels objectifs pédagogiques pour l'education prescolaire?* [Which educational aims for preschool children?] (pp. 275–294). Paris: INRP–Nathan (Coll. Pédagogie).

Pontecorvo, C. (1996b). Discorso e sviluppo. La conversazione come sistema di azione e strumento di ricerca [Discourse and development. Conversation as action system and research tool]. *Età evolutiva, 55*, 56–71.

Pontecorvo, C., & Ajello, A. M. (1994). Studying reasoning processes in group interaction. In J. Wertsch & J. Ramirez (Eds.), *Literacy and other forms of mediated action* (Vol. 2, pp. 123–133). Madrid: Fundación Infancia y Aprendizaje.

Pontecorvo, C., Ajello, A. M., & Zucchermaglio, C. (1991). *Discutendo si impara.* [Learning by discussing]. Rome: La Nuova Italia Scientifica.

Pontecorvo, C., Amendola, S., & Fasulo, A. (1994). Storie in famiglia. La narrazione come prodotto collettivo [Family stories. Narrative as a collective product]. *Età Evolutiva, 47*, 14–29.

Pontecorvo, C., Castiglia, D., & Zucchermaglio, C. (1983). Discorso e ragionamento scientifico nelle discussioni in classe [Discourse and scientific reasoning in classroom discussions]. *Scuola e Città, 34*, 447–462.

Pontecorvo, C., & Fasulo, A. (1997). Learning to argue in family-shared discourse: The reconstruction of past events. In L. B. Resnick, R. Saljo, C. Pontecorvo, & B. Burge (Eds.), *Discourse, tools, and reasoning: Essays on situated cognition* (pp. 406–442). New York: Springer-Verlag.

Pontecorvo, C., Fasulo, A., & Sterponi, L. (2001). Mutual apprentices: The making of parenthood and childhood in Italian family dinner conversations. *Human Development, 44*, 342–363.

Pontecorvo, C., & Girardet, H. (1993). Arguing and reasoning in understanding historical topics. *Cognition and Instruction, 11*(3–4), 365–395.

Pontecorvo, C., & Pirchio, S. (1997). Strategie discorsive infantili nelle dispute in famiglia [Children's discorsive strategies in the family]. *Rassegna di Psicologia, 1*, 83–106.

Pontecorvo, C., & Sterponi, L. (1997, August 26–30). *The making of thought: Learning sequences in family conversation.* Paper presented at the Seventh European Conference for Research on Learning and Instruction, Athens.

Pontecorvo, C., & Sterponi, L. (2001). Learning to argue and reasoning through discourse in educational settings. In G. Wells & G. Claxton (Eds.), *Learning for life in the 21st century: Sociocultural perspectives on the future of education* (pp. 127–140). Oxford: Blackwell

Resnick, L. B., Säljö, R., Pontecorvo, C., & Burge, B. (Eds.). (1997). *Discourse, tools, and reasoning: Essays on situated cognition.* Berlin/New York: Springer-Verlag.

Rogoff, B. (1990). *Apprenticeship in thinking: Cognitive development in social context.* New York: Oxford University Press.

Sterponi, L., & Pontecorvo, C. (1996a). Discourse at family dinner: How children are socialized through arguing. In D. Brixhe (Ed.), Savoirs et compétences en construction [Constructing knowledge and thinking skills] (special issue). *Interaction et Cognition, 7*(2–3), 329–366.

Sterponi, L., & Pontecorvo, C. (1996b). Il farsi e il disfarsi dell'argomento di discorso nelle conversazioni familiari a tavola [Doing and undoing topics in family dinner talk]. *Rassegna di Psicologia, 3,* 39–68.

16 The Role of Discourse in the Transformation of Parent–Adolescent Relationships

Manfred Hofer

The importance of verbal interaction is increasingly being recognized, particularly by social constructivists. However, the quantitative analysis of verbal exchange is not yet an established research paradigm. Research on discourse with older children, adolescents, and their parents has proved fruitful and has provided an impetus for the quantitative analysis of discourse. The research presented in this chapter draws on an approach that views discourse as a special kind of behavioral interaction. This chapter discusses why it is so important to examine discourse data in a quantitative way and then examines both conflict and planning discourse between parents and adolescents with several different coding systems. The use of multiple systems allows the examination of four specific questions. First, do patterns of parent–adolescent discourse differ from discourse patterns found in other relationships? Second, are the specific patterns of interaction that occur in discussions between parents and adolescents stable over different types of discourse? Third, can discourse help us to view the process by which individuation progresses within family relationships? Finally, are observed interaction patterns consistent with participants' subjective accounts of the interaction and relationship? The answers to these questions provide objective, generalizable evidence on the process by which adolescents and parents deal with the individuation process through everyday interactions.

The Individuation Theory Framework

The adolescent–parent relationship can be regarded as a prototypical situation for the study of discourse within a social-constructivist, individuation

Special thanks are extended to Mary Jo Pugh for her editing.

241

theory framework. The flow of thoughts and feelings exchanged provides experiences by which each party may begin to redefine the relationship from one in which parents maintain total control to one that becomes increasingly egalitarian. Adolescents establish their individuality while they retain, but alter, their relationship with parents (Grotevant & Cooper, 1986; Smollar & Youniss, 1989; Steinberg & Silverberg, 1986). Specifically, adolescents differentiate themselves as distinct persons while remaining open to parental advice and seeking parental endorsement. In addition, they alter their orientations to parental authority and distribution of responsibility. When parents are confronted with behaviors that do not meet their expectations, they try to adapt to the new demands and needs of the growing adolescent (e.g., Collins, 1990). Parents come to realize that the unilateral exercise of authority, which satisfied the demands of childhood, must be transformed into greater equality, reciprocity, and mutuality.

One means by which partners renegotiate their relationship and roles (Tesson & Youniss, 1995) is by using verbal interactions. These verbal interactions are also an expression of the underlying structure of the relationship. Hence, interactions provide an analytic tool that gives insight into the ways participants confirm and transform their relationship on both individual and dyadic levels.

On the individual level, we follow researchers who define certain behavioral indexes to grasp the adolescent's efforts to (a) be distinct from parents (separateness), (b) accept responsibility for his or her views (self-assertion), (c) understand parents' views (mutuality), and (d) be willing to accommodate to parents' views (permeability; Grotevant & Cooper, 1985). For example, a request for action in discourse is viewed as a manifestation of separateness, whereas an indirect suggestion demonstrates mutuality. Using a slightly different approach, Allen, Hauser, Eickholt, Bell, and O'Connor (1994) grouped behavioral categories according to the extent to which they promote or inhibit autonomy and relatedness among family members. For example, *clearly state reasons for disagreeing* exhibits autonomy, whereas *query* demonstrates relatedness. The Mannheim Argumentation Coding System (Hofer & Pikowsky, 1993) describes in detail strategies used by parents and adolescents when explaining their standpoints during conflict. To grasp adolescents' attempts to gain autonomy, the categories *rejection of arguments, rejection of initiatives,* and *counterarguments* are defined. With regard to parents, certain verbal acts are defined as indicators of their efforts to exert control (e.g., explanations, requests, and proposals) and their expectations for openness (e.g., questions of clarification) and responsibility (e.g., questions of justification).

On the dyadic level, discourse characteristics are viewed as reflecting features of the relationship. In particular, marked asymmetry in discourse may point to unilaterality in the relationship, whereas equal distribution of verbal acts is a sign of a more mutual relationship. The literature portrays the parent–child relationship as changing from one in which unilateral authority characterized the early relationship to one in which both partners attempt to establish peerlike mutuality. This process does not proceed in a linear fashion, however. Research indicates that sons and daughters may dominate parents during middle adolescence, especially boys in relation to mothers (Steinberg, 1987). Thus, the study of different types of asymmetry and symmetry in discourse may lead to new insight into the process by which the relationship changes.

Family Interaction in Germany

The concept of *individuation* was developed mainly in studies of families in the United States and is, to some degree, a reflection of a social-political context that is characteristic of American culture. From cross-cultural research in general, it is clear that broader social context conditions influence the determinants and consequences of education and development. The concept of individuation, however, is clearly applicable to modern societies that are structured on the premise that strong individuals know and can represent their own interests. The question then becomes "Does this paradigm generalize to other Western cultures?"

The concept of individuation, which fits so well with America's mixture of individual freedom and communitarianism, seems to clash with the stereotype of the authoritarian German family. That stereotype was advanced after World War II to explain the sordid events under the Nazi regime, and it was repeated in the works of Adorno. Although empirical evidence shows that it had some basis in reality in the 1950s, current evidence points to a liberalization of educational values and practices. German families have changed from emphasizing obedience, order, and diligence to emphasizing autonomy. Instead of physical punishment and threats as common sanctions in conflict situations, discussions of conflict are more likely to occur today. As a result, adolescents are more self-reliant, parent–adolescent relationships are closer, and mutual respect has risen.

An important change in parent–adolescent relations concerns modes of interaction. Negotiation became the principal mode of dealing with conflictual goals, and adolescents learned to use verbal means to persuade, convince, argue, compromise, and flatter parents to gain influence. In a similar manner, parents had to learn to compromise, persuade, and convince their children, because commands are no longer considered appropriate educational practice. Changes in the German family can be summarized as shifts from a *command* family toward a *discourse* family (Fischer, Fuchs, & Zinnecker, 1985). Hence, the old stereotype of the authoritarian German family appears limp and unfounded today, and concepts originally developed in the United States seem appropriate for investigations of parent–adolescent relations in German families.

Role Dependency in Discourse

Pikowsky (1998) took a closer look at the role dependency of parent–adolescent interactions by examining discourse from one sample of adolescents in different roles. Data consisted of discourse with each adolescent's mother, best friend, and younger sister in random order. The three relationships are high in closeness but differ systematically in conflict and asymmetry (Furman & Buhrmester, 1985). In the best-friend dyad, closeness and equality are highest. The mother–daughter relationship is characterized by a strong difference in power and conflict. And the sibling couple also has high conflict, but the power balance is reversed because the target adolescent may dominate her younger sister. Because confounding individual variables were held constant, Pikowsky (1998) has hypothesized that interaction patterns would differ according to the characteristics of the relationships investigated.

The sample consisted of 32 adolescent girls between 12 and 18 years of age. The dyads were asked to engage in a 10-minute discussion of a relevant conflict. The discussions were audiotaped, transcribed, and coded according to the Mannheim Argumentation Coding System. The results indicated that adolescents' verbal behavior differed markedly, depending on the partner's role. With mothers, the results were in line with those reported in the preceding section. Mothers concentrated their arguments on their daughters' behavior. Daughters confined themselves to rejecting mothers' moves and to producing counterarguments. Target adolescents modified their own positions more often and verbalized fewer counterarguments in discourse with friends compared with discourse with mothers and sisters. They were three times more likely to accept their best friend's utterances than they were to accept those of their sisters. Target adolescents switched immediately and displayed a motherlike pattern in discourse with sisters. Conflicts between sisters were less argumentative and accepting and exhibited the highest level of rejections and counterarguments. As expected, interaction symmetry was highest in discourse with best friends: There was nearly equal distribution of the speech categories between the parties.

These results are in line with those of a similar study using a planning task (Noack & Fingerle, 1994). They add evidence to the proposition that discourse is a valid mirror of relationship, as it reflects central characteristics of adolescents' important relationships (e.g., connectedness, symmetry, and conflict). Furthermore, discourse is highly discriminative between different relationships, regardless of the content or type of discourse involved.

Discourse in Different Situations

In everyday family discussions, a wide range of themes are explored (e.g., curfew, time spent studying, personal problems, hopes and dreams for the future), and the character of discourse varies. Research indicates that adolescents and parents discriminate among three types of verbal interactions (de Wuffel, 1986). *Normative rightness* deals with issues of family rules and regulations, such as curfew, obeying parents, duties, and quarreling. *Objective fact and efficiency* addresses issues such as housekeeping, homework, and school. *Subjective authenticity* pertains to problems, closeness, and free time. Because participants may have different goal patterns in these various types of discourse, they may use different methods to achieve them. Consequently, verbal behavior should vary by type of discourse.

Although the context of the discourse may vary, however, the role each person plays in the relationship (e.g., mother/daughter) is constant over all types of interactions. Thus, some degree of similarity among types of discourse can be expected due to role effects. Hofer and Sassenberg (1998) investigated how type of discourse influenced patterns of interaction between parents and adolescents using both conflict and planning discourse. Participants were 61 mother–daughter dyads in which the daughters were between 11 and 17 years of age. *Conflict discourse* refers to the world of normative rightness. In conflict, goals of the participants are contrary by definition. The adolescents' wish for separateness and the parents' wish for control may be salient because each partner wants her position to be respected. Consequently, the interaction entails negotiation, and there may be a negative emotional undercurrent. *Planning discourse*, on the other hand, refers to the world of objective fact and efficiency. Parents' and adolescents' goals probably are not opposite, so partners are willing to cooperate, and the exchange should facilitate properties of mutuality and symmetrical interactions.

Hofer and Sassenberg (1998) used the Mannheim Argumentation Category System to describe in detail strategies used by parents and adolescents when explaining their standpoints during conflict (Hofer & Pikowsky, 1993) and the system developed by Condon, Cooper, and Grotevant (1984) to analyze planning task discourse. Their findings indicated that the role-related mother–daughter pattern was highly stable across discourse types. In both tasks, mothers produced more requests than daughters did, and they dominated in reinforcing their daughters with acknowledgments. Daughters, on the other hand, were much higher in response categories, thus complementing mothers' moves. They were also more likely to accept mothers' moves than vice versa (e.g., answering their requests) and in direct disagreements. Thus, mothers gave structure to the interaction, whereas daughters responded to or complemented their moves. The same asymmetric behavior showed up in content categories. Mothers made more relevant comments and changed their perspectives more often than daughters.

Correlations between the frequencies of collapsed categories (i.e., initiatives, reactions, agreements, and disagreements) for both systems confirm these results, especially for daughters. For mothers, however, only the frequencies of initiatives and disagreements correlated significantly between both tasks. Hence, mothers consistently controlled the discourse, whereas they used agreements as signs of an individuated relationship, depending on the behavior of daughters.

To capture cross-situational stability in discourse balance, Hofer and Sassenberg (1998) subtracted mothers' relative frequency scores from daughters' relative frequency scores for each category. The categories in the planning task correlated positively with the respective categories in the conflict task. Hence, when one party dominated reactions, initiatives, agreements, and disagreements during the planning task, she also dominated in the same categories during the conflict discourse.

In terms of individuation theory, both types of discourse displayed elements of early parent–child interactions and elements of adolescent dominance. These results suggest that speech behavior varies more by role (mother vs. daughter) than by type of discourse within the same role, especially for daughters.

Continuity and Change in Discourse

The research presented so far suggests that discourse is a powerful indicator of the relationship in which an adolescent acts at a given time. This relates to the original idea of this chapter: that verbal interaction is considered a means by which participants construct their relationship and transform it if needed. This argument would be more convincing if one could demonstrate that discourse is a valid indicator of social transitions. Drawing on individuation theory, an increase in the intensity of negotiations should take place at around midadolescence. Results from cross-sectional studies suggest that conflicts between adolescents and parents increase during early adolescence (Laursen, Coy, & Collins, 1998). Furthermore, questionnaire studies show that perceived parental authority increases in the course of adolescence, reaches a peak shortly before or around midadolescence, and is followed by a systematic decline (e.g., Furman & Buhrmester, 1992). Thus, we expected a change toward more confrontational behavior during early adolescence. By the time adolescents approach the age of majority, a time when a considerable transformation of family communication can be assumed to be accomplished, interaction should reflect a more egalitarian role pattern. Indicators of closeness are expected to remain stable.

Noack and Kracke (1998) have described two longitudinal studies that shed light on these issues. In a study of early adolescents, a sample of 13-year-olds was asked to plan activities for a weekend they were to spend with their mothers and fathers. One and 2 years later, they performed a similar discourse with their parents. The discourse was categorized with an adaptation of Powers's (1982) coding system. The intensity of negotiations was expected to increase in this age period. The authors found an increase in parental directive behaviors. At the same time, adolescents acted in an increasingly conflictual manner that was most pronounced between 14 and 15 years of age. These results point to an intensification of family negotiations in the course of early adolescence.

In a study of late adolescents, parents and adolescents were followed yearly for 3 years (from 15 to 17 years of age). Planning discourse data for a total of 47 families were coded using the coding scheme developed by Condon et al. (1984). In general, there was more symmetry concerning questions in family interactions: The frequency of questions decreased across time, whereas acknowledgments became more frequent. For both parents, the category *mind reading* (or *states others' feelings*) declined across measurement points. Parents were obviously starting to take the role of active listeners more seriously, and they behaved in a more reciprocal manner. However, a higher total number of parental utterances and relevant comments indicates a slight dominance of parents throughout the years in focus. This pattern may also reflect a slow withdrawal of adolescents from the family as sons and daughters approached majority.

Overall, quantitative discourse analyses revealed a good deal of change toward asymmetry from early to midadolescence, as well as a change toward more symmetry in the late adolescent period. These findings complement results arising from both ethnographic and survey methodology.

Objective and Subjective Views on Discourse

In this chapter, discourse is treated as observed behavior and is analyzed using various category systems. The studies rest on the assumption that participants have a mental representation of their relationship and negotiate the relationship via their interactional moves. Few studies have addressed this assumption, but those that have provide valuable insights into the processes by which individuals co-construct a shared understanding of their relationship.

In the first study, Deschner (1998) interviewed adolescents between the ages of 14 and 17 and asked about the relationship with their parents in the past and the present and the kind of relationship they hoped to achieve in the future. Participants were also asked about the verbal means they use to demonstrate their desire to strive toward a symmetric relationship with their parents. Adolescents were able to articulate the degree of connectedness, separateness, and asymmetry in their past and present parent–adolescent relationships and the degree of connectedness, separateness, and asymmetry they would like to attain in the future. They also referred to specific speech acts they use to change the asymmetry of their relationship: argumentation, flattering, persuading. Thus, adolescents are generally well aware of their age-related task of transforming their relationship with their parents, and they also reflect on ways to accomplish this task (Schoenpflug, 1993).

In another study, Hofer, Sassenberg, and Pikowsky (1999) recorded discussions and collected parallel questionnaire data on the participants' subjective understanding of arguments they used in the discourse. There were substantial correlations between scales measuring participants' subjective understanding of their verbal behavior and the extent to which they used verbal categories in discourse. For example, the more daughters saw their main argument as striving toward being persons separate from their mothers, the less they accepted their mothers' arguments, the more counterarguments they produced, and the more their mothers produced rejections of daughters' arguments and counterarguments. In analyzing the relation between perceptions and verbal asymmetries, the authors computed difference scores between mother and daughter for every behavior category and correlated them with the data on subjective understanding of verbal behavior. The higher the daughters' interpretation of separateness in their verbal behavior, the more they exceeded their mothers in producing questions and the more their mothers exceeded them in accepting initiatives and arguments and rejecting initiatives. The higher the mothers' interpretation of control in their verbal behavior, the more they tended to show dominance over their daughters in producing questions, and the more the daughters exceeded their mothers in accepting initiatives.

Conclusions

The research program discussed in this chapter was conducted to explore the potential of discourse as a data source in analyzing interaction from a social-constructivist standpoint. Findings from various researchers indicate that quantitative discourse analysis is a compelling method of exploring parent–adolescent relationships on both the individual and dyadic levels. Individual discourse categories were able to trace the individuals' perceived relationship features and connect them reliably to the type of discourse that occurred among participants. Furthermore, the examination of individual discourse categories and discourse properties, such as asymmetry, shed light on the processes by which the parent–adolescent relationship is transformed. Although the elicitation, transcription, coding, and statistical treatment of discourse–especially with required sample sizes – are tedious and difficult, the research described indicates that the extra work pays off. We not only gain a richer understanding of the individuation process, but we are also able to view the actual social construction of relationships from the perspective of the participants.

Although the results described are far from conclusive, they complement previous research using different methodology. They provide a method of triangulation that strengthens confidence in the findings. The research described provides encouragement and suggests that the use of quantitative discourse analysis will provide objective, analytic, and generalizable evidence on the process by which parents and adolescents negotiate their relationship through everyday interactions.

REFERENCES

Allen, J. P., Hauser, S. T., Eickholt, C., Bell, K. T., & O'Connor, T. G. (1994). Autonomy and relatedness in family interactions as predictors of expressions of negative adolescent affect. *Journal of Research on Adolescence, 4,* 535–552.

Collins, W. A. (1990). Parent–child relationships in the transition to adolescence. In R. Montemayor, G. R. Adams, & T. P. Gullotta (Eds.), *From childhood to adolescence* (pp. 85–106). Newbury Park, CA: Sage.

Condon, S. L., Cooper, C. R., & Grotevant, H. D. (1984). Manual for the analysis of family discourse. *Psychological Documents, 14,* 2616.

Deschner, M. (1998). *Kognitionen von Eltern und Jugendlichen ueber ihre Beziehung und die Rolle von Gespraechen* [Parents' and adolescents' views on their relationship and their interactions]. Unpublished master's thesis, University of Mannheim, Germany.

de Wuffel, F. J. (1986). *Attachment beyond childhood: Individual and developmental differences in parent–adolescent attachment relationships.* Unpublished doctoral dissertation, University of Nijmegen, the Netherlands.

Fischer, A., Fuchs, W., & Zinnecker, J. (Eds.). (1985). *Jugendliche und Erwachsene '85. Generationen im Vergleich. Band 3* [Youth and adults 1985. Comparing generations]. Opladen, Germany: Leske & Budrich.

Furman, W., & Buhrmester, D. (1985). Children's perceptions of the qualities of sibling relationships. *Child Development, 56,* 448–461.

Furman, W., & Buhrmester, D. (1992). Age and sex differences in perceptions of networks of personal relationships. *Child Development, 63,* 103–115.

Grotevant, H. D., & Cooper, C. R. (1985). Patterns of interaction in family relationships and the development of identity exploration in adolescence. *Child Development, 56,* 415–428.

Grotevant, H. D., & Cooper, C. R. (1986). Individuation in family relationships: A perspective on individual differences in the development of identity and role-taking skill in adolescence. *Human Development, 29,* 82–100.

Hofer, M., & Pikowsky, B. (1993). Validation of a category system for arguments in conflict discourse. *Argumentation, 7,* 135–148.

Hofer, M., & Sassenberg, K. (1998). Relationship and family discourse in different situations. In M. Hofer, J. Youniss, & P. Noack (Eds.), *Verbal interactions and development in families with adolescents. Advances in applied developmental psychology* (Vol. 15, pp. 49–64). Stamford, CT: Ablex.

Hofer, M., Sassenberg, K., & Pikowsky, B. (1999). Discourse asymmetries in adolescent daughters' disputes with mothers. *International Journal of Behavioral Development, 23,* 1001–1022.

Laursen, B., Coy, C., & Collins, W. A. (1998). Reconsidering changes in parent–child conflict across adolescence: A meta-analysis. *Child Development, 69,* 817–832.

Noack, P., & Fingerle, M. (1994). Gespraeche Jugendlicher mit Eltern und gleichaltrigen Freunden [Adolescents' discourse with parents and friends]. *Zeitschrift fuer Entwicklungspsychologie und Paedagogische Psychologie, 26,* 331–349.

Noack, P., & Kracke, B. (1998). Continuity and change in family interactions across adolescence. In M. Hofer, J. Youniss, & P. Noack (Eds.), *Verbal interactions and development in families with adolescents. Advances in applied developmental psychology* (Vol. 15, pp. 65–81). Stamford, CT: Ablex.

Pikowsky, B. (1998). Konfliktgespraeche jugendlicher Maedchen mit Mutter, Schwester und Freundin [Adolescent girls' arguments with mother, sister, and best friend]. *Zeitschrift fuer Paedagogische Psychologie, 12,* 179–190.

Powers, S. I. (1982). *Family interaction and parental moral development as a context for adolescent moral development.* Unpublished doctoral dissertation, Harvard University.

Schoenpflug, U. (1993). Entwicklungsregulation im Jugendalter [Regulation of development in adolescence]. *Zeitschrift fuer Sozialisationsforschung und Erziehungssoziologie, 4,* 326–340.

Smollar, J., & Youniss, J. (1989). Transformations in adolescents' perceptions of parents. *International Journal of Behavior Development, 12*, 71–84.

Steinberg, L. (1987). The impact of puberty on family relations: Effect of pubertal status and pubertal timing. *Developmental Psychology, 23*, 451–460.

Steinberg, L., & Silverberg, S. B. (1986). The vicissitudes of autonomy in early adolescence. *Child Development, 57*, 841–851.

Tesson, G., & Youniss, J. (1995). Micro-sociology and psychological development: A sociological interpretation of Piaget's theory. In A. M. Ambert (Ed.), *Sociological studies of children* (Vol. 7, pp. 101–126). Greenwich, CT: JAI Press.

17 Interactive Minds

A Paradigm from Life Span Psychology

Ursula M. Staudinger

Supporting youth in their joining of society is a lofty goal that seems more than worthy and timely to pursue. Support for that pursuit can be found in a number of different research areas of developmental and life span psychology. For instance, Erikson's notion of *generativity*, an aspect of personality functioning that may develop at around midlife, highlights the importance of the transmission of knowledge and insight between generations for the young and the old, as well as for society (e.g., Erikson, Erikson, & Kivnick, 1986). Roger Säljö's chapter refers to another strong tradition in developmental research that has focused on the critical role of social interaction in learning. This research is building on a long tradition that includes the seminal works of scholars such as Baldwin, Piaget, Vygotsky, and Luria. However, although it is one of the fundamental tenets of the social and behavioral sciences that human behavior and development are at least partly a creation of social forces, social interaction, and social transmission, it is also true that theory and method do not always coincide in developmental work. Thus, there is a continuing search for the role of the social-interactive in developmental theory and research.

One persuasive example is the enrichment and transformation of social-learning theory by cognitive dimensions to better understand the social and collective foundation of action and thought (e.g., Bandura, 1998). Another example of this continuous struggle for a better match between theory and method is, as previously mentioned, the revisitation of early-20th-century social constructivist scholars such as Baldwin or Piaget (Chapman, 1988; Edelstein & Hoppe-Graf, 1993; Luria, 1976; Vygotsky, 1978; Wertsch, 1985). A third example is the ongoing mandate of interactionism (Magnusson & Endler, 1977; Pervin & Lewis, 1978) or the recent stream of postmodern efforts (Neimeyer, Neimeyer, Lyddon, & Hoshmand, 1994) at articulating reality as social construction. Finally, the recent debates about collectivism versus individualism (e.g., Cooper & Denner, 1998; Triandis, 1990) deserve mention in this context.

On the surface, then, the fundamental role of social forces and social processes in the evolutionary and ontogenetic origins of behavior and the human mind is clearly and widely acknowledged. Yet, the translation of the intellectual agenda into scientific evidence continues to be incomplete. The nonsocial, person-centered research paradigms seem to persist, for instance in the study of cognition, even when the fundamental role of context is obvious (see also Greeno, Chi, Clancey, & Elman, 1993, for debates on this issue).

Many have tried to achieve a greater match between theory and empirical methods. During the past decade, several volumes and stimulating review chapters have appeared that aim at similar goals (e.g., Baltes & Staudinger, 1996; Bar-Tal & Kruglanski, 1988; Bornstein & Bruner, 1989; Cohen & Siegel, 1991; Cranach, Doise, & Mugny, 1992; Forman, Minick, & Stone, 1993; Joiner & Coyne, 1999; Levine, Resnick, & Higgins, 1993; Light & Butterworth, 1992; Resnick, Levine, & Teasley, 1991; Rogoff, 1990; Rogoff & Lave, 1984; Sternberg & Wagner, 1994; Wozniak & Fischer, 1993).

Life span theory and research, I suggest, offers one attractive way of understanding and organizing the questions about the role of social transaction in cognition and cognitive development (cf. Baltes & Staudinger, 1996). A life span view on the study of social interactions, for instance, provides a first look at the lifelong sequencing and patterning of social contexts and their relative salience. The multidirectionality and multidimensionality of life span development are reflected in the acknowledgment that the quality and effectiveness of interactions can vary among and between different groups of individuals, and that currently functional interactions can become dysfunctional in the future and vice versa. Also, the meanings of interactions and their components can change with age. The changing role of autonomy and independence is an example in this regard (Baltes & Silverberg, 1994). Furthermore, life span research asks in which way social interactions can facilitate the activation of performance potentials beyond childhood and adolescence. Finally, acknowledging the historical and contextual embeddedness of development, for example, alerts us to the fact that interactions also change, depending on the historical time and cultural context. The concept of *developmental tasks* (e.g., Erikson, 1959; Havighurst, 1948) may be a useful template to organize the various kinds and patterns of social interaction as we move through life.

Psychological phenomena and constructs vary in the degree to which they represent the social-interactive nature of the human mind and psyche. One area of research that seems to be a prototype of a collective product is the body of knowledge and skills related to the meaning and conduct of life (Baltes, Smith, & Staudinger, 1992; Staudinger, 1996). A cultural-anthropological analysis of the concept of *wisdom*, for example, revealed that, dating back several millennia, wisdom has been seen as something that transcends the reach of any one given individual (cf. Staudinger, 1996). It became a widely shared position that individuals could not "single-mindedly" represent the kind of coalition between mind (knowledge) and virtue (character) that is necessary for wisdom to emerge. Apparently, for wisdom to emerge, be instantiated, and be recognized, social discourse and social representations in a variety of bodies of knowledge ranging from proverbs to legal documents were essential. Many manifestations of wisdom are other-oriented and include interpersonal qualities, such as advice seeking and advice giving. In addition, the acquisition of wisdom seems to be fundamentally tied to excellent mentorship by others, long-term interpersonal apprenticeship, and just being a member of a human community.

As a result of this insight into the collective nature of wisdom and other lines of argument, we attempted to translate the preceding theoretical considerations into methods of empirical inquiry (Staudinger & Baltes, 1996). Specifically, in one study we asked research participants to bring into the lab a partner with whom they usually discussed life problems. After these natural dyads were jointly or separately presented with our life dilemmas, participants were asked to engage in internal (virtual) or external (real) dialogues before individually responding to our wisdom tasks. The following is an example of such a task: "Sometimes, when people sit down and think about their life, they feel that they have not quite accomplished what they had once set out to do. What should one/the person do and consider in such a situation?" Compared with our standard paradigm, where individual participants spontaneously respond to a wisdom task, social-interactive conditions (real and virtual) led to a strong increase in performance levels (up to one standard deviation; Staudinger & Baltes, 1996). One important finding from this study is that not just any type of social interaction is helpful, which is very much in line with decades of group problem-solving research conducted in social psychology (e.g., Hill, 1982). Rather, it seems important for the facilitative effect of social interaction to unfold so that people have enough time to integrate the results of interactive cognition (external dialogue). Alternatively, they must have a lot of control over how the dialogue is sequenced and channeled from the start (internal dialogue). Sequencing interactive and individual cognition seems to play a crucial role with regard to this facilitative effect (Staudinger & Baltes, 1996). This finding also replicates results from research on child development. In this work, it was demonstrated that children profit from interactions with peers and with adults when solving a cognitive task occurring some days later (Azmitia, 1996; Rogoff & Chavajay, 1995).

In our approach, we have used the concept of *interactive minds* to describe such phenomena (see also Baltes & Staudinger, 1996). The numerous other terms available in the literature, such as *shared knowledge, mutual knowledge, society of minds, situated cognition, collective mind, collaborative cognition, distributed cognition,* or *collaborative memory* (see, e.g., Levine et al., 1993, for a review; Bar-Tal & Kruglanski, 1988; Bornstein & Bruner, 1989; Minsky, 1986; Salomon, 1993), did not seem to do justice to our understanding of the phenomenon for three reasons: (1) to keep open the outcome directionality (valence) of social interaction; (2) to develop a metaphor with good imagery involving social interaction and transaction; and (3) to preserve the unique psychological emphasis on individuals as the constituent basis for interaction.

Our definition of interactive minds implies that the acquisition and manifestation of individual cognitions influence and are influenced by cognitions of others, and that these reciprocal influences between and among minds contribute to the activation and modification of already available cognitions as well as to the development of new ones (Baltes & Staudinger, 1996, p. 7). The interaction of minds can vary along the following dimensions: internal–external, proximal (e.g., other person)–distal (e.g., artifacts, norms), explicit–implicit, unidirectional–bidirectional, and immediate–delayed; and the resulting effects on cognitive manifestations can be facilitative, neutral, or debilitative.

This definition of interactive minds suggests some boundary conditions. We as psychologists focus on individuals as units, but what are individual units? Does the interaction always involve the presence of persons? Not necessarily. Psychology also studies mental representations, which can be organized to reflect coherent knowledge about personal entities (e.g., parents, children, spouses, friends, the various voices of our conscience, protagonists in biographies). We are inclined to include such internal transactions with the mental representations we have of other persons (e.g., inner or virtual dialogues) in our conceptual territory of interactive minds. This also seems meaningful because the origins and emergence of these mental representations of other people likely involved some form of person-to-person contact at one point. This is not to say that all cognitions have social foundations or social-interactive properties. It is possible to think of cognitions (such as sensory and perceptual categories) in which evolutionary and genetic origins, as well as their ontogenetic manifestations, lie predominantly or even solely in nonsocial mechanisms of the acquisition and refinement of information (Klix, 1993).

With regard to the theme of the Johann Jacobs Foundation conference, "Joining Society: Social Interaction and Learning in Adolescence and Youth," it may be useful, based on our work of interactive minds and wisdom, to investigate the interactions that help adolescents to learn or not learn about life. Modern Western societies have become more and more void of structures such as initiation rites that create social contexts that help youth to learn about life. This is especially critical in postmodern times, when life has become increasingly complex and asks more than ever for social contexts that help youth to learn about how to lead their choice of a good life. It may be time to think about possible creative analogies of initiation rites in modern societies and even about a curriculum that provides a social context for learning about the tools necessary for composing one's good life (cf. Staudinger, 1999). It is true and there is growing research (e.g., Barkow, Cosmides, & Tooby, 1992) demonstrating that evolution has provided us with a good number of abilities to master life. At the same time, however, the human mind has been creating a degree of cultural complexity that is less than ever matched by our evolution-based capacities. More than ever, this mismatch asks for a culturally provided supply of life-compository tools. In contrast to mathematical or language skills, it seems as though life composition should come naturally; but we are not born knowing how to lead a fulfilled life and how to become a good member of society.

REFERENCES

Azmitia, M. (1996). Peer interactive minds: Development, theoretical, and methodological issues. In P. B. Baltes & U. M. Staudinger (Eds.), *Interactive minds: Life-span perspectives on the social foundation of cognition* (pp. 133–162). New York: Cambridge University Press.

Baltes, M. M., & Silverberg, S. B. (1994). The dynamics between dependency and autonomy: Illustrations across the life span. In D. L. Featherman, R. M. Lerner, & M. Perlmutter (Eds.), *Life span development and behavior* (Vol. 12, pp. 41–90). Hillsdale, NJ: Erlbaum.

Baltes, P. B., Smith, J., & Staudinger, U. M. (1992). Wisdom and successful aging. In T. B. Sonderegger (Ed.), *Nebraska symposium on motivation* (Vol. 39, pp. 123–167). Lincoln: University of Nebraska Press.

Baltes, P. B., & Staudinger, U. M. (Eds.). (1996). *Interactive minds: Life-span perspectives on the social foundation of cognition.* New York: Cambridge University Press.

Bandura, A. (1998). Personal and collective efficacy in human adaptation and change. In J. G. Adair & D. Belanger (Eds.), *Advances in psychological science: Vol. 1. Social, personal, and cultural aspects* (pp. 51–71). Hove, England: Psychology Press.

Barkow, J. H., Cosmides, L., & Tooby, J. (Eds.). (1992). *The adapted mind: Evolutionary psychology and the generation of culture.* New York: Oxford University Press.

Bar-Tal, D., & Kruglanski, A. W. (Eds.). (1988). *The social psychology of knowledge.* Cambridge: Cambridge University Press.

Bornstein, M. H., & Bruner, J. S. (Eds.). (1989). *Interaction in human development.* Hillsdale, NJ: Erlbaum.

Chapman, M. (1988). Contextuality and directionality of cognitive development. *Human Development, 31,* 92–106.

Cohen, R., & Siegel, A. W. (Eds.). (1991). *Context and development.* Hillsdale, NJ: Erlbaum.

Cooper, C. R., & Denner, J. (1998). Theories linking culture and psychology: Universal and community-specific processes. *Annual Review of Psychology, 49,* 559–584.

Cranach, M. v., Doise, W., & Mugny, G. (Eds.). (1992). *Social representations and the social bases of knowledge.* Lewiston, NY: Hogrefe & Huber.

Edelstein, W., & Hoppe-Graf, S. (1993). *Die Konstruktion kognitiver Strukturen: Perspektiven einer konstrucktivistischen Entwicklungspsychologie* [The construction of cognitive structures: Perspectives of a constructivist developmental psychology]. Bern, Switzerland: Huber.

Erikson, E. H. (1959). *Identity and the life cycle.* New York: International University Press.

Erikson, E. H., Erikson, J. M., & Kivnick, H. (1986). *Vital involvement in old age: The experience of old age in our time.* London: W. W. Norton.

Forman, E. A., Minick, N., & Stone, C. A. (1993). *Contexts for learning.* New York: Oxford University Press.

Greeno, J. G., Chi, M. T. H., Clancey, W. J., & Elman, J. (Eds.). (1993). Situated action [special issue]. *Cognitive Science, 17,* 1–147.

Havighurst, R. J. (1948). *Developmental tasks and education.* New York: Davis McKay.

Hill, G. W. (1982). Group versus individual performance: Are N+ heads better than one? *Psychological Bulletin, 91,* 517–539.

Joiner, T., & Coyne, J. C. (1999). *The interactional nature of depression: Advances in interpersonal approaches.* Washington, DC: American Psychological Association.

Klix, F. (1993). *Erwachendes Denken: Geistige Leistungen aus evolutionspsychologischer Sicht* [Thinking comes to life: Cognitive performance from an evolutionary psychology perspective]. Heidelberg: Spektrum Akademischer Verlag.

Levine, J. M., Resnick, L. B., & Higgins, E. T. (1993). Social foundations of cognition. *Annual Review of Psychology, 44,* 585–612.

Light, P., & Butterworth, G. (Eds.). (1992). *Context and cognition: Ways of learning and knowing.* Herfordshire, England: Harvester Wheatsheaf.

Luria, A. R. (1976). *Cognitive development: Its cultural and social foundations.* Cambridge, MA: Harvard University Press.

Magnusson, D., & Endler, N. S. (Eds.). (1977). *Personality at the crossroads: Current issues in interactional psychology.* Hillsdale, NJ: Erlbaum.

Minsky, M. L. (1986). *The society of mind.* New York: Simon & Schuster.

Neimeyer, R. A., Neimeyer, G. J., Lyddon, W. J., & Hoshmand, L. T. (1994). The reality of social construction. *Contemporary Psychology, 39,* 459–463.

Pervin, L. A., & Lewis, M. (Eds.). (1978). *Perspectives in interactional psychology*. New York: Plenum.

Resnick, L. B., Levine, J. M., & Teasley, S. D. (Eds.). (1991). *Perspectives on socially shared cognition*. Washington, DC: American Psychological Association.

Rogoff, B. (1990). *Apprenticeship in thinking: Cognitive development in social context*. New York: Oxford University Press.

Rogoff, B., & Chavajay, P. (1995). What's become of research on the cultural basis of cognitive development? *American Psychologist, 50*, 859–877.

Rogoff, B., & Lave, J. (Eds.). (1984). *Everyday cognition: Its development in social context*. Cambridge, MA: Harvard University Press.

Salomon, G. (1993). *Distributed cognition*. New York: Cambridge University Press.

Staudinger, U. M. (1996). Wisdom and the social-interactive foundation of the mind. In P. B. Baltes & U. M. Staudinger (Eds.), *Interactive minds: Life-span perspectives on the social foundation of cognition* (pp. 276–315). New York: Cambridge University Press.

Staudinger, U. M. (1999). Social cognition and a psychological approach to an art of life. In F. Blanchard-Fields & T. Hess (Eds.), *Social cognition, adult development and aging* (pp. 343–375). New York: Academic Press.

Staudinger, U. M., & Baltes, P. B. (1996). Interactive minds: A facilitative setting for wisdom-related performance? *Journal of Personality and Social Psychology, 71*, 746–762.

Sternberg, R. J., & Wagner, R. K. (Eds.). (1994). *Mind in context: Interactionist perspectives on human intelligence*. New York: Cambridge University Press.

Triandis, H. C. (1990). Cross-cultural studies of individualism and collectivism. In J. J. Berman (Ed.), *Nebraska symposium on motivation* (Vol. 37, pp. 41–143). Lincoln: University of Nebraska Press.

Vygotsky, L. S. (1978). *Mind in society: The development of higher psychological processes*. Cambridge, MA: Harvard University Press.

Wertsch, J. V. (1985). *Vygotsky and the social formation of mind*. Cambridge, MA: Harvard University Press.

Wozniak, R. H., & Fischer, K. W. (Eds.). (1993). *Development in context: Acting and thinking in specific environments*. Hillsdale, NJ: Erlbaum.

18 Thinking "Youth," Thinking "School"

Social Representations and Fieldwork in Educational Research

Claude Albert Kaiser

Youth as a Cultural Construction

To speak of *youth* implies that these individuals have something in common, that they share certain experiences and preoccupations. Yet everyone has his or her own particular ideas about the meaning of youth or adolescence; one can also distinguish various approaches to apprehending this concept. For example, *adolescence* can be defined in physiological or biological terms when one refers to puberty. From a sociological or economic point of view, one might define youth as a key period for the construction of a stable identity or as a stage of transition from school to work. Thus, to speak of youth is actually a way of classifying or evaluating individuals. For some, young people are a source of innovation; for others, they form a group with its own set of values and its own culture that sometimes disturbs by its behavior. There are different types of discourse about youth, and each focuses on particular categories of behavior and social phenomena.

When the focus is on sociological factors, such as family traditions or modes of access to employment, one finds considerable differences in the meaning of youth according to country or culture (see Fouquet, this volume). In other words, a person's concept of youth depends on his or her membership in specific groups, and thus youth is largely a social construction. Our position is that youth should be considered a social representation to the extent that it has a communicative function or usefulness (Moscovici, 1961, 1984; Palmonari & Doise, 1986). Thus, the term *youth* reflects specific symbolic relations within or between groups in a given social or cultural context.

Simply using the term *youth* partitions the social field into young people and adults. In accordance with the logic of social categorization (Tajfel, 1981), this partitioning can easily give rise to intergroup dynamics involving stereotyping and simplification. Thus, when one tries to determine young people's opinions concerning a particular issue, via a questionnaire for example, and renders explicit their membership in the youth category, the responses obtained will reflect not only the subjects' understanding of the group to which they belong but also their perception of adults' or society's expectations of them.

These expectations are normative to the extent that they both reflect general beliefs and values diffused in a society and determine the dimensions on which groups are defined in relation to one another (Doise, 1992). The psychosocial approach to the study of youth consists of

the descriptions of specific processes and the study of societal values which intervene in such aspects of students' identity construction. But processes and values do not really deal with adolescents as such; they only do so when the particular situations and positions of adolescents in a network of social relationship are linked to the study of processes and values. (Doise, 1992, p. 50)

Grossen, Liengme Bessire, and Perret-Clermont (1997) developed a similar position in their study of sociocognitive dynamics. Conducting research in school settings can be perceived as a symbolic encounter between the scientific community and the educational institution; the actors – students and researchers – play and interpret their roles in terms of their own perspective and what they attribute to the other.

A Study in a School Setting of Students' Opinions About Learning

To illustrate our point, we refer briefly to a survey we carried out in a technical school for the training of practitioners in mechanics and electronics (for details, see Kaiser, Perret-Clermont, & Perret, 2000; Kaiser, Perret-Clermont, Perret, & Golay Schilter, 1997). The goal of the survey was to determine the extent to which the students felt they played an active role in their studies and training. The people in charge of the system of professional schools advocated active learning, believing that the new challenge for education was to provide interactive, individualized training centered not only on the learning of content but also on the acquisition of skills. Changes in the meaning and value attributed to work were also at issue. It was hoped that students' increased participation in their own training would bring about a new attitude toward work. The ideal individual is considered to be one who knows what he or she wants, is able to project the self into the future, and anticipates personal actions: in short, an individual who makes choices and is not governed only by circumstances. Thus, learning by repetition and conditioning ought to be replaced by creativity, innovation, and a spirit of initiative. Such were the expectations of the adults regarding education in school.

From the first page of the questionnaire, it was clear that the researchers' goal was to become more familiar with young people's opinions on educational issues. They were asked to express their ideas about the process of learning and about the reasons for success and failure in various subjects. Our analysis of their responses showed a clear preference for traditional approaches of learning that are based on imitation and rehearsal.

At first glance, this finding seems paradoxical, given that these traditional values contrast sharply with the expectations expressed by the adults in charge of the school. Moreover, our results conflicted with the findings of another part of the study that is based on the observation of students' behavior (Golay Schilter, 1997; Golay Schilter, Perret, Perret-Clermont, & de Guglielmo, 1999; Golay Schilter, Perret-Clermont, Perret, de Guglielmo, & Chavey, 1997; Perret, Perret-Clermont, & Golay Schilter, 1997): What students believed or had learned to say did not correspond to what actually happened in class. For instance, in the process of carrying out a practical task imposed by the teacher, technical students constantly sought help or support from classmates. The presence of a third party often elicited decentering responses favorable to success in the task, and situations of learning through simple repetition and imitation were relatively rare.

We can account for the apparent contradictions in these findings if we take into consideration the attitudes and representations students have with respect to schools and teachers. The opinions and ideas they expressed were probably those they believed were in accordance with the model of education advocated by the teachers and directors of the institution. Although we wished to determine students' views on education and optimal learning strategies, we actually obtained elements of information about their manner of thinking about adults and schools. This obviously has important consequences with respect to the ways we might legitimately use the results of such surveys. It also points to the need for caution in other situations where similar mechanisms are at work: a job interview, for instance. The type of exchange in such a context is similar to that found in a questionnaire: The themes of conversation are generally determined in advance by the interviewer, and the interviewee merely responds to the questions, whether or not they correspond to his or her own viewpoint and concerns. Lack of concordance with the expectations of the interlocutors can have unfortunate consequences for the person being interviewed.

One might think that the solution to this problem is to provide some sort of training that encourages people to express and clarify their respective expectations. But this solution overlooks an important aspect in social interaction: the power of the context, which, as we pointed out, is mainly a symbolic encounter between different institutions or social groups.

We noticed the importance of context in a study in which students were interviewed about their future careers. These students, who were reaching the end of their compulsory schooling, had followed a program in self-evaluation that was supposed to help them develop projects for their future occupational training (for details, see Kaiser, 1997). Interviewed in small groups, the students were asked about their occupational choices and, in accordance with the preparatory self-evaluation exercises, to say which personal characteristics they believed to be their own strong points.

Almost all the students had already made their job choices, but to ascribe qualities to themselves proved to be an extremely difficult task for them, although they had had training in self-evaluation. Students in the lower-level classes tended to define their faults and weaknesses, rather than their strengths, using expressions such as "I am not." Possibly the presence of peers during the interview led them to avoid talking about their good qualities to prevent being treated as braggers or showoffs. The difficulty of expressing one's qualities was also observed in another study conducted by Guichard, Pirerotti, Scheurer, and Viriot (1988), who used individually administered questionnaires. Thus, although students had practiced self-evaluation, they did not exhibit this skill in the interviews. Perhaps they had performed the self-evaluation exercises in the same fashion as other school activities in which interaction between individuals is rarely taken into account.

In conclusion, schools, with all their actors, including directors, teachers, and students, should not be interested exclusively in the characteristics of the learners. They should pay more attention to the nature of interindividual, ideological, and institutional functioning, taking into account implicit and explicit didactic contracts, value systems, and hierarchical organizations. They should examine not only their own representations and discourse but also the concrete effects of the working conditions and the educational practices of teachers and students.

REFERENCES

Doise, W. (1992). Social psychology and the study of youth. In W. Meeus, M. de Goede, W. Kox, & K. Hurrelmann (Eds.), *Adolescence, careers and cultures* (pp. 35–53). Berlin/New York: Walter de Gruyter.

Golay Schilter, D. (1997). *Apprendre la fabrication assistée par ordinateur: Sens, enjeux et rapport aux outils* [Learning computer-assisted manufacture: Meaning, issues, and relations with tools] (Research document #13). Neuchâtel, Switzerland: University of Neuchâtel, Psychology Seminar.

Golay Schilter, D., Perret, J.-F., Perret-Clermont, A.-N., & de Guglielmo, F. (1999). Sociocognitive interactions in a computerised industrial task: Are they productive for learning? In K. Littleton & P. Light (Eds.), *Learning with computers. Analysing productive interaction* (pp. 162–178). London: Routledge.

Golay Schilter, D., Perret-Clermont, A.-N., Perret, J.-F., de Guglielmo, F., & Chavey, J.-P. (1997). *Aux prises avec l'informatique industrielle: Collaboration et démarches de travail chez des élèves techniciens* [Industrial data processing: Collaboration and working methods in technical students] (Research document #7). Neuchâtel, Switzerland: University of Neuchâtel, Psychology Seminar.

Grossen, M., Liengme Bessire, M.-J., & Perret-Clermont, A.-N. (1997). Construction de l'interaction et dynamiques socio-cognitives [Construction of interaction and sociocognitive processes]. In M. Grossen & B. Py (Eds.), *Pratiques sociales et médiations symboliques* [Social practices and symbolic mediation] (pp. 221–242). Bern/Berlin: Peter Lang.

Guichard, J., Pirerotti, M., Scheurer, E., & Viriot, M. (1988). *L'orientation éducative de la sixième à la troisième* [Educational orientation for adolescents]. Issy-Les-Moulineaux, France: Ed. EAP.

Kaiser, C. (1997). *Education des choix. Rapport d'évaluation* [Educating choice. Evaluation report]. Geneva: Department of Public Education, Unit for Educational Research.

Kaiser, C., Perret-Clermont, A.-N., & Perret, J.-F. (2000). Do I choose? Attribution and control in students of a technical school. In W. Perrig & A. Grob (Eds.), *Control of human behavior, mental processes and consciousness* (pp. 427–442). Mahwah, NJ/London: Erlbaum.

Kaiser, C., Perret-Clermont, A.-N., Perret, J.-F., & Golay Schilter, D. (1997). *Apprendre un métier technique aujourd'hui: Représentations des apprenants* [Learning a technical trade today: Learners' representations] (Research document #10). Neuchâtel, Switzerland: University of Neuchâtel, Psychology Seminar.

Moscovici, S. (1961; 1976, 2nd ed.). *La psychanalyse, son image et son public* [Psychoanalysis, its image and its public]. Paris: Presses Universitaires de France.

Moscovici, S. (1984). The phenomenon of social representation. In R. M. Farr & S. Moscovici (Eds.), *Social representation* (pp. 3–69). Cambridge: Cambridge University Press.

Palmonari, A., & Doise, W. (1986). Caractéristiques des représentations sociales [Characteristics of social representations]. In W. Doise & A. Palmonari (Eds.), *L'étude des représentations sociales* [The study of social representations] (pp. 12–33). Neuchâtel, Switzerland/Paris: Delachaux et Niestlé.

Perret, J.-F, Perret-Clermont, A.-N., & Golay Schilter, D. (1997). *Interactions entre maître et élèves en cours de travaux pratiques* [Interactions between teacher and pupils during practical work] (Research document #6). Neuchâtel, Switzerland: University of Neuchâtel, Psychology Seminar.

Tajfel, H. (1981). *Human groups and social categories.* Cambridge: Cambridge University Press.

VI

PATHWAYS TO ADULTHOOD IN NATIONAL CONTEXT

19 Joining Society in Europe

Convergence or Sustainability of National Specificities

Annie Fouquet

Each country in Europe has its own understanding of what *youth* is. To be young is not the same in the United Kingdom or in Italy, as their transition policies indicate. In the United Kingdom, policies address youngsters between 16 and 18 years old; meanwhile, in Italy and Spain, they concern young people from 18 to 30 and even 32 years of age. In European research meetings devoted to integration policies, British colleagues are often surprised to hear a Spanish colleague speaking about the transition for 30-year-old youngsters.[1] They consider it improper. Mutual knowledge of these societal pecularities is still in the early stages, and European policies proposed by the European Union have not taken all of them into account.

Several factors explain this different understanding of what youth is. They have their roots in family traditions, school and training systems, modes of access to employment and of management of professionnal mobility, or labor market segmentation. Thus, the following contrasting situations have to be considered: Northern countries with nuclear families versus Southern countries with extended families; countries with general and undifferentiated compulsory schooling versus countries with differentiated tracks; countries with a tradition of apprenticeship managed by enterprises versus countries where vocational training is managed mainly by the school system; countries with a professional labor market versus internal markets or an informal labor market in local networks.

[1] Author's personal experience in Orleans, January 1997.
I thank professors Jacques Perriault, Paul Ryan, and Dragan Popadić for their helpful critiques and comments on an earlier version of this chapter

These elements are linked in national combinations that have their own balance, according to a long tradition. Recent economic development and technical change have displaced these balances. Some systems seem to adapt more easily to new ability and skill requirements and development of new activities. The unemployment rate of young people is used as the indicator of a country's performance in youth integration. This chapter demonstrates that deeper analysis is required, because this indicator narrowly depends on the way young people are integrated into employment and at what age they enter business life.

Introduction

Until recently, leaving school, getting a first job, and establishing one's own family occurred almost at the same time. Nowadays, the transition period has expanded, becoming more complex, with back-and-forth moves between initial and final statuses. Intermediary situations between the end of compulsory schooling and the first job have become more numerous and interspace training and job experiences. In private lives, young people go back and forth between their family and peer lives, with or without cohabitation, before they start a family. These steps are no longer earmarked by transition rites and legal obligations, such as military service, engagement, and wedding.

An Approach Centered on Structures Rather Than on Individual Behavior

All European countries have known this extended transition period between childhood and responsible adult life. The reasons for the period's becoming so extended are numerous. Some of them are demographic changes, such as the growth of life expectancy or use of birth control, which led to greater participation of women in education and economic life. Technical progress keeps on changing the production processes: employment shifts from industry to the service sector; skills requirements change in both quantity and quality; unemployment expansion in Europe. All of these factors played the same part in European countries. They modified the previous balances specific to each country among training systems, family traditions, labor markets, and employment systems. Transitions became difficult, and youth unemployment grew.

Extended and more complex transitions can be analyzed according to two approaches: one in terms of individual behavior and adjustments, the other in terms of structures and institutions. These two approaches are complementary (see the following section). This chapter explores, in a comparative way, the institutional context of transition between training and employment and, more generally, between education and work. The issue is to determine if the same factors of change do or do not weaken specific national features.

Individual Behavior Adjustments or Institutional Constraints

Faced with structural changes, young people – individuals as well as whole cohorts – have lost their benchmarks and have to invent new ways of entering adult life. To anticipate new realities, young people have to create new ways to reproduce and build their identities.

In order to account for this increasing complexity of transitions, longitudinal analyses, such as biographic trajectories, have been developed over the past few years. They stress the adjustment of individuals to social constraints (Mayer, 1994).

American studies (Rindfuss, Swicegood, & Rosenfield, 1987) have shown that an extended transition goes with increasing disorder in steps. In their German literature survey on transition, Heinz and Nagel (1995) point out two approaches to explain such increased disorder. The first one is a postmodern approach that explains it as individualizing and destructuring the phases of youth (Comte & Helsper, 1991); the second one analyzes it as an extension and diversification of pathways from school to adult life (Hitmeyer & Olk, 1990).

Diversified individual pathways and biographic analysis tend to overestimate the actor's part in the negotiation of an individual trajectory, whereas structural constraints remain as indicators of social, gender, or ethnic inequalities. That is why Heinz (1994) prefers to analyze biographies in terms of pathways, allowing the setting of compromises between different requirements and constraints of the transition from school to employment. He identifies four types of transition behavior:

Strategic: clear-cut vocational choices and occupational goals are formulated.

Step-by-step: choices are reversible; occupational goals are not clearly identified.

Taking chances: choices toward demanding training or educational attainments.

Wait and see: no definite choices are made.

Methodology and Data

This chapter is based on the following complementary sources:

- Statistical data set up by Eurostat (public authority of the European Union that is devoted to statistics) on labor forces (1997) and on education (1995). These data depend on the way national categorization of school levels, grades, and credits is set up in each European country (Duru-Bellat, Kieffer, & Mearelli-Fournier, 1997).
- A metastudy of local debates and research in three European countries on the relation between education and work; this study was initiated at French CNRS (Centre National de la Recherche Scientifique [National Center for Scientific Research]) by Lucie Tanguy (Jobert, Marry, & Tanguy, 1995).
- The first outcomes of the European Science Foundation Network on Transitions in Youth. The first meeting was held in Berlin (CEDEFOP, 1994) and the third one in Marseille (Werquin, Breen, & Planas, 1997).
- The economic research program held by IRES and CEREQ[2] on youth integration policies in Europe and their convergence (Lefresne, 1995).

These studies are recent, and research issues are numerous. I intend to link theses studies with previous comparative studies on labor markets. For that I refer to works such as those using the societal effect approach of Maurice, Sellier, and Sylvestre (1982) and the professional labor market approach of Eyraud and Marsden (Eyraud, Marsden, & Sylvestre, 1990; Marsden, 1989; Marsden & Ryan, 1991). These works specify several ways of matching labor supply and demand, such as professional markets, internal markets, and local markets. My hypothesis is that the relation between education/training and work, which distributes young people into occupational statuses, has to do with the way labor markets are set up in each economy.

Few studies link social and household dimensions in a comparative way. European studies on family policy and employment focus on women's employment or on childhood (Hantrais & Letablier, 1996a, 1996b). The European Science Foundation network gave up this track after its first meeting, where papers on this matter were very tentative and nationally oriented (Kieffer & Marry, 1994), except for that of Heinz (1994), which compares Germany with the United Kingdom. After providing a rough overview of

---

[2] IRES: Institut de Recherches Économiques et Sociale (trade union research center); CEREQ: Centre d'Étude et de Recherches sur les Qualifications (public research center dedicated to the relations between education and employment; in charge of longitudinal surveys of school leavers and statistics on continuous formation).

national specificities, as indicated in the following European statistics, I classify different societal patterns of transition and then describe these patterns for three countries taken as examples.

Overview: To Be Young in Europe

In the United Kingdom, 80% of an age group enter working life between 16 and 18 years of age. People regard those who keep on studying without professional experience as being reluctant to work. To extend their abilities, young workers use vocational training, either part-time after working hours or full-time between two jobs. For that reason, the activity rates of United Kingdom youngsters between 16 and 18 years old are the highest in Europe, except for Denmark. Consequently, the issue of transitions concerns only the 16- to 18-year olds (Jobert et al., 1995).

At the opposite end of the spectrum are the Latin countries, where family solidarity plays an important role much longer (even after marriage) in the frame of the extended family. The most extreme case of this occurs in southern Italy, where half of the 30-year-old men, married or not, live with their parents. Thus, the local transition policies for young people concern 18- to 30-year olds and sometimes extend to 32-year-olds. In Latin countries, significant youth unemployment goes along with extended schooling and family; youth participation rates in the labor market are among the lowest.

Youth Participation and Unemployment Rates in Europe

In the yearly Labor Force Survey, Eurostat defines young people as the group from 15 to 24 years old. According to this authority, youth participation rates in 1995 appeared to be rather low in France (36%), Italy (39%), and Spain (41%) and much higher in the United Kingdom (see Table 19.1, column e). At the same time, unemployment rates appeared to be very high in Spain (42%), Italy (33%), and France (27%) and very low in Germany (8%) and the United Kingdom (10%). This description is partly wrong, however, because these sets of figures cannot be compared at face value for two reasons:

- *Institutional reasons.* In Germany, apprentices, who train within entreprises, are considered part of the working population, whereas the French system of alternative training (*alternance*) – partly in school, partly in an enterprise – accounts for them in the school population. This artificially increases the discrepancy.

Table 19.1 Percentage of Youngsters Engaged in Various Levels of Work-Related Activity in European Countries

| | Of 100 Youngsters | | | | Eurostat Ratios of Active Population | |
| | Learning (General or Vocational Training) (n) | With a Job (n) | In Search of a Job (n) | Inactives Not Learning (n) | Participation Rate (%) | Unemployment Rate (%) |
Country	(a)	(b)	(c)	(d)	(e) = (b) + (c)	(f) = (c) / (e)
France	60	26	10	4	36	27
Italy	53	26	13	7	39	33
Spain	54	24	17	5	41	42
Germany	43	48	4	5	52	8
Netherlands	33	50	8	9	58	13
United Kingdom	28	54	10	6	64	15
Denmark	23	66	7	4	73	10

Note: $N = 100$. Based on Eurostat (1997). Author's calculations are in columns a to d. For more countries and details on part-time and full-time jobs, see Figure 19.1.

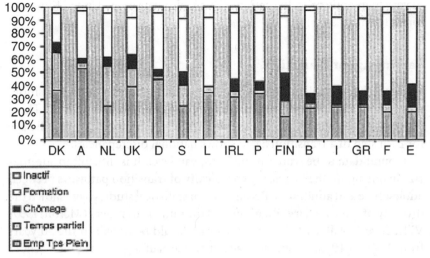

Figure 19.1. Occupation and activity for 15- to 94-year-olds, Europe, 1995. From Eurostat (1997). In these countries, vocational training is organized heterogeneously. It is carried out in general schools, training centers, the so-called dual system, or simply as on-the-job training in the workplace. In France, the greater part of vocational education takes place within the general education system, whereas in Denmark, Germany, and Austria, the dual apprenticeship system is the dominant form, which leads to a clear separation between general education and vocational training. In the Netherlands, Luxembourg, Belgium, and Sweden, vocational training takes place primarily in vocational schools. In Italy, the United Kingdom, and Ireland (as well as in the United States), many beginners enter employment directly and acquire occupational qualifications through on-the-job training at the workplace.

- *Calculation reasons.* The ratio of young people looking for a job to the whole population of young people differs significantly from the ratio of young people looking for a job to those who already have one. Again, this last category is small in Southern European countries. In the first case, the unemployment ratio varies from 42% in Spain to 8% in Germany. In the second case, this ratio varies from 17% in Spain to 4% in Germany. The gap between countries is much smaller, and in this complete description of the occupational status of young people, the youth unemployment rate is the same in France and the United Kingdom – 10% – which official statistics do not show.

This picture has to be completed to provide deeper insight into the content of national categories; the boundary line between training and employment differs for each culture. For instance, in Germany's so-called dual system, the lines are very fluid between scholars, apprentices, and workers because of very frequently mixed situations. This is also true in the United Kingdom for different reasons.

Varying Age of Transition

What are the interrelations between the two main dimensions of transition: from education to work and from parent's household to a new family? These two types of transition are not as synchronous as they used to be. The age for each step of a transition again shows national discrepancies.

I found data to be scarce at the European level. It is difficult to summarize in one figure the increasing complexity of transition pathways between adolescence and adulthood. Recent French statistical studies have shown the diversity of intermediary situations and the numerous moves (Méron, 1997; Villeneuve-Gokalp, 1997). One outcome should be noted: In the 20 years from 1975 to 1995, the median age at which half a generation left school increased by about 3 years, from 18 to 21 years of age. The increase is similar for the median age for establishing a family, rising from 22 to 25 years old.

Data on a particular country's education system are more numerous (Eurostat, 1995). They highlight the previous numbers that detail youth activity by specific national features. Age can be a good indicator of educational attainment in countries with an undifferentiated education system and no doubling. This explains the widespread use of such an indicator in the United Kingdom, where the schooling stream is automatically linked to the age of the pupils. Moreover, with British training categories being very heterogeneous, the British take the time "as a common unit to identify and measure the different types of education" (Tanguy, 1995). Furthermore, with full-time training dropout rates being very high after age 16, age is a good indicator of the level of educational attainment.

A more differentiated system and/or extended full-time schooling weaken this indicator. In such cases, the pertinent criterion of attainment is the type of institution (e.g., general education, further advanced education, polytechnic, university). This is the case in Germany, where, at the age of 18, the distribution of youngsters is bimodal. In France, where general education is widespread and extended, the schooling rate at age 20 is one of the highest (see Table 19.2).

Table 19.2 shows that the time schedule in education varies by country. In the United Kingdom, schooling is primarily linked to age: 17% of the 18-year-olds go to a university in the United Kingdom, whereas only 8% of the 20-year-olds do so in Germany. It is important for people to be "on time" in their initial education in the United Kingdom, although second chances may

Table 19.2 Institutional Places of Education/Training According to Ages

	United Kingdom (1992)	Germany (1994)	France (1994)
At age 16	Full-time education: 71%	*Hauptschulen*:14%	1st cycle[a]: 42%
	Dont	*Gesamtschulen*: 6%	2nd cycle general[b]: 42%
	General educ: 46%	*Realschulen*: 17%	Ses, Cppn, Cpa: 3%
	Further adv: 25%	*Gymnasien*: 28%	Apprentceship: 2%
	Tertiary: 0.1%	*Berufsschulen* (dual	Cap-Bep[c]: 4%
	Part-time: 16%	system): 22%	Technique long[d]: 1%
	Total in education: 88%	Full-time vocational: 9%	Total in education: 99.5%
At age 18	Full-time: 33%	Total in education: 98%	1st cycle: 4%
	Dont	Gymnasien: 25%	2nd cycle general: 47%
	General educ: 4%	Berufsschule: 43%	Ses, Cppn, Cpa: 1%
	Further adv: 12%	Berufsfachschulen: 6%	Apprenticeship: 10%
	Universities: 8%	Fachoberschulen: 7%	Cap-Bep: 21%
	Polytechnics: 9%	Faschulen: 2%	Technique long: 9%
	Part-time: 14%	Higher educ: 1%	Higher educ: 2%
	Total in education: 48%	Total in education: 85%	Total in education: 95%
At age 20	Full-time: 24%	Gymnasien: 3%	1st cycle: 0.5%
	Dont	Berufsschule: 23%	2nd cycle general: 12%
	General educ: 0.3%	Berufsfachschulen: 2%	Ses, Cppn, Cpa: 1%
	Further adv: 3%	Fachoberschulen: 3%	Apprenticeship: 3%
	Tertiary: 20%	Faschulen: 4%	Cap-Bep: 7%
	Part-time: 14%	Higher educ: 12%	Technique long: 16%
	Total in education: 38%	Total in education: 46%	Higher educ: 35%
			Total in education: 75%

[a] Lower secondary general education.
[b] Upper secondary general education.
[c] Lower secondary vocational education.
[d] Upper secondary vocational education.
Source: Duru-Bellat, Kieffer, and Mearelli-Fournier (1997).

occur later in life. Late entries to a university are numerous; in the United Kingdom, 25% of new entrants to higher education are more than 30 years old (Eurostat, 1995, p. 188).

Conversely, in France, early university entrances are the most frequent pattern: 40% of new entrants into higher education are 18 years old (or less), and no one enters after age 25. The level of diploma obtained in initial education determines a person's whole life, and second chances, if any, occur through continuous professional training (law of 1971). In general, the median age for entering higher education is 19 in France, 21 in the United Kingdom, and 22 in Germany, where entries are more spread out over time.

General education is more expanded in France. At the age of 18, general education is provided to 52% of the French, 26% of the Germans, and only 12% of the British. Not only is general education weak in the United Kingdom, but the participation rate in professional training there also is no higher than in other countries for persons of that age. Vocational training (either full-time or part-time) concerns 35% of British 18-year-olds, 40% of the French, and 58% of the Germans.

Vocational education, partly in school and partly in a work situation, concerns a large majority of 18-year-old Germans, 31% of the French at that age, and only 14% of the British (part-time). German apprentices are 6 months older than their French counterparts. In both countries, the median age has increased by $2\frac{1}{2}$ years in 20 years. From now on, apprenticeship will begin later. From 1970 to 1993, the median age of apprentices rose from $16\frac{1}{2}$ to 19 years in Germany and from 16 to $18\frac{1}{2}$ years in France (Duru-Bellat et al., 1997).

Training for Working Life at School or at Work?

An Analytical Grid of Education/Formation and Certification Systems

Educational systems generate streams of differentiated individuals to take various places in the social structure. Muller (1994) uses three criteria to compare national education systems: means of differentiation (vertical vs. horizontal), explicit or implicit effects of education, and types of certification. To these criteria, Duru-Bellat et al. (1997) add types of organization (unified or decentralized).

According to Muller (1994), "Differentiation relates first to the structure of the various established educational institutions and pathways and second to the distribution of the population according to these courses and pathways" (p. 207). It is common to distinguish at least a vertical-hierarchical and a horizontal-functional dimension of education differentiation. *Vertical differentiation* refers to the amount of education that each individual receives and its division into socially recognized packages, such as levels of education or prestige of the educational institution.

Horizontal differentiation refers to the division into qualitatively different tracks of education that are intended to prepare students for different functional tasks, such as the various kinds of baccalaureat in French secondary schools. The proliferation of specialized vocational training programs in polytechnic schools or universities is a response to the increasing specialization of knowledge and of number of professions. To what extent do systems of educational differentiation interact with labor market segmentation to produce nationally specific education/labor market relationships? This is a question for future research.

Education is assumed to provide different types of learning, depending on the kinds of curricula the students follow. These types of learning are general basic skills (e.g., reading, writing, logical reasoning, and information processing); specific instrumental skills (e.g., accounting, computers, foreign languages, techniques, or crafts); knowledge (e.g., history, politics, physics); and socialization in values, norms, and social behavior (these last effects are most often implicit). Such learning can take place either at school or at work. The problem presented by the convergence of education systems is to find how to combine them most efficently for both places.

The question involving certification concerns how credits are used to differentiate tracks, levels, and contents of education attained either at school or at work. The specific question to be asked is, how are they stratified in relation to the social occupational status hierarchy? The extension of education has an escalator effect: All students move up but keep the same relative place (Mayer & Konietzka, 1998). *Stratification* refers to the extent of streaming in the educational system and to the proportion of a cohort that attains the highest qualification level. *Standardization* is the degree to which the quality of educational meets the same nationwide standards. Among countries, the relation between educational differentiation and labor market segmentation differs, and the path toward the first job depends on the respective place of training and certification at school or at work. Who certifies skills and abilities? Is the certification attained in an enterprise recognized elsewhere? Is the certification standardized or not? Later, I will use a grid containing descriptions of national systems to answer these questions.

Transition Patterns: School Model or Apprenticeship Society?

Unlike the national systems, I prefer to use three dimensions proposed by Blossfeld and Muller (CEDEFOP, 1994, pp. 2–4): a long, nonselective period of basic education for everybody versus early selectivity and subject differentiation; general schooling systems without vocational curricula versus dual firm/school vocational training, integrated, or mixed systems; and standardized versus specific certification.

European countries are scattered between two opposite patterns: the *school model*, where schooling is lengthy, and the *apprenticeship societies*, where vocational training is attained outside the schooling system (Blossfeld, 1993, p. 27). In the school model, the majority of vocational education takes place within the general education system (e.g., in France and Spain) or in special vocational schools (e.g., in the Netherlands, Luxembourg, Belgium, and Sweden). In apprenticeship societies, vocational training is separate from the schooling system, and employers as well as employees are responsible for it. Note the following two cases. In Italy, the United Kingdom, and Ireland (as well as the United States), occupational beginners enter employment directly and acquire occupational qualifications through on-the-job training. In Denmark, Germany, and Austria, with the dual apprenticeship system, vocational training is organized within enterprises and training institutions that are clearly separate from general education.

The Parallel Evolutions

These same trends affect the national systems (Lefresne, 1995):

1. *The extension of initial education far beyond compulsory schooling.* Italy is an extreme case; compulsory schooling ends at age 14, but the great majority of youngsters remain in school far longer. Even in the United Kingdom, where school leavers are younger, the schooling rates after age 16 have been increasing in the past few years for two reasons. Skill requirements are increasing in this information society; and young people stay longer in school to avoid unemployment and the low value of vocational certification.
2. *The increasing value of vocational training in all countries except Germany, where it was always recognized.* In Sweden, now and for the foreseeable future, vocational tracks will have a value equal to that of general education tracks. In Spain and France, vocational tracks lead to the baccalaureat level. In Italy, the Progretto Reform has added or reinforced general subject matter content in technical tracks (41% of secondary students are in a vocational track). In the United Kingdom, where vocational training used to be provided outside the school system in various institutions by local authorities (generally known as *nonadvanced further education*), an attempt was made in 1983 to introduce vocational training at school by the Technical and Vocational Education Initiative.
3. *Alternative periods in established enterprises for students under school auspices are expanding in school model societies.* In Spain, a 1987 agreement between trade unions and employers opened the way to periods of practical training in enterprises. In France since 1986, vocational baccalaureats and *alternance* periods have been expanded in vocational secondary schools. In Italy, a 1993 agreement opened the way to *alternance* in the Progretto track. In Sweden, the 1991 school law established a requirement for students to spend up to 15% of their vocational training time in enterprises.

These three processes accompanied an explicit charge to develop partnerships among the leaders of the educational system, enterprises, unions, and local authorities.

●

National Specificities Remain

Besides these changes and converging evolutions, specific national interactions occur between initial training and job entry. In Latin countries, extended schooling appears to be an answer to unemployment, and the increasing value of vocational tracks and *alternance* have not yet narrowed the gap between initial education and work. Conversely, the dual systems in Sweden and Germany still appear to be central to youth integration and efficient from an economic point of view. The dual system is often referred to as *the* ideal model in French debate, whereas many German analysts describe it as *a model in crisis* because of its success. General education graduates are increasingly taking advantage of apprenticeship; but by doing so, they freeze the upward career process that was the grounds for social compromise. The system increases labor market rigidity: New professions are scarce; when not in the system, underqualified, excluded people cannot come back. Women fare less well in this process. But the dual system partners (i.e., teachers, enterprises, unions, and public authorities) wish to improve it. In the United Kingdom since the apprenticeship collapse, the low level of youth attainment appears to be a major problem (Steedman & Hawkins, 1994).

School Model and Transition

The main feature of the school model is the high percentage of an age group that goes to school. For example, more than 90% of the 17-year-olds are at school in Sweden or France. In this model, grades play a decisive role, signaling the distribution of young people into jobs. The labor market is organized according to grade levels, the content of which is guaranteed by national standards. Nevertheless, initial vocational training is hardly valued by enterprises. Youth integration policies are trying to remediate that situation. In France, for example, public authorities partly fund social constitutions of working contracts for young people (*contrats de travail aidés*), provided that the enterprises where they work trains them. Enterprises are now in favor of apprenticeships to avoid the negative effects of an initial training that may have been too school-oriented or too far removed from practical skills. Now the issue is integrating into a national system of grades the certification of knowledge and abilities built up on the job, because the French certification system is based on the training that a profession requires and not on a person's performance in a work setting (Merle, 1994). The situation in the United Kingdom is the exact opposite.

Apprenticeship Society and Transition

In the United Kingdom, the apprenticeship system collapsed because enterprises lost interest in it and wanted to keep out of what they thought was a rigid corporate system. This collapse led successive governments to develop training policies for compulsory school leavers (CGS O level) who found no jobs or apprenticeship apportunities. These youth training schemes were unappreciated because they did not provide increased skills and were not recognized by enterprises.

The youth labor market has two difficulties: First, young people in the United Kingdom generally have low qualifications; second, they have no way and no documents to demonstrate the types and levels of skill that they have built up through work experience. Cities and guilds grant vocational credits (*certificats de métiers*) that acknowledge abilities in a job situation, given a normative description of professional techniques and activities. This certification is used mostly for blue-collar upgrading. It does not transfer well. Some professions offer certification by the Business and Technicians Education Council (e.g., professions in commerce, industry, and administration) and by the Royal Society of Arts (e.g., clerks, salespeople). Validation of skills and abilities is split up, disseminated, deconcentrated, and sends a weak message to employers. That explains the attempt to set up a national system to validate abilities and skills: the NVQS (National Vocational Qualification System), which is expected to replace the role of professional branches that failed to organize professional markets. NVQS aims to set up an information device needed for the functioning of an efficient labor market, which involves monitoring trials and errors in matching job supply and demand. This involves progressively creating national standards of certification that are both independant of training and transferable. Unlike the French situation, certification in the United Kingdom is separated from training. It is based on ability patterns that are validated under conditions "as similar as possible to a real job situation."

The European attempt to promote such a validation system for Europe fails to consider the national contexts in which certification systems are elaborated, as well as the important role played by social partners in building up existing patterns, namely in France in the CPC (Commissions Consultatives Paritaires) and in Germany in negotiations of the dual system.

Apprenticeship in the German Dual System

In Germany, a special period dedicated to developing qualifications lies in the time between school leaving and obtaining a full-time job. This institutional framework, called *apprenticeship*, organizes the path to adult life for young boys and girls who do not enter higher education. Professional teaching is formally organized in 420 professions, covering almost all blue- or white-collar jobs that do not require higher education. Apprenticeship is a dual system with an average length of 3 years. It includes training courses given inside an enterprise as well as courses organized by public authorities in vocational schools (*berufsschule*). Practical and theoretical examinations establish the status of a qualified worker or a qualified employee. This mode of validation is standardized and valid outside the enterprise that delivers the training under the auspices of a public authority. Sixty percent of young Germans between 16 and 20 years of age who leave school enter the apprenticeship system, which simultaneously supplies professional qualifications, skills, work standards, and an accreditation that can be used throughout life, even in different work settings.

Employers appreciate the *social skills* abilities attained during the apprenticeship period. This dual system is the outcome of negotiations among teachers, employers, public authorities, and trade unions. Hamilton and Hurrelman (1993) stress that negotiation occurs in a process of conflict resolution that embraces many dimensions, namely, education values, globalization, technical progress, and financial aspects. According to the authors, this explains how the dual system overcomes the challenges of change, thanks to a continuous internal transformation.

Dual System Shortcomings

- An apprenticeship locates girls in traditionally female activites (e.g., hairdressing, sales, clerking), that is, in low-paid jobs with little future. In the past few years, girls' participation in the dual system has increased from 30% to 70% (Beret, 1997). After apprenticeship, girls often move on and shift from unemployment to temporary jobs or to housewife status.
- If the dual system facilitates careers in internal labor markets, namely, in large and midsized enterprises, it definitively excludes those who had no opportunity to enter apprenticeship. Unlike the French situation, where

lifelong continuous training is financed by enterprises and comanaged by trade unions, the German dual system does not offer second chances.

A Model in Crisis?

A training system that is segmented by branches leads to dangerous labor market rigidities when qualification changes become intense and immediate. For example, women have difficulty returning to the labor market after an interruption. A good level of general education with transferable abilities appears to help those who encounter rapid changes in required qualifications. That gives more value to general education and calls the dual system into question.

But the dual system also has had success. More and more young people coming out of general education with an *Abitur* grade (high school diploma signifying the end of general education) choose the dual system to extend their training. In 1971, most apprentices came from a *hauptschule* (upper primary school), and only 1% came from a *gymnasium* (senior high school). Now 40% graduate from *hauptschule*, 40% from a *realschule* (medium or junior high school), and 16% from *gymnasium* (senior high school with general education; *Abitur* graduates). After an apprenticeship program, more and more young people continue their studies to gain additional qualifications. The percentage of students coming from an apprenticeship program increased from 25% in 1985 to 34% in 1990. The massive numbers of young graduates with a general education block the upward mobility of midlevel staff (e.g., prevent technicians from becoming engineers). This calls into question the social mobility mechanisms of the dual system. Thus, the social compromise that grounded the system is greatly weakened, which, in turn, weakens the balance between enterprise training and school training. On one side, apprentices are no longer motivated to train inside an enterprise because it does not guarantee later employment. On the other side, high-level apprentices have more training opportunities outside an enterprise, which frequently provokes breaks with training enterprises. That also increases the likelihood that enterprises will lose the apprentices they have trained.

Muller (1994) summarizes the situation as follows:

It may be an irony of societal development that the general trend towards extended general schooling, which originally was motivated by manpower requirements arguments, but was more forcefully pushed forward by family aspirations and political motives, in the end appears to fit well with much later development and requirements of technological restructuring and occupational upgrading. It might also create an opportunity for a convergence of the education–employment linkage in Europe. (p. 213)

Conclusion

Joining society in a changing world is a complex process. Young people play their part by inventing new processes through which to enter adult life. School systems, enterprises, teachers, and social partners change to match new transition patterns. How can work experience or life experience be recognized by institutions? All European countries face this same question. Because of specific national backgrounds, the answers cannot all be the same. European research can play an important role in showing how changes in transition paths interact with institutional structures and how youngsters develop new abilities to overcome such difficulties in an ever more complex transition process.

REFERENCES

Beret, P. (1997, June). *Formation et marché du travail en France et en Allemagne* [Education, training and labor market in France and in Germany]. Communication of the Séminaire du Lasmas-IdL. Paris: IRESCO.

Blossfeld, H. P. (1993). Changes in educational opportunities in the Federal Republic of Germany: A longitudinal study of cohorts born between 1916 and 1965. In Y. Shavit & H. P. Blossfeld (Eds.), *Persistent inequality: Changing educational attainment in thirteen countries* (pp. 51–74). New York: Westview Press.

CEDEFOP. (1994). *The determinants of transitions in youth: Papers from the 1993 conference organized by the ESF Network on transitions in Youth.* CEDEFOP (European Centre for the Development of Vocational Training) and GRET (Universitat Autonoma de Barcelona). Berlin: Panorama.

Comte, A., & Helsper, W. (1991). *Hermeneustische Jugendforschung. Theoretische Konzepte und methodologische Ansätze* [Research on young people. Theoretical concepts and methodological issues]. Opladen, Germany: Verlag.

Duru-Bellat, M., Kieffer, A., & Mearelli-Fournier, I. (1997). Le diplôme, l'âge et le niveau: Sens et usages dans les comparaisons des systèmes éducatifs [Diploma, age and attainment level: Meaning and use when comparing education systems]. *Sociétés Contemporaines, 26,* 42–72. Paris: IRESCO.

Eurostat. (1995). *Bildung in der europäischen union. Daten und kennzahlen/Education across the European Union: Statistics and indicators/Education dans l'union européenne: Statistiques et indicateurs.* Luxembourg: Author.

Eurostat. (1997). *Enquête Forces de travail. Résultats 1995* [Labor Force Survey, 1995 outcomes]. Luxembourg: Author.

Eyraud, F., Marsden, D., & Sylvestre, J. J. (1990). Marché professionnel et marché interne en Grande-Bretagne et en France [Professional labor market and internal labor market in Great Britain and in France]. *Revue Internationale du Travail, 129,* 551–571.

Hamilton, S., & Hurrelman, K. (1993). Auf der Suche nach dem besten Modell für den Ubergang von der Schule in den Beruf: ein amerikanisch–deutscher Vergleich [Toward the best model for the pathway from school to work: A German–American comparison]. *Zeitschrift für Socialisationforschung und Erziehungsoziologie, 13*, 326–340.

Hantrais, L., & Letablier, M. T. (1996a). *Families and family policies in Europe.* London: Longman.

Hantrais, L., & Letablier, M. T. (1996b). *Familles, travail et politiques familiales en Europe* [Families, work and family policies in Europe] (Cahier 36). Noisy-le-Grand, France: Centre d'Etudes de l'Emploi.

Heinz, W. R. (1994). Transition behaviour and career outcomes in England and Germany. In CEDEFOP, *The determinants of transitions in youth: Papers from the 1993 conference organized by the ESF Network on transitions in Youth* (pp. 159–167). CEDEFOP (European Centre for the Development of Vocational Training) and GRET (Universitat Autonoma de Barcelona). Berlin: Panorama.

Heinz, W. R., & Nagel, H. (1995). Changements et modernisation des transitions école-travail [Changes and modernization in transitions from school to work]. In A. Jobert, C. Marry, & L.Tanguy (Eds.), *Education et Travail en Grande-Bretagne, Allemagne et Italie* [Education and work in Great Britain, Germany and Italy] (pp. 84–100). Paris: Armand Colin (Bibliothèque Européenne des Sciences de l'Education).

Hitmayer, W., & Olk, T. (Eds.). (1990). *Individualisierung von Jugend* [Individualization of young people]. Weinsheim/Munich: Juventa.

Jobert, A., Marry, C., & Tanguy, L. (Eds.) (1995). *Education et Travail en Grande-Bretagne, Allemagne et Italie* [Education and work in Great Britain, Germany and Italy]. Paris: Armand Colin (Bibliothèque Européenne des Sciences de l'Education).

Kieffer, A., & Marry, C. (1994). French women entering the labour process and setting up household in the 1980s. In CEDEFOP, *The determinants of transitions in youth: Papers from the 1993 conference organized by the ESF Network on transitions in youth* (pp. 168–179). CEDEFOP (European Centre for the Development of Vocational Training) and GRET (Universitat Autonoma de Barcelona). Berlin: Panorama.

Lefresne, F. (1995). Comparaison européenne des dispositifs d'insertion profession-nelle des jeunes [European comparison of professional integration schemes for youth people]. *Revue de l'IRES, 17*, 97–133. Noisy-le-Grand, France: IRES.

Marsden, D. W. (1989). *Marché du travail, limites sociales des nouvelles théories* [Labor market, social limits of new theories]. Paris: Economica.

Marsden, D. W., & Ryan, P. (1991). The structuring of youth pay and employment in six European countries. In P. Ryan, P. Garonna, & R. C. Edwards (Eds.), *The problem of youth* (pp. 82–112). London: Macmillan.

Maurice, M., Sellier, F., & Sylvestre, J. J. (1982). *Politique d'éducation et organization industrielle en France et en Allemagne* [Education policies and industrial organization in France and Germany]. Paris: PUF.

Mayer, K. U. (1994). Perspectives on systems, institutions and changes. In CEDEFOP, *The determinants of transitions in youth: Papers from the 1993 conference organized by the ESF Network on transitions in Youth* (pp. 1–11). CEDEFOP (European Centre for the Development of Vocational Training) and GRET (Universitat Autonoma de Barcelona). Berlin: Panorama.

Mayer, K. U., & Konietzka, D. (1998). Le modèle dual est-il en crise? [Occupational training and early careers: Models of Germany in crisis?]. *Revue Française de Sociologie,* *39*(2), 269–304.

Merle, V. (1994). Commentaires autour de l'article d'Hilary Steedman et Julia Hawkins [About Hilary Steedman and Julia Hawkins's paper]. *Formation et Emploi, 46,* 23–25. Paris: La Documentation Française.

Méron, M. (1997). Les trajectoires des jeunes: distances et dépendances entre générations [Youth trajectories: Length and dependancy between generations]. In M. Méron (Ed.) [special issue], *Economie et Statistique,* 304–305 (pp. 20–23). Paris: INSEE.

Muller, W. (1994). The process and consequences of education differenciation. In CEDEFOP, *The determinants of transitions in youth: Papers from the 1993 conference organized by the ESF Network on transitions in Youth* (pp. 207–213). CEDEFOP (European Centre for the Development of Vocational Training) and GRET (Universitat Autonoma de Barcelona). Berlin: Panorama.

Rindfuss, R. C., Swicegood, C. G., & Rosenfeld, R. A. (1987). Disorder in the life course: How common and does it matter? *American Sociological Review, 52,* 785–801.

Steedman, H., & Hawkins, J. (1994). Réforme de la formation professionnelle des jeunes britanniques. Une première évaluation [Youth training reform in Great Britain: A first evaluation]. *Formation et Emploi, 46,* 9–21. Paris: La Documentation Française.

Tanguy, L. (1995). Construction de la catégorie de formation dans un contexte de chômage en Grande-Bretagne [Building a training concept in the British unemployment context]. *Sociologie du Travail, 4,* 715–738.

Villeneuve-Gokalp, C. (1997). Le départ de chez ses parents: définitions d'un processus complexe [Departing from home: Definitions of a complex process]. In M. Méron (Ed.) [special issue], *Economie et Statistique,* 304–305 (pp. 149–162). Paris: INSEE.

Werquin, P., Breen, R., & Planas, J. (Eds.). (1997). *Youth transitions in Europe: Theories and evidence. Third ESF Workshop of the Network on Transitions in Youth* (Document 120). Marseille: CEREQ.

20 The School-to-Work Transition
Problems and Indicators

Paul Ryan

The *school-to-work transition* is a catchall term for the activities of young people as they bounce around or struggle along between full-time schooling and full-time, possibly career, employment. The activities in question include vocational education, work experience, unemployment, labor market programs, casual work, and fixed-term employment. The transition has become the focus of considerable interest, both academic and policy-oriented.

In some accounts, the school-to-work transition has become longer and more tortuous, at least in advanced economies (Organization for Economic Cooperation and Development [OECD], 1996, 1998). A leading transition attribute, youth status in the labor market, is said to have deteriorated in virtually all OECD countries (Blanchflower & Freeman, 2000). Others emphasize cross-country differences in transition patterns, with German and Japanese institutions performing particularly well (Ryan, 2001).

The accuracy of such generalizations is an empirical issue. Their evaluation would be helped if it were possible to quantify transition attributes comprehensively and consistently. This chapter discusses two sets of measurement problems: those involved, first, in gauging employment-related difficulties and, second, in summarizing national transitions at a particular time in a way that permits comparisons across countries and periods. The evidence concerns teenagers in eight advanced economies, supplemented by historical data for the United Kingdom.

The OECD's assistance in providing access to unpublished data is gratefully acknowledged, as are the comments of participants at the Johann Jacobs Foundation conference at Marbach Castle, Germany.

Youth Employment Problems

The first step in measuring the employment problems facing any age group has traditionally been the unemployment rate: the share of the labor force that lacks paid work while showing interest in finding work and being available for work if it is found.

On that criterion, youth employment problems appear serious in many advanced economies. In 1997, the teenage unemployment rate was in double figures in all eight of the countries surveyed in Table 20.1 except Germany. It was particularly high in Southern Europe. In Italy and Spain, around one-third of teenage workers were unemployed. In the same region, female unemployment rates were particularly high. Unemployment accounted for about two-fifths of teenage workers in France and Spain and fully three-fifths in Italy.

The difficulties confronted by an assessment of youth employment problems are illustrated here by focusing on two counties, France and the United States, for which the familiar contemporary perception is one of labor market failure and success, respectively. Unemployment rates broadly support that view. Teenage unemployment rates were much higher in France than in the United States in 1997, particularly for girls (Table 20.1). At the same time, because unemployment rates in the United States were hardly low by absolute standards, youth employment problems were also apparent there.

It is widely recognized that unemployment rates provide only a limited indicator of employment difficulties. In the case of young workers, the first limitation concerns the size of the youth labor force. When few young people are members of the labor force (as a result, for example, of extensive participation in full-time education), not even a high unemployment rate affects many young people.

Returning to the Franco–American comparison, against the much higher female youth rate in France must be set the fact that only 4% of teenage girls' work in France, as opposed to 51% in the United States. The unemployed, therefore, constitute less than 2% of female teenagers in France but nearly 8% in the United States (see Table 20.1, columns 4–6). Youth employment difficulties appear less marked from this standpoint in France than in the United States. In Spain and the United Kingdom, however, serious problems remain visible, with at least 10% of the teenage population unemployed.

Second, even when measured relative to population, unemployment offers only a partial guide to employment problems. The youth labor force shrinks when jobs are hard to find. The main dimension of adjustment is enrollment in full-time education. Enrollments rise as labor market slack

Table 20.1 Teenage Unemployment by Country, 1997 (% of 16- to 19-Year-Olds)

	(1)	(2)	(3)	(4)	(5)	(6)
	Boys			Girls		
	Unemployment Rate[b] (U/L)	Labor Force Participation Rate (L/N)	Unemployed Share of Population (U/N)	Unemployment Rate (U/L)	Labor Force Participation Rate (L/N)	Unemployed Share of Population (U/N)
France[a]	19.9	9.4	1.9	38.9	4.3	1.7
Germany[a]	8.3	34.6	2.9	8.8	26.7	2.3
Italy[a]	30.9	21.5	6.6	42.9	16.5	7.1
Japan[a]	10.3	18.9	1.9	10.3	16.8	1.7
Spain	36.5	30.4	11.1	59.3	21.3	12.6
Sweden	28.2	26.2	7.4	26.7	26.2	7.0
U.K.	18.2	63.7	11.6	14.0	60.9	8.5
U.S.	16.9	52.3	8.8	15.0	51.0	7.7

Note: U denotes unemployment, L employment, and N population.

[a] Fifteen- to 19-year-olds.

[b] On the standardized ILO/OECD definition (i.e., out of work, looked for work in last 4 weeks, ready to start work in next 2 weeks).

Source: Bowers, Sonnet, and Bardone (1999), Tables 10, 12, and author's calculations.

288

increases, driven partly by the difficulty of finding work and partly by improved prospects of finding work through increased skills and educational credentials. In the United States, the effect is weak, because many students work part-time; in France, it is strong, because few students do so (Blanchflower & Freeman, 2000).

Our Franco–American comparison of youth unemployment rates, which became more favorable to France when the basis was changed from the labor force to the population, therefore swings back in favor of the United States. The small size of the teenage labor force and the high rate of educational enrollment in France not only relieve the youth employment problem but also reflect its severity.

Third, the definition of unemployment requires consideration. How interested in work and available for work must a jobless person be in order to be considered an unemployed member of the labor force rather than an inactive nonmember? The International Labour Organization/OECD (ILO/OECD) definition of unemployment requires at the time in question both some active job search during the previous 4 weeks and readiness to start work during the coming 2 weeks. If either criterion is not satisfied, a workless individual is classed as inactive rather than unemployed.

These interest and availability criteria classify as inactive those people whose labor market attachment fails either test but is not zero on either. Low attachment is more common among the young than the middle aged, reflecting the greater importance of schooling, leisure, and labor market programs for young people, as well as the lower household responsibilities of youth. The issue has attracted particular attention in the United States, where large numbers of young people, especially nonwhite inner-city residents, are economically inactive, lacking links either to school or to legitimate employment even in tight labor markets (Rees, 1986).

Even if a young person's work interest and availability are both zero, an employment-related problem may still be judged to be present. A teenager who is educationally as well as economically inactive may be seen as wasting his or her time at a formative stage of the life cycle. A government that promotes self-reliance rather than dependence on public income support (or criminality) may view such a choice as mistaken and seek to move such young people toward the labor market.

Such considerations favor using the term *joblessness*, a potentially more comprehensive indicator of youth employment problems than *unemployment* (Rees, 1986). One variant is the total nonemployment rate, measured on a population basis (i.e., $1 - (E/N)$, where E is employment and N is population). For teenagers, the usefulness of that indicator is reduced by

Table 20.2 Unemployment, Inactivity, and Joblessness among Teenage Boys, 1997

	(1)	(2)	(3)	(4)
		Out-of-School	Jobless	Inactive as Share of All Jobless (%)
	Unemployed	Inactive[a]	(1) + (2)	(2)/(3)
France	4.5	2.3	6.8	34
Germany	2.2	2.4	4.6	52
Italy	6.8	6.5	13.3	49
Japan	1.9	1.5	3.4	44
Spain	9.7	3.9	13.6	29
Sweden	3.6	9.9	13.5	73
U.K.	8.6	10.8	19.4	56
U.S.	3.2	4.5	7.7	59

Note: Columns 1–3 are percentages of the 16- to 19-year-old male population.
[a] Not enrolled in an educational program and not unemployed under the ILO definition.
Source: Bowers, Sonnet, and Bardone (1999), Figure 3 (original data provided by OECD from individual country microdata).

high rates of educational participation, which are only partly attributable to employment problems. A superior indicator is provided by inactive joblessness, with inactivity defined with respect to education as well as to the labor market (i.e., $1 - \{(E + S)/N\}$, where S is nonemployed students).

Table 20.2 juxtaposes the inactive and the unemployed within the out-of-school jobless population as a whole. The data are restricted to boys, among whom family formation and household responsibilities have less influence on inactivity rates than among girls.

Inactivity is substantial in all eight countries surveyed, accounting for about one-half of teenage male joblessness in the group as a whole. Its importance varies considerably across countries. In the United Kingdom and Sweden, the approximately 1/10th of young men who are inactive actually outnumber their unemployed peers and constitute a recognized policy problem (Bentley & Gurumurthy, 1999). The inactive also outnumber the unemployed in the United States and Germany, although smaller proportions of young people are involved than in Sweden and the United Kingdom. In Spain and France, by contrast, most jobless youth are unemployed, and unemployment alone thus provides a less limited guide to youth employment problems than elsewhere.

Revisiting our Franco–American comparison, the higher inactivity rate of youth in the United States than in France cancels any U.S. advantage in terms of unemployment alone (Table 20.1). The French joblessness rate of

6.8% in 1997 suggests youth employment problems that – for boys at least – were no worse, and possibly slightly better, than for their counterparts in the United States, where the rate was 7.7%.

The pursuit of more accurate measures of youth employment problems must continue further.[1] Three additional adjustments are potentially important. First, out-of-school inactivity may reflect choices (e.g., leisure and foreign travel) rather than constraints. Where constraints are involved, they may be independent of, rather than encouraged by, labor market slack. The ranks of the inactive should therefore be pared down further by removing the former category in each dichotomy. The evidence required for the task has yet to be compiled for most countries.

Our Franco–American comparison is potentially affected in this respect by compulsory military service for French boys and exceptionally high incarceration rates among American boys, both of which raise the national youth inactivity rate. An adjustment for these factors would probably favor France, not least because U.S. incarceration rates are more readily attributable, if only in part, to poor youth labor market opportunities than are French conscription rates (Freeman, 1996).

Second, in many countries, labor market programs take some young people out of unemployment and inactivity without providing regular employment. The share of young people participating in such programs – most of whom would presumably have preferred employment – has been higher in France than in the United States. In 1997–1998, youth program entrants amounted to 2.9% of (all age) employment in France, as opposed to only 0.6% in the United States (OECD, 1999, Annex Table H). Adjustment for public intervention increases the imbalance, in terms of youth employment disadvantages, of France relative to the United States.

Finally, the dynamics of joblessness are potentially important. Low outflows from joblessness and long durations therein are particularly likely to indicate employment problems, such as the inertia, stagnation, and waste involved in long-term unemployment. High outflows and short durations suggest, by contrast, not so much employment problems as employment improvement, associated with job search and job-worker matching in the youth labor market.

---

[1] An initial requirement would be to reconcile discrepancies in the data. The unemployment-population ratios for teenage males differ markedly between Tables 20.1 and 20.2 for some countries, notably France, Sweden, and the United States. Although these intracountry discrepancies partly reflect differences in age categories in the two tables (15 to 19 as opposed to 16 to 19), divergent definitions and data sources also probably contribute to the discrepancies.

This consideration pushes the Franco–American comparison even further in favor of the United States. In 1994 the outflow rate in youth (16- to 24-year-olds) unemployment in the United States was more than 10 times as large, and the long-term unemployment rate only one-eighth as large, as its French counterpart (OECD, 1995, Tables 1.8, 1.9). Moreover, because France undoubtedly has a higher share of young workers following various sequences of unemployment, inactivity, and labor market programs without finding employment, its comparative deficit in terms of long-term joblessness is even greater than that in long-term unemployment.

Our assessment of comparative Franco–American youth employment problems, which moved in favor of France when unemployment was replaced by inactive joblessness as the indicator, has swung back strongly in favor of the United States as a result of taking into account labor market programs and turnover among the jobless. A full research project would be required, however, for an exhaustive assessment of the issue. Although this discussion has not attempted that task, it illustrates the difficulty of measuring youth employment problems and shows the desirability of supplementing data on youth unemployment with evidence of the scale and dynamics of inactive joblessness in particular.

The Duration of the School-to-Work Transition

The OECD paints a picture of "longer and more complex transitions than existed in the past" (1996, p. 41). A tendency for more young people to spend more time bouncing around or struggling along is consistent with such conjunctural and structural developments as depressed labor demand and experience-biased trends in labor demand (Ryan, 2001).

Differences between national transition attributes are also potentially important. At one pole stand the traditional Japanese and British patterns, in which most young people leave school early and move directly to regular employment. The middle ground is occupied by Germany and neighboring countries, many of whose young people spend well-defined periods traveling along apprenticeship-based pathways from full-time schooling to employment. At the other pole stand the late and prolonged transitions of France, Italy, and Spain, where young people typically percolate through a variety of intermediate statuses in quest of regular employment.

Qualitative evidence can be cited in support of these generalizations. The feasibility of quantitative evidence is also of interest. How might these comparisons of transition patterns across time and place be quantified? Do the generalizations survive quantification?

Quantitative indicators have certainly been widely exploited. For example, since the early 1970s, the average time taken by French school leavers to find a permanent job (*contrat à durée déterminée*) in longitudinal microdata has increased sharply and become more dependent on prior scholastic qualifications, implying an increase in both the mean and the inequality of transition durations (Affichard, 1981; Minni & Vergnies, 1994). Similar tendencies have been observed in the United Kingdom (Payne, 1995).

Even in Germany and Japan, countries whose national school-to-work institutions proved particularly resilient during the difficulties of the 1990s, various indicators suggest a lengthening of transitions. In Germany, although apprenticeship still provides a mass vehicle for the school-to-work transition, the growth of multiple pathways (e.g., apprenticeship followed by higher education) and the rise in unemployment among young adults imply some lengthening of average durations and some increase in duration inequalities (Büchel & Helberger, 1995; Franz, Inkemann, Pohlmeier, & Zimmerman, 2000). In Japan, placement rates for students graduating from secondary schools and tertiary institutions have declined, and youth employees quit their jobs more often (Kariya, 1999; Mitani, 1999), although these changes have probably not been enough to increase the OECD's duration measure.

These symptoms of lengthening transitions are, however, both partial and nationally specific. Most research has been limited to a single country, occasionally two (Büchtemann, Schupp, & Soloff, 1993). But the OECD (1996) has proposed a comprehensive measure of the transition that can be used for comparisons across time and place. Its approach treats the school-to-work transition as an aggregate national attribute. The transition is defined as starting at the lowest age by which one-quarter of the cohort has left full-time schooling and as ending at the lowest age by which a majority are no longer involved in schooling and have found regular employment. The duration of the transition is defined as the difference between these two ages in the life of a population cohort. Microdata, drawn typically from household surveys, are then used to determine the two ages. The results can be compared across countries and time.

On this definition, in 15 advanced countries (from which the 7 countries in Table 20.3 are drawn) in 1994, the school-to-work transition started at an average age of 17 and finished at age 23, lasting for an average of 6 years (Table 20.3). These estimates suggest a protracted process.

International differences also correspond to expectation. Although the starting age was similar in all countries in 1984, by 1994 dispersion had increased, with France showing the biggest rise. Differences in the ending

Table 20.3 Timing and Duration of National School-to-Work Transition According to the OECD Definition, by Country, 1984 and 1994 (*Ranked by Average Duration in 1994*)

	(1)	(2)	(3)	(4)	(5)	(6)
	Average Starting Age[a]		Average Ending Age[b]		Average Duration (Years of Age)	
					(3) − (1)	(4) − (2)
	1984	1994	1984	1994	1984	1994
Spain	16	17	26	27	10	10
Italy	16	17	23	25	7	8
U.K.	16	16	20	22	4	6
France	17	19	22	24	5	5
Germany	17	17	20	22	3	5
U.S.	16	16	21	21	5	5
Ireland	17	18	20	22	3	4
Average[c]	16	17	22	23	6	6

[a] Age at which the share of the cohort that is in full-time school and not in employment falls below 75%.

[b] Age at which the share of the birth-year cohort that is in employment but not in school rises to 50%.

[c] Unweighted mean (including eight countries not included here).

Source: OECD (1996), p. 72.

age were marked in both years, with Spain, Italy, and France as the latest and the United States and the United Kingdom among the earliest.

Other results were less readily anticipated. The average duration of the transition across countries did not increase, registering 6 years for both 1984 and 1994, even though the duration estimate increased for the United Kingdom and Germany. What did change during the period was timing: The average starting age rose from 17 to 18 years and the ending age from 22 to 23 years.

The United Kingdom is not distinctive nowadays for either the earliness or the brevity of its transition period. Its starting age of 16 was the earliest in both 1984 and 1994, but neither was exceptional among advanced economies. The United Kingdom's transition duration was shorter in both years than those of Spain and Italy, but even so, it exceeded those of Germany, Ireland, and (by 1994) France. Another possibly surprising feature of Table 20.3 is that the United States did not share the European tendency for either the starting age or the duration of the transition to increase between 1984 and 1994.

The OECD's estimates are valuable for various reasons: for facilitating cross-national and historical comparisons; for painting a vivid and broadly plausible picture; and for correcting some erroneous generalizations. The OECD methodology does, however, contain a flaw. It picks up not only differences across time and place in individuals' transition patterns – the variable of interest – but also the distorting effects of differences in the dispersion of school-leaving ages.

The problem is illustrated here with historical evidence for the United Kingdom. The limited availability of longitudinal microdata for earlier periods prevents the measurement of transition patterns on the same basis as for 1984 and 1994. Cross-sectional data on educational participation and unemployment by age in earlier periods, however, provide a reasonable approximation to longitudinal evidence: The lower the rate of change in transition attributes is in a particular period, the better the cross-sectional patterns by age mirror the experience of a particular cohort as it ages.

More than 50 years ago, in 1951, the share of British – strictly, English – youth enrolled in a school or college declined from 99% at age 14 to 35% at age 15 (Table 20.4). By the OECD's definition, the start and end of the transition therefore coincided at 15 years of age, which was when the share of the

Table 20.4 Proportion of Age Group in Formal Schooling: Great Britain, 1951 and 1957–1958 (% of Population in Age-Sex Group)

Year	Course Type	Age[a]	Boys	Girls	All
1951[b]	Full-time only	14	98.7	98.1	98.4
		15	32.7	33.9	33.3
		16	18.6	17.9	18.3
		17	9.7	10.8	10.2
	Full- and part-time[c]	14	98.7	98.2	98.5
		15	34.8	34.8	34.8
		16	23.4	19.9	21.6
		17	17.3	13.1	15.2
1957–1958	Full-time only	15	39.8	39.7	38.8
		16	22.1	22.0	22.1
		17	13.0	10.8	11.9
		18	7.8	4.7	6.1
	Full- and part-time[c]	15	80.5	68.0	74.4
		16	71.9	52.8	62.5
		17	61.4	37.1	49.4
		18	43.7	21.5	32.7

[a] Age at last birthday.
[b] England only.
[c] Day and evening courses are included in the part-time category.
Source: General Register Office (1952), Table VIII.1; Ministry of Education (1959), Table 1.

cohort in full-time schooling fell below 75%, whereas the share (presumed to be) in employment[2] but not in schooling rose above 50%.

In 1951, the duration of the transition in Britain was thus a matter of months rather than years, and zero years when rounded to an integer. Most young people left school at the statutory minimum age (15); most who did so went straight to employment; and few who did so continued part-time in education. The situation represented the kind of traditional transition – direct and fast – that the OECD presumably had in mind when depicting transition durations as having increased in advanced economies in general. The 1951 estimate is certainly much less than the 6 years estimated for 1984 and 1994, which supports the OECD's generalization, for the United Kingdom at least, over a longer period than its own data covered.

Part of the apparent increase of 6 years for the United Kingdom between 1951 and 1984–1994 represents a rise in the dispersion of actual ages of leaving education. The distribution of school-leaving ages became less concentrated at the legal minimum. The evolution of the OECD's starting and ending ages illustrates the change. By 1990, the age at which less than 75% of young people remained in schooling had risen to 16, along with the statutory minimum leaving age. More important, increased staying on after the minimum age meant that the age at which less than 50% remained in schooling (irrespective of subsequent labor market experience) had risen to 18 years (Payne, 1995, Table 1.2). By the mid-1990s, the share of young British people entering higher education had risen to one-third, from only 5% in 1951.

The compositional contribution of increased dispersion in leaving ages to the increase in the OECD duration measure since 1951 can be estimated by considering a counterfactual: continued full employment. School leavers would then have been able to move directly into work: That is, school-to-work transitions would have remained nearly instantaneous at the individual level, as they have actually continued to be in Japan (Mitani, 1999), a country for which compositional effects would be expected to dominate if

---

[2] This conclusion is not based on any direct observation of employment outcomes. Given full employment, however, the vast majority of early school leavers in 1951 clearly found employment directly. Indirect (if not wholly consistent) evidence is provided by government estimates that among 15-year-olds during 1951, 456,000 individuals acquired national insurance coverage by entering employment for the first time, whereas only 425,000 had ceased educational activity (General Register Office, 1952, Table VIII.1; Ministry of Labour, 1952, p. 341). The employment condition within the OECD's "above 50%" criterion for the ending age, therefore, can be taken to have been satisfied in 1951.

suitable data were to be analyzed. In that case, the OECD duration measure for the United Kingdom would still have risen by 2 years between 1951 and 1990. The implication is that increased differentiation in school-leaving ages generated roughly one-third of the postwar increase in the OECD duration measure. The remaining 4 years reflect the pure lengthening of individual transitions, associated with the increased difficulty of finding employment, and a greater incidence of short-term employment contracts and labor market programs.

The compositional change actually occurred in the United Kingdom soon after 1951. Similar data for 1957–1958 suggest that the terminal age on the OECD definition had already increased to 17 years, assuming that early school leavers still moved en masse directly into employment during the extended postwar boom (Table 20.4).[3] The increase in transition duration reflected the rapid dissemination of part-time postcompulsory education during the 1950s, primarily in the form of part-time courses taken at further education colleges by young male employees and apprentices.

The OECD's aggregate measure of transition durations suffers from poor focus. It caters to the need for a summary indicator for use in comparisons across time and place, but it requires conversion into a truly aggregative variable, unaffected by changes in the distribution of school-leaving ages. A promising prospect is the simple average of the experiences of individual young people within particular national age cohorts: for example, how long they spend on average between leaving full-time schooling (or passing the statutory minimum leaving age) and attaining some specified length of service in a regular job while having ended their formal education. Some such adaptation of the OECD's approach is both more promising and – given that microdata are required anyway for the calculation of the OECD measure – computationally only slightly more arduous.

Conclusions

The difficulties of comparing the school-to-work transition across time and place have been illustrated in terms of two attributes: the extent of youth employment-related problems and the duration of the national transition viewed as a whole. Both the benefits and the limits of quantification are visible in each case.

---

[3] This conclusion must be qualified in view of (a) the different geographical coverage of the 1951 and 1957–1958 estimates and (b) the limitations of cross-sectional data as a guide to longitudinal patterns in times of rapid change, such as the 1950s.

REFERENCES

Affichard, J. (1981). Quels emplois après l'école: La valeur des titres scolaires depuis 1973 [What type of work after schooling: The value of educational qualifications since 1973]. *Économie et Statistique, 134,* 7–26.

Bentley, T., & Gurumurthy, R. (1999). *Destination unknown: Engaging with the problems of marginalized youth.* London: Demos.

Blanchflower, D., & Freeman, R. B. (Eds.). (2000). *Youth unemployment and joblessness in advanced economies.* Chicago: University of Chicago Press.

Bowers, N., Sonnet, A., & Bardone, L. (1999). Giving young people a good start: The experience of OECD countries. In OECD, *Preparing youth for the 21st century: The transition from education to the labour market* (pp. 7–86). Paris: OECD.

Büchel, F., & Helberger, C. (1995). Bildungsnachfrage als Versicherungstrategie [Demand for apprenticeship as an insurance strategy]. *Mitteilungen aus der Arbeitsmarkt- und Berufsforschung, 1,* 32–42.

Büchtemann, C., Schupp, J., & Soloff, D. (1993). De l'école au travail: Une comparaison entre l'Allemagne et les Etats Unis [From school to work: A comparison between Germany and the United States]. *Formation Emploi, 44,* 37–51.

Franz, W., Inkemann, J., Pohlmeier, W., & Zimmerman, V. (2000). Young and out in Germany: On youths' chances of labour market entrance in Germany. In D. Blanchflower & R. B. Freeman (Eds.), *Youth unemployment and joblessness in advanced economies* (pp. 381–425). Chicago: University of Chicago Press.

Freeman, R. B. (1996). Why do so many young American men commit crimes and what might we do about it? *Journal of Economic Perspectives, 10*(1), 25–42.

General Register Office. (1952). *1951 census, one per cent sample tables.* London: HMSO.

Kariya, T. (1999). Transition from school to work and career formation of Japanese high school students. In D. Stern & D. Wagner (Eds.), *International perspectives on the school-to-work transition* (pp. 273–309). Cresskill, NJ: Hampden Press.

Ministry of Education. (1959). *15 to 18.* Report of Central Advisory Council for Education (England). London: HMSO.

Ministry of Labour. (1952). Young persons entering employment. *Ministry of Labour Gazette, 60*(10), 341–343.

Minni, C., & Vergnies, J.-F. (1994). La diversité des facteurs de l'insertion professionnelle [The variety of the determinants of occupational entry to the labor market]. *Économie et Statistique, 277,* 45–61.

Mitani, N. (1999). The Japanese employment system and youth labour market. In OECD, *Preparing youth for the 21st century: The transition from education to the labour market* (pp. 305–328). Paris: OECD.

OECD. (1995). *Employment outlook, July 1995.* Paris: Author.

OECD. (1996). *Education at a glance: Analysis.* Paris: Author.

OECD. (1998). Getting started, settling in: The transition from education to the labour market. In *OECD employment outlook, June 1998* (pp. 81–122). Paris: Author.

OECD. (1999). *OECD employment outlook, July 1999.* Paris: Author.

Payne, J. (1995). *Options at 16 and outcomes at 24: A comparison of academic and vocational education and training routes.* (Youth Cohort Report #35). Sheffield, UK: Department for Education and Employment.

Rees, Λ. (1986). An essay on youth joblessness. *Journal of Economic Literature, 24*(2), 613–628.

Ryan, P. (2001). The school-to-work transition: A cross-national perspective. *Journal of Economic Literature, 39*(1), 34–92.

21 To Be Young in Yugoslavia
Life After a Social Chernobyl

Dragan Popadić

The problem of transition from youth to adulthood has many different aspects. Among the numerous factors that determine it, Fouquet (this volume) concentrates on those that are most important: modes of access to employment and management of professional mobility, and the school and training systems. With respect to only these important factors, there are great variations among European countries, which are convincingly shown in collected statistical data. Clearly, youth have different transitional and integration problems in different countries, and differences in integration modes that exist among countries complicate their coordination with each other. In the first part of this chapter, I elaborate on some general sociopsychological aspects of growing up; in the second, I make some comparisons between Yugoslavia and countries mentioned in Fouquet's chapter.

Fouquet's first sentence settles into a discourse in which youth is seen as something culturally constructed. And although, in lay psychology, some may believe that just waiting to reach a certain chronological age is all one has to do, that is not the right way to become an adolescent or adult. Although it is obvious that chronological age matters, it is not essential: The occurrence of significant events that correspond with it is what is really important. Not only the period of youth but also the whole age stratification can be viewed as socially constructed. The border between adolescence and adulthood is especially fuzzy, because biological factors (which can play an important role in separating childhood from adolescence and adulthood from old age) are of no importance in this case.

In some cultures, adolescence and/or childhood does not exist sociologically. As Philip Aries (1962) convincingly claimed, the idea that children are somehow different from adults was not generally accepted until the 17th century. Earlier, 5- to 6-year-old children were divested of infant's attire and quickly included in adulthood, because they had to take an equal part in the activities and responsibilities of elders. According to Aries, the modern notion of childhood was determined primarily by two factors: the establishment of modern schools and of the bourgeois-type family.

Even if we accept the claim of some researchers (e.g., Schlegel & Barry, 1991) that adolescence is a universal phenomenon, we can also see it as invented (Fasick, 1994), because its marks, duration, social importance, and attributes are defined and strongly influenced by culture. The socioeconomic context seems to be the most important determining cultural factor.

In simple, stable social structures such as those with a basically agrarian economy, children acquire necessary skills and knowledge relatively easily and quickly. If these societies happen to be poor, entry into early adulthood is accentuated because of strong pressure from their members to become economically productive as soon as possible, thus lessening the burden on the others. These societies may be considered *adultocentric* in the sense that shared social values urge young men to look forward to becoming adults as soon as possible. In rural Yugoslav areas, where, as in all cultures, age categories are organized around institutions, marriage used to be, and still is, the most important marker and the most generally accepted passage to adulthood. (Military service is another passage, with marriage just preceding or following it.) Seen in this light, a socially established age for marriage may be used as a very sensitive instrument for registering subtle economic changes. For example, as Yugoslav ethnologists have noted, the average age for marriage has changed more quickly than any other social norm, going arm in arm with overall economic changes (Erlich, 1971).

In areas of greater urbanization and industrialization, however, people encounter more complex social relations and impose different claims. Even if an individual is biologically mature, he or she is not recognized as fully competent for the various complex demands modern society requires of its members. In these conditions, education starts to play the most prominent role. It serves to prove that an individual is capable of working in complex social and economic conditions, of integrating into the work process, and of assigning appropriate social positions to himself or herself. Because the process of education is lengthy, and because there is a permanent tendency to lengthen it further (the more complex technologies are, the more a competent work force is needed), adolescents excluded from the job market and the world of adults while acquiring needed skills and knowledge develop their own culture and lifestyle, which establish them as a separate age/social group.

Social development and associated problems complicate the process of youth integration. Societies try to solve this problem by adjusting the educational system to meet new demands. Fouquet (this volume) has given us detailed descriptions of several strategies that are expected to prepare young people for entering the job market and to create adequate education–employment linkage. This description, with the comparisons of the schooling models, is especially illuminating. Clearly, there is no simple solution, and, with accelerated development, a solution would be harder to find. Technological innovations change much more quickly than do generations of workers. How do we educate young people to be prepared for imminent changes that, together with their consequences, are unimaginable now? The existing cultural pattern corresponds to one that Margaret Mead labeled *prefigurative culture*; in it, the older generation has less and less to offer in terms of guidance and advice; in some respects, adolescents become more current with scientific advances, and elders have to learn from them. As Mead aptly described, configurative parents used to say "You know, I have been young, and you have never been old," whereas prefigurative youth may answer, "You never have been young in the world I am young in, and you never can be" (Mead, 1970, p. 63).

Globally speaking, it can be said that desynchronization is the fundamental characteristic of the moment. The criteria that used to define the discussed social categories become more numerous, more complex, and less mutually dependent. For this reason, not only adulthood but also other age categories lose their benchmarks. Thus, one of the important and socially relevant elements of people's individual and group identity loses much of its clarity. Especially in periods of deep and prolonged social crisis (as was the case in Yugoslavia), desynchronization of age criteria becomes very pronounced and has its own regularity. It is said that children in these circumstances mature early: Not able to escape facing various life difficulties, they have to participate in adult activities instead of playing. But other criteria of maturity become inaccessible, even to adults: For many of them, it is now almost impossible to find a job, to separate and become economically independent from their parents. In these respects, they retain the status of child, even though they have already formed their own families.

But social identities can be even more strongly challenged in communication with other cultures. My brief description of different age conceptions suggests a chronological order among the described cultures. But viewed in this way, European states are so diverse now that past and future meet in them, even within one country (and I think this is the rule rather than the exception). Extremely heightened opportunities for communication and information exchange enable and even prompt people easily and incessantly to make social comparisons far broader than those within the frames of their own group/culture. Many positive effects of this state of affairs are obvious, but some less favorable effects are also possible. For example, such "comparison from a distance" may either threaten the previously formed social categorizations that have an important function in the culture where they originated or lessen those socially meaningful aspects of social identity that they positively value.

Integration of youth is opposed to maladaptation or generation conflict. Fouquet's chapter implicitly warns that such conflict is possible if education and employment do not continue to play their integrative role. A similar situation occurred in the 1960s, and it generated the sudden appearance of a student movement (unanticipated by sociologists) that launched many important questions and analyses related to youth, generation lag, subcultures, and so on. Recently in Yugoslavia, these topics have become very important.

Compared with the other countries analyzed by Fouquet (this volume), the overall situation in Yugoslavia is radically different, which is why Yugoslavia might be a valuable case study. The processes that are at work in this country are as dynamic and fundamental as are those in the rest of Europe; unfortunately, however, they are developing in the opposite direction. Such conditions impose a very different setting for growing up (i.e., transitional behavior) than do those we find in other European countries; and, at the same time, they produce serious problems for integration into Europe.

While the European Community is occupied with fostering existing integration processes in Europe (both between and among countries and social groups), the urgent problem in Yugoslavia is how to stop the powerful processes of disintegration that have lasted for almost 10 years. To view this through a metaphor, that of a "social Chernobyl" unchaining series of disintegration on all levels, seems very appropriate. The former Yugoslavia has been broken into five parts (and in the state that retained the name Yugoslavia, further partitioning is still possible). The new Yugoslavia broke its ties with the rest of world, culminating during a period of sanctions imposed by the international community from 1992 to 1996, when Yugoslavia was expelled from all international organizations. Accompanied by war, these sanctions have produced the further decay of normal social functioning.

The peculiarity of the situation may be illustrated by several facts noted in Lazić (1995). From 1990 on, the gross national product of Serbia started to fall steeply (indexes: 1990/1989 = 92; 1991/1990 = 92; 1992/1991 = 74; 1993/1992 = 70 in 1990 prices). A similar development took place in employment (1990/1989 = 97; 1991/1990 = 93; 1992/1991 = 96; 1993/

1992 = 97) and especially in real wages (1992/1991 = 53; 1993/1992 = 43 for the first 10 months). Under conditions of industrial production (which, in 1997, was about one-third of 1990 production); of a poverty coefficient rising from 15.3% in 1978 and 19.5% in 1990 to an estimated 70% in 1995; of hyperinflation (which, at its peak, reached 15 digits; and in some months, prices jumped 60% every day), it is almost unthinkable to develop either individual or institutional coping strategies.

In Yugoslavia, the current unemployment rate has reached 25.7%; but, of the 2 million employed persons, 400,000 do not receive any salary, although they go regularly to their jobs; at least 500,000 are surplus workers who may lose their jobs; and 200,000 people receive less than the minimal wage (Jakobi, 1997). If one takes all this into account, it becomes obvious how difficult it is for a young person to get a job. Needless to say, even if someone gets a job, it does not provide much help in becoming economically independent. Under such conditions, leaving the parental home and starting one's own family, which are considered other important marks of reaching adulthood, are also difficult to accomplish.

There are other forms of the disintegration of social tissue. Deep political transformations and differences in the socialization of youngsters and seniors, followed by enormous social problems, have caused more and more evident alienation of youth from the adult world. The youth blame their parents' generation for the world in which they have to live, and their dissatisfaction resulted in many massive protests from 1992 to 1998 in which not only university students but also secondary and even elementary school students participated. Some of these protests took a dramatic form (Popadić, 1997). In one national survey conducted in 1993 (Mihailović, 1994), after an unknown number of youth had already emigrated, 56% of our youth declared that they wanted to leave the country, permanently or for a long time. No data exist on the number of people who left Yugoslavia during the war, but according to estimates, around 12,000 people with a postsecondary education left Yugoslavia between 1991 and 1996.

Unfortunately, large parts of the statistical data presented here are incomplete and misleading in the sense that they picture reality in a more positive light. Almost all these analyses exclude Kosovo, the region of Serbia where approximately 17% of its population live (at least 90% of them are ethnic Albanians). Long-lasting ethnic conflicts in Kosovo have resulted in a state of apartheid. Albanians refused to acknowledge the Yugoslav state and established their own parallel political, economic, financial, cultural, health, and educational systems, which are treated as illegal by the official Serbian governance. Since 1989, all official statistics lack data from Kosovo.

The parallel education system in Kosovo started in 1989, and it covers all levels from kindergarten to the university. There are no precise data on the enrollment level of students in that parallel education system. Unofficial information suggests, however, that up to 100,000 children, or 22%, are out of the system and that the dropout rate is estimated at 30%, rising from fifth to eighth grade. Although such withdrawal from the educational system is understandable under conditions of extremely high unemployment, dominance of the gray economy, and little recognition of school certificates, its negative effects are long-lasting and detrimental.

Besides these problems of integration into their own society, there are serious obstacles to the integration of Yugoslav youths with their European peers, because the overall sociopsychological climate in which they have been living is very unfavorable. They have minimal opportunities for traveling abroad and social exchange; since childhood, they have been exposed to powerful nationalistic and war propaganda; United Nations sanctions fostered among many of them, especially those with less education, xenophobic attitudes and a ghetto mentality.

Despite these dark shades in describing Yugoslavia's young generation, I believe that their most prominent characteristic is a resilience to unfavorable conditions. In spite of the extremely bad social conditions and pressures to which they are exposed, they show a surprisingly high level of openness toward the world, a democratic orientation, and creativity. Take, for example, an investigation comparing the value systems of elementary school pupils in 1988 and in 1994 (Kuzmanović, Popadić, & Havelka, 1995). Although significant changes were registered within ideologically relevant values (e.g., religious orientation, orientation toward private property), as well as an increase in utilitarian-hedonistic values and a decrease in prosocial values, it is safe to conclude that the amount of these changes is significantly small compared with the degree of social changes occurring during the same period. We assumed that schools were institutions with a prominent role in reducing the influence of mass media and the social climate in given circumstances.

I do not mean to say that the educational system has been completely opposed to the disintegrative social processes. On the contrary, research has shown how some elements of textbooks and curricula were conceived to foster authoritarianism, discrimination, and ethnocentrism (Rosandić & Pešić, 1994). But on the whole, the educational system is one of the rare social institutions that continues to have an integrative function. Partly because it is a rather conservative and slow-changing institution, the education system continues to transmit the old social values, including recognition of ethnic, religious, linguistic, and other differences within one's own community. It is insensitive to social anomie and to values and activities outside school walls; and, in this sense, it serves as a preserver of a value system corresponding to the previous (and future, I hope) state of a multiethnic and pluralistic community. Changes in curricula consisted primarily of replacing historical highlights and models for social values (many of yesterday's national heroes became yesterday's villains); however, values stayed the same, appropriate to living in a stable and peaceful society.

More important than the unchanged content of education is the fact that the process of education is resistant to extreme particularization. Historical events, artistic masterpieces, or scientific facts cannot be restricted to one's own ethnic or political group or to a narrow segment of time. Even when it deals solely with the transmission of specific knowledge and skills, the hidden and inevitable part of the curriculum is teaching that areas of human knowledge are diverse but integrated; that science and art survive states and wars; and that scientific improvements are impossible without continual exchange and cooperation. Education makes people more suspicious of those who despise culture and knowledge; less dependent on irrational authorities; and more capable of communicating with others.

In periods of great social turmoil, this dimension of education related to values may be more important than preparing for adequate jobs by acquiring appropriate knowledge and skills. This role of education can be an especially important counterbalance to the processes of homogenization and ghettoization. The social Chernobyl (i.e., the process of releasing powerful and overspreading centripetal forces) did not start, I believe, with some extraordinary social event. It started when a society not equipped with the democratic mechanisms for dealing with complex social conflicts accepted the formula that was supposed to be the panacea for all social conflicts: "Either homogenization or separation." First promoted by political leaders as the solution for interrepublic conflicts, this formula, denying the possibility of the existence of plural societies, was gradually applied to all other differences – ethnic, religious, ideological – and for many people, it soon gained the status of frequently repeated and self-evident truth.

In this chapter, I have called attention not only to the dangerous consequences of forming isolated social systems but also to the stability of such systems. The more encapsulated the system is, the more resistant it is to change. Yugoslav youth currently have to live in an isolated society in the midst of European integrative processes. Will these conditions change, and what will their future life in Europe look like? Unfortunately, that depends on political decisions that are beyond their control.

REFERENCES

Aries, P. (1962). *Centuries of childhood*. New York: Vintage.
Erlich, V. (1971). *Jugoslovenska porodica u transformaciji* [The Yugoslav family in transition]. Zagreb: Liber.
Fasick, F. A. (1994). On the "invention" of adolescence. *Journal of Early Adolescence, 14*, 6–23.
Jakobi, T. (1997). Preraspodela siromastva [Redistribution of poverty]. *Republika, 9*(164), 5–6.
Kuzmanović, B., Popadić, D., & Havelka, N. (1995). Social changes and changes of values. *Psihologija, 28*, 7–26.
Lazić, M. (Ed.). (1995). *Society in crisis: Yugoslavia in the early '90s*. Belgrade: Filip Visnjic.
Mead, M. (1970). *Culture and commitment*. New York: American Museum of National History.
Mihailović, S. (1994). Zrtvovana generacija – omladina u epicentru negativnih posledica drustvene krize [The scarred generation: The young at the epicenter of negative consequences of the social crisis]. *Sociologija, 3*, 315–323.
Popadić, D. (1997). Studentski protesti: Uporedna analiza studentskih protesta 1992 i 1996/97 [Student protests: A comparative analysis of student protests 1992 and 1996/97]. In M. Lazić (Ed.), *Ajmo ajde svi u setnju* [Let's all keep walking] (pp. 65–76). Belgrade: Medijacentar.
Rosandić, R., & Pešić, V. (Eds.). (1994). *Warfare, patriotism, patriarchy: An analysis of elementary school textbooks*. Belgrade: Center for Antiwar Action.
Schlegel, A., & Barry, H., III. (1991). *Adolescence: An anthropological inquiry*. New York: Free Press.

22 Youth and Unions in North America's Service Society

Stuart Tannock

The typical youth workplace in North America's service society today is likely to be a fast-food restaurant or mall retail outlet. Sixty-eight percent of working youth (ages 16 to 24) in the United States now work in the service and retail sectors (U.S. Bureau of Labor Statistics, 1996). Many of these youth work in what are commonly referred to as *dead-end jobs* or *McJobs*: low-wage, low-skill jobs, frequently characterized by high levels of stress, repetitive tasks, limited opportunities for learning and advancement, great uncertainty in hours and scheduling, and few if any benefits. Turnover in these jobs often surpasses 100% per year.

The most common policy response to the issue of dead-end jobs has been to stress the importance of increased educational opportunities and improved school-to-work bridging programs for today's youth. Education and bridging programs, it is said, will help youth move up and out of entry-level service and retail jobs into high-wage, high-skill career track jobs. Although this may be true for some youths, education and school-to-work programs do little to change conditions within low-wage, low-skill service jobs themselves, and economic forecasts predict a continued expansion of this sector of the economy.

Union leaders argue that an alternative response to the issue of working conditions of dead-end jobs would be organizing youth service workers into unions. Unions have generally avoided the youth sector of the economy for several reasons: high turnover, rabid anti-unionism on the part of management, and low wages (meaning low dues payments). Faced with a declining and aging membership, however, labor leaders in both Canada and the United States have recently come to recognize that the future of the labor movement depends on the ability of unions to reach out to and work with a new generation of workers. Organizing youth work thus holds potential significance not just for youth but for unions as well.

In my research, I have explored the possibilities that unionism holds for improving youth service work by studying the experiences of youth workers who are already members of service sector unions (Tannock, 2001). I have worked with two union locals: a Canadian local that represents young fast-food workers and a U.S. local that represents a large number of young supermarket workers. Studying these two union locals offers the possibility of gaining comparative insight into the experiences of unions and youth across the Canadian and American national contexts. Widespread and critical concern with youth unemployment and a greater sense of the power and presence of unions currently distinguish the Canadian from the U.S. scene. I have also compared two very different unions. The Canadian union is recognized in Canada as having made some of the greatest inroads of any union in organizing youth in the fast-food industry: Union local leaders speak of youth in terms of opportunity and provide a well-funded labor education program, as well as (in theory at least) an activist and democratic steward system. The U.S. union, on the other hand, has not had a history of explicitly targeting youth in its organizing efforts: Union local leaders often speak of the difficulties of engaging young members, offer limited labor education opportunities, and work with a relatively weak and undeveloped steward system.

Research on youth employment tends to be quantitative and top-down; descriptions of youth experiences in the workplace are rare, and descriptions of youth experiences in unions are virtually nonexistent. My goal has been to take an ethnographic approach in addressing the two main questions of my research: How do youths experience work in the (unionized) service sector, and how are unions in a service society succeeding and/or failing in reaching out to and working with youth? Through interviews with and observations of youths participating in their workplaces, union meetings, training programs, and social events, I have explored how they position themselves with respect to their unions, coworkers, and employers; how they evaluate their work and union activity; and how they develop both task-based skills and a broader understanding of the social worlds of their workplaces.

Youth, Education, and Work

The research literature on youth and work is often less concerned with work itself than with the trajectories of youths into, through, and out of various working situations: that is, what Griffin (1993, p. 28) calls the "one Big Question: the incidence and explanation of the inequalities in the move from full-time education to waged work." Without denying the obvious importance of such a question, I suggest that it is paramount to ask other questions simultaneously: not just "*how* and *why* young people take the restricted and often meaningless available jobs" (Willis, 1977, p. 182), but also "in what ways are these jobs meaningless and restricted, and to what extent do they have to be so?" I am concerned that the questions and concepts used in the youth and work literature frequently presuppose (1) that a certain hierarchy of jobs is natural and inevitable and (2) that the current conditions characterizing any type of work are also natural and inevitable. All too often, it is implied that change and reform can take place only in education and not in the workplace itself.[1]

Educational researchers, in accepting without question a hierarchy of "good" and "bad" jobs, participate in reproducing the very inequalities they seek to redress. As a young service worker, who had helped to organize a union at her fast-food restaurant, responded when asked by a journalist why she did not simply get a better job, "Somebody's got to work at [the fast-food restaurant]. Why the hell shouldn't it be me? And why the hell shouldn't I have a livable wage to do it?" In the context of North American education and training, customer service work is often dismissed – not wholly without

---

[1] The major streams of youth and work literature in the United States assume that current working conditions characterizing "bad" jobs and "good" jobs are natural and inevitable *to the extent that* they cannot or should not be changed by and for workers (bottom-up change). Since the 1990 publication of *America's Choice: High Skills or Low Wages!*, mainstream school-to-work policy papers have called on U.S. companies to transform themselves into *high-performance* workplaces. But change in this literature is top-down, employer- and policy-centered, and motivated by employer (productivity) concerns. If there is a mismatch between young worker and workplace, it is generally assumed that the worker either needs to move or to change. Moreover, as Bailey and Bernhardt (1997, p. 180) point out, research describing high-performance models has generally ignored low-end service and retail industries.

The reproduction and resistance literature on youth and work (see Borman, 1991, for an overview) calls for sweeping but vaguely defined structural changes in society and the economy but pays scant attention to concrete, local possibilities of changing workplaces. Because the critical problem in this literature is generally seen as the act of becoming a laborer (e.g., manual, clerical), rather/more than the current conditions of such jobs, there is little sense of embracing a job to change it. As a predominantly school-based research tradition, this literature has paid little attention to either the individual or collective, informal or institutional ways in which young workers can and do act to change their workplaces (see Wexler, 1983, and Weis, 1990, for critiques on the absence of change in the reproduction literature).

reason – as dead-end work, a disfavored alternative to college-track and trades jobs, and the very reason that people should stay in school.

This notion of a *dead-end job* requires unpacking, for the term accepts uncritically a historical (and gendered) pattern of devaluing service work as not being "real" work, "skilled" work, or good "career" work (Cobble, 1991, 1993; Macdonald & Sirianni, 1996). It negatively affects the working conditions of customer service jobs by sanctioning notions of superiority among customers over "lowly service workers," and it functions as a write-off concept, discouraging attempts to investigate and improve working conditions in these jobs. The challenge for researchers investigating youth service work is to give credence to those aspects of the work that young workers find rewarding and attractive without either writing these off as some kind of false consciousness (e.g., Krahn & Tanner, 1996) or glossing over the many limiting and exploitive aspects of service jobs (e.g., Widalvsky, 1989) that young service workers are equally able and willing to detail.

None of the young workers I have interviewed want to stay in their current positions for any length of time. These jobs are universally seen as temporary, stepping-stone, or stopgap jobs. Some young workers do, however, speak eloquently about wanting careers in other areas of customer service. But for careerists and temporary workers alike, the dead-end label is disabling: The positive aspects of their work need appreciating, and the negative aspects need changing.

Investigating how workers might go about changing the conditions under which they work is a critical part of developing the kind of work education that Dewey (1915/1977, pp. 38–39) called for long ago: a work education that encourages "the development of such intelligent initiative, ingenuity and executive capacity as shall make workers, as far as may be, the masters of their own industrial fate" and that "will first alter the existing industrial system, and ultimately transform it." Educational researchers have expressed concern that work education programs "socialize students for the role of diligent and obedient employee" and offer "no place for students to acquire the capacity to be socially critical" (Koziol & Grubb, 1995, p. 135). The problem, of course, is not one solely of education programs but of the vast majority of North American workplaces and, in particular, of those low-wage, low-skill places where most youths work. In these workplaces, worker reflection and activism are not likely to be encouraged, especially in cases where reflection and activism challenge or go beyond corporate goals and prerogatives. One motivation for my research was to examine whether a union presence could make a difference in providing young workers with increased opportunities for reflection, activism, and learning.

Unionization and Young Workers

Does unionization significantly improve working conditions for youth workers in customer service jobs? The answer is mixed at best. To a great extent, I found my research to be a process of documenting absences: the absence of unions from the daily lives of young unionized service workers, and the absence of young workers from the concerns and activities of service sector unions. For the most part, the two union locals I studied do little to actively involve their membership, young or old, on a day-to-day basis; have little shop floor presence; and have limited effect on working conditions beyond wages and benefits. As with many North American unions, challenges of internal organizing and union democracy have attracted limited attention from union leadership. Often young union members hardly know that they are in a union, and in the U.S. supermarket local, the only contact many had with their union was a threatening letter received when they failed to pay their dues and initiation fees. Young workers encounter the same institutionalized and individual age-based prejudice and bias in their unions as in their workplaces. Older workers, shop stewards, and union staff can hold extremely negative views of the work ethic and union commitment of younger workers and, in some cases, blame younger workers for accepting weak contracts. Young workers, particularly in the U.S. supermarket local, are explicitly excluded from some contract protections and often pay higher dues than older workers; with almost no representation among union representatives, staff, and stewards, the needs and interests of younger workers are frequently overlooked.[2] For many older union members, young workers are not even considered to be real workers.

But I also found clear signs of the possibilities that unionism raises for young workers. Most young workers recognize that their unions raise their wages and benefits, and some can tell moving stories about how their union protected them from being fired or mistreated in the workplace. Especially in the Canadian fast-food union, 16-, 18-, 20-, and 24-year-olds have become shop stewards, served on bargaining committees, joined health and safety

---

[2] Age bias in contract provisions comes via the close correlation of age with job classification in the grocery industry; baggers and stockers, who tend to be the youngest workers in the supermarkets, are, for example, denied (in this union local) premiums for unscheduled overtime granted other job classifications. Age bias in dues rates is created by the local's decision to have a wage-based rather than an earnings-based monthly dues rate, and by the correlation of age, job classification, and hours worked per month. The ratio of monthly dues to hourly wage is roughly the same for a low-wage bagger as it is for a higher-wage journeyman produce clerk; but because the bagger is likely to work far fewer hours in a month than the produce clerk, the ratio of monthly dues to monthly earnings tends to be much higher for the bagger.

committees, and participated in labor educationals. For these youths, union activism has brought learning opportunities (ranging from the specifics of contract language and grievance procedures to general reflections on working conditions across North America), increased roles and responsibilities (educating and helping coworkers resolve workplace concerns and grievances), and raised immediate and local challenges (of how to address problems in work organization, personality conflicts, and contradictory messages from both management and union leadership). The tiny group of young union activists who are invited to attend the labor educationals run by the Canadian union are able to meet and interact with workers from diverse industrial sectors in a participatory classroom environment. In this setting, they can learn to identify common and divergent issues with other types of workers, and address such broad social justice issues as human rights, women's concerns in the workplace, and challenges of technological change.

If either of these two locals were to move to a model of full member participation and education, were to focus on distributing knowledge and responsibility downward throughout their memberships, and were to listen carefully to younger workers, invite them to speak up and take action in their workplaces, I believe there would be considerable interest and appreciation from many young members. Financial and geographical constraints – both locals represent workers in fairly small work units spread out over large areas – place undeniable limitations on the two locals' membership involvement efforts (although these limitations are probably less determinative than local leadership tends to believe). Busy schedules, competing outside interests, and self-identification as being only temporary workers would undoubtedly limit immediate widespread and extensive involvement of young workers in union activities. But among the young workers I interviewed, there is considerable interest in learning more at work, in developing more community through social activities, and in having a greater voice in shaping both their own working conditions and the services and products provided to customers.

Although the lack of youth participation in the union is often blamed by older workers on a creeping generational apathy, it is clear from my observations that opportunities for youth participation simply are not made available in the U.S. local and are made available only to a small elite in the Canadian local. If unionization were to follow a model of full member participation and education, it would have the potential to transform that unhealthy cynicism toward work that many youth and work researchers fear dead-end service jobs create among young workers (see, e.g., Greenberger & Steinberg, 1986) into a positive motivation and an opportunity for learning and change.

Postscript: Reflections on the 1997 Johann Jacobs Foundation Conference

One of the frequently expressed concerns of participants in the 1997 Johann Jacobs Foundation conference, "Joining Society: Social Interaction and Learning in Adolescence and Youth," was a need to move from the vision of social stasis implied in the first part of the conference title, "Joining Society," toward a more dynamic understanding of changing society. Change or transformation, participants suggested, is just as critical to consider as are problems of continuity or reproduction. This chapter likewise urges a shift in attention from the problems of youth joining the workforce to the challenges of youth changing the workplace.

But if change was a frequent concern at the Johann Jacobs conference, bottom-up change (in the context of youth moving into the marketplace and workplace), worker-driven change, and youth-driven change at work were not. Instead, discussion at the conference was notable for being business- and employer-centered. Our host, Klaus Jacobs, set the tone for the discussion in opening the conference by explaining his interest in the conference's theme as a chairman of one of the world's largest temporary employment agencies, noting his concern as a leaser of labor for (I paraphrase here) "fitting the right people to the right work." During the conference sessions that followed, participants frequently framed their discussion with reference to the needs and concerns of corporate leaders in the United States and in Europe; they portrayed business as an innovator and a leader in fostering teamwork and learning opportunities in the workplace; and they discussed the possibilities opened up by school–business partnerships. The discussion was such that, by the final session of the conference, one participant felt compelled to "state for the record" that he did not wish to have his participation in the conference taken to be an endorsement or a celebration of capitalism.

Throughout the conference, this positive view of the (actual and potential) role of business in the lives of youths rarely ever confronted or came into dialogue with a more pessimistic view of the role of business in creating the basic social and economic realities facing working youth in North America (and Europe) today: for example, declining real wages and rising income inequality in the context of record corporate profits; declining job stability in the context of corporate downsizing and reengineering; and high levels (in the United States at least) of labor law violations by employers (especially with respect to laws covering child labor, union organizing, and wages and working hours). It is with the purpose of focusing attention both on the more troublesome aspects of the relations between business leadership and youth workers, and on the more hopeful possibilities of bottom-up, worker-driven changes, that I would like to revisit one idea discussed widely during the Johann Jacobs conference: that of *social entrepreneurship*.

The idea of social entrepreneurship was introduced to the conference by Shirley Brice Heath (this volume), who pointed to examples of youth-run artists' companies and urban farming cooperatives in the United States:

Social enterprise represents entrepreneurial efforts by neighborhoods to build responsible, aesthetic, locally grounded opportunities for resource development within impoverished communities. Simply put, those engaged in social enterprise efforts work to find ways to put local energies to work for the community without waiting for external educational, governmental, or multinational corporate forces. (pp. 42–43)

The idea of social entrepreneurship can be useful; and in calling attention to these small enterprises, Heath makes a valuable contribution. But during the conference discussion, the concept of *social* entrepreneurship was freely linked to a prevailing interest in entrepreneurship in general (particularly the role of small business as an engine of economic growth) and was swept into a blanket understanding of youth leadership in the workplace as being constituted by, or synonymous with, the entrepreneurial spirit.

Herein lies my concern with the concept. Entrepreneurship is already the dominant model in North America of youth leadership in the workplace. The notion of social entrepreneurship not only does nothing to displace this model, but also leads too easily to the glossing over of potentially significant differences in the internal organization of various "social" enterprises (e.g., cooperative vs. capitalist) and does nothing to question the possibly devastating effects of large-scale entrepreneurialism on the impoverished communities in which these small-scale enterprises are emerging.

There is a critical need to consider models of youth leadership in the workplace as alternative or additional models to that of youth as entrepreneurs. One such model is that of the young worker as labor organizer, activist, and pursuer of social justice. To find examples of such a model, we can turn to Canada, where, over the past few years, there has been a small wave of youth labor organizing. In 1993, 17-year-old Sarah Inglis attracted considerable media attention when she led a unionization drive at the McDonald's where she worked in Orangeville, Ontario. Management harassment, favoritism, and arbitrarily reduced working hours were primary motivations. That same year, 19-year-old David Coburn led a union drive at a Harvey's hamburger restaurant in Toronto. Coburn and his coworkers were fed up with management harassment and outraged to find that some of them were being paid a below-minimum wage. Since then, young workers have spearheaded union drives at mall fashion outlets (e.g., Limité, Levi's 1850, Suzy Shier) in the suburbs of Toronto; at Wal-Mart and the casinos in Windsor, Ontario; at Starbucks outlets in Vancouver; and at a McDonald's in Squamish, British Columbia, to name only the most prominent examples.[3]

Some of these efforts have ended in failure, with store closings or legal defeats, whereas others have gone on to win union recognition and to negotiate first contracts. But everywhere the issues are similar: wages, hours, scheduling, management harassment, and favoritism. This wave of youth labor organizing has been predominantly youth driven rather than labor driven; in fact, young workers have often found unions reluctant to become involved in their issues. Sarah Inglis, for example, contacted four different unions before finding one that would take on her case. Gradually, though, these youth initiatives are beginning to have an impact on the Canadian labor movement. The Canadian Labor Congress (an umbrella organization of trade unions in Canada) created a youth caucus at one of its recent conventions; and larger unions, such as the Canadian Auto Workers, have developed policy papers on how best to attend to youth issues in the workplace.

Forming a union at one's workplace, as this chapter should attest, is by no means a panacea and can bring its own set of problems. There are also countless other ways – informal as well as institutional, individual as well as collective, with lasting effect or of fleeting significance – in which young workers act on a daily basis to change and improve the conditions in which they work. The point I wish to make here is that, if researchers and policymakers really want to address the often dire social and economic circumstances facing young workers today, they need to turn away from a monopolizing focus on the young entrepreneur and to consider carefully these alternative examples of youth leadership at work.

---

[3] See Cross (1995), Inglis (1994), Klein (1995), Lorinc (1994), and McArthur (1997) for more information on these efforts. There have been similar efforts in the United States. Young workers at Noah's Bagels in Berkeley, California, voted in the late 1990s to form a union, and workers (many in their 20s) have been engaged in union drives at Borders Books and Music across the country (Irvine, 1997). In the spring of 1998, 19-year-old Bryan Drapp became an overnight media celebrity when he led 15 of his coworkers out on strike against the Macedonia, Ohio, McDonald's where he worked. As *People* magazine (!) reported, by the fifth day of the strike, the franchise owner "had agreed to most of the workers' demands, including raising the base pay, posting work schedules four days in advance, granting one week's paid vacation after a year on the job and requiring managers to attend 'people skills' workshops" (Fields-Meyer & Sweeney, 1998, p. 138).

REFERENCES

Bailey, T., & Bernhardt, A. (1997). In search of the high road in a low-wage industry. *Politics & Society, 25*(2), 179–201.

Borman, K. (1991). *The first "real" job: A study of young workers.* Albany: State University of New York Press.

Cobble, D. S. (1991). *Dishing it out: Waitresses and their unions in the twentieth century.* Urbana: University of Illinois Press.

Cobble, D. S. (Ed.). (1993). *Women and unions: Forging a partnership.* Ithaca, NY: ILR Press.

Cross, V. (1995, July). People like us: Diary of a casino strike. *Our Times,* pp. 36–40.

Dewey, J. (1977). Education vs. trade-training: Dr. Dewey's reply. *Curriculum Inquiry, 7,* 37–39. (Original work published 1915)

Fields-Meyer, T., & Sweeney, S. (1998, May 18). McHoffa. *People,* pp. 137–138.

Greenberger, E., & Steinberg, L. (1986). *When teenagers work: The psychological and social costs of adolescent employment.* New York: Basic Books.

Griffin, C. (1993). *Representations of youth: The study of youth and adolescence in Britain and America.* Cambridge: Polity Press.

Inglis, S. (1994, June–July). McDonald's union drive-through: Sarah Inglis tells her story. *Our Times,* pp. 19–28.

Irvine, M. (1997, August 18). Rising number of young employees see unions as way to go in workplace. *Seattle Post-Intelligencer,* Section B, p. 4.

Klein, N. (1995, February). Salesgirl solidarity. *This Magazine,* pp. 12–19.

Koziol, K., & Grubb, W. N. (1995). Paths not taken: Curriculum integration and the political and moral purposes of schooling. In W. N. Grubb (Ed.), *Education through occupations in American high schools* (pp. 115–140). New York: Teachers College Press.

Krahn, H., & Tanner, J. (1996). Coming to terms with marginal work: Dropouts in a polarized labor market. In D. Kelly & J. Gaskell (Eds.), *Debating dropouts* (pp. 65–83). New York: Teachers College Press.

Lorinc, J. (1994, June). Fast food, slow bargaining. *This Magazine,* pp. 25–30.

Macdonald, C., & Sirianni, C. (Eds.). (1996). *Working in the service society.* Philadelphia: Temple University Press.

McArthur, J. (1997, May–June). Walmart: A new face in the union. *Canadian Dimension,* pp. 44–45.

Tannock, S. (2001). *Youth at work: The unionized fast-food and grocery workplace.* Philadelphia: Temple University Press.

U.S. Bureau of Labor Statistics. (1996). *Employed persons by detailed industry, sex, and age, annual average 1996.* Washington, DC: U.S. Department of Labor.

Weis, L. (1990). *Working class without work: High school students in a de-industrializing economy.* New York: Routledge.

Wexler, P. (1983). Movement, class and education. In L. Barton & S. Walker (Eds.), *Race, class and education* (pp. 17–39). London: Croom Helm.

Widalvsky, B. (1989, Summer). McJobs: Inside America's largest youth training program. *Policy Review,* 30–37.

Willis, P. (1977). *Learning to labor: How working-class kids get working-class jobs.* New York: Columbia University Press.

23 Joining Society

With What Certainty?

Saul Meghnagi

The Deinstitutionalization of Life Paths

In all Western countries, the dynamics of demographic trends indicate that the past few decades have seen a substantial increase in life expectancy. This structural change has been accompanied by other changes, with obvious repercussions on people's ways of living and on their conception of the social system, the labor market, and the culture of civil society.

Research on the subject (see references in Ritter, 1997) has long dwelled on the implications of changes in the length, structure, and level of standardization of people's lives in the past century. One study in particular (Saraceno, 1991) has identified two processes covering different periods of time: an initial process whereby the structure and chronology of the lives of individuals and social groups became increasingly standardized as a result of demographic and normative institutionalization and regularization; and a later process, still underway, whereby previously established standardized models are being deregulated.

The first of these two processes – the *institutionalization of life paths* – began slowly, strengthened itself, and became consolidated in the 1950s and 1960s. It was the result of various interconnected phenomena, including increased control over life paths by the labor market, enterprises, and the state through the introduction of regulations on the structure, periods, and specific ages for choices of life and events. We can cite, for example, the definition of specific ages at which people entered and left the labor market, of minimum ages at which people could enter and leave the education system, and of minimum ages at which people could get married and assume mutual duties between spouses and among generations as established by law. Culturally shared rules on the appropriateness of certain sequences (e.g., you study first and then work; if you are a man, you get a job first and then marry; first you marry and then you have children) and the behavior appropriate to a particular age reinforced and, in many cases, determined the rules that were gradually established.

The duties stemming from all the foregoing control mechanisms were accompanied by forms of social security that guaranteed greater security with regard to the social risks of illness, unemployment, and inability to work.

All these phenomena and other related ones, particularly those concerning infant and adult mortality that were a consequence of changes in access to food and sanitation, were the basis for developing the *normal* contemporary life cycle in which we can identify *suitable ages* and *normal life patterns* (i.e., concerning work, family life, and education).

Exclusion from access to the principal resources of such normality for people outside the labor market, either partly or totally, for underemployed and unemployed youths and adults, for workers in the black market economy, for some of the rural classes, and for virtually all immigrants has emerged as a problem for the consolidation of an ideal model at which to aim. *Expedients*, in the form of social welfare activities and allowances, were thus introduced and consolidated to supplement a more respectable and secure way of living and working. The widespread diffusion of this model, in terms of both fact and value systems, in the 1960s may also have been the result of workers' struggle for a more secure and predictable life pattern. This, not merely working hours, was the cause and product of industrial conflicts on the regulation, monitoring, and length of the working day: the immediate objective of so many demands.

Family roles and the labor market structure were complementary both to the work organization that required availability of time and geographical mobility from workers and to the very structure of the welfare state. In this system, women played the key role in caretaking and securing reproduction, including reproduction required for the development of the welfare state. This is the source of the general model, which has been referred to as the *family/labor system of social security*, underlying the ways of standardizing and guaranteeing life cycles that were developed during the first half of the 20th century.

The second process, the *deinstitutionalization* of life cycles during the 1970s and 1980s, was a reversal of the former trend. It consisted of the introduction of the differentiation in life cycles and in a concomitant relaxation of regulations that had previously guaranteed standardization and stability.

There were various structural and cultural reasons underlying this change, but we refer to only some of the most important.

Within the social context, women have played a key role in changing the ways of conceiving relationships between men and women, including production, reproduction, time to work, and time to care. Within the labor market, there has been a change in both demand and supply. With growing unemployment, people achieving occupational integration are generally faced with less security in terms of the actual length of employment, less predictability of career paths and opportunities, and greater demands for flexible working times. The fact that people have less to say about their working conditions is accompanied by a gradual decline in the conditions, resources, and forms of protection previously provided by the welfare state. The demand of individuals for more flexibility and less institutionalization of the life paths is partly the result and partly the cause of these processes that are taking place at cultural and structural levels.

Alongside the previous model, based on security, stability, and standardization, other models emerge, linked to desires and interests that, by contrast, give pride of place to opportunities for change, for picking up old threads, in training, work, and relationships, and choosing how many children to have and how to bring them up. From this point of view, breaking away from traditional patterns of study and work is emblematic: People are changing the sequences and models of normality governing particular phases of life or ages and adapting them to what they feel is appropriate or right for them.

Reduction of Opportunities

Flexibility and unpredictability in life paths differ for men and women and from individual to individual. Flexibility in working life is demanded by groups of both sexes who have the resources and courage to define their own plans for the future, but it is opposed by those who fear a return to previous conditions of uncertainty or the impossibility of achieving long-desired objectives. The situation seems to be aggravated by a contradiction that remains unresolved in the sharing of tasks between men and women.

It is undeniably true, however, that the younger generations of women now see participation in working life as totally acceptable and no longer as a transgression of the prevailing model of female social identity. The ensuing creation of new models of normality has had an impact on all the life paths resulting from women's emerging expectation of reciprocity with men regarding task sharing and the new resources that enable people to plan their own lives.

By contrast, young people seem to be less concerned by the growing instability of intimate relationships, which is another phenomenon that has shaken the traditional life patterns of both men and women and which generally creates more difficulties for women, who seem to have fewer opportunities to remarry than men do. The problem seems to affect the elderly, those with young children, and those having little training and occupational experience: that is, people who are unable to get reasonably paid, relatively secure jobs. More and more frequently, however, young people find themselves in situations that are likely to produce increasingly different scenarios compared with the past, as well as conflicts between generations. The nature of these situations has psychological roots, as studied in depth in the past, plus new and complex cultural and structural roots.

For all these reasons, the word *flexibility*, in its connection with the individual nature of opportunities and choices of life, which is widely used to indicate an attitude to be adopted to tackle ongoing changes in our society, is an ambiguous expression and formulation. Although flexibility in people's lives may be perceived and formulated as something desired by people having appropriate vocational, cultural, and family resources, in many other cases it is merely a necessity and not a choice. The consequence of these phenomena may be not only (Rossi, 1997) a strengthening of old inequalities but also the creation of new ones between youths and adults, between men and women, and among classes and groups of different ethnic origin, coming from different geographical areas or different age groups.

The consequent undermining of hard-won citizens' rights, of recently and partially secured guarantees, of equality between men and women, and of economic security produces not only nonlinear life patterns but also inevitable conflicts among the different generations struggling for space and access to social, economic, and occupational opportunities. This has led to a gradual increase in studies on social differences, complexity, and identity to overcome the crisis affecting the interpretive paradigms of contemporary change and to identify defined categories of analysis more clearly. In the field of labor studies, for example, academics have abandoned (see references in Accornero, 1997) the simplistic distinction between employment and unemployment and have recognized the need to take into account the relations among the sequential organization of working hours in the long term, the day-to-day organization of working hours, the varying relational and symbolic worlds of the individual, the forms of identification made possible by job experience, and the characteristics of work. Similarly, changes in the overall configuration of people's personal lives and relationships have been linked to the cultural changes affecting our society, both for structural reasons and to allow critical consideration and analysis of various groups, including young people.

In brief, investigations show that structural and cultural factors work in different ways to change the dynamics of relationships among generations, the features of male–female relationships, and the structure and nature of marriage in terms of length and reproductive function, with a consequent variety in life patterns. Longer life spans enable people to extend the number of choices they can make or to repeat some of them. The chronological order in which choices are made varies from individual to individual, with fewer and fewer common features in terms of both space and time, because either people can remain in a situation previously considered appropriate to a younger age (e.g., living with their parents) or they can make choices that used to be made when people were older (e.g., to engage in sexual activity).

The structuring of people's lives – dictated by society, its rhythm established according to age, and based on the prevailing, fragmented tasks allocated by society to each age group (e.g., training for young people, production and reproduction for adults, and the rest for the elderly) – is now undergoing radical changes in the distribution of activities according to age, thereby shifting functions previously undertaken earlier in life to older age groups. All these factors are associated with assessments of the past, images of the present, and perceptions of the future in which working conditions and sociorelational dynamics are connected.

The reallocation of roles and life tasks is obviously largely determined by the types of changes currently taking place in the social environment. The naturalness of most human behavior is conditioned by beliefs, customs, and explicit or implicit rules that play a decisive role, particularly in the structuring of systems of etiquette within which given personal choices are determined. As we have shown, in advanced contemporary societies, this interdependence, which may be defined as anthropological, is identified by examining the factors of the institutionalization and the deinstitutionalization of life paths.

The result of this state of affairs is that each individual's predominant social identity seems to be mutable, changing with prevailing external and internal conditions and events. Even the indicator of belonging to a certain age group, which is beyond any doubt from a purely biological point of view, provides only a very partial description of conditions, attitudes, behavior, and ways of seeing and perceiving reality. The variables of gender, schooling, qualifications, and residence are intertwined with the nature of a people's family commitments, the nature of the phase they are going through in their working lives, whether or not they are part of the labor market, and whether their jobs are full-time or part-time, secure or insecure. A youth may be a young manager, an office clerk, a blue-collar worker, an undergraduate, a working student, a student worker, or a dropout; and the same person may also be a woman or a man, have a partner or be single, have children or be childless.

This is the premise of studies (see references in De Leonardis, 1998) on social differences, complexity, and identity to overcome the crisis affecting the interpretive paradigms of contemporary change and to define the categories of analysis and target groups clearly.

Knowledge as an Instrument of Protection

The outline provided so far is aimed at highlighting two issues affecting all Western countries: the reduction (or the deinstitutionalization) of forms of welfare and the decrease in stable and guaranteed job opportunities. Hence, we ask if training is useful. If the answer is yes, what type of training is useful for the guidance of a young person?

The guidance and self-guidance of a person are part of his or her competence and, consequently, are the result of knowledge acquired in various ways: experience consolidated through action and decision-making processes, and the ability to make assessments, solve problems, and make decisions when faced with new situations. Competence has been defined as *conceptual*, related to the field of action, and as *strategic*, with regard to the possible forms of decision making and action.

In recent years, researchers (see references in Ajello & Meghnagi, 1998) have analyzed the strategies of reasoning and focused on the comparison between the problem solution of a novice (i.e., a person with a starting knowledge of a specific subject) and that of an expert. Studies have shown that there is a close connection among knowledge structure, reasoning, and problem solving. Researchers have also investigated the matter in depth, attempting to understand better the structural features of the different fields of knowledge; the different modalities of problem setting and solving, together with an understanding of the forms and models of problem recognition (i.e., how a person recognizes and redefines it); and the processes involved in decoding ill-structured and difficult problems. In reality, as in the social sciences, problems are ill-structured; that is, objectives are unclear, and experts have reached no consensus on their solution. The redefinition of a problem gives rise to a new representation that differs from person to person. Therefore, the problem cannot be solved with the help of algorithms following prescribed steps on which everyone agrees, as in other sciences.

Instead, the problem-solving process consists of an argumentation of the reasons that a person gives to confirm that the solution proposed and applied in a given practical situation is correct. Being an expert means using one's own competence in several ways of varying level and nature, from knowing how to do something concretely to knowing how to tackle a problem, even if ill-defined, by representing it in a different way, in order to be able to formulate interpretations and solutions. It means knowing how to explain the nature of a problem and how to justify the reasons for one's choices, actions, and decisions.

In this sense, guidance is part of our competence, intended as situated knowledge, in which context determines the effectiveness of knowledge, guides its manifestation, addresses its application, and defines its effectiveness. On the other hand, it should be noted that everyone builds his or her other abilities and knowledge within the framework of a process that is limited not only to contact with material or symbolic reality but also through social mediation favored by more competent people or peers who provide elements of reflection, analysis, and reasoning. At this point, guidance takes on or fails to take on the character of an action in support of transition processes. To this end, it is essential to consider both elements of potential development related to the way in which past experiences have been structured through knowledge strategy processes based on symbolic systems and related forms of socialization.

All individuals reelaborate the information they receive from the environment, reorganizing it for broader hypotheses and using strategies that are not always identifiable or foreseeable in an orderly, giving–acquiring process. In the field of adult education, this is also part of the debate on the relevance of existential situations, living and working contexts, in the development of the demand for knowledge and cognitive processes capable of producing changes in knowledge. In confirming this thesis, innovative experiences (Schwartz, 1995) have proved that it is possible to work effectively for the guidance and training of people with a low level of education. This has been achieved by starting from the acknowledgment that, whatever the level of education and basic skills, an individual always has a set of competences that he or she has mastered and on which action can be focused.

Every individual observes, remembers, acts, and reacts to the surrounding reality, filtering and selecting the information that he or she receives through the sensory organs, building notions and pictures. This process, however, clearly of an individual nature, does not take place outside definitions and representations that, to a significant extent, are shared by many members of a community and that guide the processing of information and the building of ideas.

The representations used to fit new perceptions, images, and information into an organized context of ideas and judgments make it possible to transform them from unknown to partly known and to control their inclusion in the overall framework of knowledge and understanding. The building of a representation tends to make customary what actually is not customary in order to master it and encompass it in a mental universe that is enriched and transformed in this way.

In conclusion, social representation and knowledge are characterized by a synergy between persistence and innovation, related to history and memory, and are configured as the supporting structure of our culture, our way of being, and our access to knowledge. This may guarantee greater employment opportunities and overall greater opportunities to find one's social and professional place.

Conditions for Building Socially Useful Knowledge

The related cognitive and practical instruments are composed of elements of the historical development of culture; based on variously integrated theories, they are used both consciously and unconsciously every time they are put into practice at a social level, in relations, analyses, summaries, and judgments. The same forms of reasoning and argumentation are obtained according to criteria and rules accepted within a given culture; they follow widely acknowledged conventions and are developed within the framework of shared paths of relations and socialization. Language is both the vehicle for and the instrument of processing, as well as a resource with cultural connotations, the bearer of social representations and images of reality.

As a result, the development of knowledge varies from person to person, but it is based on a substantial sensitivity to the cultural context, to the extent that it is necessary to analyze how people share knowledge and forms of reasoning with others. If, according to a knowledge-building assumption, every acquisition is the outcome of individual strategies of reasoning, it may similarly be held that personal experience, related to events, is only a part of what constitutes the basis for this processing. People build up knowledge, starting from what is given to them by others orally, in writing, and through pictures or gestures.

It is not merely by chance that the idea is taking root that knowledge is disseminated among individuals through interactions that give rise to judgment and to decision-making and problem-solving processes, through the blurring of the boundaries between disciplines and subdisciplines and among other closely related fields.

Every cognitive act should ultimately be seen as a specific response to a set of specific circumstances. Learning should be viewed as an activity within the social framework of a particular practical situation. For these reasons, knowledge is a form of protection for the young, to help them find their social and professional places. The acquisition of knowledge, however, not only depends on the young but also requires, among other things, two essential conditions, which will now be discussed.

Offers and Opportunities for Related Rich Job Experiences

Expertise grows in relation to the situation in which one is called to operate. The context of experience is not irrelevant to the practice of a skill. On the contrary, it determines its manifestation, favors its consolidation, and promotes its growth. The gradual increase in the areas of experience and their richness makes it possible to increase knowledge and arrange it differently. The organization of ideas is related to the different activities that people learn to perform, the difficulties of the tasks they carry out, and the frequency of such difficulties. The way thought works is the outcome of the interiorization of knowledge and notions related to the cultural context with which people come into contact, the concrete realities in which they operate, and the different communities with which they deal. If rich in stimuli and opportunities to put one's knowledge to the test, a job experience is essential to allow the young to project themselves into their possible future and to place this future in the present in the form of ideas, projects, and hypotheses from which behavior, choices, and decisions stem. Whoever is excluded for a long time from skilled job opportunities, even if temporarily, is potentially excluded from employment. This exclusion increases in time and underlies many forms of marginalization and understandable rebellion and violence against others and against oneself.

Training Based on Cross-Sectional Competences

The notion of *cross-sectional competences* is not univocal. It may be used to indicate the ability to use knowledge pertaining to different fields, thereby crossing the boundaries between one discipline and another. In that context, it means the knowledge that can be defined as basic or vocational concerning the protection of workers (or potential workers) who do not have (or are very unlikely to have) full-time, nonfixed-term jobs. How can these workers, atypical in the past (especially in Europe), consolidate their basic or vocational training? How can they secure a pension? How can they secure income in case of illness, especially prolonged illness? All of these and similar problems are the subjects of debate and analysis in all the countries that have more or less generous welfare states. The feeling of insecurity of youth with regard to their employment prospects goes hand in hand, in these cases, with a more general uncertainty regarding various aspects of their future. A survey conducted by the European Trade Union Confederation (ETUC, 1998) focuses on a comparative analysis of this issue. The underlying assumption is that the participation of youth in society is a problem not only for young people but also for society itself. The forms of protection, even through knowledge and experiences that help increase it, are an essential condition for allowing them to take their place in society and a necessity against exclusion and marginalization.

REFERENCES

Accornero, A. (1997). *Era il secolo del lavoro* [It was the century of labor]. Bologne: Il Mulino.

Ajello, A. M., & Meghnagi, S. (1998). *La competenza tra flessibilità e specializzazione* [Competence between flexibility and qualification]. Milan: Angeli.

De Leonardis, O. (1998). *In un diverso welfare* [In a different welfare]. Milan: Feltrinelli.

ETUC. (1998). *Les competences transversales* [Cross-sectional competences]. Final Research Report, European Economic Community Leonardo Da Vinci Program. Brussels: Mimeo.

Ritter, G. A. (1997). *Storia dello stato sociale* [History of the welfare state]. Bari, Italy: Laterza.

Rossi, N. (1997). *Meno ai padri più ai figli* [Less to fathers, more to sons]. Bologne: Il Mulino.

Saraceno, C. (1991, April). *Dalla istituzionalizzazione alla de-istituzionalizzazione dei corsi di vita femminili e maschili?* [From institutionalization to deinstitutionalization of female and male life courses]. Speech delivered at the European Economic Community International Conference "I tempi, i lavori, le vite" [Times, works, lives]. Turin, Italy.

Schwartz, B. (1995). *Moderniser sans exclure* [Modernizing without excluding]. Rome: Anicia.

Index

accountability, and family conversation, 230, 231

adolescence: border between adulthood and, 300; definition of, 259; discourse and transformation of relationships with parents, 241–249; learning as discursive practice and concept of, 213

Adorno, T., 243

adultocentric societies, 301

adults and adulthood: and communities of practice, 19–23; definition of, 14; overview of pathways to in national context, 35–37. *See also* socialization; transition

age: categories of in Yugoslavia, 301; and family discourse, 231; and job classification in grocery industry, 312n2; and labor union membership, 312; structuring of life paths according to, 322; of transition to adulthood, 274–276, 293–297. *See also* adolescence; adults and adulthood; childhood; youth

alienation: modern education and life experiences, 187–188; and preapprenticeship program, 170–171; and socialization gap, 13

Allen, J. P., 242

alternance periods, and vocational training, 278

alternative training (*alternance*), and apprenticeship in Europe, 271

altruism, and social construction of self, 144

America's Choice: High Skills or Low Wages! (1990), 310

anthropology: and concept of wisdom, 254; and study of youth-based organizations, 46, 47

anxiety, and fear of losing identity, 148

apprenticeship: and social distribution of knowledge, 123; and transition patterns in Europe, 277–278, 279, 280–281; and youth employment in Germany, 271, 276. *See also* Dual System; preapprenticeship

appropriation: of lifestyles by counterculture youth groups, 95–100; discursive practices and social, 192

Aries, P., 300–301

arts: government support for, 67n12; and youth-based organizations, 48, 60, 69

asymmetry, in parent–adolescent discourse, 243, 247–248

athletic/academic youth-based organizations, 48, 60

Australia, and acquisition of literary skills by aborigines, 104. *See also* Youth in Search